"You will be my witnesses"

A Festschrift in Honor of the Reverend Dr. Allison A. Trites on the Occasion of His Retirement

“You will be my witnesses”

A Festschrift in Honor of the Reverend Dr. Allison A. Trites on the Occasion of His Retirement

edited by

R. Glenn Wooden
Timothy R. Ashley
Robert S. Wilson

Mercer University Press
Macon, Georgia USA
May 2003

ISBN 0-86554-690-8 MUP/H511

"You will be my witnesses"
A Festschrift in Honor
of the Reverend Dr. Allison A. Trites
on the Occasion of His Retirement.

Mercer University Press, Macon GA 31210-3960 USA

Printed in the United States of America

The paper used in this publication meets the minimum requirements of American National Standard for Information Sciences—Permanence of Paper for Printed Library Materials, ANSI Z39.48-1984.

Library of Congress Cataloging-in-Publication Data

You will be my witnesses : a festschrift in honor of
the Reverend Dr. Allison A. Trites on the occasion of his retirement
/ edited by R. Glenn Wooden, Timothy R. Ashley, Robert S. Wilson.
pp. cm.
Includes bibliographical references.
ISBN 0-86554-690-8 (alk. paper)
1. Theology. I. Trites, Allison A., 1936– .
II. Wooden, R. Glenn, 1957– . III. Ashley, Timothy R., 1947– .
IV. Wilson, Robert S., 1943– .
BR50.Y68 2003
230'.61--dc21

2003004129

Contents

Abbreviations

AB	Anchor Bible
ABD	*Anchor Bible Dictionary*
ANET^3	J. B. Pritchard, *Ancient Near Eastern Texts Relating to the Old Testament*, 3rd ed. (Princeton: Princeton University Press, 1969)
AUA	Baptist Archives, Acadia University
BaptQ	*The Baptist Quarterly*
BARev	*Biblical Archaeology Review*
BASOR	*Bulletin of the American Schools of Oriental Research*
BBB	Bonner biblische Beiträge
BDB	Francis Brown, S. R. Driver, and Charles A. Briggs, *A Hebrew and English Lexicon of the Old Testament* (Oxford: Clarendon, ^{1}1907; corr. repr. 1962)
BHS	*Biblia Hebraica Stuttgartensia*
BMM	*Baptist Missionary Magazine of Nova Scotia and New Brunswick*
Bib	*Biblica*
BibTod	*Bible Today*
BKAT	Biblischer Kommentar: Altes Testament
BNTC	Black's New Testament Commentaries
BRMT	Blackwell Readings in Modern Theology
BSac	*Bibliotheca Sacra*
BWANT	Beiträge zur Wissenschaft vom alten und neuen Testament
BZAW	Beihefte zur Zeitschrift für die alttestamentliche Wissenschaft
CAD	*Chicago Assyrian Dictionary*
CBC	Cambridge Bible Commentary
CBQ	*Catholic Biblical Quarterly*
CGTC	Cambridge Greek Testament Commentary
CM	*The Christian Messenger*
CNT	Commentaire du Nouveau Testament
CV	*Christian Visitor*
DJG	J. B. Green and S. McKnight, *Dictionary of Jesus and the Gospels* (Downers Grove IL: InterVarsity, 1996)
DNB	*Dictionary of National Bibliography*
DPHL	G. F. Hawthorne, R. P. Martin, and D. G. Reid, *Dictionary of Paul and His Letters* (Downers Grove: InterVarsity, 1993)
EVV	English Versions
GKC	Gesenius, Emil Kautzsch, and Arthur E. Cowley, *Gesenius' Hebrew Grammar*, 2nd ed. (Oxford: Clarendon, 1910; corr. repr. 1963)
HALOT	Ludwig Köhler et al., *The Hebrew and Aramaic Lexicon of the Old Testament* (Leiden: Brill, 1994–2000)
Hermeneia	Hermeneia: A Critical and Historical Commentary on the Bible
HNT	Handbuch zum neuen Testament
HSM	Harvard Semitic Monographs
IBC	Interpretation: A Bible Commentary for Teaching and Preaching
IBS	*Irish Biblical Studies*
ICC	International Critical Commentary
JBL	*Journal of Biblical Literature*
JHI	*Journal of the History of Ideas*

JSNT	*Journal for the Study of the New Testament*
JSNTSS	Journal for the Study of the New Testament, Supplement Series
JSOT	*Journal for the Study of the Old Testament*
JSOTSup	Journal for the Study of the Old Testament, Supplement Series
JTS	*Journal of Theological Studies*
KB	Ludwig Köhler and W. Baumgartner, *Lexicon in Veteris Testamenti Libros* (Leiden: Brill, 1958)
KEKNT	Kritisch-Exegetischer Kommentar über das neue Testament
LCC	Library of Christian Classics
LXX	Septuagint
MNTS	McMaster New Testament Studies
MT	Masoretic Text
NCB	New Century Bible Commentary
NEB	New English Bible
NICNT	New International Commentary on the New Testament
NIDNTT	*The New International Dictionary of New Testament Theology*. Ed. Lothar Coenen et al.; trans. Colin Brown (Exeter: Paternoster, 1975–1978)
NIGTC	New International Greek Testament Commentary
NIV	New International Version
NovT	*Novum Testamentum*
NovTSup	Novum Testamentum, Supplements
NTAbh	Neutestamentliche Abhandlungen
NTCW	Allison A. Trites, *The New Testament Concept of Witness*, SNTSMS 31 (Cambridge: Cambridge University Press, 1977)
NTS	*New Testament Studies*
NTTS	New Testament Tools and Studies
OG	Old Greek
OTL	Old Testament Library
OTP	James H. Charlesworth. *Old Testament Pseudepigrapha* (Garden City: Doubleday, 1983–1985)
Pesh	Peshitta
REB	Revised English Bible
RelPos	Religion and Postmodernism
SBT	Studies in Biblical Theology
SNTSMS	Society for New Testament Studies Monograph Series
STDJ	Studies on the Texts of the Desert of Judah
TDNT	Gerhard Kittel and Gerhard Friedrich, editors, *Theological Dictionary of the New Testament*, 9 vols., trans. Geoffrey W. Bromiley (Grand Rapids: Eerdmans, 1964–1974)
Th	Theodotion
TNTC	Tyndale New Testament Commentaries
Vg	Vulgate
VT	*Vetus Testamentum*
VTSup	Vetus Testamentum, Supplements
WBC	Word Biblical Commentary
ZAW	*Zeitschrift für die alttestamentliche Wissenschaft*

Foreword

Principal Lee M. McDonald
Acadia Divinity College

The publication of this volume celebrates thirty-seven extraordinary years of teaching at Acadia Divinity College and more years than that of dedicated service to the church. It is a joy to honor the lifetime service of Allison Trites for his ministry of teaching and service to the church. His commitment to the work of Christ has been an encouragement to all of his colleagues, fellow workers, and students, not to mention his fellow church members at the Wolfville United Baptist Church.

Allison has made many important contributions to biblical scholarship and is known widely for his interest in the church's witness for Christ. His own publications, which will be shared presently, are widely known and cherished by scholar, student, and layperson alike.

His commitments to excellence in teaching and writing have been equally matched by his Christian commitment to his church both locally and internationally. This is evidenced by his eager willingness to preach in our churches, to make trips to our mission fields to teach or preach, and by the churches of the Convention of Atlantic Baptist Churches electing him as their president. He is a deacon in his home church and those of us on the Faculty remember well how anxious he was about faculty meetings going too long because he had Wednesday night commitments at his church. Just a year ago, he was invited to come without pay to teach at a mission school in Latvia which had a special and urgent need for a professor to teach a course and he joyfully accepted the invitation after requesting permission to be absent from graduation ceremonies.

On several occasions as I have traveled for Acadia Divinity College, several biblical scholars have asked me if I was from the school where Allison Trites teaches. I received a letter from a New Testament scholar from Australia when I arrived here in Nova Scotia congratulating me on coming to a school with such an outstanding New Testament scholar present. When I was recently visiting a seminary in California for the Association of Theological Schools, a mature New Testament professor asked me to convey his appreciation to Dr. Trites for his publications that were instrumental in his own decision to enter theological education. Last year as I attended the Baptist World Alliance held on Prince Edward Island in Canada a seminary president saw my name tag with the location of my place of service and he immediately asked me to greet Dr. Trites for him, saying that Dr. Trites's book on the church's witness was a pivotal book in his spiritual journey. A well-known dean of a seminary in the USA came for a visit to our home and with no prompting asked if he could pay a visit to Allison Trites.

Such stories, and there are many more, serve to illustrate Allison Trites's commitment to the church and to biblical scholarship. Allison has taught New Testament studies to more than a generation of pastors in our convention. Indeed, more than eighty percent of all of our pastors who are currently serving in our churches have taken their New Testament courses from Dr. Trites. As with his former students, Dr. Trites is recognized by his current students as well for being a dedicated professor known for his scholarship, Christian commitment, and generous hospitable spirit. He has been a model to the rest of us who serve here. I freely admit that on several occasions I have gone to his office for advice and counsel on a variety of matters related to the College. His ability to speak with grace and genuine wisdom that has been impacted by his walk with Christ has been one of the College's rich treasures over the years. When he retires, we will all miss that very much, but we are greatly encouraged that he and Gene live across the street and just a short walk from the College!

Around the Divinity College, Allison is affectionately known for his courtesy, grace, and hospitality. Allison and Gene, his dear wife, are known for their gracious hospitality. I do not know of any faculty or staff member who has not been invited by them to be a guest at their dinner table. For years the faculty and staff have gathered at Allison's and Gene's lakeside cabin for an annual faculty meeting in the summer and on several occasions we have been invited to join him in a canoe ride! Allison's gracious and hospitable spirit has led many of us at the College to refer to Allison as our professor without guile.

He is always present at our Wednesday morning faculty prayer gatherings at the College and he is a faithful attendee and frequent participant in the College chapel services. He has also been an essential part of our annual Regatta with our neighbor seminary, the Atlantic School of Theology, in Halifax. Allison has not only been an active cheerleader for our team, but also on several occasions he has taken first place in the canoe races and has always been in the first two or three to finish! His daily swims at the University pool have kept him in good condition over the years. Students have especially loved his involvement in the various school activities on the University campus. It is not uncommon still to see Allison and Gene at Acadia University sports activities cheering on the University team.

We at the College, who serve with him in the ministry of the school, are delighted to share in the publication of this volume that honors him on his retirement and also highlights his years of faithful service for Christ. Several of the papers in this volume were presented at our annual Hayward Lectures in the fall of 2001 to honor Allison's thirty-seven years of service at Acadia. He is a model to all of us in his scholarship, commitment to the church and society, and in his collegial spirit. We congratulate him on the completion of a successful and highly productive career in Christian service at Acadia Divinity College and we all wish him and Gene God's very best in a well-deserved retirement.

Christmas 2001

Editors' Preface

R. Glenn Wooden
Timothy R. Ashley
Robert S. Wilson

This volume is an expression of the esteem with which colleagues and scholars in North America and in Great Britain hold the Rev. Dr. Allison Albert Trites. Few people build an academic career—much less a ministry—in one institution. Allison Trites, a son of New Brunswick, has laboured for thirty-seven years in one small theological college, not because he lacked opportunities at larger, more prestigious institutions, but because he believed that God had called him to be a witness in that place. What mattered to him was faithfulness, not prestige and the size of the institution. Few will come up to the standard that Allison has set.

His placement in a small theological college at the edge of the continent was offset by his regular attendance and participation in scholarly conferences. He also "religiously" observed the scholarly discipline of the sabbatical leave, usually going to a larger school for a year of networking, and scholarly and ecclesiastical effort. Each time, he came back refreshed and celebrating the venue, yet convinced that he was where God had placed him.

The three editors considered it a privilege to work on this project for our colleague. The impetus for a *Festschrift* came after one of the editors, Timothy Ashley, returned from a meeting of the Society of Biblical Literature where one had been presented to a former professor. We have been gratified by the acceptance of invitations to contribute, as well as the completion of articles that were promised. We thank the contributors for all their hard work. We are also grateful to the present and past principals of Acadia Divinity College (Drs. Lee McDonald and Andrew MacRae), to the Board of Trustees of Acadia Divinity College, and to the Atlantic Baptist Historical Committee who provided support for the project. It seemed fitting that a Baptist university press should be the publisher of this volume, and we are grateful to Mercer University Press, especially Marc Jolley, assistant publisher, and Edmon L. Rowell, Jr., senior editor, for immediate interest in this project, for their patience, and for bringing it to print.

The *Festschrift* is a diverse volume that will interest different people on different levels. Altogether, the contributions reflect Allison's interests in Old and New Testament studies, history, and theology. The theme of witness has been a topic of interest to Allison since his Oxford dissertation on the subject. In the following essays, that theme is broadly rather than narrowly defined, so it is rehearsed and played in a whole range of ways.

We should make one brief note on style and spelling. We agreed, early on, to let contributors speak in their own voice. There are writers from Canada, the UK, and the USA. Spelling and style are, therefore, Canadian, British, and American. Although this may grate on some purists, it does represent the writers more faithfully.

We commend this volume to all readers—especially those who will read these essays and remember the life and work of the honouree.

Introducing the Man

Andrew MacRae, former principal
Acadia Divinity College

How easily we identify individuals by their occupations, their professions, or their career achievements. We think of them as scholars, or teachers, or physicians, or builders, or politicians, or actresses, or musicians. While that gives many insights into the persons and their interests, talents, and contributions to society, quite frequently that kind of identification fails to introduce us to the persons we remember as real live persons. With that awareness, let me introduce Allison Trites, or "Allie" to some of his closest friends and associates, in rather personal terms, with a view to explaining his very long tenure at Acadia.

Allison is a Maritimer, who has retained for a lifetime his affection for his native New Brunswick, and for his roots in Atlantic Canada. He was born in September 1936, and raised in Fredericton, where he graduated in Philosophy and History from the University of New Brunswick. It was there he was ordained to Christian ministry in 1961. His preaching, teaching and study sojourns to the USA, Europe, the Middle East, and Lithuania, for example, have added enrichment to his life, but have, in no sense, reduced his affinity to his origins. This identification with Atlantic Canada has led him to be recognized by his peers, academic and church-related, in many ways, not least in his period of service as president of the United Baptist Convention of the Atlantic Provinces in 1987–1988.

Allison is an Acadia man! Although his academic horizons were wide, and took him, in student days and on sabbaticals, from the University of New Brunswick, to Eastern Baptist Theological Seminary, in Philadelphia, to Oxford, Cambridge, and Louisville, he has made Acadia, of which he is not a graduate, his first love, and has devoted thirty-seven remarkable years to teaching on its campus. Not only so, he has probably covered more laps in the Acadia pool, with his energetic daily dips, than the rest of the faculty of Theology put together! And he has been a most loyal supporter of every Acadia team he could fit into his schedule as a fan and vocal supporter! Despite all the attraction and appeal of the wider academic and theological world, Allison has stayed with his commitment to Acadia, on the campus of which he has established the widest and strongest interfaculty and interpersonal relationships.

Allison is a family man. He and his wife Eugenie ("Gene" to everyone), a native of Lancashire, England, and a warm and caring part of the local church and community scene in Wolfville, have two sons, Jonathan, a surgeon in Halifax, and Ian, a member of the diplomatic service, assigned to service in Japan, and three grandchildren, children to Jonathan and Suzanne. It would be hard to conceive of a more closely knit family, or a home more characterized by open and welcoming hospitality than theirs.

Allison is a bookworm par excellence. For more than twenty years he has been the most regular book reviewer for the *Atlantic Baptist*—the official publication of the Atlantic Baptist community and Canada's oldest Christian publication—who has introduced a wide lay readership to many writers most would never have encountered otherwise. But though he devours books with the enthusiasm some others reserve for hamburgers, lobster, or coffee, he has shared the fruit of his brand of bookishness with the wider world, in many articles in prestigious dictionaries, in journal articles, and in several books from his own hand.

Allison is an optimist. His warm, friendly, outgoing, but essentially modest nature leads him to take quite a benevolent view of life, of people (even of awkward people), and of students. Sometimes, I have thought he imagined that students were constitutionally possessed of the same voracious love of learning that is his own, and capable of the same amount of reading and intellectual digestion and reproduction as he. I really do not think he has ever lost that optimistic expectation, although it is evidently not supported by real-life evidence. Nonetheless, his enthusiasm has lit a flame in many flickering student lives, which has continued to burn brightly throughout their subsequent ministries. Of course, his optimism led him to expect far too much of his students, sometimes to their considerable initial discomfort, but, later, their undying gratitude. He never could conceive that students, who were carrying five courses, were incapable of carrying five times the amount demanded in his course. But his optimism and his encouragement have produced many new scholars through the years!

Allison is a great sport. Behind his academic exterior lies a great deal of fun, waiting to get out. An enthusiast for everything he tackles, whether it be his research, chopping down decaying trees on his property, swimming every day, taking time for a vigorous game of ping-pong, or causing waves by taking part in the now established annual canoe races in competition with the Atlantic School of Theology, he approaches everything with the vigour of a man determined to win, but with the complete acceptance and joy in the success of another when he loses. In my early years at Acadia, beginning in 1980, by which time Allison had already been fifteen years on the faculty, he and I used to team up at the ping-pong table, and could usually defend the honour of the older crowd pretty well. Allison always sounded astonished when he missed an easy shot, which would never happen in translating Greek! But his astonishment always led to redoubled effort. Sadly, for me, my appointment as Principal and Dean in 1985 all but ruled out ping-pong. "A great sport," I said. Why, he and his patient English wife, Gene, have even deigned to eat haggis at our table! That is being a great sport!

Allison is an unashamed delegator! If Allison has a task that needs to be completed, and his attention, in his view, can be better given to preparing to preach or in carrying out a piece of research, he will not hesitate to seek help. Staff members would not say so, but I have seen some of his course "revisions," given to a member of staff to decipher and then to produce in intelligible form, and I have heard the benign groans, and even helped to decipher his medical-style hieroglyphic hand-scrawl. If someone else can do it, and leave Allison at peace to get on with the really important item in his mind or on his agenda, then "God's in His heaven, and all's right with the world."

Allison is a visionary churchman. There is not a mean, arrogant, or superior bone in his body when it comes to relating to persons from other Christian traditions. Allison's vision of the church, the Gospel, and the community of faith is very wide. I would entrust to him, without hesitation, the task of speaking to, relating to, and communicating with persons from every part of the Christian spectrum. His great respect for the history, the heritage, and the traditions of the old, established, hierarchical, and highly liturgical churches, and his complete openness to the "free" and the "contemporary" churches, which cling tightly to their faith but lightly to convention, custom, and predictability, and his ability to speak the language of all, without a trace of double-talk, and with complete integrity, make him a remarkable resource for building positive relationships across the chasms that too often divide Christians and separate them from one another. This breadth of vision is seen clearly in his record of having been a visiting professor or teacher at such varied institutions as King's College in Halifax, Nova Scotia (Anglican), the Presbyterian

College in Montreal, Quebec, Southern Baptist Theological Seminary in Louisville, Kentucky, Carson-Newman College in Tennessee, and the United Theological College in Aberystwyth, Wales. Furthermore, he has served on the Ecumenical Council of Canada, and has been an energetic supporter of the interchurch activities in his own area of residence over many years.

Allison is a great colleague. When I arrived in Canada in 1980, with my wife and family, to teach at Acadia, Allison was on sabbatical, but on his return, I quickly discovered what a willing, cooperative, and encouraging colleague he was. Over the years, he has taken his place and played his full part in the diverse life of a small, and very busy faculty. On the faculty he was everyone's friend, and could be counted on to get to know the "new kid on the block" very quickly, and make that person feel very much at home. He always played his part on faculty committees, and in the daily life and the social functions of the College. One of the additional marks of his collegiality was that it continued, following the graduation of students who had majored in New Testament, to offer support and encouragement to such persons in their early years of ministry or in their further graduate level studies. I suspect he has written more academic references to graduate schools for his former students than most faculty members have done, and has continued to be an encourager. I pay my own tribute to his collegiality because of the special opportunities that were mine to observe and experience it, on my appointment as Principal and Dean of Theology from 1985 to 1998. Throughout these years, Allison could be counted on to pull his weight, to give diligent attention to all his responsibilities, and to meet any expectations I, in my role, may have made on him. Through all the years, Allison was a symbol of reliability, loyalty, unselfish support, and willing service.

Allison is a preacher. Not only so, he is a popular preacher. Not too many academics, it seems, remain connected enough with the grass roots of church life to maintain an effective and relevant preaching ministry. Allison Trites has done so, to a remarkable degree. He is in constant demand among the churches of his own denomination, and beyond it. It is reckoned that he has preached in more than 300 churches in what is now named the Convention of Atlantic Baptist Churches.

Allison is an outstanding New Testament scholar. This book would not have been compiled if it were not so. It honours him, not simply because he is the longest serving member of our faculty, and for the personal qualities to which I have made reference, but because he has made a significant contribution to New Testament scholarship in Canada and internationally. During his Oxford days, he was the recipient of a Beaverbrook Overseas Scholarship, and was also recognized with scholarly awards from the Lilly Foundation, the American Philosophical Society, and the Canada Council.

He has written several books, monographs, and many scholarly articles, and their subject areas reveal the breadth of his academic, professional, and scholarly interest. He has written extensively on the theme of witness, prayer, the Johannine writings, the charismatic movement, Christian citizenship, the ascension, Christian baptism, women in ministry, church growth, angels, and more. Most of all, he is known for his fascination with, and his expertise in, Luke and Acts, and is widely known as a Lukan scholar.

It was partly in recognition of his scholarship, but also his other qualities as a teacher, preacher, and faculty member, that I recommended to the board in 1991 that he be named the Payzant Distinguished Professor of Biblical Studies, a position he held until his retirement in June 2002.

Publications of Allison A. Trites

Bible

1968

"The Idea of Witness in the Synoptic Gospels: Some Juridical Considerations." *Themelios* 5:18-26.

1969

"Awareness of God's Self-Disclosure." *Journey into Life: Seven Studies in Christian Experience*, ed. Abner J. Langley and Theo T. Gibson, 3-12. Saint John: Jubilee Journey Committee, United Baptist Convention of the Atlantic Provinces.

1970

"Biblical Basis of the Church's Mission." *This Is Tomorrow: A Sequel to the Home Missions Digest*, ed. C. Alvin Armstrong, 3-24. Brantford: Baptist Federation of Canada.

"Two Witness Motifs in Acts 1:8 and the Book of Acts." *Themelios* 7:17-22.

1973

"*Martus* and Martyrdom in the Apocalypse: A Semantic Study." *Novum Testamentum* 5:72-80.

1974

"The Woman Taken in Adultery." *Bibliotheca Sacra* 131:137-46.

1975

"The Importance of Legal Scenes and Language in the Book of Acts." *Novum Testamentum* 16:278-84.

1975–1978

"Gather, Scatter." *The New International Dictionary of New Testament Theology*, ed. Lothar Coenen et al. English edition, 2:31-35. Exeter: Paternoster.

"Witness, Testimony." *NIDNTT* 3:1047-51.

1977

The New Testament Concept of Witness. Society for New Testament Studies monograph series 31. Cambridge: Cambridge University Press.

"Some Aspects of Prayer in Luke-Acts." *Society of Biblical Literature 1977 Seminar Papers*, ed. Paul J. Achtemeier, 59-77. Missoula: Scholars.

1978

"The Prayer Motif in Luke-Acts." *Perspectives on Luke-Acts*, ed. Charles H. Talbert, 168-86. Danville: Association of Baptist Professors of Religion.

1979

"The Transfiguration of Jesus: The Gospel in Microcosm." *Evangelical Quarterly* 51:67-79.

"The Witness Theme in the Gospel of John." *Verdict* 2/2:7-14.

1983

New Testament Witness in Today's World. Valley Forge: Judson.

1987

"The Transfiguration in the Theology of Luke: Some Redactional Links." *The Glory of Christ in the New Testament*, ed. Lincoln D. Hurst and Norman T. Wright, 71-81. Oxford: Oxford University Press.

1988

"Church Growth in the Book of Acts." *Bibliotheca Sacra* 145/578:162-73.

1990

"Church Growth in the Acts of the Apostles." *McMaster Journal of Theology* 1:1-18.

1992

"The Blessings and Warnings of the Kingdom (Matthew 5:3-12; 7:13-27)." *Review and Expositor* 89:179-96.

"Witness." *A Dictionary of Biblical Tradition in English Literature*, ed. David L. Jeffrey, 842-43. Grand Rapids: Eerdmans.

"Witness." *Dictionary of Jesus and the Gospels*, ed. Joel B. Green, Scot McKnight, and I. Howard Marshall, 877-80. Downers Grove: InterVarsity.

1993

"Witness." *Dictionary of Paul and His Letters*, ed. Gerald F. Hawthorne, Ralph P. Martin, and Daniel G. Reid, 973-75. Downers Grove: InterVarsity.

"Witness." *The Oxford Companion to the Bible*, ed. Bruce M. Metzger and Michael D. Coogan, 805-806. New York: Oxford University Press.

1994

The Transfiguration of Christ: A Hinge of Holy History. Hantsport: Lancelot.

1995

"Angel of the Lord." *The Complete Who's Who in the Bible*, ed. Paul Gardner, 43-44. London/Grand Rapids: Marshall Pickering/Zondervan.

"Angels." *The Complete Who's Who in the Bible*, 44-49.

"Apostles." *The Complete Who's Who in the Bible*, 52-56.

"Barnabas." *The Complete Who's Who in the Bible*, 75-76.

"Luke." *The Complete Who's Who in the Bible*, 422-28.

"Stephen." *The Complete Who's Who in the Bible*, 633-36.

"Timothy." *The Complete Who's Who in the Bible*, 648-51.

1996

"Church Growth in the Book of Acts." *Vital New Testament Issues*, ed. Roy B. Zuck, 44-54, 244-45. Grand Rapids: Kregel Resources.

"Proclaiming Ephesians: God's Order in a Needy World." *Southwestern Journal of Theology* 39:43-50.

1997

"The Resilient Christ: A Study in Mark's Gospel." *What's Cooking: A Festschrift in Celebration of the 75th Birthday of Mary Ella Milham*, ed. James S. Murray, 43-54. Fredericton: University of New Brunswick Libraries.

1998

"Witness and Resurrection in the Apocalypse of John." *Life in the Face of Death: The Resurrection Message of the New Testament*, ed. Richard N. Longenecker, 270-88. Grand Rapids: Eerdmans.

2000

"Fornication." *Eerdmans Dictionary of the Bible*, ed. David Noel Freedman, Allen C. Myers, and Astrid B. Beck, 469b. Grand Rapids: Eerdmans.
"Governor." *Eerdmans Dictionary of the Bible*, 524.
"Persecution." *Eerdmans Dictionary of the Bible*, 1030.
"Saints." *Eerdmans Dictionary of the Bible*, 1151-52.
"Thanksgiving." *Eerdmans Dictionary of the Bible*, 1295-96.
"Theater." *Eerdmans Dictionary of the Bible*, 1296.

2001

"Witness." *Oxford Guide to Ideas and Issues of the Bible*, ed. Bruce M. Metzger and Michael D. Coogan, 551-52. New York: Oxford University Press.

History-Theology

1962

"B. B. Warfield's View of the Authority of Scripture." ThM Thesis, Princeton Theological Seminary.

1967

"The Art of Meditation." *The Watchman Examiner* 149:335-36.

1980

"The New Brunswick Baptist Seminary (1835–1895)." *Repent and Believe*, ed. Barry M. Moody, 103-23, 172-206. Hantsport: Lancelot.

1985

"An Assessment of the Baptist-Reformed Dialogue." *Reformed World* 38:385-95.

1988

"Calvin Goodspeed: An Assessment of His Theological Contribution." *Costly Vision: The Baptist Pilgrimage in Canada*, ed. Jarold K. Zeman. Burlington: G. R. Welch.

"A Forgotten Founder: A Biographical Study of Professor Calvin Goodspeed." *Southwestern Journal of Theology* 30:20-24.

"A Forgotten Scholar: Professor Calvin Goodspeed." *An Abiding Conviction: Maritime Baptists and Their World*, ed. Robert S. Wilson, 197-210. Hantsport: Lancelot.

1994

"The Life and Work of William Harris Elgee." *A Fragile Stability: Definition and Redefinition of Maritime Baptist Identity*, ed. David T. Priestley, 115-29. Hantsport: Lancelot.

"To Promote Intelligence and Harmony: The Life and Work of J. E. P. Hopper." *A Fragile Stability: Definition and Redefinition of Maritime Baptist Identity*, ed. David T. Priestley, 37-55. Hantsport: Lancelot.

In addition, Allison has published popular material in the *Atlantic Baptist* (articles and numerous reviews), the *Baptist Leader*, the *Canadian Baptist*, *Christian Week*, the *Second Mile*, *Decision*, the *Communicator*, the *Fredericton Daily Gleaner*, and *Christianity Today*. He also was an abstractor for *Religious and Theological Abstracts* (Myerstown, Pennsylvania) from 1968 to 1983.

Biblical Studies

"A Friend in Need: Pastoral Practice in the Face of Doubt"

Timothy R. Ashley
Minister, First Baptist Church, La Crosse, Wisconsin

This study is about one model of pastoral practice.[1] The goal of pastoral practice is "bringing others to fuller life in Christ," and includes most different kinds of professional ministry such as preaching, teaching, evangelism, counselling, discipling, and pastoral care, but is not meant to exclude ministry done by others than professionals. What follows is an exercise in thinking out one or two implications of the biblical story of Job, in order to draw conclusions for the practice of ministry in the contemporary world. This does not aim to be an "academic" study of either the book or the character of Job, although I hope its approach is scholarly. The aim of the study is application. I chose to contribute this kind of study to a book honouring my colleague Allison Trites, because *his* interest in biblical studies, like mine, is directed toward the practice of ministry in the real church, rather than toward the study of an ancient series of documents from the Near East in and for the academy. This composition is about *friendship* because Allison has been a colleague and fast friend for two decades now.

The Old Testament contains a number of models that are useful for pastoral practice. The stories of Samuel and David (1 and 2 Samuel) teach about wise pastoral practice that listens and follows *before it leads*. The so-called *Confessions* of Jeremiah the prophet[2] teach about pastoral practice that incarnates a people to God, and, in a sense, God to a people. Again, the mysterious figure of the Servant of Yahweh in Isaiah 40–55 teems with lessons for ministry. The Servant models the kind of practice that serves *alongside* people. The Servant is a gentle proclaimer

---

[1]This paper was presented as one of the G. K. Simpson Lectures at Acadia Divinity College in February 1999. The reader will detect signs of its origins in oral discourse. Bible translation is from the NRSV (1989/1990) compared with the Hebrew text.

[2]Jer 11:18–12:6; 15:10-21; 17:14-18; 18:18-23; 20:7-13; 20:14-18.

rather than an "overpowerer" of people. Every one of these models is worthy of consideration.

The current study focuses, as was said above, on the story and character of Job. Job was a virtuous man of faith (Job 1:1). Fundamental to any study of the man Job is the lesson that faith is, basically, not a state of knowing the "right" content, but of having a relationship with the living God. In order to determine whether Job simply serves God because of what he has always known, God allows the Adversary[3] to test Job in almost unbelievable ways. He loses everything he has—and almost lets go of that faith, but does not.[4] Job's words drip with irony. Readers know that Job is not wrong.

As human beings live, their experience leads them to develop *primary faith affirmations* growing out of their experience with God (e.g., God exists, God is good). With further experience, these *primary affirmations* come to be expressed in *theological formulations* (e.g., God exists as Holy Trinity, God's goodness is seen in divine fairness/justice). These *theological formulations* are confirmed or denied in "what happens to us" in life. When the *theological formulations* are confirmed, all is well. However, when experience denies them, then people can experience *cognitive dissonance*, when the *theological formulations* do not seem to fit their experience. This may lead to modification of these *theological formulations*, or perhaps to rejection of them in favour of other *theological formulations* that are less dissonant with experience. If experience is strongly dissonant,

---

[3]The term השטן (the adversary) is translated rather than transliterated as "the satan," or simply "Satan." This character is a member of the divine court and not simply "the devil."

[4]The mainline historical-critical consensus concerning Job is generally acceptable. The Book of Job has its origins in an ancient tale of a righteous man who loses everything, but who, through faithfulness, regains all he lost and more. This tale survives in the prologue (1:1–2:13) and the epilogue (42:7-17). The real creative work in the book is taken up in the poetry of 3:1–42:6, which disagrees with the view of suffering in the prologue and epilogue. These later chapters were written by a wisdom writer, perhaps as a result of the Babylonian Exile, in the 6th century BC or a bit later. See, e.g., O. Eissfeldt, *The Old Testament: An Introduction*, trans. P. R. Ackroyd (New York: Harper & Row, 1965) 454-70, or, more recently and simply, V. H. Matthews and J. C. Moyer, *The Old Testament Text and Context* (Peabody: Hendrickson, 1997) 182-88.

persons may come to the point of what I would call *pistic dissonance*, where it is not simply the *theological formulations* that are in danger, but the *primary affirmations* as well.

The Wisdom Tradition and Wisdom Literature of Israel in general has a practical, horizontal outlook. By "horizontal" I mean that the Wisdom writers generally do not look for solutions to all of life's problems from a transcendent direction. This literature looks for solutions to this world's problems in terms of *this world*. One of the ways to see this is the relatively few times the name of God occurs in Wisdom texts as compared to legal, narrative or prophetic texts in the Old Testament. Proverbs, on average, only mentions God once every ten verses, as opposed to either Amos or Deuteronomy that mention God about once every verse. The *wisdom outlook* in Israel entailed a basic confidence in the human ability to find out about life and the world by searching and observing.[5] Within such an outlook, Proverbs provides the baseline. The vast majority of the proverbs set out the most fruitful ways to search for the good life, drawn from observation of the world. A proverb is a general truth in a specific example. But, what happens when, because the proverbs are in God's Book, people mistake these general truths in specific examples for laws or promises? What happens when proverbs (small or capital "p," for that matter) are thought to provide *the best way*, or the *only way* to lead a godly life? People who want the good life must do A, B, and C. Although such an approach is dangerous, it may work as long as life is on an even keel and people are comfortably oriented in their world.

But, then something happens that violates the rules. A comfortable orientation is upset by painful disorientation. The result is at least *cognitive* and, perhaps even *pistic dissonance*. Job reacts against using formulae such as found in Proverbs as theological orthodoxy and orthopraxy, and seeing this kind of wisdom methodology as *the* way to the good life. Job may best be read and understood when "the times are out of joint" and people are painfully disoriented.

Very few would claim that there are *no* good ways to assure a good life, and the author of Job cannot be accused of saying there are none. Job reacts, however, against Wisdom as a set of rigid propositions that one simply follows to obtain the good life—living life by formulae that may be

---

[5]On this theme see W. Brueggemann, *In Man We Trust: The Neglected Side of Biblical Faith* (Richmond: John Knox, 1972).

unerringly applied to every situation of life. In other words, Job reacts against the "wisdom" that sees living in certain well-traced patterns, as just so much "plugging in your quarter and getting out your blessing." Job is sure there *must be* ways in which the good life may be found, but objects that he has plugged the cosmic candy machine chock full of quarters and nothing but misery has dropped out. He has done everything normally necessary, he has "named and claimed" every precious promise, and is still suffering. Thus for Job, and others like him, it was necessary in the light of what life really looked like to call into question the adequacy of the well-tested ways. In short, Job *doubted* that these traditional ways were right. At the very least, Job was experiencing *cognitive dissonance*. However, Job's doubt is not necessarily to be thought of as antithetical to faith and a great evil, but, rather, as something which, so long as it remains a "way station on the road to faith," can be useful in discovering and fighting through to a stronger faith. Job, most especially, outlines this kind of *doubt in the interest of faith*. In this context *faith* is, as was said above, not a state of "knowing the right content," but of having a living relationship with God.

This kind of doubt is different from *unbelief*, which refuses to hold that faith is of any human use. This kind of doubt is also different from *pessimism*, which doubts so radically that the *good* becomes impossible to conceive of as strong enough to carry the day. Most of all, this doubt is different from *cynicism*, which doubts so radically that good and evil become irrelevant choices. Ronald T. Habermas differentiated doubt, the sincere question, from unbelief, the unwillingness to hear an answer.[6] Philip Phenix (born 1915), an educator at Columbia University in New York City, differentiated between *constructive* and *destructive* doubt. Constructive doubt is seen in the attitude of the father of the possessed son in Mark 9:24 who cried out, "I believe, help my unbelief." Destructive doubt is, according to Phenix, the view of cynics who are

> essentially faithless, in the sense that they presuppose the futility of any sustained quest for faith. . . . Abandoning the search for ultimate

---

[6]R. T. Habermas, "Doubt is not a four-letter word," *Religious Education* 84 (1989): 402-10. Habermas's categories were based on P. de Vries, "The deadly sin: unbelief is hazardous to health, but doubt can give hope," *Christianity Today* 31 (1987): 22-24.

> certainties, the sceptic unwittingly cuts the ground from under serious inquiry itself, thus discrediting his [or her] own activity of doubting.[7]

The literati, of course, knew of this *doubt in the interest of faith*, and its travail to bring forth a greater and more robust faith that is, at the same time, not credulity. Two excerpts of nineteenth-century poetry will show this. The first, from Philip James Bailey (who died in 1902), is from a poem called "A Country Town":

> Who never doubted never half believed.
> Where doubt there truth is—'tis her shadow.

The second is from that prince of Victorian poets, Alfred, Lord Tennyson, whose great poem "In Memoriam A. H. H." was written on the death in 1833 of one who was, at least, Tennyson's friend, Arthur Henry Hallam:

> There lives more faith in honest doubt,
> Believe me, than in half the creeds. (XCVI.3.3-4)

It sometimes takes others longer to "catch on" than it does our poets.

The Harvard social psychologist, Gordon W. Allport (1897–1967), posited some of the causes of doubt from his own perspective. He wrote that (1) Doubts may be attributed to a history of personal traumas. (2) Doubts are generated through unconscious attitudes toward parent figures (thus showing that he was influenced by Freud). (3) Doubts often correlate with an egocentric self-worshiping personality. (4) Doubts can be initiated by public hypocrisy and failure of institutional religion. (5) Doubts arise in the conflict between faith and science.[8]

The purpose of mentioning these educationalists, the social scientist, and the poets, is not to discuss their findings as such, or to complicate the issue of doubt, but rather to show how many different kinds of persons from many different perspectives have discussed the matter, and for how long (the poets are from the nineteenth century, Allport's work is more than fifty years old, etc.). It is interesting to see how many points of contact these vastly different persons have with the Hebrew Wisdom

---

[7]P. Phenix, "Transcendence and the Curriculum," in *Curriculum Theorizing the Reconceptualists*, ed. W. Pinar (Berkeley: McCutchan, 1975) 331.

[8]See G. W. Allport, *The Individual and His Religion: A Psychological Interpretation* (New York: Macmillan, 1950) 117-33.

literature (without any overt recognition of these points of contact). To add a theologian to the mix, Paul Tillich (1886–1965) worked with faith as the dynamic state of being "ultimately concerned," and saw certain sorts of doubt as contributing to faith that is really *concerned* with the *Ultimate* (that is, God).[9] Tillich's views are well known.

Another educator, John Westerhoff III, in a slim volume called *Will Our Children Have Faith?* (written more than a quarter-century ago) speaks of four kinds, or styles, of faith: (1) Experienced Faith (he means experiencing someone else's, e.g., parents' faith); (2) Affliative Faith (join up and see); (3) Searching Faith (see below); and (4) Owned Faith (see below as well).

Westerhoff's third style of faith, Searching Faith, is crucial. Three things characterize Searching Faith: doubt/critical judgment, experimentation, and the need to commit to persons and causes. These three are not airtight categories, and bleed into one another. Let me cite what Westerhoff wrote about doubt:

> Sometimes painful and sometimes celebrative, those with searching faith need to act over against the understanding of faith acquired earlier. We seem to know this, at least in terms of adolescent family behaviour, but we have neglected it when considering faith. For example, my teenagers sometimes think I am quite stupid and misguided. And while that is not easy to live with, it is important for them to believe it in order to acquire their own identity. The same is true of faith that is our own, we need to doubt and question that faith. At this point, the "religion of the head" becomes equally important with the "religion of the heart," and acts of the intellect, critical judgment, and inquiry into the meanings and purposes of the story and the ways by which the community of faith lives are essential. Serious study of the story, and engagement with historical, theological, and moral thinking about life becomes important. The despairs and doubts of the searching soul need to be affirmed and persons need to join others in the intellectual quest for understanding.[10]

---

[9]Two of Tillich's smaller books are quite helpful in the discussion: Tillich, *The Courage to Be*, based on the Terry Lectures at Yale (New Haven: Yale University Press, 1952) esp. 48-50, 76-77, 174-77, et passim; also his *Dynamics of Faith*, World Perspectives 10 (New York: Harper, 1956) esp. 16-22, but the whole book may be consulted with profit.

[10]J. H. Westerhoff, *Will ur Children Have Faith?* (NewOYork: Seabury, 1976)

Again, the last style of faith in Westerhoff's schema is Owned Faith, and this comes only as a result of maturation *through the process* of searching faith, never without it or in spite of it, or by denying the process. Importantly, the dynamics of the previous style are never wholly outgrown. In other words, doubts come back through life.[11]

Westerhoff ended the citation above with an important sentence for the current matter—our own understanding of our response to our own doubts and those of others. I repeat that sentence now for emphasis:

> The despairs and doubts of the searching soul need to be affirmed and persons need to join others in the intellectual quest for understanding.[12]

The answer is *community*. *Community* functions in ways that are beyond a simple intellectual understanding and extends to the whole experiential dimension of life. Pastoral practice occurs *in community*, not apart from it or over against it. The practitioner who is not a part of a community will not be able to function pastorally in that community.

Let us now turn to Job. Job the righteous sufferer disputes with three "friends"—Eliphaz, Bildad, and Zophar—throughout the dialogues of the Book of Job (chapters 3-31). His friends' airtight theology stated that all suffering is brought on by the sin of the sufferer. Because of his own suffering, Job *doubts* their theological formulation is adequate to explain his experience (*cognitive dissonance*). At the end of the whole series of messy incidents (including Job's so-called dialogues with Eliphaz, Bildad and Zophar, and Elihu's monologues), God arrives in a whirlwind and confronts Job with the divine presence. Some scholars see in this confrontation the real *answer* to the problems of God's justice in the world, and to the theology of suffering brought out in the dialogues. For example, Davidson and Lanchester saw God's answer as both rebuking Job's impious attitudes and resolving the tensions raised by Job's challenges to God

---

96-97.

[11]Westerhoff acknowledges his indebtedness to the researches of James Fowler. Fowler's work is now nicely summarized in the book J. W. Fowler, *Stages of Faith: The Psychology of Human Development and the Quest for Meaning* (San Francisco: Harper & Row, 1981).

[12]Westerhoff, *Will Our Children Have Faith?*, 97.

throughout chapters 3-31.[13] If this *is* an *answer*, it is not the kind of answer that includes a kind of informational exchange that brings *new* rational reasons to believe rather than to doubt. There is no such informational exchange in the transaction between God and Job, and the reasons to believe are a belief in divine creation and providence—hardly new. The resolution of Job's doubt is rather in the antithesis spoken by him in Job 42:5 (near the end of the poem): "I had heard of you (Yahweh) by the hearing of the ear, but now my eye sees you." What was it that Job had heard "by the hearing of the ear" all his life? The answer to this question will demand a closer look at Job 28.[14]

Job 28 is a poem about wisdom. This poem is understood by most scholars to be an independent composition—either by the same author or by someone else—dealing with wisdom, and placed here for reasons that are not always made clear.[15] The poem neither sounds like Job, nor is its structure similar to the surrounding dialogues. It is, therefore, probable that the author borrowed a poem or song from elsewhere.[16] The Wisdom poem of chapter 28 is crucial to the development of the theological argu-

---

[13]A. B. Davidson and H. C. O. Lanchester, *The Book of Job* (Cambridge: Cambridge University Press, 1918) 297-98.

[14]My seminary Old Testament professor suggested the following approach to chap. 28 many years ago. His approach is discussed in a remarkable short study to which this section owes much. See R. B. Laurin, "Theological structure of Job," *ZAW* 84 (1972): 86-89.

[15]S. R. Driver and G. B. Gray, *A Critical and Exegetical Commentary on the Book of Job together with a New Translation*, ICC (Edinburgh: T. & T. Clark, 1921) 1:xxxviii. See, e.g., Rowley (citing several others), who sees chap. 28 as out of place in its present location, even if the author of the rest of the poems wrote it. H. H. Rowley, *Job*, NCB (Grand Rapids: Eerdmans, 1976) 178-79. "Virtually all critics are agreed that the poem on wisdom, xxviii, is extraneous" (M. H. Pope, *Job: Introduction, Translation, and Notes*, AB 15 (Garden City: Doubleday, 1965) xvii).

[16]C. Westermann, *The Structure of the Book of Job: A Form-Critical Analysis*, trans. C. A. Münchow (Philadelphia: Fortress, 1981) 136. A similar problem arises with the "doxologies" now in Amos at 4:13; 5:8-9; 9:5-6, which may also have their sources elsewhere, but are best read where they are in the current book. See, e.g., J. D. W. Watts, *Vision and Prophecy in Amos* (Leiden: Brill, 1958) 170-77.

ment of the book, and it therefore seems most cogent to try to explain the poem where it stands in the text (whatever its source).[17]

All of his life Job had heard that Yahweh alone was the possessor of Wisdom. Humans should forget having wisdom to any real extent, except as God doled it out. Chapter 28 breaks into three sections: Verses 1-12 detail human capacity in what might be called technology, especially mining. Verses 13-20 contrast this capacity with human *in*capacity to mine wisdom. It is not underground, it is not for sale, even for the precious metals that *are* discovered underground. Each of these sections ends (vv. 12 and 20) with the refrain "Where shall wisdom be found? And where is the place of understanding?" The third section, vv. 21-28, proclaims the answer: There are two types of wisdom, one that deals with God's workings with the inner secrets of the cosmos (including divine providence), and one that deals with a kind of practical wisdom for living in the world. God alone has the first kind of wisdom. Many people think true wisdom includes insights into the *whys* of the universe. That kind of wisdom and knowledge can be sought, but not found. Yet, God has revealed *some* wisdom to humans, the only wisdom that is needed to live meaningfully on the earth. This kind of wisdom is summed up in the old proverb "Behold the fear of Yahweh, that is wisdom; and to depart from evil is understanding" (28:28; cf. Proverbs 1:7a; 9:10).

According to Westermann, chapter 28 is the only pure wisdom speech in the book. It is an expansion of the kind of proverbial sayings encapsulated in a riddle made up of the content of verses 12, 21, 23:[18]

> But where shall wisdom be found?
>   And where is the place of understanding? . . .
> It is *hidden* from the eyes of all living,
>   and concealed from the birds of the air. . . .
> God understands the way to it,
>   and he knows its place.

---

[17]See below. Many recent commentators interpret the chapter as integral to its context, e.g., N. C. Habel, *The Book of Job: A Commentary*, OTL (Philadelphia: Westminster, 1985) 391-401.

[18]Westermann, *The Structure of the Book of Job*, 136.

There is a kind of wisdom that all but God may *hear of*, but not possess (see v. 22). The only kind of wisdom that is accessible to human beings is that kind of wisdom summed up in v. 28 that consists in fearing Yahweh and shunning evil. This view makes divine wisdom and human wisdom two distinct categories.

Job and his friends would likely agree on such a view. See, for example, the words of Zophar from chapter 11:

> Can you find out the deep things of God?
> Can you find out the limit of the Almighty?
> It is higher than heaven—what can you do?
> Deeper than Sheol—what can you know? . . .
> If you direct your heart rightly,
> you will stretch out your hands toward him. . . .
> Surely then you will lift up your face without blemish;
> you will be secure, and will not fear. . . .
> But the eyes of the wicked will fail;
> all way of escape will be lost to them,
> and their hope is to breathe their last. (vv. 7, 8, 13, 15, 20)[19]

Here are Job's own words in chapter 23:

> If I go forward, he is not there;
> or backward, I cannot perceive him;
> on the left he hides, and I cannot behold him;
> I turn to the right, but I cannot see him.
> But he knows the way that I take;
> when he has tested me, I shall come out like gold.
> My foot has held fast to his steps;
> I have kept his way and have not turned aside.
> I have not departed from the commandment of his lips;
> I have treasured in my bosom the words of his mouth.
> But he stands alone and who can dissuade him?
> What he desires, that he does.
> For he will complete what he appoints for me;
> and many such things are in his mind. (vv. 8-14)[20]

---

[19]See also 5:8-9; 8:20; 22:12-13; 26:5-14.
[20]See also 9:4-12; 12:7-10.

Job is the paragon of the upright life; the prologue describes Job as "one who feared God and turned away from evil" (1:1), later set forth as the conditions for having wisdom (28:28). In general, the Old Testament insists that God and God alone be worshiped, and that holy living brings divine blessing (see, e.g., Exodus 20:1-6; Deuteronomy 10:12-11:32). God's speeches in Job 38:1–40:2 and 40:6–41:34 especially emphasize divine power. In 40:9-14 God tells Job that, if he can govern the world as wisely as God can, then God will acknowledge Job's case.

Job's problem is not with such theological generalities, but with his friends' specific interpretation of what it means to fear God and turn from evil. According to their interpretation, Job needed to fear God by turning away from the evil that his current suffering showed he had committed. It was precisely the conflict between what his friends claimed to be true and his own experience that gave rise to Job's doubt and distrust of the system of wisdom itself. To sum up Job's response throughout—in many and various forms: "I've done everything I can, and I'm still suffering." Job can have neither God's own wisdom nor normal human wisdom, even though he has feared God, turned from evil, and lived the upright life. The deck seems stacked against Job.

What chapter 28 does, then, at a point when Job and his friends have said about all that they could say and were still at an impasse, is to summarize the issue at debate: the meaning of the traditional wisdom doctrine. The friends were prepared to accept it as it was, but Job was not so easily convinced. He doubted that the traditional wisdom theology really met his life experience. It may have once been sufficient to explain life, but no longer. He had, in Westerhoff's terms, moved from an earlier stage of faith to *searching faith*. Chapters 29–31 summarize Job's problem with God's apparent inconsistency and capriciousness. Job used to know (chapter 29), but now he does not (chapter 30), in spite of the fact that he has followed the wisdom ways of chapter 28 to the letter, and lived uprightly (chapter 31).

In 42:5, Job says that *he sees* that wisdom is not as simple as he *had heard* it was. His primary experience of life (seeing) made his secondary experience inferred from others' experience to be nonsense. It is *not* just a matter of formulae—of plugging in one's quarter and getting out a blessing, as if God were the cosmic candy machine. That way had become too neat, too pat, for Job's primary life-experience. It is interesting how much of a *minority report* Job's statement is. The major biblical metaphors for receiving divine revelation have more to do with *hearing a word* than with *seeing a person*. It was common to "*hear* Yahweh's word." It was agreed, "No one may *see* [God] and live" (cf., Exodus 33:20). Job contrasts the reality of face-to-face encounter with hearsay, and invests the "seeing" metaphor with primary relevance.

Would-be pastoral practitioners should understand that theology, even moderately good theology, has and may continue to play a stifling role, if a relationship with God (the primary experience and affirmation) is confused with the formulation of certain propositions about God (even orthodox ones). Face-to-face relationship is what God brings in chapters 38–42. And it is in such a relationship that an *answer* to the problem of doubt and suffering emerges.[21] Job learns no new doctrine in his encounter with God. He simply meets God ("now my eye sees you"). Meaningful faith through doubt comes not *simply* (and not always) by the proclamation (or acceptance) of certain facts about God, true though they may be.

Chapter 28 provides such a collection of facts in a hymnic creedal form. But more than creed is needed for thoughtful, involved people, as Job shows in chapters 29–31. Faith finds its basic ground only in a personal encounter with God.[22]

This realization enables Job to carry on with life. Pastoral practice involves enabling people to "carry on with life" in the presence of God. And, so, after teasing the reader a bit with Elihu, who does little but put off the inevitable (chapters 32–37), Job does have that encounter with God (38:1–42:6).

To summarize, Job 42:5 is the key to understanding the last part of the Book of Job, and is a significant clue to an experiential understanding of the character of Job himself. Further, in the Wisdom poem of chapter 28, the narrator of the final form of the book contributed the old familiar case of what had started out to be a living, vital way to a relationship with God, but had ended as being ossified and legalistic—something to be "heard by the hearing of the ear." What do these conclusions contribute to our understanding of Job's struggle for faith? And what does Job's

---

[21]On the whole problem of theodicy that the book raises, see, e.g., J. L. Crenshaw, *Theodicy in the Old Testament*, Issues in Religion and Theology 4 (Philadelphia: Fortress, 1983). Crenshaw's own introduction to the problem (pp. 1-16) is especially valuable.

[22]Laurin, "Theological structure of Job," 88.

struggle for faith say to a contemporary search for a paradigm of pastoral practice in the community of faith? To come to answers to these questions, we need to explore a different part of the story of Job. The other characters in the dialogues of chapters 3–31 are Eliphaz, Bildad, and Zophar. They are called Job's "friends" nine times in the book.[23] The core of Job is made up of the "interactions" between Job and these friends. What goes into making a friend?

> Now when Job's three friends heard of all this disaster that had come upon him, they came each from his own place. . . . They made an appointment together to come to sympathize with him and comfort him. And when they saw him from a great distance, they did not recognize him; and they raised their voices and wept; and they tore their robes and sprinkled dust on their heads toward heaven. And they sat with him on the ground seven days and seven nights, and no one spoke a word to him, for they saw that his suffering was very great. (2:11-13)

The three started out on a positive track. Many people in the world find faith difficult. If Job's acquaintances had contented themselves with *being with Job* to comfort him without trying to explain things to him that were not known to them (and could not really be known), if they had simply "wept with those who weep," they would have been much better "friends," and better remembered by successive generations of readers. Their problem was that, from whatever motive, they decided that Job the doubter needed answers more than he needed community, and arguments more than he needed presence. The result of the decision that Job needed to be argued out of his doubts is found in chapters 3–31. God himself did not underwrite such an example of pastoral practice:

> After Yahweh had spoken these words to Job, Yahweh said to Eliphaz the Temanite: "My wrath is kindled against you and against your two friends; for you have not spoken of me what is right, as my servant Job has." (42:7)

In all his doubting, Job had spoken more of what was *right* of God than had Eliphaz, Bildad, and Zophar.[24] Job had *searching faith*, to use

---

[23]The first occurrence is in 2:11. The Hebrew word is רע, which is related to the word for "to have to do with one another" (רעה); *HALOT*, 1253-56, 1262.

[24]The word here is נכונה, "what is firm, reliable, true," *BDB*, 465b.

Westerhoff's term, but he did have faith. Job's friends did not understand faith-in-the-questioning-key at all. Whereas there is a place for content in godly living, and there well may be a role for intellectual argument in helping people with some kinds of intellectual doubts, the fundamental attitude for pastoral practice in the community should be a willingness to *be with* doubters through their doubts, more than to argue them out of these doubts. Were Eliphaz, Bildad, and Zophar really friends of Job at all, then? Were they really those who "had to do with" Job in his suffering in any important way?

Job has a stout, and some find disturbing, view of what goes into making a radical or "true" friend.[25] Chapter 6 is the locus of this discussion. The friends have been introduced in the prologue as people of high social standing like Job, who gathered from all over to be with Job in his sorrow and suffering (see above, 2:11-13). These so-called friends were comfortable with Job until he decided, in his agony, to *express* his doubt of the system. Then, at the crunch, when Job *needed* a friend in the very worst way, he was met instead by rigid theologians, and when he *called for* sympathy, he was given a lecture on doctrine. Eliphaz, Bildad, and Zophar—and their modern counterparts—seem to have thought that they were required to defend God against the impious doubter.[26]

Chapters 6–7 contain Job's response to the first speech of Eliphaz. When Job first responds to him, it is not to his theological *argument* that he responds in some anger, but to his perceived betrayal *of a friend*. In 6:2-4, Job sets the scene for the discussion of friendship by saying that his suffering is immense, and God, in fact, is the cause (which readers of the prologue know to be true, at least in part). What is required in the face of such a situation is illustrated in 6:5-7 by the saying that cattle do not bellow when they have enough fodder, and—with change of detail—neither do people. Job has looked for sympathy and has been met with the "tasteless fodder" of argument, so he has bellowed, so to speak. He

---

[25]These paragraphs owe much to an important article by N. C. Habel, " 'Only the Jackal Is My Friend': On Friends and Redeemers in Job," *Interpretation* 31 (1977): 227-36.

[26]Habel, "Only the Jackal Is My Friend," 229. Through the author's years of seminary teaching, quite a number of students (as well as practicing pastors) have reacted negatively to the suggestion that it is not good pastoral practice to argue with people who make theological errors while in the throes of anguish.

needed a "friend," but has found none, so he would be better off, he says, if God would put him out of his misery and kill him (6:8-11), because he has neither the inner strength nor the outer resources (i.e., friendship) to face his life (6:11-13). His doubts were getting the better of him through his suffering. He was teetering on the brink of *pistic* disaster.

It is in 6:14 that we come onto the startling definition of friendship that is necessary in the face of doubt, and with which the current discussion will conclude. This verse is pivotal to the whole chapter. Scholars have variously translated it. Indeed, some commentators and translators find what the text says so distasteful that they modify the text in the interest of something more palatable.[27] The AV is somewhat confusing: "To him that is afflicted pity *should be shewed* from his friend; but he forsaketh the fear of the Almighty." The NASV reads: "For the despairing man *there should be* kindness from his friend; lest he forsake the fear of the Almighty." The NRSV reads: "Those who withhold kindness from a friend forsake the fear of the Almighty." In the NRSV this verse is accompanied by the note that this translation is drawn from the Syriac and Latin versions, since the Hebrew is obscure. The text is not only a little obscure, it is shocking. The REB (following its NEB predecessor) gets closer: "Devotion is due from his friends to one who despairs and loses faith in the Almighty." So does the NIV: "A despairing man should have the devotion of his friends, even though he forsakes the fear of the Almighty." Norman Habel has suggested the following translation: "A despairing man needs the loyalty of a friend when he loses his faith in the Almighty."[28]

What a powerful definition of a friend! A friend is one who shows love and covenant loyalty (Hebrew חסד) to one who is despairing to the point of giving up his/her faith in God. And this is not just seen as the extreme case. *When* that faith is lost is exactly *when* the loyalty of a friend is needed, and by extension, given. The lovely Hebrew word חסד describes

[27]One wonders whether, e.g., Dhorme's excision of this verse as a marginal gloss does not have to do with its "unorthodoxy": see E. Dhorme, *A Commentary on the Book of Job*, trans. H. Knight (London: Nelson, 1967) 84-85.

[28]Habel, "Only the Jackal Is My Friend," 230. In his commentary in the Old Testament Library (*Book of Job*, 138-39, 148-49), Habel enriches the discussion in the light of his later thought. The Hebrew text is למס מרעהו חסד ויראת שדי יעזוב:, "to a despairing one (is) loyalty from a friend, when (and) he loses his fear of Shaddai."

that loyalty which guarantees covenant bonds and relationships. In Habel's words,

> It includes a basic trust which enables people to live by the spirit of a covenant relationship rather than the letter. This chesed is the ultimate force of Jonathan's friendship with David. At the moment of potential disaster he says to David, "If I am still alive, show me the chesed of Yahweh so that I may not die; and do not cut off your chesed from my house forever." (1 Sam. 20:14-15)

Job looks for this kind of support to help him work through his doubt-on-the-way-to-becoming-fuller-faith (his searching faith). He does not get it, so that the rest of chapter 6 spells out his disgust at these "so-called" friends. Job is looking for redemptive friendship. When it becomes obvious that his earthly friends will not provide him with such, this "friend" paradigm is transposed, so to speak, into a heavenly key, and, in chapter 16, Job looks for such a redemptive friend from heaven:

> Even now my witness is in heaven; my guarantor is on high. My interpreter, my friend before God when my eye is dripping; he will arbitrate for persons with God as a human being does for his friend. (16:19-21)[29]

And, indeed, in the famous Redeemer passage in 19:23-27, although this passage is very difficult, it is clear that this Redeemer figure is drawn on the paradigm of the ultimate friend.[30] What Job is looking for is one who can be a friend in the following sense:

> To be a friend is to be co-human in a dehumanized situation where a despairing [human being] has lost his [or her] religion as a source of inner support.[31]

When, at least in the moment, such a friend does not appear, Job sighs in his last lament: "The jackal is now my brother; the owl is my friend" (30:19). The only compassionate companions he has are the

---

[29]Habel, "Only the Jackal Is My Friend," 233. See his commentary in the Old Testament Library, 263, for a somewhat adjusted reading.

[30]On this passage see, e.g., N. C. Habel, *The Book of Job*, CBC (London: Cambridge University Press, 1975) 103-05. Habel's older comments are often different from his comments in his newer commentary, but equally valuable.

[31]Habel, "Only the Jackal Is My Friend," 230.

creatures of the wilderness that hoot and howl in the night. How many persons that we know in the Christian community feel that their only friends are their pets, because only they will listen without arguing?

To repeat, the lesson of Job is that proper pastoral practice with doubters is one of *being with them* rather than one of arguing with them. Doubters are hardly ever argued out of their doubts or into the kingdom anyway, because it is not a matter of sheer information and assent that brings them out of doubt and into the light of the kingdom. It is a matter of will and of heart. In the contemporary world many summaries of doctrine are available (as in Job 28), but all of them may only be "hearing with the ear," when divorced from an encounter with God.

Although Habel's work on Job has been quite thoroughly cited already, nonetheless, there can be no better conclusion than what Habel calls his "Closing Comments." They were a tremendous challenge to pastoral practice when they were first written, and remain so today.

> The poet of Job forces us to consider friendship as a radical option for life in an age of increased anonymity and contrived sensitivity. His word is more than a nostalgic glance at what appears to be a vanishing species. If education in the art of friendship is dangerous, the task of seeking a friend may be even more precarious. We, like Job, may find it relatively easy to discover redeemers who will save our property or life from disaster. Advocates for the oppressed are likewise available, at least in small numbers. Counsellors and lifeline operators will provide hours of anonymous compassion across a desk or over the telephone. But finding or being a friend who is more than a mate, more loyal than a kinsman, more empathetic than a redeemer, more trustworthy than a priest, involves the ultimate risk. Trusting a friend without reservation in the face of an alien world is a major concern for Job. Our temptation is to assume that we could be a loyal friend to others in need; the greater problem is our inability to trust anyone to be a radical friend. We have lost faith in trust. Recent studies reveal that among the clergy this weakness is epidemic. In exposing three friends, the poet was speaking to all professional "friends." He spoke in uncomfortable terms that are difficult to internalize. His wisdom is tantamount to heresy: It is better to suffer with a friend than to defend his God.[32]

---

[32]Ibid., 236.

The challenge in this and any generation is to be such friends. Pastoral practitioners who have learned from Job will learn to help doubters by seeing them with their eyes, not only hearing what these "poor benighted folk" are like with the hearing of the ear. One model of pastoral practice for the new millennium should be that of radical friend of the friendless.[33] In fact, although this would require another study, our Lord himself showed the same stance toward those he served.

---

[33]In his recent book, *No Longer Servants but Friends: A Theology of Ordained Ministry* (Nashville: Abingdon, 1999), Edward C. Zaragoza attempts to construct the pastoral model of "friend." Unfortunately, much of what Zaragoza accomplishes in the book is a critique of a so-called "servant model," and is more a critique of a model drawn from corporate and business sources than from biblical sources. The book does a disservice to the servant model of ministry. Except for the last chapter (and the appendixes), the book is largely a disappointment for one looking for an exposition of biblical texts.

The Witness of Daniel in the Court of the Kings

R. Glenn Wooden
Acadia Divinity College

In 1983 I sat in the office of Dr. Allison Trites, my New Testament professor, talking about the directions that I might take for graduate studies. He encouraged me to pursue one of the areas that I had indicated was of interest to me, namely, the study of apocalyptic literature. As a result of that conversation, I went on to do a masters thesis on Ezekiel 38–39, and then a dissertation on Daniel. It is with deepest gratitude that I dedicate this paper to Allison, Christian gentleman, churchman, professor, and colleague.

In the Book of Daniel, the main character functions in three roles: as a court diviner who interprets dreams and riddles (chapters 1–5); as an administrator (chapter 6); and as the receptor of dreams and visions that must be interpreted for him (chapters 7–12). In the first two roles, Daniel is a witness to the God of his fathers in the courts of the Mesopotamian kings. In this essay, I will focus on the role of the diviner in chapter 2, for it is in this chapter that the patterns are set for chapters 4 and 5, and in which we are given insight into the character's own revelatory experiences in chapters 7–12.

It was Hans-Peter Müller and John J. Collins who focused the attention of scholars on the role of Daniel as a diviner.[1] The phrase used for

---

[1]H.-P. Müller, "Magisch-mantische Weisheit und die Gestalt Daniels," *Ugarit-Forschungen* 1 (1969): 79-94; idem, "Mantische Weisheit und Apokalyptik," in *Studies in the Religion of Ancient Israel*, VTSup (Leiden: E. J. Brill, 1972) 268-93; idem, "Marchen, Legende und Enderwartung," *VT* 26 (July 1976): 338-50; J. J. Collins, "Jewish Apocalyptic against Its Hellenistic Near Eastern Environment," *BASOR* 220 (1975): 218-34; idem, *The Apocalyptic Vision of the Book of Daniel*, HSM 16 (Missoula: Scholars, 1977); idem, *Daniel: A Commentary on the Book of Daniel*, Hermeneia, ed. F. M. Cross (Minneapolis: Fortress, 1993). See also F. H. Cryer, *Divination in Ancient Israel and Its Near Eastern Environment: A Socio-Historical Investigation*, JSOTSup 142, ed. D. J. A. Clines and P. R. Davies (Sheffield: Sheffield Academic, 1994); L. L. Grabbe, *Priests, Prophets, Diviners, Sages: A Socio-Historical Study of Religious Specialists in Ancient Israel* (Valley Forge: Trinity Press International, 1995); A. Jeffers, *Magic and Divination in*

this function is usually "mantic wise man," a diviner who predicts the future.[2] Based upon the work of others,[3] Müller and Collins contended that the stories of Daniel came from the Mesopotamian Diaspora, and were developed among circles of Jews who served or aspired to serve in the administrations of the kings of the Persian and Hellenistic eras. The stories reflect the self-understanding and ultimate aspirations of such functionaries: they knew their God was superior, and they aspired to be in roles such as those in which Daniel found himself. It has been suggested that the stories were actually developed and circulated among Jewish mantics who eventually found their way back to Palestine sometime before the tumultuous years of Antiochus IV Epiphanes in the second century BCE.[4]

This view, as espoused most fully by Collins, assumes a positive portrayal and appraisal of the role of the court diviners by these Jews,[5]

Ancient Palestine and Syria, Studies in the History and Culture of the Ancient Near East 8, ed. B. Halpern and M. H. E. Weippert (Leiden: E. J. Brill, 1996) on divination in the Hebrew Scriptures; and esp. J. C. VanderKam, *Enoch and the Growth of an Apocalyptic Tradition*, Catholic Biblical Quarterly Monograph Series 16, ed. B. Vawter (Washington: Catholic Biblical Association of America, 1984) on manticism in the Jewish tradition of Enoch.

[2]For a discussion of the phrase, see R. G. Wooden, "The Book of Daniel and Manticism: A Critical Assessment of the View That the Book of Daniel Derives from a Mantic Tradition" (PhD diss., University of St. Andrews, 2000) 1-26.

[3]For example, W. L. Humphreys, "A Life-Style for Diaspora: A Study of the Tales of Esther and Daniel," *JBL* 92 (1973): 211-23; and S. Niditch and R. Doran, "The Success Story of the Wise Courtier: A Formal Approach," *JBL* 96 (1977): 179-93.

[4]Collins, *Daniel*, 47-52, provides a concise and accessible overview of the issues. P. L. Redditt, "Daniel 11 and the Sociohistorical Setting of the Book of Daniel," *CBQ* 60 (1998): 463-75, offers an update with new insights into the issue.

[5]Note the following from Collins, *Daniel* (the emphases are added): "The high offices of Daniel and his companions probably reflect the *aspirations* rather than the actual situation of the authors, but the problems envisaged are largely those that confronted Jews in the service of the empire, and it is reasonable to suppose that they were *relevant to the tradents' position in life*" (48). "Daniel's attitude to this Babylonian wisdom is *much more positive* than that of Deutero-Isaiah, although he too insists on its inferiority. . . . Their methods may be inferi-

although they did not think highly of the individuals who filled the roles. Thus, in these stories the diviners fail each time. Nonetheless, the roles were something to which a Jew could aspire; at the least, one like Daniel was one in whom a Jew could take pride, and who could be a role model to those working in the service of foreign kings.

In this essay we will reconsider the portrayal of the diviners and of Daniel. Using Daniel 2, I will attempt to demonstrate how the view presented in the book is that the very *raison d'être* of the professions of the diviners was without foundation. In distinction from them, Daniel is portrayed as a person who received divine revelations directly from his God, and not as a diviner who read the indirect messages sent by gods through various phenomena. In his role as the receptor of direct revelations, Daniel served as a witness to the uniqueness of the God of Israel.

Daniel 2 launches the reader into the professional life of Daniel the diviner. Chronologically, it is set during the time of the training of the captives, in the second year of Nebuchadnezzar's reign, at least one year before the end of the three-year training period. This chronology has long been considered a problem, but as part of the longer narrative of chapters 1–6 it presents an interesting scenario that fits with the portrayal of the four young men in Daniel: even before they finished their training, they were shown to be better than the practising experts, and were promoted to high positions that were to be taken up upon completion of their training.[6] In this scenario, 1:17 becomes more than a description of unproven gifts, it is a telescoping of the events of chapter 2 in which Daniel prays for, and is given both the king's dream and understanding of it, while he is still in training. In a similar way, chapters 7 and 8

---

or, but they are *not denounced in principle*" (50). "To say that the tales present a life-style does not necessarily mean that they were models for direct imitation. The situations envisaged in the tales would not arise very often in the life of a typical person. The patterns of behavior and priorities advocated, however, were more broadly applicable. There is an element of fantasy in the tales, which suggests another function: they are affirmations of group identity. Jews who had been deprived of their homeland and their temple *could take pride in the success of Daniel and his friends and their superiority in wisdom* over the Babylonians" (51).

[6]D. N. Fewell, *Circle of Sovereignty: Plotting Politics in the Book of Daniel*, 2nd ed. (Nashville: Abingdon, 1991) 37, notes how this scenario is not followed through at the end of the chapter.

chronologically precede chapter 5, taking place in the first, third, and last years respectively of Belshazzar. By so arranging the visions before the events of chapter 5, the editors provided Daniel with the needed revelations for him to interpret the "writing on the wall."

Chapter 2 is built around Nebuchadnezzar's demand that his professional diviners provide and interpret his troubling dream. Mesopotamian kings and officials did in fact have dreams that they thought held important messages from the gods. A. Leo Oppenheim published a translation, with discussion, of a dream-interpretation book that diviners would have used during the period of the Assyrian and Babylonian kings.[7] Thus, Nebuchadnezzar's desire to have his troubling dream interpreted is quite in keeping with what we know happened. But chapter 2 is significantly different from chapter 4 where another dream is interpreted for this king. In chapter 4, Nebuchadnezzar tells the diviners the content of his dream; in chapter 2, however, he expects them to tell him the content of the dream as well!

Nebuchadnezzar summoned the "*ḥartoms* and exorcists, that is, those of the Chaldeans who practice sorcery" to interpret his dream.[8] However, he withheld the dream from them as a test, and expected them both to relate it to him and to interpret it.[9] The religious experts, however,

---

[7]A. L. Oppenheim, "The Interpretation of Dreams in the Ancient Near East with a Translation of an Assyrian Dream-Book," *Transactions of the American Philosophical Society* 46 (1956): 179-373; idem, "New Fragments of the Assyrian Dream-Book," *Iraq: British School of Archaeology in Iraq* 31 (1969): 153-65. Such interpretation was done through consulting texts or relying upon "the oral tradition of the masters." See S. Parpola, *Letters from Assyrian Scholars to the Kings Esharhaddon and Assurbanipal*, Alter Orient und altes Testament 5, ed. K. Bergerhof, M. Deitrich, and O. Loretz (Kevelaer: Butzon & Bercker, 1970–1983) 1:11; 2:18, #13. Oppenheim, "Interpretation of Dreams"; idem, "New Fragments," 153-65; A. R. Millard, "Daniel and Belshazzar in history," *BARev* 11 (1985): 73-78.

[8]See below for this translation of the Hebrew.

[9]Cf. A. Bentzen, *Daniel*, Handbuch zum alten Testament 19 (Tübingen: J. C. B. Mohr [Paul Siebeck], 1952) 225; Fewell, *Circle of Sovereignty*, 24; Collins, *Daniel*, 156. Whether this is a test of the religious experts or a plea for their assistance in remembering a forgotten dream depends upon the meaning of מלתא מני אזדא (vv. 5, 8). LXX, Th, Vg, and KJV translated אזדא as if it were from the root אזד = אזל "to go," so, "the thing has gone from me," i.e., "I have forgotten

needed to know the content of the dream, and so they pleaded with him to divulge it. He then stated:

> I know with certainty that you are trying to gain time, because you see I have firmly decreed: if you do not tell me the dream, there is but one verdict for you. You have agreed to speak lying and misleading words to me until things take a turn. Therefore, tell me the dream, and I shall know that you can give me its interpretation. (2:8-9 NRSV)

The reason for the test is that Nebuchadnezzar does not trust the diviners. Omens were open to many interpretations. The king here tells the religious experts that he suspects they play for time by giving vague or false interpretations,[10] then when something takes place that fits into the interpretation, they take the glory for having predicted the future. Therefore, he wanted them to tell him the dream, and if they could do that he had assurance that they truly had access to the communications of the gods and could interpret the dream.

This was not an unknown part of Mesopotamian court life. The legendary Naram-Sin doubted his diviners, although he was sternly reprimanded by the gods for this through defeat.[11] Several letters from religious experts to Mesopotamian kings reveal a similar suspicion. One relates how the king "closed his ears" against an omen interpretation, but the expert boasted that the omen had come true within the month. Sennacherib's suspicion of collusion among diviners led him to separate his diviners into four groups in order to obtain a reliable report on an important question.[12]

---

it" (cf. J. A. Montgomery, *A Critical and Exegetical Commentary on the Book of Daniel*, ICC [Edinburgh: T. & T. Clark, 1927] 147). It is now known to derive from Persian *azdā* meaning "well known; conception, notion" (*HALOT*). In the Dan context it means something like, "My decree *has been made known*," i.e., the decree that they will die (2:5), or it means "*a well-known thing* has been decreed by me," i.e., it has been made known and is firm. (Even the NKJV has adopted this meaning.) Given this understanding of the word, it is not necessary to maintain that Nebuchadnezzar forgot the dream. That the author/editor wanted to portray the king purposely withholding the dream fits better with the challenge that if they can relate it to him, he knows they can interpret it too.

[10]Cf. letters ##12, 65, and 66 from diviners to kings in Parpola, *Letters from Assyrian Scholars*, 1:9 and 43, and the commentaries at 2:14-15, 70-71.

[11]*ANET*^{3}, 648, ll. 85ff.

[12]A. L. Oppenheim, *Ancient Mesopotamia: Portrait of a Dead Civilization*, 2nd

In one letter a diviner wrote to the king: "As reg[ards what the king, my lo]rd, wrote to me: '[Why] have you never told me [the truth]? [When] will you (actually) say to me [what] it is?'. . . . "[13] Yet another wrote: "But perhaps the king, my lord, does not believe (me)! The rear side of the Moon should be shown to one (of the) eunuch(s) . . . the king, [my lord], [will] soon [believe me]."[14] The diviners went to great lengths to provide a favourable reading of omens, and doubtless this was evident to those who did not provide the interpretations. Oppenheim observed, "when one reads through their reports to the Assyrian kings, one can be amused at their efforts to interpret bad omens in a favourable sense by means of complicated reasoning."[15] So Nebuchadnezzar's mistrust is not merely a literary creation; Mesopotamian kings had misgivings that any faithful Jew would have gladly exploited.

Nebuchadnezzar's mistrust of the diviners prepares the scene for Daniel's part in the story. The king sets up the impossible test, and the impossibility of passing that test highlights the inability of the other court diviners and their professions. However, that part of the scenario also becomes part of the critique of the very professions, which also highlights Daniel's abilities.

The critique is accomplished in several ways. It is clearest when it is offered by the professionals themselves during their dialogue with the king.

> There is no one on earth who can reveal what the king demands! In fact no king, however great and powerful, has ever asked such a thing of any *ḥartom* or extispex or Chaldean.[16] The thing that the king is asking is too difficult, and no one can reveal it to the king except the gods, whose dwelling is not with mortals. (2:10-11 NRSV modified)

---

ed. (Chicago: University of Chicago Press, 1968) 227; cf. *CAD*, B:122a.

[13]Parpola, *Letters from Assyrian Scholars*, 1:9, #13, with commentary at 2:16-19.

[14]Ibid., 1:13, #14, with corrections at 2:507 and commentary at 2:19-21.

[15]Oppenheim, *Ancient Mesopotamia*, 227.

[16]For the translation of the titles, see Wooden, "Book of Daniel and Manticism," 128-57.

Here they admit outright the limitation of their professions: they have no access to the gods and had no hope of telling the king the dream.[17]

Daniel offered a similar critique. When he finally appears on the scene to reveal the dream and its meaning, the reader can expect one of two possibilities. Either he would use his superior grasp of the information that made him ten times better than the experienced *ḥartoms* and exorcists (1:20), but was nonetheless of the same nature as theirs; or he would rely upon his special God-given ability to interpret dreams and visions (1:17). The story moves in the latter direction: Daniel receives a revelation of the dream and its interpretation. When he tells it to the king, he makes the following comments:

> No experts, exorcists, *ḥartoms*, or extispices[18] can show to the king the mystery that the king is asking, but there is a God in heaven who reveals mysteries, and he has disclosed to King Nebuchadnezzar what will happen at the end of days. . . . But as for me, this mystery has not been revealed to me because of any exceptionally greater wisdom[19] that I have more than any other living being. . . . (2:27-28a, 30 NRSV modified)

Not even wisdom ten times better than that of everyone else was equal to the task.[20] It was not, then, a failure of other professionals to have mastered the correct body of knowledge and skills, it was a failure of the very professions themselves to be able to deliver what was expected.[21] The other professionals were correct about the inscrutability of the Divine, but the Divine did not have to dwell among people for

---

[17]J. N. Lawson, " 'The God Who Reveals Secrets': The Mesopotamian Background to Daniel 2:47," *JSOT* 74 (1997): 61-76, argues that these diviners did believe that they were aided by the gods (cf. Oppenheim, "Interpretation of Dreams," 221). His point, although valid, is not relevant to this examination of the literary portrayal of the diviners in Dan, which is an ethnoreligious critique, not a phenomenological study.

[18]See above, n. 16.

[19]Reading בי יתירא מן־כל־חייא with 4QDan[a] and Pesh.

[20]Collins, *Daniel*, 157, suggests that this was hyperbole.

[21]Contra ibid., 50, cited above in n. 5 ("inferior, but not denounced in principle").

diviners to have access to that knowledge. The Divine had only to reveal what was needed to someone like Daniel (2:30).

Such statements from both Daniel and the religious experts make it clear that the perspective of the stories is not favourable to the learned professions. They had no real access to the Divine. To Jews, for whom the prophetic tradition was important (as evidenced in Daniel by the use of the prophetic materials in chapters 7–12),[22] this inability to access the realm of God was the tell-tale sign of fraud.

The critique of the professions is also found in the use of several words in the chapter. Immediately after the self-critical dialogue of the professionals, the narrator relates the command of the king: "Because of this the king flew into a violent rage and commanded that all the *wise men* of Babylon (לכל־חכימי בבל) be destroyed" (2:12). It is important to note the switch from "Chaldeans" to "wise men" at this juncture. Up to vv. 12-13 there are references to the following: "Chaldeans" כשׂדים, 1:4; 2:4, 5, 10a; "*ḥartoms* and exorcists" החרטמים והאשׁפים, 1:20; "the *ḥartoms* and exorcists, that is, the sorcerers of the Chaldeans" לחרטמים ולאשׁפים ולמכשׁפי כשׂדיים,[23] 2:2; and "*ḥartom* and exorcist and Chaldean" לכל־חרטם ואשׁף וכשׂדי, 2:10b. However, when the king issued orders to execute those belonging to those professions, it was not an order to kill "every *ḥartom* and exorcist and Chaldean," but "all the *wise men* of Babylon." That is the first occurrence of חכימין "wise men, experts" in Daniel. Rather than understanding the חכימין to be a separate profession ("sages"), it is better to understand them as "experts" in the court, that is, it is an inclusive term, an adjective that can be used of any person who is skilled or knowledgeable in some way. The terms חכם and חכים are used often in the Hebrew/Aramaic Scriptures to refer to those who were experts, and to those who were advisors in such settings as the courts of rulers.[24] This general use is found at 5:7 where "wise men" refers back to a list of diviners: "The king cried aloud to bring in the exorcists, *ḥartoms*, Chaldeans, and

[22]See Wooden, "Book of Daniel and Manticism," 273-324, for a discussion of the use of Jer, Hab, Isa, and Hos.

[23]Reconstructed version, on which see the discussion below.

[24]See *HALOT*.

extispices;[25] and the king said to the wise men of Babylon, . . . " (NRSV modified).

What is significant is that the point where the court "experts" demonstrate a lack of expertise is where the king angrily orders that those failed "experts" be put to death. Also, when Daniel speaks of the inabilities of the professions in 2:27, we have the first of only two instances of חכים occuring in a list of diviners rather than as a general reference to them. The second such occurrence at 5:15 is equally incongruent with the expected usage of this term: it is at the beginning of a sentence that explains that the "experts" could not do that at which they were supposed to be expert. Placing the word at these points in the stories seems to be sarcasim that contrasts what one should expect of such professionals with their failure to deliver: the so-called "wise men, experts" were neither wise nor expert.

Further critique occurs in the list of diviners at 2:2 where we find the lone occurrence of מכשפים in Daniel. This word is a piel participle of כשף, "to practise sorcery." The verb is found 6 times in the Masoretic Text, the noun "sorcery" 6 times, and "sorcerer" once.[26] These are related to the Akkadian *kaššāpu* "sorcerer," one who practised *kišpū* "witchcraft" or "sorcery,"[27] whose intent was the harm of others. Given the malevolent nature of these "experts,"[28] it is surprising to find them among the religious experts in Daniel 2:2. A textual corruption seems to have obscured the original intent for מכשף, however. In OG the list is τοὺς ἐπαοιδοὺς καὶ τοὺς μάγους καὶ τοὺς φαρμακοὺς τῶν Χαλδαίων "the enchanters, Magi, and charm preparers of the Chaldeans."[29] In this form

[25]Reading לחרטמיא with 4QDan^a, supported by OG. On the translation of the titles, see above, n. 16.

[26]Verb: Exod 7:11; 22:17 [18]; Deut 18:10; Mal 3:5; Dan 2:2; 2 Chr 33:6. The first five occurrences are participles. Nouns: 2 Kgs 9:22; Isa 47:9, 12; Mic 5:11; Nah 3:4$^{2\times}$; and Jer 27:9.

[27]*HALOT*; see *CAD* K:284, 292, 454-56, 598 on this term.

[28]In the Assyrian law code and Hammurapi's law code, black magic and those who practiced it were both outlawed. See *ANET*^{3}, 184 and 166, respectively.

[29]On the translation of the Greek titles, cf. A. McCrystall, "Studies in the Old Greek Translation of Daniel" (DPhil diss., Oxford University, 1980) 190-213.

of the list "Chaldean" defines the previous terms; it is not a separate profession. The 1QDan^a fragment supports a similar *Vorlage*.[30] The first word on the fragment is כשדיים, which is at variance with the Masoretic Text's ולכשדים: it lacks both the conjunction and preposition. The fragment begins at this word and has none of the previous line, and so, whether the previous word was in the construct state (ולמכשפי) cannot be determined with certainty. In light of OG, however, it is reasonable to conclude that the *Vorlage* read לחרטמים ולאשפים ולמכשפי כשדיים. Whether מכשף is a substantive ("sorcerers"), or the description of the activity ("those who practice sorcery"), it is, nonetheless, a negative assessment of the *ḥartoms* and exorcists by the Jewish author, because those professions consisted of Chaldean sorcerers.[31]

One further means of critique has been noted independently by Avalos and by Coxon. Both have suggested a comedic function for lists in Daniel.[32] Only Avalos focused specifically on this feature, however. He argued that the lists of officials in Daniel 3 were meant to portray them as automatons who were summoned, and who dutifully and mindlessly filed into the king's presence.[33] The list at 2:2 is too early to be comedic

---

[30]D. Barthélemy and J. T. Milik, *Qumran Cave 1*, Discoveries in the Judaean Desert 1 (Oxford: Clarendon, 1955) 150-51.

[31]This explanation takes the *vav* on ולמכשפי as explicative, "that is," on which see *BDB* s.v. 1.b.; *HALOT* s.v. §5; H. Bauer and P. Leander, *Grammatik des biblisch-Aramäischen*, (repr.: Hildesheim: Georg Olms, 1969) §70r. See also D. W. Baker, "Further Examples of the *waw explicativum*," *VT* 30 (1980): 129-36, who has amassed examples of, and references to the explicative function of ו in Hebrew and Aramaic together with references to Ugaritic, Akkadian, and Greek. He shows from his own and others' studies that this function of the conjunction is not rare. In Dan he notes 1:3 (ומן); 4:10 (וקדיש); 6:29 (ובמלכות); 7:1 (וחזוי); and 8:10 (ומן). J. E. Goldingay, *Daniel*, WBC 30, ed. D. A. Hubbard, G. W. Barker, and J. D. W. Watts (Dallas: Word Books, 1989) 5 and 122, supports him in his findings for Dan and adds two more: 8:24, and 11:38. B. E. Colless, "Cyrus the Persian and Darius the Mede in the Book of Daniel," *JSOT* 56 (December 1992): 115, argues that 6:28 has a *vav explicativum*. He supports the contention that one is found at 7:1 and suggests that 6:9 (ואסרא) also contains one.

[32]P. W. Coxon, "The 'List' Genre and Narrative Style in the Court Tales of Daniel," *JSOT* 35 (1986): 95-121; H. I. Avalos, "The Comedic Function of the Enumerations of Officials and Instruments in Daniel 3," *CBQ* 53 (1991): 580-88.

[33]Avalos, "Comedic Function," 584.

on a first reading, but on subsequent readings it does become one of the many lists, and so participates in the overall portrayal of the Mesopotamian officials (religious and administrative) as toadies of the king, in contrast to Daniel and his friends. In chapters 2, 4, and 5, the King summons "*all* the wise men of Babylon," whose professions are then listed. They faithfully answer the summons each time, and each time they fail. In chapter 2 they even stand before the king and plead with him to tell them the dream so that they can interpret it. Daniel, on the other hand, seems never to answer the first summons, and he succeeds each time. Here, then, the Mesopotamian religious experts are portrayed as "pathetic, passive, and gutless" individuals who were exposed as "mindless automatons" who are at their wits end when the king asked something out of the norm. The Jewish Daniel, however, was an assertive individual who succeeded where they failed, and who let nothing concern him.

So, through the use of explicit critiques of the abilities of any such professionals, the sarcastic use of "wise men" as a general term for the inexpert professionals, and the description of them as "practicers of sorcery," this chapter in Daniel presents a significant negative critique of the professions. The use of lists in the stories further advances this critique.

This portrayal of the diviners is in line with other Jewish material. The *Sibylline Oracles* 3:218-233 is a particularly relevant example because it seems to come from the same period as the final composition of Daniel.[34]

> There is a city . . . in the land of Ur of the Chaldeans, whence comes a race of most righteous men. They are always concerned with good counsel and noble works for they do not worry about the cyclic course of the sun or the moon or monstrous things under the earth nor the depth of the grim sea, Oceanus, nor portents of sneezes, nor birds of augurers, nor seers, nor sorcerers, nor soothsayers, nor the deceits of foolish words of ventriloquists. Neither do they practice the astrological predictions of the Chaldeans nor astronomy. For all these things are erroneous, such as foolish men inquire into day by day, exercising themselves at a profitless task. And indeed they have taught errors to shameful men from which many evils come upon mortals on earth so that they are misled as to good ways and righteous deeds. (*OTP* I, 367)

---

[34]J. J. Collins, "Sibylline Oracles," *OTP* 1:354-55.

An earlier example is that of the court magicians in Exodus 7–8 where they were portrayed as buffoons. This is clear when that story is compared with the Papyrus Westcar account of the magical acts of Ḥor in the second Demotic tale of Setna-a-em-wese. When the magicians of Ethiopia conjured up fire, another produced water to put it out; when another created a thick darkness, another brought back the light, and so forth.[35] Thus, when Moses changed the water of the Nile into blood and the Egyptians had nothing to drink (Exodus 7:17ff.), Pharaoh's magicians should have turned it back into water, instead of doing 'the same thing by their spells' (v. 22). When Moses brought swarms of frogs (Exodus 8:3ff.), the magicians should have rid the kingdom of them, not brought more upon the land (v. 7).[36] Having the Egyptians exacerbate the problems by parroting Moses and Aaron was a satirical portrayal.

In the contest between Elijah and the prophets of Baal in 1 Kings 18:17-40, the author actually tells the reader that Elijah "mocked" them (v. 27), and relates how he did it. Again, what the prophets of Baal could not do, the prophet of Yahweh could, even after making the task harder still by pouring water on the wood that should ignite.

Images of gods and the process of making them are derided in Isaiah 41:21-29; 44:6-20; and 46:1-10 (cf. Jeremiah 50:38). At the same time the author declared that what the foreign gods could not do, Yahweh could. But the two most relevant passages speak specifically about religious experts in Babylon. In Isaiah 44:25-26a, we learn that Yahweh works against the Babylonian religious experts by confounding them, and works for his own servants by bringing about what they pronounce. This parallels well what happens in Daniel where the foreign experts fail, but the divinely gifted Jew not only understands what the others could not, he also has his prophecies come true. In the second passage, Isaiah 47:10-15, Babylon, who felt secure with all her magic and divination, is told that her experts could do all they wanted, but to no avail, because their arts were worthless: "there is not one that can save you" (v. 15). It is this

---

[35]Müller, "חַרְטֹם," *TDOT* 5:178.

[36]Y. T. Radday, "On Missing the Humour in the Bible: An Introduction," in *On Humour and the Comic in the Hebrew Bible*, ed. Y. T. Radday and A. Brenner, JSOTSup, ed. D. J. A. Clines and P. R. Davies (Sheffield: Almond, 1990) 21-22.

derision of the inability of the Babylonian religious experts that the stories of Daniel illustrate.

This comedy or satire further illustrates that the professions of religious experts in the courts of Mesopotamia are not portrayed in Daniel for emulation. When a *real* revelation was given, the learned interpretation of the Mesopotamian religious experts was not equal to it. However, faithful Jews who knew the Revealer of true mysteries were up to the task because their God could reveal his will to one of them, and Daniel was one such person.

Now, it is true that in the stories Daniel[37] was a member of the professions that were critiqued. He was compared with the "*ḥartoms* and exorcists" (1:20), was one of "the experts" who was sought out to be killed (2:13), was made the "chief prefect over all the wise men of Babylon" (2:48), and was referred to as the "chief of the *ḥartoms*" (4:6 [9]), and "chief of the *ḥartoms*, exorcists, Chaldeans, and extispices" (5:11). However, Daniel was also differentiated from those professionals.

A basic differentiation is that of ethnicity. The narrative makes it clear at 1:3-6; 2:25; 3:8; 5:13; and 6:13 that Daniel was from the Judean royalty or nobility and was forced into exile; he was not Mesopotamian. This ethnic origin serves to contrast him with some of the other characters. Note should be taken of the use of כשׂדים, כשׂדי "Chaldean," which occurs numerous times in Daniel. At Daniel 5:30 and 9:1 the term is used as a reference to the people of Babylon in general.[38] At 3:8, there is also

---

[37]Except in passing, reference will not be made to Hananiah, Mishael, and Azariah, because they play a secondary role in this chapter. It is clear from the story that they were part of the faithful group that received the revelation, and Daniel did include them in two places (vv. 23, 36). This serves to make it clear that the four from Judaea were the one group who could and did respond successfully to the king's demand. However, Daniel is nevertheless distinct from the three, because only he receives the vision of the night (v. 19) and is rewarded for that: Daniel was promoted to a high administrative position and put in charge of all the experts, while, at the request of Daniel, the three were given only administrative positions.

[38]The Chaldeans were a people from southern Babylon who rose to power and formed the last dynasty of the Babylonian empire (629–539 BCE). They were the ethnic group to which Nebuchadnezzar belonged. It is in this way that the term כשׂדים is used approximately seventy-six times outside Dan in the Hebrew

an explicit contrast that seems to be ethnic, rather than professional, because that chapter is about a religious conflict between Babylonian and Jewish administrators, not about the abilities of diviners. Another occurrence of this use is found in 2:2, for which we earlier adopted a variant reading in which it is specified that the *ḥartoms* and exorcists were "of the Chaldeans." We also commented above about a shift in terminology in chapter 2. The shift from "Chaldean" to "wise men" also serves to explain why the Jews did not appear with the others when summoned: they were Jews, and it was the Chaldeans who were summoned.

Another use of "Chaldean" in Daniel is as the title of a diviner. Over time the name "Chaldean" came to be associated with the recording of astronomical events, thus connecting this people with astrology.[39] It was in this sense that the term Chaldean was used by the better known Greek historians.[40] Thus, in the second century BCE Cato (*De Agricultura* 5.4) listed the Chaldeans among various types of religious experts, as did Josephus (*Wars* 2.7.3 [112]). The occurrences of כשדי in Daniel 4 and 5 are in lists of diviners, and seem to be the Hellenistic use of the term for astrologers.

This mixing of the two uses in Daniel is not unique. Strabo (*Geography* 16.1.16; first century BCE) also used the name for both a profession and a people. However, we would argue that it is not just a mixing of an ethnic and professional designation, rather, in Daniel there is a nuanced use. When it refers to professionals, it was used in the pregnant sense of Babylonian diviners, and was meant to exclude Jews.

At 1:4 "Chaldean" may be an ethnic reference to the language and literature of the people of Babylon; it may also designate the astrologers' texts and the language training required to understand and use them. In the context of the chapter it is more likely the latter, the Hellenistic use of the term, because in 1:20 it is the religious experts with whom the four

---

scriptures. The fifth-century Greek historian Hellanikos, in *Persika* (F. Jacoby, *Die Fragmente der griechischen Historiker*, Teil 1 [Berlin, 1923] 122, no. 4 F 59), as well may have used "Chaldean" to denote a people.

39O. R. Gurney, "The Babylonians and Hittites," in *Divination and Oracles*, ed. M. Loewe and C. Blacker (London: George Allen & Unwin, 1981) 161-62; J. Oates, *Babylon*, Ancient Peoples and Places 94, ed. G. Daniel (London: Thames & Hudson, 1986) 112-13.

40Herodotus, *Histories* 1.181.5; Ctesias, *Persika* 2; Diodorus 2.29-31.

boys are compared. However, in this context it is most probable that the term has the pregnant sense that encompasses both referents: it was Babylonian diviners with whom the Jewish trainees were compared.

In the self-standing occurrences at 2:4, 5, and 10, the term could either be used as a comprehensive one for all the religious experts, just like חכים,[41] or it could be a reference to only one profession, that is, astrologers.[42] Here too, however, it is a reference to the ethnic background of the referents. Even in the list at 2:10 the occurrence of the word could be ethnic or political rather than professional: it is the "Chaldeans" who speak and then who refer to "*ḥartoms*, enchanter," and then in a more inclusive way "Chaldean. . . . " Just after this (2:12), the Jewish Daniel is grouped among the "wise men of Babylon," which is the first occurrence of the term חכים in the book. By so differentiating between designations that can exclude and include Jews, the reason is given for Daniel's not appearing when "all the *ḥartoms* and exorcists, that is, the sorcerers of the Chaldeans" were summoned to interpret the King's dream: he was not a Chaldean; he was a Jew.[43] Then, because the professions (not the specific professionals) were deemed fraudulent by the king, he made no such ethnic differentiation and wanted all the members of each group to be killed.

The ethnic difference has one other aspect to it. These Jewish young men were not members of these professions by choice. They were taken

---

[41]G. Behrmann, *Das Buch Daniel*, Handkommentar zum alten Testament in Verbindung mit anderen Fachgelehrten, ed. D. W. Nowack (Göttingen: Vandenhoeck & Ruprecht, 1894) 7; Montgomery, *Daniel*, 144; Goldingay, *Daniel*, 46; Jeffers, *Magic and Divination*, 58.

[42]R. H. Charles, A *Critical and Exegetical Commentary on the Book of Daniel* (Oxford: Clarendon, 1929) 13-15; and Collins, *Daniel*, 137-38. The NIV translates it "astrologers" at Dan 2:2, 4, 5, $10^{2\times}$; 3:8; 4:4 [EVV 7]; 5:7, 1; and as "Babylonian(s)" at 1:4; 5:30; 9:1.

[43]Cf. D. K. Marti, *Das Buch Daniel Erklärt*, Kurzer Hand-Commentar zum alten Testament 18, ed. I. Benzinger et al. (Tübingen: J. C. B. Mohr [Paul Siebeck], 1901) 8, 11; and Collins, *Daniel*, 139. If our observations on its use are correct, then it would seem it was under the influence of the Hellenistic understanding of the term in the lists of chapters 4 and 5 that a later copyist "corrected" or inadvertently harmonized the occurrence at 2:2, thus giving us the list in the Masoretic Text, and thereby obscuring the excluding usage in the rest of chapters 1 and 2.

to Babylon and forced to train for the professions of which they became members. This detail from 1:3-6 may be significant for the contrast of Daniel and the Babylonian diviners, because it answers the question, If these professions were worthless, why were faithful Jews serving in them?

The second distinguishing point about Daniel is the reprieve that he was granted by the king. In chapter 1, explicit reference is made to such special treatment as the result of divine intervention: the overseer of the captives was affected by God, and thus he allowed Daniel and his friends to eat something other than the king's food (v. 9). Although not referred to explicitly in chapter 2, divine favour is also present there.[44] One of the inconsistencies in the story is that the diviners were denied time (2:8) to come up with an answer, yet Daniel was granted it (2:14-16). In light of the results of divine intervention in chapter 1, this should be understood as a sign of divine intervention as well—the hearer/reader is left to read between the lines.

The final, and most significant difference between Daniel and the other diviners is that he alone received divine revelations in chapter 2. Chapter 1 prepared the hearer/reader for when God gives the four special abilities (v. 17), and specifically gave Daniel the ability to interpret dreams and visions,[45] the very thing needed to fulfil what was demanded of the experts in chapter 2. There, Daniel was graced with the humanly

---

[44]Fewell, *Circle of Sovereignty*, 27.

[45]The MT points the text as a hiphil perfect, thus making the final part of the verse a new statement: ודניאל הֵבִין בכל־חזון וחלמות, "Now, Daniel understood all kinds of visions and dreams." This could be an editorial insertion, or simply an observation on Daniel's abilities without any reference to their source. I read the text with the OG and point the hiphil as an infinitive הָבִין that is coordinated with the statement about the four boys (the verb 'gave' is repeated) καὶ τοῖς νεανίσκοις ἔδωκεν ὁ κύριος ἐπιστήμην καὶ σύνεσιν φρονήσεως ἐν πάσῃ γραμματικῇ τέχῃ· καὶ τῷ Δανιὴλ ἔδωκε σύνεσιν ἐν παντὶ ὁράματι καὶ ἐνυπνίοις καὶ ἐν πάσῃ σοφίᾳ. J. Ziegler, O. Munnich, and D. Fraenkel, "Susanna, Daniel, Bel et Draco," *Septuaginta: Vetus Testamentum Graecum* 14/2 (Göttingen: Vandenhoeck & Ruprecht, 1999); cf. T. J. Meadowcroft, *Aramaic Daniel and Greek Daniel: A Literary Comparison* (Sheffield: Sheffield Academic, 1995) 255. The Hebrew text would then be translated: "Now, the four young men, God gave them knowledge and understanding of all kinds of writing and wisdom, and Daniel, *God gave him* understanding of all kinds of visions and dreams."

impossible solution to the demand of the King, and it came through a direct revelation in a night vision (2:19). In the examination by Niditch and Doran of the type of folktale into which this story falls, they noted that this one is significantly different in one respect. While the wise people in such stories succeed by means of their ingenuity, here they achieved success by means of asking and receiving from God.[46] This difference is actually a major emphasis of this chapter and so will receive more attention in our analysis.

At 2:10-11 the Chaldeans made two points: there is no one able to do what the king demanded; and, were the gods to reveal such knowledge, they would have to dwell with humans. Thus, when Daniel asked for time so that he might interpret the dream, the task had been set up as an impossibility from the Mesopotamian perspective; it was outside the domain of humans, regardless their natural or professional abilities.

Daniel was undaunted by the task, and he enlisted his friends to pray for mercy in the matter of the king's "mystery" (2:18). The word רז "mystery" occurs for the first time in Daniel at 2:18.[47] Given what it was that the king demanded from his diviners, what the four requested, and what Daniel received from God (2:19), the term רז included both the content of the dream and the interpretation of it. That it came to Daniel in a night vision, is an echo back to 1:17 where Daniel's special abilities from God included the interpretation of visions.

After receiving the "mystery," Daniel burst forth with a psalm of praise, which we will take up shortly. Once the praise is expressed to God, Daniel carried out his role as mediator of the רז. However, when he went to Nebuchadnezzar, he again set himself apart from everyone. In 2:27-28, he repeats what the other religious experts had said about the limits of their profession in 2:10-11. He then revealed to the king that

---

[46]Niditch and Doran, "Success Story," 190-91. What this difference also highlights is the contrast between revelation and mere learning. In this chapter there is a development of the concept of חכמה "wisdom" and what it means to be a חכים "wise man." Although the other experts are sarcastically afforded the title "wise men" in vv. 12-13, the hymn in vv. 20-23 makes it clear that only those who receive wisdom from Daniel's God are truly wise men.

[47]Dan 2:18, 19, 27, 28, 29, 30, $47^{2\times}$; 4:6. See R. E. Brown, *The Semitic Background of the Term "Mystery" in the New Testament*, Facet Books: Biblical Series 21, ed. John Reumann (Philadelphia: Fortress, 1968).

there is a God who could, and had revealed what had been asked. Daniel was careful to note, however, that it was not revealed to him because he had בי יתירא מן־כל־חייא בחכמה די־איתי[48] "an exceptionally greater wisdom in [him] than all other living beings," but because God wanted Nebuchadnezzar to know about the future (2:30). Daniel's ability to tell the king what he wanted, therefore, was not due to skill in learned interpretation, that is, a form of human wisdom in which he was trained and in chapter 1 was said to excel; it was interpretation through direct revelation for which he could take no credit as one trained to be a wise man. Nebuchadnezzar reiterates this point in 2:47 where he professes that Daniel's God enabled Daniel to reveal the mystery.

The reception of the dream and its interpretation is followed by a hymn of praise.[49] Although there is some debate about whether it is original to the chapter,[50] in the final form of the text it serves as the hermeneutical lens through which the hearer/reader is to understand what God gave to Daniel in 1:17, and how Daniel knew what he did in chapter 2. In the hymn we find themes and terminology that are echoed in this chapter and in subsequent chapters. It moves from praise of God, to acknowledgement that it is God who makes people wise by giving them wisdom, and finally to thanks that Daniel had been the recipient of such wisdom.

20 a May the name of God be blessed for ever and ever,
b For wisdom and prowess belong to him
21 c He changes the times and seasons;
d He deposes kings and establishes kings;
e He gives wisdom to the wise and knowledge to those who can understand.
22 f He reveals what is deep and hidden,

---

[48]See n. 19.

[49]On the form see C. Westermann, *Praise and Lament in the Psalms*, trans. K. Crim and R. N. Soulen (Atlanta: John Knox, 1981) 102n.55, and J. J. Collins, *Daniel with an Introduction to Apocalyptic Literature*, Forms of the Old Testament Literature 20, ed. R. Knierim and G. M. Tucker (Grand Rapids: Eerdmans, 1984) 51, 108, and 111.

[50]Cf. W. S. Towner, "Poetic passages of Daniel 1-6," *CBQ* 31 (1969): 317-26.

g And[51] knows what is in the darkness,
h And the light resides with him.
23 i To you, O God of my fathers, I give thanks and praise,
j because you have given wisdom and prowess[52] to me.
k Now you have made known to me what we asked of you;
l you have made known to us what the king wanted.

The second line of the poem, seems to have been originally intended as a preface to lines c-e:[53] God's wisdom (חכמתא; line bα) is revealed through those to whom he gives it (line e); and God's prowess (גבורתא; line bβ) is displayed in his rule over the seasons and political processes of the world (lines c-d). In its present context, however, line *b* prepares for *j* where God is praised for giving prowess and wisdom to Daniel.

The term גבורתא, translated here as "prowess," is generally taken as a reference to God's power over the world.[54] However, unless Daniel's mediating of information about the end of kingdoms is understood as "power," he does not display any in these stories. There is another semantic field to which גבורה belongs, however. In certain contexts it is a wisdom term: at Proverbs 8:14 it belongs to wisdom; at Job 12:13 it occurs with חכמה "wisdom," עצה "counsel," and תבונה "understanding"; and at Isaiah 11:2, it occurs with חכמה "wisdom," בינה "understanding," עצה "counsel," and דעת "knowledge."[55] It was rendered in the Greek by σύνεσις at 2:20 (Theodotion) and at Job 12:13;[56] and by φρόνησιν at 2:23 (OG). There is also evidence of this usage in some of the Dead Sea Scrolls. The parallel passages in CD 13.8 גבורות פלאו "his mighty wonders" and 1QS 9.18 רזי פלא "mysteries of wonder" suggest a semantic overlap of גבורה and

---

[51]4QDan[a] וידע, cf. OG, Pesh, and Vg. MT ידע.

[52]MT וגבורתא. E. Ulrich, "Daniel Manuscripts from Qumran. Part 1: A Preliminary Edition of 4QDan[a]," *BASOR* 268 (November 1987): 26, suggests the possibility of נהירתא, which might explain φρόνησιν in the OG; however, he notes that the form נהירא (not תא־) occurs at 2:22 in both the Masoretic and Qumran texts. Nor is φρόνησιν the rendering of either of these forms anywhere. Charles, *Daniel*, 38, suggested that harmonization may have occurred with the phrase in 2:20.

[53]Cf. Job 12:13-25. There are other links to Job 12 as we will note below.

[54]See 2 Chr 20:6. Cf. Marti, *Daniel*, 13; Charles, *Daniel*, 36-37.

[55]Cf. 1QSb col. 5, l. 25.

[56]Cf. Job 22:2 where the MT has גבר (although one MS reads דעת) and the Greek renders it with σύνεσιν.

רז.[57] Also, at *Manual of Discipline* (1QS) 4.3 it modifies חכמה and could have the meaning "wondrous, mysterious."[58] The parallels also have relevance to Daniel. In 2:17-30 רז is used six times (vv. 18, 19, 27, 28, 29, 30) of that which God revealed (גלה) to Daniel. Within the hymn of praise (vv. 22-23), however, it is only "wisdom," "prowess," and what the king wanted to know that were given (יהב) and made known (ידע) to him. The גבורה in this poem, then, was not physical or political power, but exceptional intellectual ability, mental prowess.

Lines c and d relate generally to the context, that is, not only nature, but also politics is under the control of God who brings about changes of monarchs like the changes of the seasons. These lines serve as preparation for the revelation in this chapter, and as background for the many political changes dealt with throughout the book, including what is related at the beginning of chapter 1. Line e moves back to the wisdom theme. In a self-standing poem the recipients of God's wisdom originally may have been wise Jews generally, just as in 1:4 similar attributes belonged to all those who came into the king's training program. However, the phrases now serve to prepare for the more specific revelation to Daniel who is the truly wise man in this context. As we noted before (note 46), there is a progression in the use of the term "the wise men" in Daniel: although the word is used as a term for all the professions, it is incongruous with how they functioned, but Daniel, the receiver of wisdom and prowess from God, was the real wise man. Thus the implication is that real wisdom is not learned, it is received from God.[59]

---

[57]C. Rabin, *The Zadokite Documents: I. The Admonition, II. The Laws*, 2nd ed. (Oxford: Clarendon, 1958) 65. Cf. ברזי פלאו "by his mysteries of wonder," at CD 3.18.

[58]P. Wernberg-Møller, *The Manual of Discipline Translated and Annotated with an Introduction*, STDJ 1, ed. J. P. M. van der Ploeg (Leiden: E. J. Brill, 1957) 74-75; C. A. Newsom, *Songs of the Sabbath Sacrifice: A Critical Edition*, Harvard Semitic Studies 27, ed. F. M. Cross (Atlanta: Scholars, 1985) 220, adopted his conclusions.

[59]There is a similar differentiation in chap. 1 between those who are "insightful" generally (1:4) and those who receive insight from God (1:17). Not all the "insightful" Jews who entered the king's training program were faithful to their God. However, Daniel and the three were, and they were given special insight into all kinds of literature.

Lines f-h relate directly to the story of chapter 2: God knows and reveals what is inaccessible. In these lines four metaphors are used for wisdom. The adjective עמיק "deep" connotes hidden knowledge. It is related to the Akkadian stem *nēmequ(m)* "wisdom," and is close in form to the stems *emqu*, "experienced, skilled, educated, wise, wily," and *imqutu*, "ability."[60] The pael passive participle מסתרתא "hidden" (√סתר, "to hide") connotes a similar idea. In Deuteronomy 29:28 it is said that the "hidden things" (√סתר) belong to God, but the revealed things (√גלה) to humans. Job 28:21 speaks of wisdom being hidden both from people (√עלם) and from the birds (√סתר), and its location is known only to God (Job 28:23-24). In lines g and h we have a complementary contrast of darkness and light. Carrying on from line f, God is said to know what is in darkness, that is, what is deep and hidden. More significantly, נהור (Q נהיר) "light,"[61] which is needed to expose what is deep and hidden in darkness, dwells with God. That word is cognate with נהירו "light" in 5:11: just as wisdom belonged to God and was given to Daniel (2:21, 23), so too, the "light" was God's and was also evident in Daniel as a divine gift (5:11).

According to lines f-g, it is Daniel's God who knows and reveals those things that are inaccessible to the creation. The verb גלא "to reveal" is used eight times in Daniel, and of those, six occur with רז "mystery."[62] In Daniel the mystery, i.e., the dream and its interpretation, was not accessible to humans, because it came from the divine realm. However, Daniel's God revealed it to him (v. 27).

The poem moves to the specific reason for praise at line i. The God who gives (יהב) wisdom to the wise (line e), gave (יהב) wisdom and intellectual prowess to Daniel (line j); and the God who knows (ידע) what is in darkness (line g), let Daniel know (ידע) what he and his friends had requested. The other court wise men were wise in name only, but Daniel was truly wise, because he had wisdom and mental prowess from God; he knew the רז, because God gave him it.

---

[60]See Montgomery, *Daniel*, 160, and *BDB* (Hebrew עמק) on *nēmequ(m)*. See *HALOT* (Hebrew עמק) on *emqu* and *CAD* for *imqutu*. The phrase גלא עמיקתא should be compared with מגלה עמקות in Job 12:22.

[61]See Job 12:22.

[62]They occur together in 2:19, 28, 29, 30, 47^2. In addition, גלה occurs in 2:22 with עמקה and מסתרה (cf. Deut 29:28), and in 10:1 with דבר; and רז occurs in 2:18 without a verb and in 4:6 with אנס.

This poem, then, functions as an exposition of what took place in the revelation of the רז to Daniel. Although true wisdom and light are in the purview of God, he gave them to Daniel. In addition to explaining this account of revelation, these themes are picked up again in 5:11 where Daniel is recalled as one having wisdom like the wisdom of God (the gods), and as one in whom there was light.

Through the critique of the professions of the diviners, and through the portrayal and explanation of what Daniel does, the narrative sets Daniel apart from all others. He was not just a better diviner than they; he functioned in a way that no other could. He did not just have a superlative understanding of books, wisdom, dreams, and visions, he was recipient of the wisdom of God, and he could even receive the dreams and visions that had been sent to others. Daniel was not a diviner when he interpreted omens, he was more like a prophet of God. So, although Daniel may have been portrayed as one to be emulated by those who found themselves in the service of foreign powers, it was not really in his role as a court diviner. Nor are the positions of the other diviners held up for emulation. Even though he is said to be among them, and in chapters 4 and 5 is said to be at the head of those in these professions, Daniel does not function as they do. Daniel acts more like a prophet who received direct revelations from his God, unlike the diviners who had no such access to the gods. The message to the recipients of the stories and of the book was that they were to maintain their Jewish identity and methods in whatever they did, even for the interpretation of dreams and omens.

What was the result of Daniel's presence in the court of the kings of Mesopotamia? In Daniel, Nebuchadnezzar goes from being the conqueror of Israel (1:1-2), to the deporter and patron of those whom he wanted in his courts (1:2-17); to the tester of the four, whom he learns excel beyond the abilities of his own people (1:19-20); to the one who acknowledges that Daniel's God is the God of gods and Revealer of mysteries (chapter 2); to the protector of those who worship the God of Hananiah, Mishael, and Azariah (chapter 3); to the one who praises the God of Israel as (if) a convert (3:32-33 [4:2-3]; 4:31-34 [34-37]).[63] He also goes from a character that has no voice in chapter 1, to a speaking character in third-

---

[63]Cf. Fewell, *Circle of Sovereignty*, 63-80. She leaves open the question whether the story implies a conversion or merely prudence on Nebuchadnezzar's part.

person narratives in chapters 2–3, to the narrator of a first-person account (with some third-person narration interspersed, that is, 4:16-30 [19-33]) in chapter 4. The changes in Nebuchadnezzar's relationship to the God of Israel are portrayed as due to the influence of the four, especially Daniel, upon the king as he is slowly "converted" to viewing the God of Daniel as "God of gods and Lord of kings, and a Revealer of mysteries" (2:47); the "Most High God" (4:2, 34); "the King of heaven" (4:37). This is the God like whom "there is no other god who is able to deliver in this way" (3:29); and who "does according to his will in the host of heaven and among the inhabitants of the earth" (4:37). Contrasted with this portrayal of Nebuchadnezzar is that of his "son" Belshazzar in chapter 5.[64] That king shuns his "father's" beliefs, is chastised by Daniel as he interprets God's indictment, and dies when "Darius" takes the kingdom.

Daniel, then, acts as a witness to Nebuchadnezzar and as a witness against Belshazzar as he fulfils a prophetic role as the receiver of revelations and as a forthteller of the judgements of the God of Israel. Mesopotamian religious expertise is shown to be worthless—devoid of any value for Jews except as the focus of ridicule, even when such Jews practised it. Practitioners who believed in it were merely charlatans to be jeered or buffoons to be laughed at, not professionals to be emulated. Contrary to the consensus view of scholars, then, the religious experts in Daniel are *not* portrayed in such a way that their professions could be considered as viable options for faithful Jews. The view of Daniel 1–6 seems to be summed by Isaiah 44:25-26a where we hear about the God

> who frustrates the omens of liars,
>   and makes fools of diviners;
> who turns back the wise,
>   and makes their knowledge foolish;
> who confirms the word of his servant,
>   and fulfills the prediction of his messengers. . . . (NRSV)

---

[64]See ibid., 85-94; and Wooden, "Book of Daniel and Manticism," 263-66.

Jesus the Servant—Vicarious Sufferer: A Reappraisal

John Tudno Williams
United Theological College
Aberystwyth, Wales

It has long been believed in Christian circles that the Suffering Servant of Deutero-Isaiah, and especially the portrayal of him in the fourth and final song in Isaiah 52:13–53:12, prefigured in great detail Jesus of Nazareth in his passion. Indeed this has long been the critical orthodoxy, or should we rather say the uncritical orthodoxy? There have been voices, however, and on the whole they have been lone voices,[1] which have questioned this particular way of linking the old and the new in the testaments, although they have increased in recent years.[2]

Morna Hooker in her famous MA thesis published as *Jesus and the Servant* in 1959 was one such voice, albeit not by any means the first in the twentieth century,[3] and she has stated recently that she has maintained her position over the past forty years.[4]

Her work presupposed three things: (a) after the fashion of the time she based her collectivist interpretation of the Servant on the notion of corporate personality whereby the Servant could be identified with the nation Israel or a righteous remnant within it and with its leader as head of the returning exiles;[5] (b) that the term "Servant of the Lord" should

---

[1]Including H. M. Orlinsky, "The So-called 'Servant of the Lord' and 'Suffering Servant' in Second Isaiah," in *Studies on the Second Part of the Book of Isaiah*, VTSup 14 (Leiden: Brill, 1967) 1-133.

[2]See most recently the valuable collection of essays in W. H. Bellinger, Jr. and W. R. Farmer, eds., *Jesus and the Suffering Servant* (Harrisburg: Trinity Press International, 1998).

[3]See also F. J. Foakes-Jackson and K. Lake, eds., *The Beginnings of Christianity* (London: Macmillan, 1920–1933) 1:381-92; 5:364-70; and R. Bultmann, *Theology of the New Testament*, vol. 1, trans. K. Grobel (London: SCM, 1952) 31.

[4]M. D. Hooker, "Did the Use of Isaiah 53 to Interpret His Mission Begin with Jesus?," in Bellinger and Farmer, *Jesus and the Suffering Servant*, 88.

[5]The way in which this notion of corporate personality was applied to the study of the OT has come under severe criticism in recent years: see J. R. Porter, "The Legal Aspects of the Concept of 'Corporate Personality' in the Old

not be used as a quasi-title alongside other personal titles; and (c) that the Jews before the Christian era had no belief in a suffering Messiah.[6]

Her main conclusions were as follows. (a) In the Synoptic Gospels "there is no certain reference to the [Servant] Songs themselves, which in any way suggests that Jesus was identified with a Messianic interpretation of the Servant, or which is concerned with the significance of his suffering and death."[7] "The use which is made of . . . quotations from Deutero-Isaiah [in these gospels] does not support the suggestion that they imply an identification of Jesus with the 'servant.' "[8] So "there is no justification for assuming that individual words, even though they may be thought to derive from the Servant Songs, point to such an identification."[9] Thus "there is . . . no sufficient evidence to uphold the traditional view that Jesus thought of himself as the 'suffering Servant' of Deutero-Isaiah."[10]

Testament," *VT* 15 (1965): 361-80; and J. W. Rogerson, "The Hebrew Concept of Corporate Personality: A Re-examination," *JTS* 21 (1970): 1-16. It is deemed by R. E. Clements, "Isaiah 53 and the Restoration of Israel," in Bellinger and Farmer, *Jesus and the Suffering Servant*, 43, to be "a false trail in the path of exegesis."

[6]M. D. Hooker, *Jesus and the Servant: The Influence of the Servant Concept of Deutero-Isaiah in the New Testament* (London: SPCK, 1959) 56-57; cf. also H. H. Rowley, *The Servant of the Lord and Other Essays on the Old Testament* (London: Lutterworth, 1952) 59-88; E. Lohse, *Märtyrer und Gottesknecht: Untersuchungen zur urchristlichen Verkündigung vom Sühntod Jesu Christi*, Forschungen zur Religion und Literatur des alten und neuen Testaments 46 (Göttingen: Vandenhoeck & Ruprecht, 1955) 108; H. W. Robinson, *The Cross in the Old Testament* (London: SCM, 1955) 89; H. H. Rowley, *From Moses to Qumran: Studies in the Old Testament* (New York: Association Press, 1963) 100; and F. Hahn, *The Titles of Jesus in Christology: Their History in Early Christianity* (London: Lutterworth, 1969) 56 and 64n.18; and more diffidently M. Hengel, *The Cross of the Son of God* (London: SCM, 1986), 247. Contrast W. Zimmerli and J. Jeremias, *The Servant of God*, SBT 20 (Naperville IL: Alec R. Allenson, 1957) 77-78; and W. D. Davies, *Paul and Rabbinic Judaism: Some Rabbinic Elements in Pauline Theology*, 4th ed. (Philadelphia: Fortress, 1980) 274-84, who claims it is "at least possible."

[7]Hooker, *Jesus and the Servant*, 149.

[8]Ibid., 149.

[9]Ibid., 149; cf. also 155.

[10]Ibid., 154.

(b) "No sure reference to any of the Servant Songs exists in those passages where Jesus speaks of the meaning of his death; there is no evidence that either he or the evangelists had the suffering of the Servant in mind."[11] Even, when as in Luke 22:37 Isaiah 53:12 is quoted, nothing is made of it in relation to the meaning of Jesus' death.[12] That is why H. J. Cadbury found it unbelievable that the one time Luke in his gospel quotes Isaiah 53 he "escapes all the vicarious phrases with which that key passage abounds."[13] Also when Isaiah 53:4 is quoted at Matthew 8:16-17 there is no allusion to expiation of sin or vicarious suffering on the part of the Servant. To the contrary it is applied rather loosely to Jesus' healing ministry.[14]

(c) Similar conclusions are on the whole drawn from a consideration of the evidence of other New Testament writings. Here there is "little evidence that the identification of Jesus with the Servant played any great part in the thinking of St. Paul, St. John, or the author of the Epistle to the Hebrews."[15] The two notable exceptions to this state of affairs are found in Acts 8, where the fourth Servant Song (53:7-8) is clearly linked with Christ's suffering (Acts 8:32-35), although there is no mention there "of the vicarious nature of the Servant's sufferings."[16] It is the humiliation of the Servant, his submission to suffering and injustice, and his death which is depicted here, but the passage immediately before this about the

---

[11]Ibid., 149-50; see also Hooker, "The Use of Isaiah 53," 92.

[12]Hooker, *Jesus and the Servant*, 86.

[13]Cadbury, *The Beginnings of Christianity* 5:366.

[14]Hooker, *Jesus and the Servant*, 83; see also D. Juel, *Messianic Exegesis: Christological Interpretation of the Old Testament in Early Christianity* (Philadelphia: Fortress, 1988) 120-21, 128-29; and Hooker, "The Use of Isaiah 53," 90.

[15]Hooker, *Jesus and the Servant*, 127. Cf. B. H. McLean, "The Absence of an Atoning Sacrifice in Paul's Soteriology," *NTS* 38 (1992): 549; cf. also 542n.34, where the following statement of p. 549 is repeated more or less word for word!: "It is remarkable that in all of Paul's letters, there does not exist a single clear allusion (let alone quotation) to any verse of Isaiah 53 that could be interpreted in the light of the crucifixion or atonement." However, for H. Hübner, "Rechtfertigung und Sühne bei Paulus: Eine hermeneutische und theologische Besinnung," *NTS* 39 (1993): 87, Isa 53 is often in Paul's ken. Cf. also L. L. Carpenter and A. H. Godbey, *Primitive Christian Application of the Doctrine of the Servant*, Duke University Publications (Durham: Duke University Press, 1929) 85.

[16]Hooker, *Jesus and the Servant*, 127.

onlookers' verdict on the Servant's sufferings with their suggestion of vicariousness is omitted, rather "strangely," says Hooker.[17] Hence, C. F. Evans's verdict: "Neither in [the] gospel nor in Acts is the death of Christ given sacrificial or atoning value."[18] It is in fact in 1 Peter 2:22-25 that we are actually provided with "the earliest definite proof for the full identification of Jesus with the Servant in all its Christological significance."[19] It is to be noted that Hooker's views are now modified with regard to Romans 4:25,[20] and a recent consensus on this point is noted by Breytenbach.[21]

From now on I propose to narrow the issue under consideration to the question of whether the New Testament doctrine of the vicarious suffering of Jesus can be based directly on that allegedly posited of the Suffering Servant in Isaiah 53.

In 1978, Norman Whybray questioned whether there was indeed such a concept of vicarious suffering in the Old Testament as a whole, and Hooker had also noted "very little use" being made "of the idea of vicarious suffering" in connection with the Servant in Jewish literature.[22] It would surely have considerably strengthened Hooker's case if she had had at her disposal the evidence provided by Whybray which appears to indicate that this concept of vicarious suffering was entirely absent from the literature of the Old Testament, and that not just in connection with the Servant. This feature has been, it appears to me, hardly noted until recently by New Testament scholars.[23] We must also return briefly later

---

[17]Ibid., 113-14; see also Hooker, "The Use of Isaiah 53," 91-92.

[18]C. F. Evans, *Explorations in Theology: 2* (London: SCM, 1977) 48. The essays edited by D. D. Sylva, *Reimaging the Death of the Lukan Jesus*, BBB, Bd. 73 (Frankfurt am Main: Anton Hain, 1990), raise the question of a theological rationale for the lack of atonement theology in Luke–Acts.

[19]Hooker, *Jesus and the Servant*, 127; and Hooker, "The Use of Isaiah 53," 92.

[20]Hooker, "The Use of Isaiah 53," 101-103.

[21]C. Breytenbach, "Versöhnung, Stellvertretung und Sühne: Semantische und traditions-geschichtliche Bemerkungen am Beispiel der paulinischen Briefe," *NTS* 39 (1993): 70; cf. also Hengel, *Cross of the Son of God*, 223-24.

[22]Hooker, *Jesus and the Servant*, 155-56.

[23]For example, there is no mention of Whybray's work in the detailed treatment of D. J. Moo, *The Old Testament in the Gospel Passion Narratives* (Sheffield: Almond, 1983). The publication of Bellinger and Farmer, *Jesus and the Suffering*

to ask what evidence there might be in Jewish extracanonical literature for this concept, especially in connection with the Servant or the Messiah.

Have we, therefore, been justified in believing all along that the concept of vicarious suffering is found in the Old Testament as a whole, or at least in Isaiah 53?

Let us now review the evidence for it in the Old Testament itself, by following closely Whybray's research on the matter. We begin with the Hebrew phrase נשׂא עון, found some thirty times in the MT, but not in Isaiah 53 or in any other Servant passage. However, it has often been claimed to be a phrase that indicates the presence of the notion of vicarious suffering in the Old Testament. Literally it means, "to carry or bear iniquity." We note also that it is sometimes used interchangeably with נשׂא חטא, which actually does occur in Isaiah 53:12.[24] (a) There are seven cases where it clearly means, "to forgive," when God is the subject of the verb (Exodus 34:7; Numbers 14:18; Psalms 32:5; 85:3; Isaiah 33:24; Hosea 14:3; Micah 7:18).[25] (b) Often (fourteen times) it refers to people bearing their own iniquity in the sense of being punished by God for their own sins: Exodus 28:43; Leviticus 5:1, 17; 7:18 (LXX 8); 17:16; 19:8; 20:17, 19; 22:16; Numbers 5:31;[26] 30:15; Ezekiel 14:10; 44:10, 12.[27]

In this group there are examples of the phrase that are deemed to be contentious, since they have been taken to indicate a form of vicarious suffering. We may dismiss two examples of them immediately. In Ezekiel 14:10 the false prophet and the apostate inquirer must bear an equal punishment (LXX λήμψονται τὴν ἀδικίαν αὐτῶν [A αὐτοῦ]). We find a more difficult example in Numbers 30:15. Chapter 30 discusses the subject of vows and in particular the responsibility of a woman, whether married or unmarried, for the vows she had made. If her father or

---

Servant, has rectified the situation somewhat.

[24]R. N. Whybray, *Thanksgiving for a Liberated Prophet: An Interpretation of Isaiah Chapter 53*, JSOTSup 4 (Sheffield: University of Sheffield, Department of Biblical Studies, 1978) 31, 57.

[25]Whybray, *Thanksgiving for a Liberated Prophet*, 32.

[26]Mistakenly given as 3:31 in W. Zimmerli, "Zur Vorgeschichte von Jes. LIII," in *Congress Volume, Rome, 1968*, VTSup 17 (Leiden: Brill, 1969) 239n.3.

[27]See also O. Hofius, "Das vierte Gottesknechtlied in den Briefen des neuen Testamentes," *NTS* 39 (1993): 416. Hofius, by the way, has no reference at all to Whybray's work in his article.

husband disapproves of her vows, then they are annulled forthwith. If, however, he fails to express his disapproval of them immediately when he hears them, and only does so later, then he himself has to bear the consequences of his own inaction (30:16, EVV 15: λήμψεται τὴν ἁμαρτίαν αὐτοῦ: thus the LXX correctly). The MT has the feminine suffix which could give the misleading rendering "he shall bear her sin (guilt, punishment)," whereas it is probably to be taken as a so-called "genitive of nearer definition"[28] with the meaning "he bears guilt which he has incurred with regard to her."[29] Thus, this can hardly be a case of vicarious suffering because the husband was at all times responsible for his wife's words and actions.[30]

(c) There now remain twelve examples of the phrase נשׂא עון which, it has been held, may suggest vicarious suffering (Exodus 28:38; Leviticus 10:17; 16:22; Numbers 14:34; 18:1, 23; Ezekiel 4:4-6$^{3\times}$; 18:19, 20$^{2\times}$.

(i) Chapter 28 of Exodus describes the regalia attached to the high priesthood, and in the course of the description of the "flower" or plate of gold which is to be attached to the front of the high priest's turban by a lace of blue there occurs the statement: "And Aaron shall bear the guilt (נשׂא עון) of the holy things which the children of Israel sanctify as their holy gifts" (literal translation of 28:38). (Certainly the REB does not suggest any vicarious suffering with its rendering: "[Aaron] has to bear the blame for defects in the rites with which the Israelites offer their sacred gifts.") It appears therefore to be the high priest's responsibility to ensure that the sacrifice offered to Yahweh is truly holy, and if it is not, then the guilt falls upon him. That is why the flower attached to the turban was to be worn in order to ward off or protect him from the consequences of this guilt (namely, it is apotropaic).[31] As in v. 43 where

---

[28]GKC §128f.

[29]See Whybray, *Thanksgiving for a Liberated Prophet*, 144n.21.

[30]G. A. Cooke, *A Critical and Exegetical Commentary on the Book of Ezekiel*, ICC (Edinburgh: T. & T. Clark, 1936) 52, had included this passage with other alleged references to vicarious suffering. W. Zimmerli, "Die Eigenart der prophetischen Reden des Ezechiel," *ZAW* 66 (1954): 9-12, terms many of these cases a "priestly formula" or divine verdict in cases of desecration of that which is considered holy.

[31]Cf. M. Noth, *Exodus: A Commentary*, OTL, ed. G. E. Wright et al. (London: SCM, 1962) 225.

it is said that Aaron and his sons shall ensure that they do not bring guilt upon themselves, it is stressed here that the high priest's task, in which the proper regalia plays a vital role, is an awesome one and the consequences of failure lead to blame, even guilt (עון), being incurred by him himself, and then lead even to death. Whybray[32] believes the verb נשׂא in v. 38 is to be translated quite literally as "to carry" and holds that the flower on the turban represents the guilt he carries. Indeed, he discerns a pattern throughout this chapter whereby Aaron is portrayed as "carrying" (נשׂא) an object or objects into the sanctuary that are in turn identified with something which they symbolize. Thus, v. 38 is deemed to fit into this pattern. It is, therefore, concluded that נשׂא עון cannot mean "to incur guilt" here and so suggest that the high priest's action is in any way vicarious: "He does not in any way substitute himself for Israel in his encounter with God."[33] Rather, he is pictured as a messenger.

This whole discussion raises the more general issue as to what the high priest was deemed to have been doing in the presence of Yahweh. We are reminded also of the depiction of the Jewish high priest's actions in Hebrews, where it is insisted that he had to offer for himself as well as for the people, thus stressing his own sinfulness and fallibility (5:3; 9:7). It could not, therefore, be a case of a vicarious sacrifice whereby he was the innocent victim suffering for the sake of a guilty people.

It could be claimed that the evidence of the LXX does not entirely support Whybray's claim that נשׂא has a uniform meaning in Exodus 28, for different verbs are used to render the Hebrew: ἀναλαμβάνω (v. 12), λαμβάνω (v. 29), φέρω (v. 30), and ἐξαίρω (v. 38, LXX 34). But, after all, such translation variants are not very unusual in the LXX, and, besides, these verbs are all well-nigh synonyms.

(ii) Leviticus 10:17 is concerned with the nature of the חטאת or sin-offering, and the phrase נשׂא עון of (in this case) the congregation is parallel to "to make atonement (כפר) for them." In this case the LXX translation with the verb ἀφαιρέω suggests the correct rendering of נשׂא עון, not as "bearing guilt/punishment," but as "taking away the guilt." Aaron's sons, who are being chastised in this context, "have been given the חטאת so they may, as the principal agents in the performance of the rite, take

[32]Whybray, *Thanksgiving for a Liberated Prophet*, 33-42.
[33]Ibid., 40.

away or remove the עון of the people, so making atonement." They "are in no way involved in vicarious guilt."[34]

(iii) The example of the scapegoat (Leviticus 16) may suggest to some the strongest case for the notion of vicarious suffering in the Old Testament. However, this is the only Old Testament passage where an animal is the subject of the verb in the phrase נשׂא עון. "It is nowhere stated [in the Old Testament] that an animal slaughtered in sacrifice 'bears the guilt' of the person(s) for whom the sacrifice is offered,"[35] nor can it be assumed that when, for example, the priests ate the victim's flesh they were in some way absorbing, and so "bearing," the עון of the people which had been transferred to its flesh.[36] No such transference of עון to a sacrificial victim seems to have been envisaged in the laws of the Old Testament. On the contrary, the victim was deemed always to be pleasing and acceptable to Yahweh.[37] McLean says, "Traditional interpretations are unable to supply an image that combines the idea of vicarious atonement through death with that of a victim becoming accursed."[38] The sacrificial victim does not atone for personal sin.[39] The second goat mentioned in the Yom Kippur ritual is laden with the sins of the nation and dispatched into the wilderness so that they are carried away as far as possible from the sinner. No "suffering" or "punishment" appears to be imposed upon the goat. Indeed, it is never mentioned as being killed: it is only in the later Mishnah that this is stated. Thus, this goat cannot have been a propitiatory sacrifice nor was it in any way vicarious. The implication of נשׂא here, despite the LXX's λαμβάνω, has to be "carry away" rather than the "bear" of RSV and NRSV, for it is after all taken "to a barren region" (NRSV, Leviticus 16:22).[40] Thus, basically it is an apotropaic ritual.

(iv) In Numbers 14:26ff. Moses and Aaron are bidden to tell the Israelites that apart from Caleb and Joshua they are all to die before reaching the promised land. Their "little ones," that is, those under

---

[34]Ibid., 46.

[35]Ibid., 48.

[36]Cf. ibid., 46.

[37]Cf. ibid., 46.

[38]McLean, "The Absence of an Atoning Sacrifice in Paul's Soteriology," 539; see further 540-42.

[39]Ibid., 542.

[40]Whybray, *Thanksgiving for a Liberated Prophet*, 48-49.

twenty (v. 31), also will be permitted entry into the land but only after they have borne (נשׂא; LXX ἀναφέρω) the (religious) fornication (whoredoms) of their fathers (v. 33; translated as "suffered for your faithlessness"; cf. NRSV and NIV). The fathers, however, will bear their iniquity (נשׂא עון, λαμβάνω) there in the wilderness for forty years (14:34). This cannot, therefore, be a case of vicarious suffering, despite Zimmerli's suggestion that it is so,[41] but of the innocent children suffering the consequences of their fathers' sins: in fact the punishment befalls both generations.[42]

(v) Ezekiel 4:4-6 portrays a symbolic action of the prophet whereby he is to lie on his left side for 390 days, representing the years of Israel's punishment, and then he is to do so on his right side for forty days, representing the years of Judah's punishment. What the prophet seems to be doing is representing the exiled nation in "bearing its punishment" (נשׂא עון).[43] In no way does he take away or lessen the suffering of the nation—a point conceded by Zimmerli,[44] although Zimmerli and G. A. Cooke still believe this is a case of vicarious suffering.[45] The former sees clear parallels between this passage and Isaiah 53 especially with regard to vicarious suffering.[46] He also points to the similarities between Ezekiel 3:26-27; 24:27; 33:22; and Isaiah 53:7.[47] Indeed he holds Ezekiel to be an *Urbild* of the Servant of Isaiah 53.[48]

In fact, a parallel may be admitted here between the sharing by the individual prophet of his compatriot's suffering with the situation in Isaiah

---

[41]Zimmerli, "Die Eigenart der prophetischen Reden des Ezechiel," 10n.1.

[42]Whybray, *Thanksgiving for a Liberated Prophet*, 47-48; cf. also G. B. Gray, *A Critical and Exegetical Commentary on Numbers*, ICC (Edinburgh: T. & T. Clark, 1903) 163.

[43]See also Hofius, "Das vierte Gottesknechtlied," 416n.12.

[44]Zimmerli, "Zur Vorgeschichte von Jes. LIII," 243.

[45]Cooke, *Ezekiel*, 52.

[46]Zimmerli, "Zur Vorgeschichte von Jes. LIII," 240-43.

[47]Zimmerli, *Ezekiel: A Commentary on the Book of the Prophet Ezekiel*, 2 vols., trans. R. E. Clements, ed. F. M. Cross and K. Baltzer, Hermeneia (Philadelphia: Fortress, 1979, 1983) 1:165a.

[48]Zimmerli, "Zur Vorgeschichte von Jes. LIII," 243; and idem, *Ezekiel*; cf. also K. W. Carley, *Ezekiel among the Prophets: A Study of Ezekiel's Place in Prophetic Tradition*, SBT 2nd series 31 (London: SCM, 1975) 75.

53 where the Servant in fact shares (albeit more intensely and severely) the suffering of his fellow exiles. As the prophet has suffered his paralysis, so must the people themselves suffer the paralysis of the exile that comes as a consequence of their own sins.[49] This interpretation of the action seems to be confirmed by the MT of Ezekiel 4:4a which reads: "You shall lay the punishment of the house of Israel upon it" (שׂים . . . עון . . . עליו, θήσεις τὰς ἀδικίας . . . ἐπ' αὐτοῦ), which is followed in the second part of the verse and in the following two verses by the phrase, again addressed to the prophet, "You shall bear the punishment of the house of Israel" (or Judah, as the case may be) (נשׂא עון, λήμψῃ τὰς ἀδικίας) (cf. also v. 5b). Thus the prophet is bidden both to impose and also to bear the punishment of these two nations. It is not surprising that Zimmerli[50] feels it necessary to emend the שׂים עון of v. 4a to another נשׂא עון on the grounds that since the prophet is the one who bears the עון, he can hardly be the one who imposes it as well.[51] In contrast Steck points out that in Ezekiel 4 it is not said that guilt or punishment are taken away.[52]

None of the above five cases, which are among those suggested by Zimmerli as doing so, actually appear to support the contention that the notion of vicarious bearing of the guilt of others is found in the Old Testament, although they were among his prime candidates in this respect. In six further cases (Numbers 18:1^{2x}; 18:23; Ezekiel 18:19, 20^{2x}) נשׂא עון is used in what Zimmerli terms a weakened sense to mean, "to assume responsibility."[53] In Numbers 18:1 the priests are to take care when performing their sacred duties; otherwise they commit עון (iniquity).[54] It is a similar situation in the case of the Levites later in the same chapter (v. 23): they have to "shield the people from the consequences of their approaching the holy things. If they incur עון, it will be their own

[49]Cf. Whybray, *Thanksgiving for a Liberated Prophet*, 50-52.

[50]Zimmerli, *Ezekiel* 1:164-65.

[51]Note also the emendation conjectured by RSV (similarly NEB): "I will lay the punishment . . . upon you." This is not retained in NRSV or in REB.

[52]O. H. Steck, "Aspekte des Gottesknechtes in Jes 52,13-53,12," ZAW 97 (1985): 56n.62.

[53]Zimmerli, "Die Eigenart der prophetischen Reden des Ezechiel"—a notion dismissed by Whybray, *Thanksgiving for a Liberated Prophet*, 43, as "especially improbable."

[54]Cf. Whybray, *Thanksgiving for a Liberated Prophet*, 43.

עון, not one transferred to them from the people."[55]

The form נשא בעון is found uniquely in the Old Testament three times in Ezekiel 18:19, 20[2x]. Whybray suggests it means, "to bear some of the punishment," i.e., share it, in these verses,[56] and LXX has λαμβάνω τὴν ἀδικίαν every time. Thus, even if the notion of vicarious punishment is broached in these examples, it is rejected, for no generation will, according to the prophet, be made to suffer for the iniquity of its predecessors or successors: each has to face up to the consequences of its own sins. That is indeed the burden of the discussion in this chapter arising from the proverb quoted in 18:2. Thus any sense of vicarious suffering or vicarious punishment is totally rejected and individual responsibility is very much to the fore here.

Having reviewed the alleged examples of vicarious suffering in the Old Testament outside Isaiah 53, we have to conclude that this notion is not present in any of them.[57]

Now what of the language of Isaiah 53 itself? In its interpretation, so much depends on the identity of the speakers in the first part of the chapter and also who the Servant is deemed to be. Generally, if the speakers are Gentiles then the Servant will be identified with the nation Israel, whereas if it is Jews who are represented as speaking, then the Servant will be an individual.[58] In addition, one has to assess the possibility of whether such an advanced concept as vicarious suffering could here have been attributed to Gentiles, and indeed whether on the basis of what has been argued already any Jews even might have been capable of such sentiments as early as the time of the Babylonian exile.

Not unnaturally Whybray adopts a theory regarding the identity of the Servant and of the speakers in this chapter that supports his conten-

---

[55]Ibid., 45.

[56]Ibid., 55-56.

[57]Cf. the remark of McLean in "The Absence of an Atoning Sacrifice in Paul's Soteriology," 549: "As a rule, the Old Testament rejects the concept of vicarious atonement on the grounds that 'a person may die only for his own sins' (Deut 24:16; cf. 2 Kgs 14:6; 2 Chr 25:4)."

[58]See recently on the identity of the 'we' and 'the many' of this Fourth Servant Song, Steck, "Aspekte des Gottesknechtes in Jes 52,13-53,12," 39-41; and H. G. Reventlow, "Basic Issues in the Interpretation of Isaiah 53," in Bellinger and Farmer, *Jesus and the Suffering Servant*, 29.

tion that it is not possible to sustain the arguments for the existence of vicariousness here. Of necessity, this has to be the weakest, because it is the most speculative, part of his thesis. For him the Servant is the prophet (Deutero-Isaiah) himself and the speakers are fellow members of the Jewish nation, indeed friends and acquaintances of his. Thus any suffering he is described as undergoing would have to be a more acute form of the suffering that the rest of the nation in Babylon was also experiencing at the time of the Exile.[59] "He 'bore the sins of many' not in the sense of suffering instead of the many but of enduring additional and exceptional suffering."[60] So the notion of vicarious suffering is not truly represented here because both parties are involved in the suffering. Thus, says Orlinsky, "the central element in the phenomenon of vicariousness, that the wicked go unpunished, is lacking altogether here."[61]

The other side of the argument presented by Whybray is of course one in which it is stressed that the "we," who in the chapter confess their sins, are made to recognize the Servant's innocence. However, that can only be a comparative innocence in Whybray's eyes, for he is at pains to deny the Servant's absolute sinlessness[62] (whatever that precisely may mean outside a Christological context). Although "he had done no violence, and there was no deceit in his mouth" (v. 9), the suffering Servant cannot be entirely whitewashed. Otherwise, the terms innocent and guilty suggest too strongly the notion of vicarious suffering.

We turn now to consider the pertinent phrases of chapter 53 as they relate to the question of vicariousness, and we shall begin at the end of the chapter (v. 11b), where in fact Yahweh is the speaker. (The change of speaker from observers to Yahweh occurs at v. 11b:[63] "He shall bear their iniquities" עונתם הוא יסבל, LXX τὰς ἁμαρτίας αὐτῶν αὐτὸς

---

[59]Whybray, *Thanksgiving for a Liberated Prophet*, 30; cf. also C. R. North, *The Suffering Servant in Deutero-Isaiah: A Historical and Critical Study* (London: Oxford University Press, 1956) 203.

[60]R. N. Whybray, *The Second Isaiah*, Old Testament Guides 1 (Sheffield: JSOT, 1983) 78.

[61]Orlinsky, "The So-called 'Servant of the Lord' and 'Suffering Servant' in Second Isaiah," 59.

[62]Whybray, *Thanksgiving for a Liberated Prophet*, 144n.8.

[63]Ibid., 163n.3.

ἀνοίσει).[64] The only other example of the phrase סבל עון in the Old Testament is Lamentations 5:7, which suggests that subsequent generations of the Jews suffer the consequence of the sins of their forefathers. A similar sentiment is reiterated in the popular proverb of the time: "The fathers have eaten sour grapes, and the children's teeth are set on edge" (Ezekiel 18:1; Jeremiah 31:29). In the context of Lamentations this can hardly imply undeserved suffering on the part of the generation of the exile, for v. 16 of the same chapter states: "The crown has fallen from our head; woe to us, for we have sinned" (NRSV).

Obviously synonymous with the phrase סבל עון is the נשׂא חטא of Isaiah 53:12c: "He bore the sin of many" (LXX αὐτὸς ἁμαρτίας [ℵB ἀνομίας] πολλῶν ἀνήνεγκεν).[65] In the remaining eight passages in the Old Testament where the phrase נשׂא חטא occurs (Leviticus 19:17; 20:20; 22:9; 24:15; Numbers 9:13; 18:22, 32; Ezekiel 23:49), and they all happen within the context of priestly legislation, it always refers to bearing/incurring the consequences of one's own guilt, and so is entirely irrelevant to the point at issue.[66] The usage in Isaiah 53:12 appears, however, to be entirely different, for it is the only example where a person is said to bear or incur the חטא of others.

This is an appropriate place to mention the discussion of the identity of the "many" (רבים, LXX πολλοί) in vv. 11b and 12c. They will have included the Babylonian exiles, and so both examples would, if the Servant is an individual, refer to suffering which is actually shared, and thus cannot be vicarious.[67] Again, the interpretation of the phrases depends very much on one's presuppositions regarding the identity of the Servant and of the speakers (= transgressors) in the body of the poem.[68]

---

[64]"The penalty for their guilt," according to G. R. Driver, "Isaiah 52:13–53:12: the Servant of the Lord," in *In Memoriam Paul Kahle*, ed. M. Black and G. Fohrer, BZAW 103 (Berlin: Töpelmann, 1968) 104.

[65]See further Hofius, "Das vierte Gottesknechtlied," 415-16.

[66]Cf. Whybray, *Thanksgiving for a Liberated Prophet*, 30-31; cf. also Hofius, "Das vierte Gottesknechtlied," 416n.12.

[67]Whybray, *Thanksgiving for a Liberated Prophet*, 30.

[68]For J. W. Olley, " 'The Many': How Is Isaiah 53.12c to Be Understood?," *Bib* 68 (1987): 353-54, the "many" include the nations, with their rulers, but also rebellious Israel. For Zimmerli, "Zur Vorgeschichte von Jes. LIII," 236, it is the believing community of the Servant that speaks in chap. 53.

We now turn to similar statements in v. 4a: "Surely he has borne our griefs/infirmities (חלינו הוא נשא, LXX τὰς ἁμαρτίας ἡμῶν φέρει) and carried our sorrows/diseases" (ומכאבינו סבלם, LXX περὶ ἡμῶν ὀδυνᾶται). The LXX in fact paraphrases and certainly nothing corresponds in the MT to the περί of the Greek: "He faces pain for our sakes." In the quotation in Matthew 8:17 the passage follows the MT more closely. It is the word order of this verse, with its object ("our griefs") coming first in the sentence followed immediately by the pronoun הוא, with the object again in the prior position in the second half of the poetic line, which appears to underline the vicarious nature of the Servant's suffering. Whybray[69] tries to counter this argument by pointing to the metaphorical use of the words חלי and מכאב in other passages describing conditions in the exilic period: these are words which also echo the physical afflictions of the Servant described in the previous verse (v. 3).[70] Again, Whybray stresses that all this suffering is shared by both the speakers (that is, the nation) and the Servant alike, albeit in a more intense form by the Servant.

Verse 6b possibly causes the greatest difficulty to Whybray's view: "The Lord has laid on him the iniquity of us all." The hiphil of פגע, which is found here, is rare in the Old Testament (there are only six examples). In the example at the end of the song at v. 12 it is rendered by the NRSV "and made intercession for the transgressors." Christian eisegesis has suggested that the Servant through his suffering and death made intercession or intervened on behalf of the transgressors.[71] However, on the analogy of his prophetic predecessors such intercessory activity by the Servant does not necessarily imply any vicarious suffering on his part.[72] We may note also the use of the same verb in Isaiah 59:16, where it is actually Yahweh who acts in that capacity. The LXX of v. 12 retains the same rendering of the Hebrew verb as in v. 6: παραδίδωμι, a favourite word of the translator. Hence LXX renders here "He was handed over because of their sins." Returning to v. 6b we note that the qal of the verb means basically "to meet" and so the hiphil must express the meaning "to

---

[69]Whybray, *Thanksgiving for a Liberated Prophet*, 58-60.

[70]Contrast K. Seybold, חָלָה in *TDOT* 4:405-406.

[71]Cf. C. R. North, *The Second Isaiah: Introduction, Translation, and Commentary to Chapters XL-LV* (Oxford: Clarendon, 1964) 246; and C. Westermann, *Isaiah 40–66: A Commentary*, trans. D. Stalker, OTL (London: SCM, 1969) 269.

[72]Whybray, *Thanksgiving for a Liberated Prophet*, 71-74.

cause to meet." KB[73] suggest: "to cause a thing to encounter a person": hence "to lay upon" and here most probably עון bears the sense of penalty for the sins of all the speakers[74] (cf. also v. 11). We note that the LXX form of this verse—παρέδωκεν αὐτὸν ταῖς ἁμαρτίαις ἡμῶν—could be translated "The Lord delivered him up to our sins," and so would not clearly reflect an interpretation conveying a vicarious understanding of the phrase.[75] It is worth noting, as Whybray does,[76] that the writer is not using here language with sacrificial or ritual associations. The usage of הפגיע in v. 6 is indeed unique and the adoption of this particular and unusual verb also suggests a play on the word, which, as indicated already, has a wholly different connotation in v. 12. Such use of homonyms in totally different senses is common in this chapter: נענה, "was afflicted" and "showed himself submissive"; הפגיע, "inflicted" and "interceded"; נגע, "struck down" physically and judicially; and possibly רבים, "many" and "great."[77]

The preposition מן has been rendered in a way that tends to support a vicarious interpretation of the whole passage. Thus we generally find in English translations "wounded for our transgressions" and "crushed for our iniquities" in v. 5 and "stricken for the transgression of my people" (v. 8), and in the first two instances the LXX's διά with the accusative tends to support this. However, the LXX renders the example in v. 8 more literally with ἀπό. It is probable that the proper rendering of מן here should be causal, that is, "as a result of, in consequence of";[78] it would be the *beth pretii* or 'beth of exchange' which would normally give us the meaning "for" in such contexts.[79] Thus a more accurate rendering of מן weakens

---

[73]L. Köhler and W. Baumgartner, *Lexicon in Veteris Testamenti Libros* (Leiden: E. J. Brill, 1958) 751.

[74]Cf. A. Gelston, "Isaiah 52:13–53:12: An Eclectic Text and a Supplementary Note on the Hebrew Manuscript Kennicott 96," *Journal of Semitic Studies* 35 (1990): 194, 201.

[75]S. K. Williams, *Jesus' Death as Saving Event: The Background and Origin of a Concept*, Harvard Dissertations in Religion 2 (Missoula: Scholars, 1975) 113.

[76]Whybray, *Thanksgiving for a Liberated Prophet*, 60.

[77]Driver, "Isaiah 52:13–53:12," 96.

[78]C. F. D. Moule, *An Idiom Book of New Testament Greek* (Cambridge: Cambridge University Press, 1959) 73.

[79]Orlinsky, "The So-called 'Servant of the Lord' and 'Suffering Servant' in

considerably the vicarious sense.[80] All we are now stating is that the Servant suffers as a consequence of the sins of others. Indeed, מן never has the sense of 'in exchange for, in payment for.'[81] The only ב in vv. 4-6, that in v. 5 ("By his bruises we are healed"), "can hardly be made to prove anything" for vicariousness, according to Orlinsky.[82] This is not a *beth pretii* meaning 'in exchange for,' but a *beth instrumenti.*[83]

While on the subject of prepositions we might well ask whether the על (LXX ἐπ' αὐτόν) in the phrase "the chastisement that makes us whole was upon him" (v. 5) has any specific vicarious connotation. For Zimmerli[84] it contains the picture of the bearing of a load. Again, the general tenor of the interpretation must decide the issue rather than a consideration of the phrase in isolation from its context.

We now have to consider v. 10b: אם־תשים אשם נפשו. The Hebrew is rendered by NRSV: "When you make his life an offering for sin." Thus the Servant is called an אשם in v. 10, the cultic term for a guilt-offering,[85] thus suggesting a sacrifice, and the LXX has περὶ ἁμαρτίας, which is the normal LXX translation of this Hebrew ritual term. However, the λύτρον of Mark 10:45, which, it is often suggested, is based on this אשם, is never a sacrificial term in the LXX,[86] and the two terms are unconnected.[87]

Second Isaiah," 57 ; and Whybray, *Thanksgiving for a Liberated Prophet*, 61-62.

[80]See also Hooker, "The Use of Isaiah 53," 96-97.

[81]Cf. Whybray, *Thanksgiving for a Liberated Prophet*, 61.

[82]Orlinsky, "The So-called 'Servant of the Lord' and 'Suffering Servant' in Second Isaiah," 58. The LXX has a simple dative without a preposition: τῷ μώλωπι αὐτοῦ ἡμεῖς ἰάθημεν.

[83]Whybray, *Thanksgiving for a Liberated Prophet*, 149n.138.

[84]Zimmerli, "Zur Vorgeschichte von Jes. LIII," 238.

[85]D. Kellermann, "אָשָׁם" in *TDOT* 1:429-37, esp. 435. Not so Hofius, "Das vierte Gottesknechtlied," 417.

[86]Hooker, *Jesus and the Servant*, 76.

[87]Ibid., 77. Cf. ἀντίψυχον in *4 Maccabees*: Hooker, *Jesus and the Servant*, 78. See further C. K. Barrett, "The Background of Mark 10:45," in *New Testament Essays (T. W. Manson Festschrift)*, ed. A. J. B. Higgins (Manchester: Manchester University Press, 1959) 5; Barrett, *New Testament Essays* (London: SPCK, 1972), 20-21; and D. Hill, *Greek Words and Hebrew Meanings: Studies in the Semantics of Soteriological Terms*, SNTSMS 5 (London: Cambridge University Press, 1967) 80. Contrast Lohse, *Märtyrer und Gottesknecht*, 119, and 192n.3; and Hahn, *Titles of Jesus in Christology*, 57.

The construing of this sentence is difficult. If, on the one hand, the subject of the verb שׂים is assumed to be נפשׁ, then we would have the rendering "If (or when) his soul (= he himself) makes an offering for sin."[88] However, the phrase שׂים אשׁם represents a wholly unique usage for the Old Testament since שׂים is never employed with the name of a sacrifice as its object.[89] Besides, the phrase as construed has no object to correspond with the victim to be sacrificed, for now the Servant is the subject of the verb, not its object, and thus all that it would be suggesting would be that the Servant makes a guilt-offering, thus obliterating any vicarious sense.[90] In addition, the imperfect of the verb suggests a future action, whereas the previous part of the poem describes his past actions.[91] On the other hand, the rendering of the phrase as "When you make [him] his life an offering for sin" (NRSV) is to be rejected as a possible translation.[92] It would presumably be addressed to Yahweh, and it is indeed odd to find this sudden address to him where no other is found in

---

[88]This conveys the right sense according to North, *Second Isaiah*, 232; cf. also KJV[mg] and RV[mg]. For the emendation ישׂים for תשׂים, see Hofius, "Das vierte Gottesknechtlied," 417n.17. This is adopted in RSV: "when he makes himself an offering for sin." NIV interprets the third person as Yahweh and introduces him explicitly into its rendering, and thus we have "and though the Lord makes his life a guilt offering." JB has "If he offers his life in atonement" (NJB: "if he gives his life as a sin offering"). REB adopts with the *BHS* apparatus an emendation that derives originally from J. Begrich, *Studien zu Deuterojesaja*, BWANT 77 (Stuttgart: Kohlhammer, 1938) 58: "and healed him who had given [made, NEB] himself as a sacrifice for sin." This rendering is also favoured by Driver, "Isaiah 52:13–53:12," 96-97, 104.

[89]Whybray, *Thanksgiving for a Liberated Prophet*, 64. R. E. Watts, "Jesus' Death, Isaiah 53, and Mark 10:45: A Crux Revisited," in Bellinger and Farmer, *Jesus and the Suffering Servant*, 139, believes it closely parallels the δοῦναι τὴν ψυχὴν αὐτοῦ of Mark 10:45. Cf. also Zimmerli and Jeremias, *The Servant of God*, 96; and Moo, *Old Testament in the Gospel Passion Narratives*, 122-26.

[90]Whybray, *Thanksgiving for a Liberated Prophet*, 64-65.

[91]Ibid., 65.

[92]Driver, "Isaiah 52:13–53:12," 96, calls it "to all intents and purposes, nonsense." However, D. J. A. Clines and J. Elwolde, *The Dictionary of Classical Hebrew* (Sheffield: Sheffield Academic, 1993) 1:415, treats אשׁם as an object of the verb שׂים.

this context.[93] The very uncertainty as to the correct translation of this sentence warns us against building too much upon it.[94]

The concept of a human being as an אשם would be quite unusual in the Old Testament, and, besides, seems to portray human sacrifice, which, of course, was wholly abhorrent to the true adherents of Yahweh.[95] Snaith sought to solve the difficulty posed by the term אשם by stating that here it means "compensation, substitution. The so-called 'guilt-offering' was actually a compensation offering. . . . The Servant was an innocent substitute for the guilty. The prophet is not concerned about what happens to the sinners, nor does he say that the Servant suffered and died for the sinners in order to save them. There was nothing vicarious in this sense about the suffering and death of the Servant nor is there anything to do with atonement."[96] He went on to describe the suffering as "an interlude in the life of the Servant. . . . His sufferings were indeed an אשם, but not in any sense in which the so-called guilt-offering is usually understood. They were a substitute; he paid the penalty of their sins. This was not *in order that* the guilty might go free. It is just a fact that he did suffer the consequences of sins that were not his."[97]

In v. 11b the hiphil of צדק may indicate that the Servant will make the many "to be acquitted" (though guilty),[98] "make righteous, bring to righteousness,"[99] or "deliver."[100] If taken with the following line, "he will bear their iniquities," it is to be seen in vicarious terms.[101] However, it

[93]Cf. Whybray, *Thanksgiving for a Liberated Prophet*, 64.

[94]Cf. Orlinsky, "The So-called 'Servant of the Lord' and 'Suffering Servant' in Second Isaiah," 61n.1; and Whybray, *Thanksgiving for a Liberated Prophet*, 66.

[95]Whybray, *Thanksgiving for a Liberated Prophet*, 65.

[96]Snaith, "Isaiah 40–66: A Study," 196.

[97]Ibid., 204-205.

[98]Cf. J. Muilenburg, "The Book of Isaiah. Chapters 40–66," in *The Interpreter's Bible*, vol. 5, ed. G. A. Buttrick (New York/Nashville: Abingdon, 1956) 630.

[99]North, *Second Isaiah*, 244-45.

[100]J. L. McKenzie, *Second Isaiah*, AB 20 (Garden City: Doubleday, 1968) 131, 136.

[101]Cf. Whybray, *Thanksgiving for a Liberated Prophet*, 67 and 150n.155. "It seems difficult to avoid some vicarious note" (J. W. Olley, *'Righteousness' in the Septuagint of Isaiah: A Contextual Study*, SBL Septuagint and Cognate Studies Series 8 [Missoula: Scholars, 1979] 50).

usually means, "to acquit" an innocent party rather than "to let off" a guilty one: the latter indeed, it is claimed, would be an abhorrent sin.[102] We can compare the wise (משׂכלים) of Daniel 12:3 who bring צדקה to the many and do so through their teaching rather than their suffering.[103] Whybray himself finds it difficult to distinguish between two renderings of the verb here: either "My Servant being guiltless acted righteously for the many," or "My Servant brought the many salvation."[104] Thus does he arrive at the conclusion that the concept of vicarious suffering is not clearly or certainly found in Isaiah 53.[105]

We now have to ask whether the Suffering Servant is described as actually dying. Clearly if he did not do so, talk of vicarious death is inappropriate. Certainly in the early descriptions of him in the Fourth Servant Song (53:2-3, with which 52:14b should be linked) the impression seems to be given that every conceivable indignity and pain had been imposed upon him; indeed, the descriptions here of his wretched appearance and condition appear to have been exaggerated on purpose.[106] The Servant certainly suffered violent action against his person, but it is open to question whether he actually suffered death itself.[107] The participle מחלל (a wholly unique poal participle) in v. 5a normally means "pierced, killed" in Hebrew (cf. the Pesh), although the LXX and Vg have "wounded" (NRSV).[108] In this case Whybray[109] accepts Driver's arguments that neither this participle nor the adjacent מדכא ("crushed")—and they are synonymous—imply the death of the victim: "Indeed, the whole context suggests that these and other expressions used to describe the sufferings of the Servant refer to physical ill-treatment and not to his death at the hands

---

[102]Whybray, *Thanksgiving for a Liberated Prophet*, 67, 70.

[103]Cf. ibid., 69-70.

[104]Ibid., 70-71 and 151n.176.

[105]Ibid., 75. Snaith, "Isaiah 40–66: A Study," 217, similarly declared: "We do not find anything vicarious there at all."

[106]Cf. Whybray, *Thanksgiving for a Liberated Prophet*, 92-94.

[107]Ibid., 92, 95-98. Cf. the brief review of research by J. A. Soggin, "Tod und Auferstehung des leidenden Gottesknechtes Jesaja 53:8-10," *ZAW* 87 (1975): 346n.2.

[108]Cf. Driver, "Isaiah 52:13–53:12," 93. Clines and Elwolde, *Dictionary of Classical Hebrew* 3:236, gives the two meanings: "be pierced, be wounded."

[109]Whybray, *Thanksgiving for a Liberated Prophet*, 98.

of his fellowmen."[110]

Again, the comparison of the Servant with a lamb in v. 7b does not suggest death as such (cf. Jeremiah 11:19). Besides the verbs here are subordinate ones in relative clauses and relate the verbs to animals and not to the Servant as such. Thus they should be translated "Like a lamb that is led to the slaughter, or like a sheep that before its shearers is silent," as in RSV, NRSV, REB,[111] and not "He was led away like a sheep, he was silent like a ewe." We might add with Snaith that "There is no reference here whatever to any temple sacrifice; the point is the helplessness and dumbness of the animal."[112]

In v. 8a the passive participle לקח ("taken, taken away") does not have to be associated with death (although one should point to 2 Kings 2:10),[113] and the phrase is understood by Whybray to mean "From (after) imprisonment (arrest) and trial (the rendering of משפט) he was taken away."[114] What then of the second part of the verse with its apparent reference to removal from "the land of the living?" The rare verb גזר ("cut off") found here does not refer to death in prose texts; it is only in four instances in laments (Ezekiel 37:11; Psalms 31:23 [EVV 22]; 88:6 [EVV 5]; Lamentations 3:54) where that could be the case.[115] Soggin has argued that, whereas כרת ("cut off") generally refers to death, גזר alludes not to death itself but to situations of apparent hopelessness from which Yahweh is believed to be able to rescue the victim. Interestingly, Jewish tradition has not in general interpreted v. 8b as a reference to the Servant's death either.[116] In addition, Driver argued that the expression "the land of the living" actually meant "human society": "the world of living men" is his

[110]Driver, "Isaiah 52:13–53:12," 94.

[111]Cf. Driver, "Isaiah 52:13–53:12," 94, 104; and Whybray, *Thanksgiving for a Liberated Prophet*, 99.

[112]Snaith, "Isaiah 40–66: A Study," 195.

[113]Cf. Whybray, *Thanksgiving for a Liberated Prophet*, 100.

[114]Ibid., 99.

[115]Cf. Soggin, "Tod und Auferstehung," 346-55; and Whybray, *Thanksgiving for a Liberated Prophet*, 101-102.

[116]Soggin, "Tod und Auferstehung," 351. See also the evidence in A. Neubauer and S. R. Driver, *The Fifty-Third Chapter of Isaiah according to the Jewish Interpreters* (Oxford: Clarendon, 1877).

actual rendering[117] (cf. REB), although Whybray[118] is by no means certain about that. Thus for Driver it refers to imprisonment rather than actual death.[119]

Then, neither does v. 9a—"They made his grave with the wicked / And his tomb with the rich"—necessarily imply that the Servant has already died.[120] The verb נתן here does not have to convey the sense of digging the Servant's grave, but merely of choosing or assigning one for him. It "does not necessarily imply that he was ever laid in it," declares Driver.[121] We also note in passing the generally accepted emendation of במתיו ("in his death") to במתו ("in his tomb" or "burial-place") adopted by NRSV.[122]

And finally, we are confronted with the verb ערה in v. 12b. Does it mean, "to pour out, empty" his נפש ("his life, himself") or "to lay bare, expose," as in REB?[123] In the only other instance in the Old Testament where the piel of ערה occurs with נפש as its object, namely, Psalm 141:8, it is rendered "do not leave me exposed" by JB. The versions take this to mean that he was delivered up to death: παρεδόθη (that favourite verb of the LXX translator) appears twice in 53:12. According to Driver this "does not necessarily imply that he was put to death, although it may have this force."[124] Similarly, Sapp admits the LXX is less definite than the Hebrew here. It "leaves some doubt as to whether the Servant was actually put to death or only led up to the point of possible death."[125] However, the full phrase contains למות ("to death") and cannot be simply

---

[117]Driver, "Isaiah 52:13–53:12," 104.

[118]Whybray, *Thanksgiving for a Liberated Prophet*, 103.

[119]Driver, "Isaiah 52:13–53:12," 95.

[120]Cf. C. C. Torrey, *The Second Isaiah* (New York: Scribner's, 1928) 420-21; Orlinsky, "The So-called 'Servant of the Lord' and 'Suffering Servant' in Second Isaiah," 62; Driver, "Isaiah 52:13–53:12," 95; Soggin, "Tod und Auferstehung," 353; and Whybray, *Thanksgiving for a Liberated Prophet*, 103-104.

[121]Driver, "Isaiah 52:13–53:12," 104.

[122]Cf. ibid., 95-96.

[123]For "lay bare, expose" see also Sa'adyah: Driver, "Isaiah 52:13–53:12," 102.

[124]Ibid., 102.

[125]D. A. Sapp, "The LXX, 1QIsa, and MT Versions of Isaiah 53 and the Christian Doctrine of Atonement," in Bellinger and Farmer, *Jesus and the Suffering Servant*, 177.

eliminated on metrical grounds as was done by Barrett.[126]

All in all, therefore, a case can be made for doubting whether the Servant is actually said to have died, while the case for denying the Servant's resurrection is a stronger one. This was a concept which was all but absent from the rest of the Old Testament and would hardly be present as early as a sixth century BC text.[127] This situation has to be confronted by upholders of the traditional interpretation. Indeed, for Orlinsky, "He shall see his offspring" (v. 10c) indicates that the Servant did not die. Moreover, talk of death is the language of hyperbole,[128] and Driver more cautiously concludes, "No phrase is used which unambiguously implies the Servant's death."[129]

We should add that there are few signs in intertestamental Judaism of the existence of the idea of vicarious suffering and atoning death, especially in connection with the Suffering Servant.[130] The *Testament of Benjamin* 3:8 reads in Sparks, *The Apocryphal Old Testament*, "In you (that is, Joseph) shall be fulfilled the prophecy of heaven [about the lamb of God and the Saviour of the world]—that one without blemish shall be offered up on behalf of sinners, and one without sin shall die on behalf of the ungodly [in the blood of the covenant, for the salvation of the Gentiles and of Israel, and he shall destroy Beliar and those who serve him]."[131] The bracketed words are those indicated as Christian interpolations by R. H. Charles, *The Testaments of the Twelve Patriarchs*[132] (cf. also

---

[126]Barrett, "The Background of Mark 10:45," 5. Contrast Watts, in "Jesus' Death, Isaiah 53, and Mark 10:45," 139.

[127]Cf. Whybray, *Thanksgiving for a Liberated Prophet*, 79-92. Cf. also Robinson, *Cross in the Old Testament*, 97.

[128]Orlinsky, "The So-called 'Servant of the Lord' and 'Suffering Servant' in Second Isaiah," 61-62.

[129]Driver, "Isaiah 52:13–53:12," 104. In contrast, Gelston, "Isaiah 52:13–53:12: An Eclectic Text," 190, believes there is a death (vv. 8c, 9a) and a resurrection (vv. 10c, 11b) of the Servant. Hooker, *Jesus and the Servant*, 46-47, also denies there is talk of resurrection in Isa 53.

[130]Cf. Hooker, *Jesus and the Servant*, 155-56.

[131]H. F. D. Sparks, *The Apocryphal Old Testament* (Oxford: Clarendon Press, 1984) 595.

[132]R. H. Charles, *The Testaments of the Twelve Patriarchs* (London: A. & C. Black, 1908) 202. See also H. C. Kee, *OTP* 1:826.

the ἀμνὸς τοῦ θεοῦ of *Testament of Joseph* 19:6, a passage generally suspected of being a Christian interpolation[133]). The heavenly prophecy is taken by Zimmerli to be Isaiah 53, and the passage is deemed by him to be the oldest testimony to an expected Messiah of Joseph.[134] However, Charles connected the passage with those in 2 Maccabees 7:38 and 4 Maccabees 6:28-29 about the vicarious suffering of the Jewish martyrs.[135] Furthermore, M. de Jonge believes the *Testaments* to be a Christian composition that incorporates a variety of pre-Christian, Jewish material. In this particular passage the Armenian definite article before the adjectives rendered in Greek by ἄμωμος ("one without blemish") and ἀναμάρτητος ("one without sin") is said to indicate a Christian hand at work on the version.[136]

The 'son of man' of the *Similitudes of Enoch* is depicted "to a large extent" says Zimmerli, quoting Billerbeck, with traits borrowed from Servant passages, including 52:13-15 and 53:11.[137] But others can see nothing there remotely resembling vicarious suffering: "It would be quite misleading to speak of a 'suffering servant' in this connection," says J. J. Collins.[138] These references owe much more to Daniel 7 (see especially vv. 9, 13) than to Deutero-Isaiah.[139] The Son of Man is apparently saved

---

[133]Cf. Jeremias, "ἀμνός" in *TDNT* 1:338; C. K. Barrett, "The Lamb of God," *NTS* 1 (1954): 215; M. de Jonge, "Christian Influence in the Testaments of the Twelve Patriarchs," *NovT* 4 (1960): 215-17; and Barrett, "The Background of Mark 10:45," 176.

[134]Zimmerli and Jeremias, *The Servant of God*, 57-58.

[135]Charles, *Testaments of the Twelve Patriarchs*, 202.

[136]M. de Jonge, *Jewish Eschatology, Early Christian Christology, and the Testaments of the Twelve Patriarchs: Collected Essays of Marinus de Jonge*, NovTSup 63 (Leiden: E. J. Brill, 1991) 295.

[137]Zimmerli and Jeremias, *The Servant of God*, 60; and P. Billerbeck, "Hat die alte Synagoge einen präexistententen Messias gekannt?," *Nathanael* 21 (1905): 107.

[138]J. J. Collins, "The Son of Man in First-Century Judaism," *NTS* 38 (1992): 465; cf. also idem, *The Scepter and the Star: The Messiahs of the Dead Sea Scrolls and Other Ancient Literature*, Anchor Bible Reference Library (New York: Doubleday, 1995) 124.

[139]Cf. M. Casey, *Son of Man: The Interpretation and Influence of Daniel 7* (London: SPCK, 1979) 99-112; J. D. G. Dunn, *Christology in the Making: A New Testament Inquiry into the Origins of the Doctrine of the Incarnation* (Philadelphia:

from the suffering of the righteous. He is "the heavenly counterpart of the righteous on earth. While they are oppressed and lowly, he is enthroned and exalted."[140]

The *Targum of Isaiah*'s interpretation of the Fourth Servant Song is of course quite idiosyncratic.[141] The entire song is expounded as a reference to the Messiah, but virtually every suggestion that the Servant will suffer has been removed. Such traces remain only faintly in two places. Indeed, the suffering has been applied to the Messiah's enemies or to Israel, whom the Servant-Messiah rescues.[142] It appears in fact to be a piece of anti-Christian polemic.[143]

It was Starcky[144] who originally alluded to an Aramaic fragment from Qumran that seems to be relevant to our discussion. It was subsequently published by Puech[145] and is now known as 4Q541 (or 4QTLevi d). Garcia Martinez renders Fragment 9, col. 1: "And he will atone for all the children of his generation."[146] Starcky claimed it interpreted Isaiah 53 eschatologically with reference to a saviour figure. Collins refutes this on the grounds that a servant does not necessarily have to be a suffering figure, nor is the one described in this and the related Fragment 24 messi-

---

Westminster, 1980) 76; B. Lindars, *Jesus, Son of Man: A Fresh Examination of the Son of Man Sayings in the Gospels in the Light of Recent Research* (London: SPCK, 1983) 9-10; and Collins, "The Son of Man in First-Century Judaism," 452, 459.

[140]Collins, "The Son of Man in First-Century Judaism," 459.

[141]For the text and a translation see J. F. Stenning, *The Targum of Isaiah* (Oxford: Clarendon, 1949).

[142]Cf. Zimmerli and Jeremias, *The Servant of God*, 68-71; and Juel, *Messianic Exegesis*, 124.

[143]Zimmerli and Jeremias, *The Servant of God*, 71.

[144]J. Starcky, "Les quatre étapes du messianisme à Qumran," *Revue Biblique* 70 (1963): 492; cf. also Hengel, *Cross of the Son of God*, 246; and Watts, "Jesus' Death, Isaiah 53, and Mark 10:45," 144n.75.

[145]E. Puech, "Fragments d'un apocryphe de Lévi et le personnage eschatologique: 4QTLévi c-d (?) et 4QAJa," in *The Madrid Qumran Congress: Proceedings of the International Congress on the Dead Sea Scrolls, Madrid 18-21 March 1991*, ed. J. C. Trebolle Barrera and L. Vegas Montaner, STDJ 11 (Leiden: E. J. Brill, 1992) 449-501.

[146]F. García Martínez, *The Dead Sea Scrolls Translated: The Qumran Texts in English*, trans. W. G. E. Watson (Leiden: Brill, 1994) 270.

anic.[147] In fact, the text concerns a leading priest.[148] However, Brooke proceeds to claim that there are in these fragments indications of pre-Christian traditions about the suffering of the eschatological priest (-messiah) that have been adopted in Palestinian Jewish Christianity and thus have influenced the New Testament itself.[149]

Nevertheless, we are obliged to concur with Büchler's verdict[150] that there is no idea of vicarious suffering or atonement in Jewish literature up to the end of the first century AD. This stands, at least as far as the Old Testament itself is concerned, and more specifically in the case of passages influenced or alluding to Isaiah 53. Nor do passages in Wisdom 2, 3, and 5, although containing echoes of the Suffering Servant[151] (cf. λογίζομαι and πλανάομαι, Wisdom 2:21 and Isaiah 53:3, 4, 6), show there is "the slightest allusion made to the atoning power of the suffering and death of the righteous one,"[152] despite 3:6 where the death of the righteous may be regarded as a sacrificial offering. Thus Hooker's verdict stands: "One of the remarkable things about Isaiah 53 is that Jewish exegesis of this chapter in the period between its composition and the first century CE seems virtually to ignore the idea that one person's suffering can have atoning power for others."[153] Moreover, evidence for the idea of vicarious atoning suffering itself (quite apart from possible influence by Isaiah 53) is equally scant.[154]

This clearly cannot be the case with reference to the Maccabean mar-

---

[147]Collins, *The Scepter and the Star*, 123-26.

[148]G. J. Brooke, "4QTestament of Levi d(?) and the Messianic Servant High Priest," in *From Jesus to John: Essays on Jesus and New Testament Christology in Honour of Marinus de Jonge*, ed. M. C. de Boer, JSNTSS 84 (Sheffield: JSOT, 1993) 86, 89.

[149]Brooke, "4QTestament of Levi d(?) and the Messianic Servant High Priest," 92-100.

[150]A. Büchler, *Studies in Sin and Atonement* (Oxford: Oxford University Press, 1928)—quoted by both Hooker, *Jesus and the Servant*, 56; and Whybray, *Thanksgiving for a Liberated Prophet*, 75.

[151]Cf. Carpenter and Godbey, *Primitive Christian Application of the Doctrine of the Servant*, 33.

[152]Ibid., 37.

[153]Hooker, "The Use of Isaiah 53," 99.

[154]Cf. Williams, *Jesus' Death as Saving Event*, 121-35.

tyrs whose suffering seems to have been interpreted as being vicarious (that is, of course, on the assumption that 2 Maccabees and 4 Maccabees are to be dated earlier than the end of the first century AD[155]). The idea of vicarious suffering is found in 4 Maccabees 6:27-29 and 17:20-22.[156]

What then are some of the implications of what we have discussed on the basis of Whybray's work in particular?

(1) The doctrine of vicarious suffering cannot with certainty be derived from the fifty-third chapter of Isaiah because it does not appear to be found in the Old Testament in general or in this chapter in particular. This point, it seems to me, has been too little noticed in contemporary New Testament scholarship.

(2) We must beware of the modern danger of isolating the Servant Songs from the rest of the chapters normally attributed to Deutero-Isaiah. They were certainly not so regarded in New Testament times and treating the Servant of the Lord or the Suffering Servant as quasi-titles for those times is an overtly modern procedure. In fact, Orlinsky believed that the concepts "Suffering Servant" and "Vicarious Suffering" are postbiblical in origin, and probably derive from a pagan, Hellenistic, not a Judaic source.[157] We need also to be reminded that the central message of this unknown prophet of the exile is that Yahweh has brought about Israel's salvation by his own creative and redeeming power, and certainly apart from the suffering of a righteous man.[158]

(3) The interpretation of Isaiah 53 depends more than most Old Testament texts on the rendering of individual words and phrases and on the actual readings and emendations of the Hebrew text adopted for deciding such central issues as the extent of the evidence for vicarious

---

[155]Ca. 60 BC for 2 Maccabees, according to O. Eissfeldt, *The Old Testament: An Introduction*, trans. P. R. Ackroyd (New York: Harper & Row, 1965) 581; and 40 AD for 4 Maccabees, according to G. W. E. Nickelsburg, *Jewish Literature between the Bible and the Mishnah: A Historical and Literary Introduction* (London: SCM, 1981) 226.

[156]Cf. Carpenter and Godbey, *Primitive Christian Application of the Doctrine of the Servant*, 55; and Hooker, *Jesus and the Servant*, 54. See further McLean, "The Absence of an Atoning Sacrifice in Paul's Soteriology," 549-50.

[157]Orlinsky, "The So-called 'Servant of the Lord' and 'Suffering Servant' in Second Isaiah," 118; cf. also 54.

[158]Cf. Hooker, *Jesus and the Servant*, 47.

suffering and whether the Servant is said to have died and possibly been resurrected. Yet, of course, such issues cannot be decided solely on the basis of the evidence of a single chapter, but this must be done in conjunction with the interpretation of evidence from the rest of the Old Testament and other Jewish literature.

(4) Eisegesis of the Old Testament from the standpoint of the New Testament and later Christian theology is a constant danger. In this respect especially, there is the urge to read Isaiah 53 in the light of the tradition exemplified by Handel's *Messiah*. The old inclination from precritical days to read back later Christian theology into the Old Testament with respect to, for example, a suffering Messiah, physical resurrection, and in this instance atonement theory,[159] still remains with us.

(5) In many ways the creative role of the early church, and, dare we say, even of Jesus, is more firmly emphasized when clear distinctions are drawn between Old Testament and New Testament categories. Here the first part of the criterion of dissimilarity or distinctiveness may well be employed in a positive fashion at least with respect to the Old Testament and Jewish background whereby "there are no grounds . . . for deriving a tradition from Judaism."[160] "Given the innovation inherent in the early Christian confession of a crucified Messiah, perhaps some more room should be allowed for creativity," comments R. E. Watts.[161] Thus, Jesus' (or that of the early church) use of the Suffering Servant motif may take its place alongside other expressions which meet this part of the criterion, such as the use of "Abba" and of "Amen" as an introductory word; Jesus' offer of salvation to the outcasts of Israel; his distinctive use of parables; and his use of the title "Son of man."[162] Moreover, whilst one would not thereby deny the role played by Isaiah 53 in the shaping of the early church's thinking about vicarious suffering as it related to Jesus, it may well be that other Jewish sources, such as the depiction of the significance

---

[159]Cf. Whybray, *Thanksgiving for a Liberated Prophet*, 75-76.

[160]E. Käsemann, *Essays on New Testament Themes*, trans. W. J. Montague, SBT 41 (London: SCM, 1964) 37.

[161]Watts, "Jesus' Death, Isaiah 53, and Mark 10:45," 144n.75. Cf. also de Jonge, *Jewish Eschatology*, 296.

[162]Cf. R. H. Stein, "The 'Criteria' for Authenticity," in *Gospel Perspectives: Studies of History and Tradition in the Four Gospels*, ed. R. T. France and D. Wenham (Sheffield: JSOT, 1980) 241.

of the suffering martyrs, played as important a role, if not also a prior role, in this thinking.[163]

(6) The ways in which the Old Testament is employed in the New need to be constantly monitored. For example, is it sufficient to look as C. H. Dodd and Lindars have taught us to do, for allusions to passages which then inevitably draw in their wider context for consideration? For example, Lindars did not regard the absence of explicit references to vicarious suffering in Acts 8 as a problem, suggesting that the "precise words are not intrinsically necessary to the argument, but stand for the whole prophecy."[164] That is, of course, assuming the whole prophecy does indeed speak of vicarious suffering! Or should we not demand signs of deliberate exegesis of a passage from the Old Testament in the New for the usage to carry real weight?

(7) And finally, what do we understand by the phrase 'vicarious suffering'? Is there not a real sense in which both victim and sinner share the suffering? The involvement of the believer with the sufferings of Christ finds expression in the gospels and is certainly a prominent theme in the letters of Paul, and no scholar has done more to illuminate the concept of 'interchange' between Christ and the believer than Morna Hooker.[165] Thus in terms of Isaiah 53 it is not a case of the Servant suffering instead of others (as their substitute), but rather of his suffering alongside them (as their representative).[166] In this way we conclude where we began by acknowledging Hooker's significant contributions together with that of the late Norman Whybray with reference to the issues reviewed in this essay.

---

[163]Cf. Barrett, "The Background of Mark 10:45," 1-18.

[164]B. Lindars, *New Testament Apologetic: The Doctrinal Significance of the Old Testament Quotations* (London: SCM, 1961) 83. Cf. also C. H. Dodd, *According to the Scriptures* (London: Nisbet, 1952).

[165]Cf. M. D. Hooker, *From Adam to Christ: Essays on Paul* (Cambridge: Cambridge University Press, 1990) 13-69. Cf. also idem, "The Use of Isaiah 53," 102-103.

[166]Cf. the views of Orlinsky, "The So-called 'Servant of the Lord' and 'Suffering Servant' in Second Isaiah," and Whybray, *Thanksgiving for a Liberated Prophet*. Cf. also Hooker, "The Use of Isaiah 53," 96.

Death, Descent, and Deliverance in Matthew 27:51b-53

Tim McLay
St. Stephen's University
St. Stephen, New Brunswick

Matthew 27:51b-53 is, without doubt, one of the most interesting, if not perplexing, passages in the first gospel.[1] Matthew supplements the Marcan account of the splitting of the temple veil and the confession of the soldier by including a dramatic chain of events that begin with an earthquake and conclude with the resurrection of the saints and their appearance to many in the holy city.[2] The past few decades have witnessed resurgence in interest in Matthew's gospel and the passion narrative in particular, but, despite the advance in our understanding of 27:51b-53,[3]

---

[1]The idea and some of the research for this paper originated in a class taught by Dr. Trites.

[2]For research in Matthew and the passion narrative in particular, see the works below as well as others listed throughout this paper. D. Senior, *The Passion Narrative according to Matthew: A Redactional Study*, BETL 39 (Louvain: Leuven University Press/Peeters, 1975); idem, "Matthew's Special Material in the Passion Story," *Ephemerides Theologicae Lovanienses* 63 (1987): 272-94; W. Schenk, *Die Sprache des Matthäus* (Göttingen: Vandenhoeck & Ruprecht, 1987); R. H. Gundry, *Matthew: A Commentary on His Literary and Theological Art* (Grand Rapids: Eerdmans, 1982); R. Kratz, *Auferweckung als Befreiung* (Stuttgart: Katholisches Bibelwerk, 1973); J. D. Kingsbury, *Matthew: Structure, Christology, Kingdom* (Philadelphia: Fortress, 1975); D. Hill, "Matthew 27:51-53 in the Theology of the Evangelist," *IBS* 7 (1985): 76-87; idem, "In Quest of Matthean Theology," *IBS* 8 (1986): 135-42; T. L. Donaldson, "The Mockers and the Son of God (Matthew 27:37-44): Two Characters in Matthew's Story of Jesus," *JSNT* 41 (1991): 3-18; J. P. Meier, "Salvation History in Matthew: In Search of a Starting Point," *CBQ* 27 (1975): 203-15; G. D. Kilpatrick, *The Gospel according to St. Matthew* (Oxford: Clarendon, 1946); E. Lohmeyer, *Das Evangelium des Matthäus* (Göttingen: Vandenhoeck & Ruprecht, 1967); H. Zeller, "Corpora Sanctorum (Mt 27,52-53)," *Zeitschrift für katholische Theologie* 71 (1949): 385-465.

[3]It has been convincingly argued that the use of typical Matthean vocabulary, style, and stock apocalyptic terms indicates that the evangelist was responsible for the special passion material and that it reflects his theological purposes. See Senior, *The Passion Narrative according to Matthew*, 307-23; Schenk, *Die Sprache*

there has been little light cast on the evangelist's odd insertion concerning the raising of the saints in v. 52.[4] Not only does the raising of the saints strike the reader as somewhat odd, the resurrection of the saints at Jesus' death is also at odds with the remainder of the New Testament, which stresses that the resurrection will take place following the Parousia.[5] In what way does Matthew intend the raising of the saints to be a witness to the resurrection?

The present paper is an attempt to cast some light on Matthew 27:51b-53 by arguing that the resurrection of the saints is the proleptic fulfilment of (what we will argue is) Jesus' promise of resurrection in Matthew 16:18. As a corollary to our main argument, we will also suggest that the passage may be linked to an early belief in Jesus' "Descent into Hades."[6]

The Origins of the Resurrection of the Saints

In order to set this investigation within an interpretive context, it is useful to note briefly some previous approaches to the passage, most of which have attempted to explain the passage based on its putative sources.[7] For example, Matthew 27:51b-53 are interpreted by G. D.

---

des Matthäus, 210; and Gundry, *Matthew*, 575-77.

[4]The oddity of the raising of the saints would seem to have been recognized at an early stage in the Christian tradition. At least this might explain the variant reading of ηγερθη in A C W 090 𝔐, which would apply the raising to Jesus.

[5]See 1 Cor 15:20-23; 1 Thess 4:13-18; 1 Pet 1:4-5; 1 John 3:2; Rev 20:11-15.

[6]Most scholars have argued that there is not enough evidence to suggest a "Descent into Hades" motif. See Gundry, *Matthew*, 577; D. Senior, "The Death of Jesus and the Resurrection of the Holy Ones (Mt 27:51-53)," *CBQ* 38 (1976): 313-29; The position has been stated most clearly by D. Hutton, "The Resurrection of the Holy Ones (Mt 27:51b-53): A Study of the Theology of the Matthean Passion Narrative" (Th.D. diss., Harvard Divinity School, 1970) 4-7. See R. C. Fuller, "The Bodies of the Saints (Mt. 27:52-53)," *Scripture* 3 (1948): 86-87, for a statement in favour of the motif. For an excellent discussion of the motif, see R. Bauckham, "Descent to the Underworld," in *ABD* 2:145-59.

[7]Senior, "Matthew's Special Material in the Passion Story," 277-84, provides a good review of various sources that have been suggested to account for vv. 51-53.

Kilpatrick as a misplaced resurrection account,[8] while others appeal to a source held in common with the *Gospel of Peter*.[9] Admittedly, Matthew does link Jesus' death and the account of the resurrection in 28:2-4 very closely. Both events are introduced with the words "And behold," and each includes an earthquake as a sign of divine intervention.[10] Both passages also employ the motif of fear on the part of the guards. However, these parallels may reveal nothing more than that the evangelist intended his readers to "link the death and resurrection of Jesus in terms of their effects."[11] We are still left to ponder the redactor's theological purposes in the passage, unless we explain it by regarding him as inept with scissors and paste.

From a different perspective, Schenk had argued for the origins of 51b-53 in a Jewish apocalyptic hymn whose roots are found in the vision of the dry bones in Ezekiel 37.[12] While Schenk's attempt to discern a hymnic fragment is less than convincing, the influence of Ezekiel 37 on our passage has attained the status of a scholarly consensus.[13] Both Ezekiel 37:1-14 and Matthew 27:51b-53 share common motifs of earthquakes, the

---

[8]Kilpatrick, *The Gospel according to St. Matthew*, 47.

[9]Hutton, "The Resurrection of the Holy Ones," 161-63; B. Johnson, "The Empty Tomb Tradition in the Gospel of Peter" (Ph.D. diss., Harvard University, 1965); J. D. Crossan, *Four Other Gospels: Shadows on the Contours of Canon* (Minneapolis: Winston, 1982) 141-42; W. Trilling, "Der Tod Jesu: Ende der alten Weltzeit," in *Christusverkündigung in den synoptischen Evangelien* (München: Kösel-Verlag, 1969).

[10]See Kratz, *Auferweckung als Befreiung*, 38-45, where he argues that the earthquake motif reflects a theophany.

[11]Hill, "Matthew 27:51-53 in the Theology of the Evangelist," 77; Meier, "Salvation History in Matthew," 209. Together the two passages represent the decisive in-breaking of God's intervention in history. For criticisms of the views of Trilling and Hutton, see W. Schenk, *Der Passionsbericht nach Markus: Untersuchungen zur Überlieferungsgeschichte der Passionstraditionen* (Gütersloh: Gerd Mohn, 1974) 75-82; and Senior, "The Death of Jesus and the Resurrection of the Holy Ones," 314-18.

[12]Schenk, *Die Sprache des Matthäus*, 76-78; M. Riebl, *Auferstehung Jesu in der Stunde seines Todes: zur Botschaft von Mt 27, 51b-53* (Stuttgart: KBW, 1978).

[13]Senior, "Matthew's Special Material in the Passion Story," 282; Schenk, *Die Sprache des Matthäus*, 210; Gundry, *Matthew*, 575-77; Hill, "Matthew 27:51-53 in the Theology of the Evangelist," 76.

opening of tombs and the resurrection of the dead, and the return to Israel (Jerusalem in Matthew), and these signs are related to a new and perfect sanctuary. However, despite the parallels with Ezekiel, it does not appear we are any closer to understanding the peculiarity of the resurrection of the saints in Matthew's gospel.

Matthew 12:40, 16:18 and the Raising of the Saints

Rather than attempting to explain the resurrection of the saints based on its putative sources or in isolation from the remainder of the gospel, I believe it is best to understand it in the context of Matthew's own theology, particularly as it is developed in other passages that are peculiar to the gospel. I would like to focus on two passages special to Matthew that prepare for the resurrection of the saints in 27:51b-53. The first passage I will examine is the sign of Jonah (12:39-42), which has a parallel in Luke 11:29-32 (the sign of Jonah and the Queen are not present in Mark). The second passage is Matthew 16:18, which is Jesus' promise that he would build his church.

There are various differences in how Matthew (12:39-42) and Luke (11:29-32) present and interpret the sign of Jonah due to their redactional purposes,[14] but the primary dissimilarity is Matthew's insertion in v. 40: "For just as Jonah was three days and three nights in the belly of the sea monster, so for three days and three nights the Son of Man will be in the heart of the earth." I interpret Matthew's insertion of 12:40 as a reference to Jesus' being in Hades, the realm of the dead,[15] and not merely as a reference to the grave.[16]

---

[14]See Gundry, *Matthew*, 242-44. Matt and Luke (cf. Luke 11:31-32) both include references to the "queen of the South" and the people of Nineveh on the day of Judgment, but in reverse order.

[15]So also W. Grundman, *Das Evangelium nach Matthäus* (Berlin: Evangelische, 1971) 334; Gundry, *Matthew*, 244.

[16]So V. Luz, *Das Evangelium nach Matthäus* (Zürich: Benziger, 1990) 2:276. There is debate concerning the relationship between the grave and Hades/Sheol. The view of some scholars that their referents are completely distinct is extreme. The modern semanticist would describe their sense relations with the term "overlapping," i.e., they are interchangeable (synonymous) in some contexts, but not in all. For a balanced perspective see, T. J. Lewis, "Dead, Abode of the," in *ABD* 2:103.

The metaphor καρδίᾳ τῆς γῆς "heart of the earth" is unique in the Scriptures, but there is little doubt that the referent is Hades, especially when we consider that the imagery is rooted in the psalm of Jonah.[17] The imagery of the journey from Sheol in the belly of the fish[18] is reflected in Matthew in various ways, and it is instructive for our purposes to examine the language Jonah uses to depict his situation. First, it is commonly noted that Matthew 12:40a is an exact quotation from Jonah 2:1 in the LXX: ἦν Ἰωνᾶς ἐν τῇ κοιλίᾳ τοῦ κήτους τρεῖς ἡμέρας καὶ τρεῖς νύκτας "Jonah was in the belly of the fish three days and three nights." This citation demonstrates the obvious influence of LXX Jonah upon Matthew.[19] Second, in Jonah 2:3b, God is said to have heard Jonah's cry ἐκ κοιλίας ᾅδου "from the belly of Hades," which not only retains the usual translation of Hebrew Sheol with the Greek word Hades (the Hebrew text has מבטן שאול "from the belly of Sheol"),[20] but also substitutes a pun that the Hebrew lacked: in the Greek, Jonah is said to be in τῇ κοιλίᾳ τοῦ κήτους "the belly of the fish" in vv. 1 and 2, but in v. 3 he

[17]For a discussion of the prayer as a psalm of thanksgiving rather than a prayer for deliverance, see D. Stuart, *Hosea-Jonah*, WBC 31 (Waco: Word, 1987) 472-73; A. J. Hauser, "Jonah: In Pursuit of the Dove," *JBL* 104 (1985): 21-37.

[18]The belly of the great fish is the means of Jonah's deliverance and the journey from Sheol took three days. See the seminal article on Jonah's journey from Sheol by G. M. Landes, "The 'Three Days and Three Nights' Motif in Jonah 2.1," *JBL* 86 (1967): 446-50.

[19]In his examination of Matt's use of the OT, Gundry reports that Matt exhibits more of a mixed textual tradition than does Mark, which is dependent upon the LXX. However, the first gospel does exhibit dependence on the LXX in 15 of 41 quotations or allusions to the OT. R. H. Gundry, *The Use of the Old Testament in St. Matthew's Gospel*, NovTSup 18 (Leiden: Brill, 1964) 148-50.

[20]Hades is a stereotyped equivalent in the LXX for the place known as Sheol (שאול) in the OT, the abode of the dead (Ps 6:5; 88:10-12; Job 26:6) and this usage has carried into the NT. In all but one of its 72 occurrences in the MT, Sheol is translated by Hades in the LXX. At the same time, Hades is reserved almost exclusively for Sheol, though according to E. Hatch, H. A. Redpath, et al. *A Concordance to the Septuagint and the Other Greek Versions of the Old Testament (including the Apocryphal Books)*, 2nd ed. (Grand Rapids: Baker, 1998) it does translate other terms on nine occasions. See the brief but complete discussion by J. Jeremias, "ᾅδης," *TDNT* 1:146-49.

prays from the κοιλίας ᾅδου "belly of Hades."[21] Jonah not only prays from Hades/Sheol in v. 3, but the play on words in the Greek also allows the reader to make an explicit identification between the belly of the fish and Hades.

The identification of καρδίᾳ τῆς γῆς as a referent for Jesus being in Hades has further support in vv. 4 and 7 of the LXX version of Jonah's psalm. We find in v. 4 of the psalm that Jonah was thrown εἰς βάθη καρδίας θαλάσσης "into the depths of the *heart* of the sea," and in v. 7 Jonah says κατέβην εἰς γῆν ἧς οἱ μοχλοὶ αὐτῆς κάτοχοι αἰώνοι "I descended into the *earth* whose bars constrain forever." So, although the phrase καρδίᾳ τῆς γῆς does not appear in Jonah's psalm, its lexical components are employed as part of the metapho ical imagery that is associated with Hades/Sheol. Given Matthew's familiarity with the LXX version of the psalm of Jonah, I would suggest Matthew borrowed from the imagery and coined the phrase καρδίᾳ τῆς γῆς "heart of the earth" as a metaphor for Hades.[22]

The affirmation that the Son of Man would be in "the heart of the earth" is the first hint of the resurrection theme that Matthew develops in 12:40 and 27:51b-53. In fact, Davies and Allison note that, although there is no explicit reference to resurrection in 12:40, "the figure of three days and nights posits an end to the time in the earth and so suggests the resurrection."[23] Some readers may object to this interpretation, because Matthew does not state the equivalent of "so the Son of Man will be three days and three nights in the heart of the earth *but then he will be raised*." However, Matthew allows the reader to infer this conclusion, because the reader is familiar with the Jonah story and that the prophet did not remain in the belly of the fish. If there is any doubt, the missing information is supplied to the reader later in the form of the threefold

---

[21]The Hebrew uses ממעי הדגה "from the belly of the fish" in vv. 1 and 2.

[22]This connection is reasonable, because the inner part of the earth was believed to be the location of Hades (Gen 37:35; Num 16:33; Ps 55(54):15; Isa 38:9-20); furthermore, there is a natural connection, since Jesus was on the earth, whereas Jonah was at sea.

[23]W. D. Davies and D. C. Allison, Jr., *A Critical and Exegetical Commentary on the Gospel according to Saint Matthew*, 2 vols., ICC (Edinburgh: T. & T. Clark, 1988, 1997) 1:356.

predictions of Jesus' suffering, death, and resurrection. The first hint of what is to follow is found in 12:40.

The linguistic connections between Matthew's gospel and the psalm of Jonah become clearer when we consider the explicit use of Hades in another passage special to the gospel, 16:18. The connections between 12:40, 16:18, and the psalm of Jonah are threefold. First, not only does the term Hades occur in 16:18, but this is also the sole occurrence of the phrase πύλαι ᾄδου "gates of Hades" in the New Testament.[24] Given Matthew's familiarity with the prayer of Jonah, I suggest that the occurrence of ἧς οἱ μοχλοὶ αὐτῆς κάτοχοι αἰώνοι "whose bars constrain/imprison forever" in Jonah 2:7 stimulated Matthew to use the more common phrase πύλαι ᾄδου in 16:18. Second, there is Jesus' reference to Peter as Simon Βαριωνᾶ "the son of Jonah" in 16:17. Commentators have offered little to explain the difference between Matthew's Βαριωνᾶ and John's ὁ υἱὸς Ἰωάννου "the son of John" (1:42), but it is explicable if Matthew is intentionally linking the saying of 16:17-18 with the psalm of Jonah. Third, it seems more than coincidental that the reference to Peter as "the son of Jonah" comes soon after the assertion in 16:4 that "a sign will not be given this generation except the sign of Jonah." The significance of Jonah for Matthew's theology is underscored by the fact that Matthew has three references to Jonah in contrast to Luke who has just the one (11:29-32).

Not only does 16:18 reinforce Matthew's dependence upon Jonah, it also focuses on the theme of resurrection. Let us examine 16:18 more closely. Some commentators and English translations give the impression that πύλαι ᾄδου οὐ κατισχύσουσιν αὐτῆς "the gates of Hades shall not prevail against it" in Matthew 16:18 means that the church will survive despite adversity and the attacks of evil forces.[25] The meaning "prevail over, overcome, have power against" for κατισχύω is the primary meaning

---

[24]The phrase appears three times in the LXX (Isa 38:10; Wis 16:13; 3 Macc 5:51). A similar expression is πυλῶν (τοῦ) θανατοῦ "gates of death" in Ps 9:14 (13); 106 (107):18; and, particularly, Job 38:17, which also contains the parallel expression πυλωροὶ ᾄδου.

[25]J. Jeremias, "ᾅδης," 927. Davies and Allison, *Matthew* 2:630-32, accept this position in their commentary. They also list twelve different interpretations of the meaning of 16:18.

offered by Liddell and Scott and it is well attested in the LXX.[26] As most commentators have acknowledged, this indicates that there is some type of struggle between the church and the gates of Hades.[27] However, should we understand demonic forces to be the referent for the gates of death?[28] It is true that there is some merging of the concepts of ᾅδης and γέεννα "hell" evident in the New Testament, which reflects developments in the pseudepigrapha, but the only explicit use of ᾅδης in the New Testament that exhibits this merging is in Luke 16:23.[29]

Against the view that Hades refers to the assembly of evil forces is the natural association of the expression πύλαι ᾅδου with the realm of the dead as it appears in the LXX. On this basis, it is better to interpret "the gates of Hades" as a metaphor for death, which is the active subject of the verb attacking the church,[30] but it will not ultimately prevail.[31] The

---

[26]Exod 17:11; Deut 1:38; 1 Kgs 19:8; OG Dan 11:5, passim. Davies and Allison, *Matthew* 2:633, also note that, in the LXX, the verb is always active when followed by the genitive.

[27]See the discussion in Davies and Allison, *Matthew* 2:630-32. Though they list twelve different views, most reflect some kind of conflict. Jeremias has been referred to above. Other examples are Schweizer, who interprets the verse to mean that death cannot put a stop to the Christian community, and Bousset, who believes it refers to the resurrection of the church. McNeile, in a similar vein, believes the gates will not prevail over the church, because Christ could not be imprisoned, so that the resurrection refers to him rather than the church. See E. Schweizer, *The Good News according to Matthew* (Atlanta: John Knox, 1975) 342; W. Bousset, *Kyrios Christos: A History of the Belief in Christ from the Beginnings of Christianity to Irenaeus*, trans. J. E. Steely (Nashville: Abingdon, 1970) 65; A. H. McNeile, *The Gospel according to St. Matthew* (London: MacMillan, 1915) 242.

[28]As McNeile, *The Gospel according to St. Matthew*, 242, notes, "it is doubtful if Hades was ever thought of as the abode of the powers of evil, from which they emerge to injure men."

[29]Davies and Allison, *Matthew* 2:633n.110, provide a seemingly impressive array of NT references to argue that ᾅδης means evil forces in 16:18, but apart from Luke 16:19-31 the other references use different terminology. Their references are Luke 8:31; 2 Pet 2:4; Jude 6; Rom 10:7; Rev 9:1-2, 11; 11:7; 20:1-3; but contrast Matt 11:23; 16:18; Luke 10:15; Acts 2:27, 31; Rev 1:18; 6:8; 20:13-14.

[30]Schweizer, *The Good News according to Matthew*, 342.

inability of death to prevail over the church in this passage is then understood to mean there will be a resurrection of the church from the realm of the dead: "I will build my church and the gates of death will not prevail against (that is, contain) it."[32] The triumph of the resurrection is fulfilled in Matthew by Jesus' death, which signals the final victory over the power of death and initiates the proleptic resurrection of the saints in 27:51b-53.[33]

In the second volume of his Narnia series, C. S. Lewis provides an excellent illustration of the interpretation that I have suggested. After Aslan is resurrected, he arrives back at the castle at Cair Paravel, leaps the gates that are shut, and proceeds to breathe life back into all the living creatures that had been turned into statues. Afterwards, the giant takes his club and smashes open the gates to release all the creatures.[34]

One of the immediate objections that may be brought against our suggested interpretation is that there is a facile equation of the church (ἐκκλησία) in 16:18 with the saints (ἅγιοι) in 27:52. To whom do these terms refer? The masculine plural substantive of ἅγιος "saint" is found only here in the gospel, while ἐκκλησία appears only three times (twice in 18:17). Elsewhere in the New Testament, when ἅγιος occurs in the masculine plural substantive it usually refers to New Testament saints. However, though this use is spread throughout the New Testament corpus, it is predominant in the epistles that are traditionally associated with the apostle Paul.[35] On the other hand, we cannot take it for granted

---

[31]We assume that the antecedent for αὐτῆς "it" is ἐκκλησίαν "church," because it is closer than πέτρᾳ and makes more sense in the context.

[32]Bousset, *Kyrios Christos*, 65.

[33]According to Meier, Matthew "depicts the resurrection of the dead as taking place proleptically at the death of Christ," as part of the evangelist's scheme of salvation-history (Meier, "Salvation History in Matthew," 209; cf. Senior, "The Death of Jesus and the Resurrection of the Holy Ones," 328-29; Kratz, *Auferweckung als Befreiung*, 76-82).

[34]C. S. Lewis, *The Lion, the Witch, and the Wardrobe* (Glasgow: Collins, 1950) 152-56. (Thanks to Glenn Wooden for reminding me of this illustration.)

[35]In more than sixty cases (forty-two times in books associated with Paul), ἅγιοι clearly refers to NT saints. See Acts 9:13, 32; Heb 6:10; 8:2; Jude 3; Rev 13:7, 10; Rom 1:7; 8:27; 1 Cor 1:2; 6:1; Eph 1:1, 4, 7; Phil 1:1; 4:21; Col 1:2, 4; 1 Thess 3:13; 1 Tim 5:10; Phlm 5, 7. References that include both the OT

that Matthew is specifically referring only to the "holy ones" of the Old Testament either,[36] though Senior offers the occurrence of ἅγιοι in Isaiah 4:3, Tobit 8:15, and Psalm 33:10 in the LXX as possible parallels for Matthew.[37] That the "holy ones," and by extension Jesus' church, could have at least included Old Testament saints is indicated by the essential continuity Matthew maintains between Jesus and the Old Testament. This connection is established in the very first verse of the gospel where it is stressed that Jesus is a descendent of David who was a descendent of Abraham, and is maintained despite Jesus' conflict with the institution of Judaism and its leaders (e.g. 5:17, 10:6, 23:23).[38]

The referent for ἐκκλησία in 16:18 is not transparent either, but, once again, we should not interpret Matthew's terminology through Pauline spectacles. Even though there is more of a local sense to ἐκκλησία in 18:17, Matthew's use of the word in both passages is in keeping with the standard sense of the LXX where ἐκκλησία can be translated simply as "people of God."[39] At the very least, in Matthew's usage, the referent of those included by the terms ἐκκλησία and ἅγιοι overlap. Therefore, it is possible to view the rising of the "holy ones" as a fulfil-

---

and the NT righteous are found in Rev 11:18; 18:20, and probably 5:8; 8:3, 4; 16:6.

[36]That the term refers to holy ones from the OT period is more or less assumed, for example, by Gundry, *Matthew*, 576; and G. Strecker, *Der Weg der Gerechtigkeit* (Göttingen: Vandenhoeck & Ruprecht, 1966) 217.

[37]Senior, *The Passion Narrative according to Matthew*, 315.

[38]See the articles by A. Segal, "Matthew's Jewish Voice," in *Social History of the Matthean Community: Cross-Disciplinary Approaches*, ed. D. L. Balch (Minneapolis: Fortress, 1991) esp. 4-8, 20-25, 30-37; and A. Saldarini, "The Gospel of Matthew and Jewish-Christian Conflict," in *Social History of the Matthean Community: Cross-Disciplinary Approaches*, ed. D. L. Balch (Minneapolis: Fortress, 1991) 38-61. As Gundry notes in the same volume, they slightly overstate the positive outlook of Matthew toward the law and Judaism, but the positive features cannot be ignored (R. H. Gundry, "A Responsive Evaluation of the Social History of the Matthean Community in Roman Syria," 62-67).

[39]See Schmidt's discussion in his "ἐκκλησία," *TDNT* 3:527-28. The addition of limiting adjectives to ἐκκλησία in the LXX to define it as an assembly of God's people is dropped in later books so that it almost becomes a technical term.

ment of Jesus' statement to Peter in 16:18 where Jesus promises to build his "church" and the gates of death will not be able to contain it.

The proleptic resurrection of the saints in 27:51b-53 is the evangelist's theological affirmation of Jesus' promise to Peter in 16:18 that death will not overcome and contain his people of God. There will be a resurrection!

A Descent into Hades Motif in Matthew?

I have argued that the resurrection of the saints is a proleptic fulfilment of Jesus' promise of the resurrection of his church/people of God from Hades in 16:18. I have also argued that 12:40 refers to Jesus' being in Hades, and implies a resurrection. The fact that 12:40, 16:18, and 27:51b-53 are all part of Matthew's special material suggests that they might be best understood from a common theological frame of reference. At the very least, it can safely be proposed that there is a resurrection motif present in the gospel, but it is possible that Matthew reflects a nascent "Descent into Hades" motif.[40]

The primary evidence to conclude that the motif is present in Matthew is provided by the gospel's dependence upon the psalm of Jonah in the LXX version. We have already given six linguistic arguments that link Matthew 12:40, 16:18, and the psalm of Jonah: (1) Matthew 12:40 quotes from Jonah 2:1; (2) the LXX of Jonah equates the "belly of the fish" and the "belly of Hades"; (3) the metaphor καρδίᾳ τῆς γῆς "heart of the earth" in 12:40 was created by borrowing from the imagery of the psalm; (4) the use of the phrase πύλαι ᾅδου "gates of Hades," which is unique in the New Testament but well known from the LXX, was motivated by its association with the image of the restraining bars in Jonah

---

[40]Most recent scholars deny there is any evidence to support the presence of the "Descent into Hades" motif in vv. 51b-53. The principle objections have been summarized by Hutton, "The Resurrection of the Holy Ones," 5-6. Hutton argues that (1) the passage is so primitive that Matthew could hardly have been aware that he was giving expression to this developing motif; (2) there is no evidence that Matthew understood that Christ was to release the people of God from Hades; and (3) the location of the passage in the narrative of the crucifixion is opposed to the earliest association of the "Descent into Hades" with Christ's resurrection. It is the second objection that constitutes Hutton's main argument and it is this issue that we now examine.

2:7; (5) Matthew identifies Peter as Βαριωνᾶ in 16:17; and (6) Matthew's dependence upon Jonah is highlighted by the threefold reference to Jonah in the gospel. However, two additional thematic connections between the psalm of Jonah and Matthew strengthen our case for Matthew's dependence on the former and indicate the presence of a "Descent into Hades" motif in Matthew.

The most obvious reason to argue for the presence of the "Descent into Hades" motif in Matthew is the fact that the motif is found in Jonah.[41] Not only is there geographical progression indicated when Jonah goes from being covered by the waters (Jonah 2:3, 5) to going down to the earth ("roots of the mountains" in MT, v. 6), but Jonah 2:6 also explicitly speaks of a "*descent* (κατέβην) into the earth/land whose bars constrain forever."[42] Each of the three Matthean passages we have considered is also linked explicitly to Hades and/or a motif of resurrection. Second, Jonah experienced deliverance/salvation from Hades,[43] just as Jesus delivers the saints/people of God.

Here, in the psalm of Jonah, are the seeds for Matthew's special material in 12:40, and 16:18 (and by implication 27:51b-53). There are three dominant themes in Jonah's prayer—death/Hades, a descent into Hades, and deliverance/salvation from Hades—which provide the necessary origins for a "Descent into Hades" motif for Matthew's gospel. As we have argued, the first and third of these themes are worked out in Matthew's special material. While the "Descent into Hades" by Jesus to free the saints remains implicit, the possibility that Matthew has borrowed

---

[41]Landes, "The 'Three Days and Three Nights' Motif," 446-50; Stuart, *Hosea-Jonah*, 475-77.

[42]Magonet points out that the sense of progressive descent is unique in Jonah as compared to Pss. He also compares the use of ירדתי (EVV 2:6, "I went down") in v. 7 with 1:3$^{2\times}$, 5, where Jonah *went down* to Joppa, *went down* in the boat, *went down* into the hold of the ship, and went down into (was hurled into) the sea. See J. Magonet, *Form and Meaning: Studies in Literary Technique in the Book of Jonah* (Sheffield: Almond, 1983) 17, 40-41.

[43]Jonah had descended through the depths until he reached the land whose bars imprison forever (vv. 3-6), when he prayed for help (v. 7), and was delivered by the fish. Thus, the introduction of the fish in 2:1 (EVV 1:17) anticipates the following psalm of thanksgiving. Landes, "The 'Three Days and Three Nights' Motif," 449; Stuart, *Hosea–Jonah*, 472-74; and Hauser, "Jonah," 28-29.

the motif from Jonah is supported by Matthew's dependence on the psalm of Jonah and by the content of the sayings in the gospel: (1) Matthew affirms the presence of Jesus in Hades in 12:40; (2) Jesus promises that the gates of Hades would not be able to contain the church in 16:18;[44] and (3) in 27:51b-53 we have Jesus' promise fulfilled by the raising of the saints upon his death.

In summary, according to Matthew, Jesus' death, as the obedient Son of God, initiates the resurrection of the saints (27:51b-53), which is the proleptic fulfillment of Jesus' promise that there would be a resurrection of his church from Hades (16:18). Jesus' descent into Hades is evidenced in Matthew's comparison of Jesus being three days and three nights in the heart of the earth, just as Jonah had spent three days and nights in the belly of the fish (12:40). Matthew 12:40, 16:18, and 27:51b-53 are all part of Matthew's special material and, based on this material and its background and linguistic connections with the psalm of Jonah, it suggests that Matthew exhibits a nascent form of the "Descent into Hades" motif.

[44]Surely, it is no coincidence that the first of the three passion predictions immediately follows this promise in 16:21.

The Samaritan Woman: An "Unorthodox" Witness (John 4:1-42)[1]

Kevin Quast
Taylor University College
Edmonton, Alberta

Introduction

Consider the women of the Fourth Gospel. They rise above their sisters in the other gospels. "In Luke, women are confined mostly to work among other women or within the house, while Mark's writings include areas limited exclusively to the roles of women played in the times of Jesus."[2] In John, by contrast, "women are main actors in scenes that are quantitatively dominating and of great theological importance."[3] For example, at the outset of John's narrative, Mary, the mother of Jesus, has the faith to approach her son for help when wine at a wedding ran out. At the bidding of Mary, Jesus foreshadowed his "hour," performed his first sign, "revealed his glory, and his disciples believed in him" (John 2:1-11). Not long after this wedding party, Jesus travels through Samaria with his new disciples. Here, he breaks the cultural and religious conventions of his time by speaking with a woman in public. What's worse, she was a Samaritan woman! Significantly, he discusses spiritual matters with her. In turn, she becomes a missionary, leading others to faith through her word about Jesus. Jesus' own disciples reap where she has sown (John 4:1-

---

[1]This lecture was presented in honour of Dr. Allison Trites as one of the 2001 Hayward Lectures, Acadia University.

[2]M.-E. Fletcher, "The Role of Women in the Book of John," *Evangelical Journal* 12 (1994): 41.

[3]T. K. Seim, "Roles of Women in the Gospel of John," in *Aspects on the Johannine Literature: Papers Presented at a Conference of Scandinavian New Testament Exegetes at Uppsala, June 16-19, 1986*, ed. B. Olsson and L. Hartman, Coniectanea Biblica: New Testament Series 18 (Stockholm: Almqvist & Wiksell International, 1987) 57. See also A. Fehribach, *The Women in the Life of the Bridegroom: A Feminist Historical-Literary Analysis of the Female Characters in the Fourth Gospel* (Collegeville: Liturgical, 1998).

42). Then, there is the woman caught in adultery. Her accusers haul her before Jesus as a test. In response, Jesus refuses to apply the Mosaic Law in a situation where it discriminated against women. She becomes a living testimony of his saving grace (John 8:1-11).

Later in the gospel narrative, another woman, Martha, displays faith and insight as she speaks with Jesus about the death of her brother, Lazarus. He tells her: "I am the resurrection and the life." She responds by confessing: "Lord, I believe you are the Messiah, the Son of God, the one coming into the world" (John 11:20-44). Soon after, while Martha serves at the table, her sister Mary anoints Jesus with costly perfume in preparation for both his "coronation" and "burial." Jesus defends Mary's insightful action when Judas criticizes it (John 12:1-8). Days later, Jesus' mother—along with three other women—follows him to the foot of the cross. All other disciples, except the Beloved Disciple, have abandoned him. By making the Beloved Disciple Mary's son, and she his mother, Jesus marks the beginning of new relationships in the family of God (John 19:25-27). After the crucifixion, Mary Magdalene is the first to discover the empty tomb, the first to see the resurrected Lord, and the first to receive a commission to proclaim the good news of the resurrection. In short, she is the first to meet the conditions of apostleship stipulated in the other New Testament traditions (John 20:1-18).

These scenes from John together make a powerful statement. The fourth evangelist, more than the other three, presents women as central witnesses to the most crucial moments in the life and ministry of Christ. These women fulfil every aspect that we can conceive of the role of a witness: they participate in theological dialogue; they confirm the historical accounts; they model faith; and they are sent to proclaim the significance of the saving work of Christ.

Given the weight assigned to the testimony of a woman in first-century courtrooms and synagogues, it is shocking enough to realize the number of times John turns to the witness of women in his narrative. However, one woman in particular rises to the top (or, should I say, sinks to the bottom) when it comes to her scandalous profile. Mary, the mother of Jesus is a saint. The sisters, Martha and Mary, solid worshippers of God, display sterling faith in Jesus. Mary Magdalene is another loyal disciple from her first to her last appearance. We can hardly say anything directly about the woman taken in adultery, even if we allow her tenuous place in the text of the gospel.[4] Then there is the Samaritan woman. . . . Why her? Here is someone who is certainly no saint. Even Jesus disagrees with her on theological matters. She avoids any talk of her personal relationship of faith in God. She has no credence with her own people, let alone Jews or Christians. She typifies the fringe of church and society. Why her? Why does John devote such a lengthy chapter of his story to her? Moreover, why choose her as our paradigm of "the woman as witness" in the Fourth Gospel? Because she models what it means to be a witness to Christ.

We will look at John 4:1-42 with a view to see how this unorthodox candidate serves as a "woman of witness" for Jesus Christ in John's unfolding drama of the Lord's saving revelation. For our purposes, we need not focus on the relationship of the Christian gospel to Judaism, or even Samaritanism. Nor need we dwell on the nature of true worship, nor the promise of the Spirit, nor even, dare I say, the full Christological claims of this narrative. As profound as these theological elements may be, we are primarily concerned with the role of a woman—an unlikely woman at that—as a witness to Christ.

Setting the Stage

In this chapter of John, we see how the offer of a new beginning moves beyond the religious borders of Judaism to the Samaritan people. Commentators have long recognized the way in which this story is like a two-act play. Besides the main story on the front stage, a subplot is developed on a back stage in both acts. A grand finale, with its final chorus, brings closure to all the stories.[5]

Some have suggested that the drama develops the standard features of betrothal scenes common to the Hebrew narrative:[6] a future bride-

---

[4]As Bruce Metzger notes: "The evidence for the non-Johannine origin of the pericope of the adulteress is overwhelming." B. M. Metzger, *A Textual Commentary on the Greek New Testament*, 3rd ed. (London/New York: United Bible Societies, 1971) 219.

[5]C. H. Dodd, *The Interpretation of the Fourth Gospel* (Cambridge: Cambridge University Press, 1953) 315.

[6]The "betrothal scene" is described by R. Alter, *The Art of Biblical Narrative* (London: Allen & Unwin, 1981) 50-51. For a representative sample of those who apply this approach to Jesus and the Samaritan woman, see J. E. Cook, "Wells, Women, and Faith. (Betrothal Type-Scenes; Isaac/Rebekah, Jacob/Leah/Rachel,

groom travels to a foreign land; he encounters a woman at a well; water is offered; the woman hurries home to report the stranger's arrival; and the bridegroom is then invited to the future father's-in-law home, sealing the betrothal. Jacob's own betrothal follows the same general lines (Genesis 29) as this scene in John 4, now at *Jacob's* own well. Adeline Fehribach, in her feminist historical-literary analysis of this passage, speaks of John's presentation of the woman "as a fictive betrothed and bride of the messianic bridegroom on behalf of the Samaritan people, as a symbolic wife to Jesus who produces abundant offspring after Jesus plants the seeds of faith in her. In such a portrayal, the Samaritan woman represents the whole Samaritan people with whom Jesus desires to establish heavenly familial ties."[7]

Both the two-stage, two-act drama and the betrothal motif reflect John's creative flair. The betrothal can be interpreted variously, as the secondary literature attests. It would be pushing things to say that Jesus is in danger of becoming the sixth husband of a slut—but then again, as we shall see, some have taken this tack in their interpretation. In any event, this is a scandalous passage. That Jesus and a Samaritan of the opposite gender should have anything to do with each other would boggle the first-century mind.

Samaritans and Jews

Samaritan descendants from the tribe of Joseph belonged to a strict religious sect.[8] These Samaritans differed sharply from their Jewish cousins

---

Moses/Zipporah, Jesus/the Samaritan Woman)," in *Proceedings, Eastern Great Lakes and Midwest Biblical Societies* (Buffalo: Eastern Great Lakes Biblical Society and Midwest Region of the Society of Biblical Literature, 1997) 11-18; D. N. Fehribach and G. A. Phillips, "Drawn to Excess, or Reading beyond Betrothal," *Semeia* 77 (1997): 23-58. L. Eslinger, "The Wooing of the Woman at the Well," in *The Gospel of John as Literature: An Anthology of Twentieth-Century Perspectives*, ed. M. W. G. Stibbe, NTTS 17 (Leiden: Brill, 1993) 165-82; N. R. Bonneau, "The Woman at the Well, John 4 and Genesis 24," *BibTod* 67 (1973): 1252-59; J. H. Neyrey, "Jacob Traditions and the Interpretation of John 4:10-26," *CBQ* 41 (1979): 25-26; M. C. Carmichael, "Marriage and the Samaritan woman," *NTS* 26 (1980): 332-46.

[7]Fehribach, *Women in the Life of the Bridegroom*, 47.

[8]For more details on the history and theology of the Samaritans, see J. MacDonald, *The Theology of the Samaritans*, New Testament Library (London: SCM, 1964); and J. D. Purvis, *The Samaritan Pentateuch and the Origin of the Samaritan*

on two main points: their choice of the holy mountain of God for worship, and their view of the Torah. Basically, the Samaritans believed that the Jews had revised the Torah to diminish the status of Mt. Gerizim, in favour of Jerusalem. Consequently, the Samaritans adopted their own version of the Pentateuch. The rivalry between Samaritan and Jew was so strong that they avoided contact with one another, even to the point that Jews would detour around Samaria when travelling between Galilee and Judea (John 4:3, 4, 7; Matthew 10:5; Luke 10:52). Yet, Jesus took his disciples straight through the region of Samaria on his way to Galilee.

Act One. Jesus Meets the Woman

The band arrives at a renowned well in the district of Samaria. The well, previously owned by the patriarch Jacob, still exists today. It is located at the foot of Mt. Gerizim just outside Shechem, about thirty miles north of Jerusalem. While the disciples go into town to buy food, a weary Jesus sits alone in the heat of the day. Along comes a woman to draw some water. Jesus asks her for a drink.

That Jesus even spoke to the Samaritan woman is significant, as the Gospel itself stresses: "The Samaritan woman said to him, 'How is it that you, a Jew, ask a drink of me, a woman of Samaria?' (Jews do not share things in common with Samaritans.)" (John 4:9). [*Later*] "his disciples came. They were astonished that he was speaking with a woman . . . " (John 4:27). Not only did Jews go out of their way to avoid Samaritans, but the rabbis consistently taught that Jewish men were not to greet women in public: "A man shall not talk with a woman in the street, not even with his own wife, and especially not with another woman, on account of what men may say."[9] Of course, common practice may not always correlate with rabbinic sayings. "In the realities of everyday life, especially in rural villages, such mores and codes are neither ironclad nor comprehensive."[10] Similar to the betrothal scenes of earlier Hebrew narratives, public conversation between a man and a woman at a well

Sect, HSM 2 (Cambridge: Harvard University Press, 1968).

[9]H. L. Strack and P. Billerbeck, *Kommentar zum neuen Testament aus Talmud und Midrasch* (München: Beck, 1974) 2:238. See also L. Morris, *The Gospel according to John*, NICNT (Grand Rapids: Eerdmans, 1971) 274.

[10]R. G. Maccini, *Her Testimony Is True: Women as Witnesses according to John*, JSNTSS 125 (Sheffield: Sheffield Academic, 1996) 132.

"could well be nothing out of the ordinary."[11]

Other rabbinical maxims showed that they thought women were not considered worthy or capable of theological conversation: "Every man who teaches his daughter Torah is as if he taught her promiscuity";[12] and "Let the words of Torah be burned up, but let them not be delivered to women."[13] What is more, Samaritan women were doubly tainted: "Samaritan women were suspected of immorality generally and a rabbinical maxim tells us that all Samaritan women were to be deemed perpetual menstruants—an unpleasant idea which suggests sterility."[14]

Jesus did not share this perspective. To the chagrin of his disciples (John 4:27), Jesus transcended social, religious, racial, gender, and sexual barriers all in this one interchange. He, an unmarried Jewish man, engages an immoral Samaritan woman in deep conversation.

Jesus Offers the Gift of God: Living Water

In order to witness, the Johannine Jesus employs a familiar method in Johannine discourse: he makes an ambiguous statement and capitalizes on the consequent misunderstanding to present a discourse on the nature of eternal life. After their initial words to each other, Jesus says: "If you knew the gift of God, and who it is that is saying to you 'Give me a drink,' you would have asked him, and he would have given you living water" (John 4:10).

The phrase "living water" commonly denoted "fresh" or "running" water, and so, with only a deep well of still water nearby, the woman's literal interpretation and concern about where Jesus will get the "living" water is appropriate. However, Jesus is not speaking merely of running water and hence we have the misunderstanding that leads to the discourse.

Sexual Relations. While it is obvious that Jesus is using the phrase "living water" figuratively, not all interpreters agree as to what he is referring. Noting that the Old Testament uses the imagery of drinking water from a cistern or well as reference to sexual relations (e.g., Proverbs 5:15-18),

---

[11]Ibid., 133.

[12]*m. Soṭa* 3:4.

[13]*y. Soṭa* 19[a].

[14]D. M. Derrett, "The Samaritan Woman's Purity (John 4:4-52)," *Evangelical Quarterly* 60 (1988): 295. For the rabbinic sources, see *m. Nid.* 4:1; *Tos. Nid.* 5:1.

Lyle Eslinger argues that here Jesus and the woman embark on a conversation laced with sexual overtones.[15] Following the imagery of Proverbs 5:15-18, Jeremiah 2:13 and Song of Songs 4:12, 15, he takes "drinking living water" to be a reference to sexual relations. In other words, when Jesus is promising "living water" to the woman, she takes it as sexual advance. She refers to her "well" and asks to see the source of his "living water." Jesus is aware of what she is thinking and continues the *double entendre* to finally make the point that he can meet her needs at a spiritual level in a way that her failing quest for sexual fulfillment never could.[16]

Torah. Another figurative interpretation of "living water" is also possible, and perhaps more palatable. "Living water" was used to refer to the Torah.[17] Moreover, the simple term 'water' frequently represented the Torah in midrashic allegories. To strengthen this association, we only need to realize that the other phrase in John 4:10—"the gift of God"—was also used in Rabbinic writings to describe the supreme gift, the Torah.[18]

Certainly, Samaritans shared a high view of the Torah with the Jews. Since the Torah was *the* important revelation of God for the Samaritans, Jesus, in effect, presented himself as the new source of God's saving revelation for both the Jews and Samaritans. The Samaritan woman stood witness to a person who was claiming to be the word of God that neither her people nor the Jews had.

Spirit. The mention of "living water" also brings the Holy Spirit into the picture. In John 1:33, Jesus said that he had come to baptize in the Holy Spirit. In John 3:5, the close connection between water and Spirit is again made. However, the most direct statement linking this water with the Spirit is found in John 7:37-39: "Jesus . . . cried out, 'Let anyone who is thirsty come to me, and let the one who believes in me drink. As the scripture has said, "Out of the believer's heart shall flow rivers of living water." ' Now he said this about the Spirit, which believers in him were

---

[15]Eslinger, "Wooing of the Woman at the Well," 168-69.

[16]But note a strong critique of Eslinger's "reader-response" analysis in Fehribach and Phillips, "Drawn to Excess, or Reading beyond Betrothal," 30-31.

[17]R. E. Brown, *The Gospel according to John: I-XII*, AB 29 (Garden City: Doubleday, 1966) 176; G. R. Beasley-Murray, *John*, WBC 36 (Waco: Word Books, 1987) 60.

[18]Brown, *John, I-XII*, 176; Beasley-Murray, *John*, 60.

to receive."

Accepting the living water of Jesus results in eternal life. Jesus describes this process in a vivid way to the woman: "[T]hose who drink of the water that I will give them will never be thirsty. The water that I give will become in them a spring of water gushing up to eternal life" (John 4:14). With vibrant, natural imagery, Jesus shows how living water, gushing up from the fountain of life himself, is necessary for abundant, eternal life. Jacob's water, and all that it stands for, cannot compare to the living water Jesus offers.

Five Husbands: Allegorical or Actual?

Our Samaritan woman hears that she must turn from the well of her ancestors to Jesus and responds by asking for his living water, "that I may never be thirsty or have to keep coming here to draw water" (John 4:15). Her request reveals, however, that her insight is limited. Jesus will draw her deeper with his own insight into her character: "Jesus said to her, 'Go, call your husband, and come back.' The woman answered him, 'I have no husband.' Jesus said to her, 'You are right in saying, "I have no husband"; for you have had five husbands, and the one you have now is not your husband.' " (John 4:16-18).

Because of the perceived extreme unlikelihood that a woman would have had as dismal a marital record as attributed to this woman, many have assumed that this whole passage is to be taken as an allegory. Because of Josephus's account in his *Antiquities of the Jews*, it has been common to interpret the Samaritan woman's life as a comment on the history of the Samaritan people. After giving an account of the destruction of Israel's government in Samaria and the settlement of the Cutheans in the land (see also 2 Kings 17:24-41), Josephus goes on to say, "When the Cutheans first came to Samaria, each of their five tribes reverenced its own god. But God sent an epidemic on them, and many died. . . . The priests [of Israel] came and taught the Samaritans to worship God, and the plague stopped immediately. These same rites have continued to this day among those called *Cuthim* in Hebrew, and Samaritans in Greek. They vary in their attitude to the Jews, calling them relatives when they are prospering, but aliens when they are in trouble."[19]

---

[19]Flavius Josephus, *Antiquites of the Jews* 9.288 in Josephus, *The Essential Writings: A Condensation of Jewish Antiquities and The Jewish War*, trans. and ed.

Hoskyns and Davey offer a modern example of this allegorical interpretation: "It is difficult to avoid detecting in the mention of her five husbands an allusion to the five heathen people, who, with their different deities, had been introduced into Samaria" (2 Kings 17:24, 28-30).[20] But, as Beasley-Murray notes: "This exegesis is not to be countenanced: 2 Kings 17:30-31 mentions seven gods, not five, but more importantly the Evangelist does not allegorize in this manner."[21] In good Antiochian fashion, it is probably best to take the narrative literally.

As an aside, if Eslinger is right about the conversation between the woman and Jesus being filled with sexual *double entendres*, then Jesus' mention of her husband fits the context much better. "At the point where she expected to get his 'living water' Jesus's command comes as a rebuke to her carnal misconceptions. Had she not been making sexual advances, had Jesus not understood them, and had the reader not understood both the reader and Jesus, his command to go call her husband would make no sense here. Jesus tells her to get her husband exactly when she expected to commit adultery against the man."[22] Jesus proceeds to completely shut down the direction she is heading and "now openly reveals his disinterest in her charms by demonstrating his supernatural knowledge of her past."[23]

Clearly, John is saying something about Christ's supernatural insight with the penetrating disclosure of this woman's marital history. However, that is not the focus of our discussion. What is relevant is that here we have a woman who would have had a tarnished reputation in her own community. She would fare even worse in the eyes of Jewish men.[24] Still, Jesus delicately yet directly addresses the issues of her life in order to prepare her to be his witness. Shocked at Jesus' insight, the woman exclaims, "Sir, I see that you are a prophet" (John 4:19). With that declaration, she moves closer to the point of faith.

Paul L. Maier (Grand Rapids: Kregel, 1988) 175.

[20]E. C. Hoskyns and N. Davey, *The Fourth Gospel* (London: Faber & Faber, 1948) 242.

[21]Beasley-Murray, *John*, 61. For a modern allegorical interpretation, see Calum Carmichael, "Marriage and the Samaritan Woman," 332-46.

[22]Eslinger, "Wooing of the Woman at the Well," 180.

[23]Ibid.

[24]Rabbinic law allowed for two, or at the most, three marriages for a woman. Strack and Billerbeck, *Kommentar zum neuen Testament*, 2:437.

True Worship

Jacob's Well was a symbolic stage setting for talk of more than living water. Being at the foot of Mt. Gerizim, it also invited dialogue about true worship. In an attempt to bring the conversation back to a less personal topic, the woman poses the question about the proper place of worship: "Our ancestors worshiped on this mountain, but you say that the place where people must worship is in Jerusalem" (John 4:20). Interestingly, in his response, Jesus offers a mild correction in support of the Jewish side of the debate when he says, "You worship what you do not know; we worship what we know, for salvation is from the Jews" (John 4:22).

However, Jesus does not leave the discussion at a simple comparison of Jewish and Samaritan worship. He goes on to proclaim that both liturgical traditions will be superseded in "the hour" (John 4:21-23). Foreshadowing what he himself is inaugurating, Jesus says that genuine worshipers will worship God "in spirit and truth."

Worship in spirit and truth must be related to the person of Jesus Christ. While the Holy Spirit is the Spirit of truth (John 14:16, 15:26, 16:12), Jesus *is* the truth (John 14:6). Not only does Jesus offer eternal life through the living water of the Spirit, but through the same Spirit, he also makes possible a true encounter with God in worship. The Samaritan woman will become a worshipper of Jesus but at the present time, she does not understand. She confesses, "I know that Messiah is coming. . . . When he comes, he will proclaim all things to us" (John 4:25).

The Messiah—"I am"

This revealing Messiah, whom she hopes for, now reveals himself to her: "I am (ἐγώ εἰμι) he, the one who is speaking to you" (John 4:26). Jesus uses words loaded with theological significance, at least for the Johannine reader. In the simple admission "I am," Jesus speaks as God speaks, taking upon himself God's name "Yahweh" ("I Am"; see also John 6:20, 8:58, and 18:5). The Samaritan woman was one of the first to hear the "I am" on the lips of Jesus. What is more, she had the unique privilege of hearing his claim to be the Messiah. This stands in sharp contrast to his consistent refusal to accept the title of "Messiah" from his fellow Jewish men.

In the dialogue of act one, the light slowly dawns on the woman. In their interchange, this woman became a witness to some profound aspects of Christ's character and mission. She met a Jewish man who treated her, a Samaritan woman, as a person worthy of theological[25] and intimate personal dialogue. She heard his claim to be the living water that she, and all, needed for eternal life. She realized that he was a prophet who knew all about her private life. He instructed her on the nature of worship "in Spirit and truth." To conclude, she could testify to Jesus' claim to be the Messiah, and she would testify to these things among her townspeople.

Act Two. Jesus and the Disciples (vs. 27-38)

Just as the woman leaves the front stage, the disciples enter from the back stage, where they were buying food. They make the surprising discovery that Jesus has been conversing with a woman. However, the focus quickly shifts from her to Jesus. Deciding not to voice their astonishment at Jesus' breach in protocol, the disciples instead offer him some of the food they have brought from town. In response to the disciples' offer of food, Jesus replies: "I have food to eat that you do not know about" (John 4:32). The misunderstanding motif surfaces again. The disciples wonder if someone has brought him food while they have been absent, missing completely that Jesus is speaking figuratively of his mission to complete God's saving work. He was eating such food by engaging the Samaritan woman in his work and empowering her to participate in it as well.

Two Proverbs

Jesus uses two agricultural proverbs to elaborate on the nature of his work. The first one, "Four months more, then comes the harvest" (John 4:35), reflects the approximate interval between sowing and harvesting. After sowing, the farmer must wait patiently for the harvest. However, Jesus contrasts the spiritual calendar with the agricultural, for there is no more waiting. The fruit for eternal life will not be gathered just among the Jews, the harvest has already started in Samaria. "One sows and another reaps" is the second proverb Jesus quotes (John 4:37). This proverb was normally cited cynically to describe life's injustices, but Jesus uses it here to make the encouraging point that the disciples are part of an endeavour that others began. There is no rivalry, only partnership, in

---

[25]On the significance of Jesus' having a *theological* discussion with this woman, see S. M. Schneiders, "Women in the Fourth Gospel," in *The Gospel of John as Literature: An Anthology of Twentieth-Century Perspectives*, ed. M. W. G. Stibbe, NTTS 17 (Leiden: Brill, 1993) 188-89.

the process of sharing the gift of eternal life. In the context of the Gospel time line, those who ministered to the Samaritans before the disciples include Jesus, John the Baptist (see John 3:23; Aenon near Salim is in Samaria), and especially the woman, who is on the other stage sowing a harvest that Jesus and his disciples are about to reap. Our Samaritan plays a central role in the fulfillment of both these prophetic proverbs. She has gone ahead to speed up the spiritual harvest in Samaria. She is the one who has sown what the other disciples are about to reap.[26]

A problem of interpretation arises in John 4:38 where Jesus says to his disciples "I sent you to reap. . . . " Drawing only from John to this point, it cannot be said that the disciples have been sent to reap anything anywhere. Perhaps Jesus, or the evangelist, is speaking retrospectively. A more venturesome suggestion is that we have an allusion to the evangelization of Samaria as recorded in Acts 8:4-24.[27] Note the parallels: Philip sows, Peter and John reap; the living water of the Spirit is received; and worship expands beyond Jerusalem. If this comparison is intentional, then it is an example of the dramatic, even allegorical, retelling of an event in the ministry of Jesus as both a precursor and interpretation of later developments in the Christian church.

The story has not ended yet. The company on the back stage is being led by the woman to the well.

Grand Finale: The Entire Cast (vs. 39-42)

Clearly, the woman was impressed by the insight Jesus had into her life, such that she not only accepted his claim to be the Messiah, but she also persuaded many other townspeople. By doing so, she was carrying out the mission Jesus was describing to his disciples; now they were to enter into her labours. An important observation about belief in Christ can be made here. Some accepted the woman's testimony, but it was only an invitation to a saving relationship with Christ. Verses 41 and 42 tell us,

---

[26]See R. E. Brown, *The Community of the Beloved Disciple* (New York: Paulist, 1979) 187. R. A. Culpepper, *Anatomy of the Fourth Gospel: A Study in Literary Design*, Foundations and Facets (Philadelphia: Fortress, 1983) 137; E. Schüssler Fiorenza, *In Memory of Her: A Feminist Theological Reconstruction of Christian Origins* (New York: Crossroad, 1983) 328.

[27]O. Cullmann, *The Early Church: Studies in Early Christian History and Theology* (Philadelphia: Westminster, 1956) 186; see also Beasley-Murray, *John*, 64.

"many more believed because of his word. They said to the woman, 'It is no longer because of what you said that we believe, for we have heard for ourselves, and we know that this is truly the Savior of the world.' "

How are we to interpret their comments to the woman? Are we to conclude that her witness was ineffectual or incomplete in some way? Was she not trustworthy? It should be noted that, being a woman in first-century Palestine, her testimony would have carried less weight than it would if she were a man but it would not have been discounted automatically. Robert Maccini has done an extensive study of women as witnesses in biblical culture, and he concludes: "Jewish women (1) were proscribed in most but not all instances from giving testimony in forensic contexts; (2) were competent to swear religious vows and oaths; (3) gave testimony in nonforensic contexts that was received sometimes positively, sometimes negatively, depending upon the circumstances; (4) were, under the influence of the Holy Spirit (or demonic spirits), widely recognized and accepted as prophets; (5) were viewed by some people as whimsical and deceitful in nature, and by others as stable and sincere."[28]

Interestingly, even a feminist interpretation that clearly establishes the Samaritan woman's role as witness also maintains that this role is diminished by the text.[29] Fehribach maintains that the fact that she is not given a personal name suggests she is less important than other witnesses in the Gospel of John.[30] That she responds defensively to Jesus and does not fully understand him are also seen to be signs of her limited role.[31] Her function as a witness who "sows" pales in comparison to the witness of the disciples who "reap."[32] Her testimony is compromised by its limited content and accompanying doubt: "Come and see a man who told me everything I have ever done! He cannot be the Messiah, can he?" (John 4:29).[33] Finally, her witness is devalued by her own townsfolk when they confess, "It is no longer because of what you have said that we believe" (John 4:42).[34]

---

[28]Maccini, *Her Testimony Is True*, 97.

[29]Fehribach, *Women in the Life of the Bridegroom*, 75-81.

[30]Ibid., 80.

[31]Ibid., 77, 80.

[32]Ibid., 75.

[33]Ibid., 76-77, 80.

[34]Ibid., 77-78, 81.

If we use these indexes to judge any other witness in John, they too would diminish. This would even include the unnamed Beloved Disciple. "That the woman's knowledge of and witness to Jesus are limited in no way denigrates them."[35] Regardless of her gender, character, or insight, the Samaritan woman's role as witness could only go so far. Inasmuch as any witness to Christ is limited in what he or she can do, the woman served in an exemplary fashion. Entrance into eternal life ultimately depends upon belief in the word of Jesus, not the word of another. Such trust cannot exist apart from a personal encounter with Jesus Christ. Therefore, "the villagers do not malign but confirm her testimony. What she told them was true, but now they know and believe much more because of what Jesus has told them. This is typical of the witness/belief pattern in John's Gospel."[36] The mission of any disciple of Christ is to bring others to the point that they can meet him for themselves. In this light, our Samaritan woman passes the test of a true, albeit unorthodox, witness to Jesus.

For their part, the rest of the Samaritan townsfolk become witnesses as well, and they declare Jesus the "Savior of the world" (John 4:42). This is the only time in any of the four gospels where Jesus is called "Savior," although we do find the term applied to Jesus in Acts and the letters.[37] Jews never called the Messiah "Savior," but in the Greek world gods or heroes were given the title. In particular, the emperor of Rome claimed to be saviour of the world.[38] The Samaritans asserted that Jesus alone was the Savior, not just of the Jew or the Samaritan, but also of the whole world.[39]

Conclusion

The narrative began with two isolated strangers who would normally have no contact at all with each other. It ended with their respective

---

[35]Maccini, *Her Testimony Is True*, 142.

[36]Ibid., 142.

[37]Acts 5:31; Eph 5:23; Phil 3:20; 1 Tim 4:10; Titus 1:4; 2:13; 3:6; 2 Pet 1:1,11; 2:20; 3:2; 3:18; 4:14; 1 John 4:14; Jude 25.

[38]Beasley-Murray, *John*, 65.

[39]S. T. Davis, " 'This Is Truly the Savior of the World': The Theological Significance of the Earthly Jesus," *Ex Auditu* 14 (1998): 97-103.

families testifying as one to their faith in Jesus as the Messiah, the Saviour of the world. Crucial to this remarkable development was the gradual transformation of an uncomprehending, indecent woman into a believing witness for Christ. "She was chosen, commissioned and sent by Christ himself."[40] "As the 'enlightened one,' she was sent out to become the first evangelist to the Samaritans."[41]

The Samaritan woman could testify to Jesus' claim to be the living water that she, and all, needed for eternal life. She realized that he was a prophet who knew all about her private life. He instructed her on the nature of worship "in Spirit and truth." Ultimately, she could testify to Jesus' claim to be the Messiah.

The witness of the Samaritan woman extended beyond the borders of her town. Maccini well concludes, "the Samaritan woman does testify, and is in fact a prominent witness to what she knows. Her testimony, as far as it goes, is true. Samaritan, Jewish, or other, it is not difficult to imagine John's readers, like the villagers, accepting her testimony and coming out to meet Jesus for themselves."[42]

The Samaritan woman is a key figure in gospel narrative. She shares her place with Mary the mother of Jesus,[43] the sisters Mary and Martha, and Mary Magdalene in the Johannine company of women witnesses to Jesus. Together, they distinguish the Gospel of John in its portrayal of women. More so than the other gospel writers, John presents women as central witnesses to the most crucial moments in the life and ministry of Christ. These women fulfil every aspect that we can conceive of the role of a witness. They participate in theological dialogue, they confirm the historical accounts, they model faith, and they are sent to proclaim the significance of the saving work of Christ.

---

[40]Fletcher, "The Role of Women," 44.

[41]D. G. Bloesch, *Is the Bible Sexist? Beyond Feminism and Patriarchalism* (Westchester: Crossway, 1982) 60.

[42]Maccini, *Her Testimony Is True*, 144.

[43]By comparison, Macicini notes of the Samaritan woman, "she is much more of a witness than Jesus' mother," ibid., 142. See also p. 44.

The Pauline Concept of Mutuality as a Basis for Luke's Theme of Witness[1]

Richard N. Longenecker
Wycliffe College, University of Toronto
Toronto, Ontario

In his *magnum opus* on the concept of witness in the New Testament, Allison Trites highlights the importance of the witness theme in the New Testament, which he finds to be "most fully developed in the Johannine and Lukan writings"—particularly in the Fourth Gospel, the Acts of the Apostles, and the Johannine Apocalypse—but "also present in other parts of the NT"—that is, in the Synoptic Gospels and the New Testament Epistles.[2] And in explaining how this witness theme came about, he points to the "juridical character" of the language in these writings, sketches out the nature of the opposition against Christianity in the first century, and proposes that Luke, in particular, but also the other New Testament writers, have "taken the original notion of bearing witness before a court of law and adapted it to the conditions of the Messianic Age."[3] Confining here our attention to his treatment of the Lukan writings, Trites's thesis is that "Luke-Acts presents the claims of Christ against a background of hostility, contention, and active persecution," using, in large part, "legal terminology" and "ideas drawn from the lawcourt."[4]

Professor Trites has ably demonstrated "a sustained use of juridical metaphor" in the Fourth Gospel[5] and that "the idea of witness" is "very

---

[1]This lecture was presented in honour of Dr. Allison Trites as one of the 2001 Hayward Lectures, Acadia University.

[2]Quoted material taken from *NTCW*, 175.

[3]*NTCW*, 133; see 128-35 for Acts.

[4]*NTCW*, 132-33.

[5]*NTCW*, 78-124. For a recent, laudatory statement of the thesis that "the dominant framework of the narrative of John's Gospel, and its most pervasive motif, is that of a lawsuit or trial on a cosmic scale," see A. T. Lincoln, "Trials, Plots, and the Narrative of the Fourth Gospel," *JSNT* 56 (1994): 3-30 (quoted summary taken from A. T. Lincoln, " 'I Am the Resurrection and the Life': The Resurrection Message of the Fourth Gospel," in *Life in the Face of Death: The Resurrection Message of the New Testament*, MNTS, ed. R. N. Longenecker (Grand

much a live metaphor in the Book of Revelation."[6] Discussion of the Johannine writings I must leave to others more qualified. My purpose in this article is to build on what Trites has proposed with respect to the Lukan writings—particularly the second of Luke's two volumes, the Acts of the Apostles—and to suggest that, in addition to the testimony terminology of the lawcourts, Luke was also influenced by Paul's understanding of mutuality with respect to the mission of Jesus and the mission of the church. Or, to state matters in a slightly different manner, that while the concept of "interchange" was significant for the church's understanding of the work of Christ and soteriology generally,[7] Paul's concept of "mutuality" was also important for the church's understanding of mission—and that, in particular, it served as an important theological basis for the theme of witness in Acts.

Rapids: Eerdmans, 1998) 135); A. T. Lincoln, *Truth on Trial: The Lawsuit Motif in the Fourth Gospel* (Peabody: Hendrickson, 2000).

[6]*NTCW*, 154-74; cf. G. B. Caird, who was Trites's mentor at Oxford: "The repeated use of the words 'witness' and 'testimony' is one of the many points of resemblance between the Revelation and the Fourth Gospel. In Greek as in English these words could be treated as dead metaphors, without any conscious reference to the lawcourt, which was their primary setting. But both these books use the words in their primary, forensic sense. The author of the Fourth Gospel, perhaps inspired by the example of Second Isaiah, presents his argument in the form of a lawcourt debate, in which one witness after another is summoned, until God's advocate, the Paraclete, has all the evidence he needs to convince the world that Jesus is the Son of God, and so to win his case. In the Revelation, the courtroom setting is even more realistic; for Jesus had borne his testimony before Pilate's tribunal [cf. 1:5 and 3:14], and the martyrs must face a Roman judge. What they have to remember as their give their evidence is that that evidence is being heard in a court of more ultimate authority, where judgments which are just and true issue from the great white throne" (G. B. Caird, *A Commentary on the Revelation of St. John the Divine*, BNTC (London: Black, 1966), 17-18).

[7]Cf. M. D. Hooker, "Interchange in Christ," *JTS* 22 (1971): 349-61; idem, "Interchange and Atonement," *Bulletin of the John Rylands Library* 60 (1976): 462-81; idem, "Interchange and Suffering," in *Suffering and Martyrdom in the New Testament*, ed. W. Horbury and B. McNeil (Cambridge: Cambridge University Press, 1981) 70-83; idem, "Interchange in Christ and Ethics," *JSNT* 25 (1985): 3-17. Note also K. Berger's expression *ein Tauschgeschäft* in his "Abraham in der paulinischen Hauptbriefen," *Münchener theologische Zeitschrift* 17 (1966): 52.

1. A Mutuality of Missions in Luke-Acts

What immediately strikes the reader of Luke-Acts is the underlying architectural structure of Luke's writings. For not only are the two volumes almost equal in size (the Lukan Gospel being the longest of our New Testament writings, with Acts only about one-tenth shorter) and almost identical in chronological coverage (about thirty-three years for both), they also, more importantly, exhibit, as Charles Talbert puts it, "a remarkable series of correspondences between what Jesus does and says in Luke's Gospel and what the disciples [mainly Peter and Paul] do and say in the Acts."[8] Talbert has set out in quite detailed fashion a large number of parallels of event and expression—even of sequence—that can be found in Luke's two volumes: (1) parallels between Jesus' Galilean ministry (Luke 4:14-9:50) and Jesus' Perean-Judean ministry of the Travel Narrative (Luke 9:51-19:10) in his first volume; (2) parallels between the church's mission to the Jewish world (Acts 2:42-12:24) and the church's mission to the Gentile world (Acts 12:25-28:31) in his second volume; and (3) parallels between the two volumes themselves.[9] In addition, he has argued that the literary genre of Luke-Acts "is similar to the biographies of certain founders of philosophical schools, that contained within themselves not only the life of the founder but also a list or brief narrative of his successors and selected other disciples."[10]

Talbert, of course, has been criticized for overdrawing the redactional parallels that can be found both within and between Luke's Gospel and his Acts, and for identifying too precisely the literary genre of Luke's two-volume work. But his main points have certainly been established: (1)

---

[8]C. H. Talbert, "Discipleship in Luke-Acts," in *Discipleship in the New Testament*, ed. F. F. Segovia (Philadelphia: Fortress, 1985) 63.

[9]C. H. Talbert, *Literary Patterns, Theological Themes, and the Genre of Luke-Acts*, Society of Biblical Literature monograph series 20 (Cambridge: Society of Biblical Literature, 1974) 1-65.

[10]Talbert, "Discipleship in Luke-Acts," 63; cf. idem, *Literary Patterns*, 125-40; idem, *What Is a Gospel? The Genre of the Canonical Gospels* (Philadelphia: Fortress, 1977); idem, "The Gospel and the Gospels," in *Interpreting the Gospels*, ed. J. L. Mays (Philadelphia: Fortress, 1981) 14-26—building on a suggestion of Hans Freiherr von Soden, *Geschichte der christlichen Kirche*, 1. *Die Entstehung der christlichen Kirche* (Leipzig: Teubner, 1919) 73.

that the architectural structure of Luke-Acts requires that the two volumes be read together, the first interpreted by the second and the second by the first; and (2) that the ministry of the early church, as depicted in Luke's second volume, be seen as having been shaped by the Jesus tradition, as portrayed in his first. Indeed, in setting out numerous parallels between Jesus' mission and the church's mission, Luke must be seen to be actually proposing the thesis that Jesus' ministry and the church's mission *together* constitute the fullness of God's redemptive activity on behalf of humanity. For though Jesus' mission and the church's mission are not to be taken as being identical, they are, nonetheless, comparable and inseparable. In fact, the very structure of Luke-Acts shouts out to the attentive reader that there exists some sort of mutuality between the mission of Jesus and that of the church—with Jesus' mission, it appears, being the announcement of God's kingdom and the effecting of human redemption, and that of the church being the proclamation, extension, and application of what Jesus has accomplished.

The other canonical Gospels, of course, each in its own way, relate the church's mission to the mission of Jesus—by implication in Mark's Gospel; by direct association of the church with the disciples in Matthew's Gospel; and by the use of the literary device of "two levels" of meaning in John's Gospel. Only Luke, however, juxtaposes the mission of Jesus and the mission of the church, setting out, in parallel fashion, that of Jesus in his Gospel and that of the church in his Acts.

It has often been asked how Luke first came to think of relating the mission of the church to the ministry of Jesus in such a fashion—that is, not just by implication, association, or allusion, but by actually juxtaposing the two missions as comparable and inseparable entities. It is the thesis of this essay that it was probably by association with Paul—or, at least, with those directly involved in the Pauline mission—from whom Luke would have heard such things as "And if we are children, we are also heirs: heirs of God and coheirs with Christ—if indeed we share in his sufferings in order that we may also share in his glory" (as in Romans 8:17); or "I want to know Christ—the power of his resurrection and participation in his sufferings, becoming like him in his death, and so, somehow, to attain to the resurrection of the dead" (as in Philippians 3:10-11); or "Now I rejoice in what was suffered for you; and I complete in my flesh what is still lacking with respect to Christ's afflictions, for the sake of his body, which is the church" (as in Colossians 1:24). Furthermore, it is our suggestion that such a concept of mutuality between the ministry of Christ and the ministries of those who follow him, once formed in his mind, would have had explosive consequences not only for Luke's understanding of discipleship[11] but also for his understanding of the church's mission. For now the thesis could be made that what was foundational in Jesus' ministry—both in his work and in his teaching; whether expressly evident or only embryonically present—was (and is) to be explicated and more fully expressed in the church's mission.

It is, in fact, just such a concept of mutuality that Luke expresses over and over again throughout the length and breadth of his two volumes, showing how what was basic in Jesus' ministry has been (and should continue to be) the pattern for all of the church's life and ministry. And it is this concept that I want to highlight in what follows by focusing attention on the three Pauline passages cited above.

2. The Concept of Mutuality in Romans 8:17

In many ways, Romans 8 is the high point of Paul's letter to Christians at Rome. Or, to use the imagery of J. A. T. Robinson, who compared the letter's structure to a series of locks in the Corinthian canal (which, of course, was dug and constructed somewhat after Paul's day): "The heights of the epistle are reached in chapter 8, a sustained climax which takes the argument across the watershed."[12] And one of the most important features of this eighth chapter is the apostle's set of statements in vv. 14-17 regarding the "adoption" of Gentile believers into God's family and their resultant status as "sons of God," "children of God," and "heirs of God," as well as "coheirs with Christ":

> [14]Those who are led by the Spirit of God are the sons of God (υἱοὶ θεοῦ). [15]For you did not receive a spirit that makes you a slave again to fear, but you received the Spirit of adoption (πνεῦμα υἱοθεσίας). It is by him we cry "Abba, Father." [16]The Spirit himself testifies with our spirit that we are God's children (τέκνα θεοῦ). [17]And if we are children (τέκνα), we are also heirs (κληρονόμοι): heirs of God (κληρονόμοι

[11]See my article, R. N. Longenecker, "Taking Up the Cross Daily: Discipleship in Luke-Acts," in *Patterns of Discipleship in the New Testament*, ed. R. N. Longenecker, MNTS (Grand Rapids: Eerdmans, 1996) 50-76.

[12]J. A. T. Robinson, *Wrestling with Romans* (London: SCM, 1979) 9.

θεοῦ) and coheirs with Christ (συγκληρονόμοι Χριστοῦ)—if indeed (εἴπερ) we share in his sufferings (συμπάσχομεν) in order that (ἵνα) we may also share in his glory (συνδοξασθῶμεν).

There is much in these verses that deserves extended treatment, particularly in any commentary study of the passage. For here we are at the very heart of Paul's gospel. The presence of the Spirit and the Spirit's activity in the believer's life are of vital importance, both in freeing one from slavery and in bringing one into relationship with God. Likewise, the theme of adoption, which is an image used to extend to Gentile Christians the Old Testament concept of God's election of Israel as his chosen people, deserves extensive consideration. And certainly the declarations that believers in Jesus are able, by the Spirit, to address God as "*Abba*, Father" and to think of themselves as "sons of God," "children of God," "heirs of God," and "coheirs with Christ" are highly significant as statements of fact and revolutionary as bases for a new self-understanding on the part of Gentile Christians.

What is important to note for our purposes, however, is that when Paul talks about believers in Jesus as "sons/children/heirs of God" and "coheirs with Christ," he adds the further statement—in somewhat parenthetical fashion—about believers also sharing in Christ's sufferings in order that they may also share in his glory. Furthermore, it needs to be noted that in this appended statement of v. 17b he strikes a distinctive note of mutuality by his use of the συν-compound verbs συμπάσχομεν, "we are sharing his [Christ's] sufferings" (present indicative active), and συνδοξασθῶμεν, "we may share his [Christ's] glory" (aorist subjunctive passive).

Scholars have been almost equally divided as to whether the conjunction εἴπερ (a joining of the conditional particle εἰ with the enclitic particle περ), which begins this appended statement, should be understood as introducing a statement of fact, and so to be read as "since" or "seeing that" (that is, "*since/seeing that* we share in his sufferings"),[13] or as

[13]So, e.g., C. K. Barrett, A *Commentary on the Epistle to the Romans*, BNTC (London: Black, 1957) 164-65; M. Black, *Romans*, NCB (London: Oliphants, 1973) 120; C. E. B. Cranfield, *A Critical and Exegetical Commentary on the Epistle to the Romans*, 2 vols., ICC (Edinburgh: T. & T. Clark, 1975, 1979) 1:407-408; see also H. Lietzmann, *Die Briefe des Apostels Paulus. I. An die Römer Erklärt*, HNT 3 (Tübingen: Mohr, 1971) ad loc.; M.-J. Lagrange, *Saint Paul: Épitre aux*

signalling a condition that exhorts something further on the basis of what has just be said, and so to be read as "provided that" or "if so be" (that is, "*provided/if so be that* we share in his sufferings").[14] On basis of the use of εἴπερ elsewhere in Paul's letters, the declarative translation "*since/seeing that* we share in his sufferings" is probably the better meaning.[15]

But whatever reading is accepted, the significant point to be noted here is that in speaking of the status of believers as "sons of God," "children of God," "heirs of God," and "coheirs with Christ," Paul adds a further statement regarding the lives and mission of those same believers: that they share in Christ's sufferings (or, ought to share in his sufferings) in order that they may share in Christ's glory! For, it seems, when Paul thinks of the status of Christian believers he also thinks of how that status works itself out in their lives and mission. And in so doing, he strikes a note of mutuality in his use of the συν-compound verbs συμπάσχομεν, "we are sharing his sufferings," and συνδοξασθῶμεν, "we may share his glory."

The reference in the expression "we are sharing his sufferings," as C. E. B. Cranfield points out,

---

Romains, Études Bibliques (Paris: Gabalda, 1931) ad loc.; O. Michel, *Der Brief an die Römer Übersetzt und Erklärt*, KEKNT (Göttingen: Vandenhoeck & Ruprecht, 1955 through [14]1978) ad loc.; H. W. Schmidt, *Der Brief des Paulus an die Römer*, Theologischer Handkommentar zum neuen Testament in Neuer Bearbeitung 6 (Berlin: Evangelische Verlagsanstalt, 1962 through [3]1972) ad loc.

[14]So, e.g., J. Calvin, *The Epistles of Paul the Apostle to the Romans and to the Thessalonians*, trans. R. Mackenzie, Calvin's Commentaries, ed. D. W. Torrance and T. F. Torrance (Edinburgh: Oliver & Boyd, 1960) 171; F. Godet and A. Cusin, *Commentary on St. Paul's Epistle to the Romans*, 2 vols. (Edinburgh: T. & T. Clark, 1881) 2:85; F. F. Bruce, *The Epistle of Paul to the Romans: an Introduction and Commentary*, TNTC 6 (Grand Rapids: Eerdmans, 1963) 167; J. D. G. Dunn, *Romans*, 2 vols., WBC 38A, 38B (Dallas: Word Books, 1988) 1:456; B. Byrne, *Romans*, Sacra Pagina series 6 (Collegeville: Liturgical, 1996) 253-54.

[15]Cf. Rom 3:30: "*since* there is only one God"; Rom 8:9: "*seeing that* the Spirit of God lives in you"; 1 Cor 8:5: "*even if there are* so-called gods, whether in heaven or on earth, as indeed there are"; 1 Cor 15:15: "but he [God] did not raise him [Christ], *if indeed* [supposedly] the dead are not raised"; 2 Thess 1:6: "*seeing that* God is just"—which, together with that of Rom 8:17, comprise the six uses of εἴπερ in the New Testament.

> is not to our suffering with Christ in the sense of our having died with Him in God's sight, nor to our having suffered (sacramentally) in baptism. Had either of these "sufferings" been in mind, a past tense would have been natural. The reference is rather to that element of suffering which is inseparable from faithfulness to Christ in a world which does not yet know Him as Lord.[16]

Or as Joseph Fitzmyer expresses it (implicitly highlighting the feature of mutuality in their respective missions), "Jesus has suffered before, and Christian suffering is only the overflow of his."[17] And the statement "that we may share his glory" refers, as Cranfield further observes, "not to life after death merely, but to something far more wonderful—the glory of the final consummation."[18]

3. The Concept of Mutuality in Philippians 3:10-11

Philippians 3 presents us with "one of the most remarkable personal confessions that the ancient world has bequeathed to us."[19] In that confession Paul enumerates the privileges of his Jewish descent and his personal achievements in relation to the law (vv. 4-6), describes the dramatic reorientation that has taken place in his life because of Christ (vv. 7-9), expresses his present desire for his own life and ministry (vv. 10-11), and states his ultimate purpose as being to "press on to take hold of that for which Christ Jesus took hold of me . . . to win the prize for which God has called me heavenward in Christ Jesus" (vv. 12-14).

It is with vv. 10-11, however, where Paul expresses—in a somewhat parenthetical fashion (as in Romans 8:17b)—his present desire for his life and ministry, that we are here most concerned:

---

[16]Cranfield, *Romans* 1:408.

[17]J. A. Fitzmyer, *Romans: A New Translation with Introduction and Commentary*, AB 33 (New York: Doubleday, 1993) 502.

[18]Cranfield, *Romans* 1:408, paraphrasing E. Gaugler, *Der Römerbrief*, 2 vols. (Zurich: Zwingli Verlag, 1958) 1:292.

[19]P. Bonnard, *L'Épître de Saint Paul aux Philippiens et l'Épître aux Colossiens*, trans. C. Masson, CNT 10 (Neuchâtel: Delachaux & Niestle, 1950) 61; P. T. O'Brien, *The Epistle to the Philippians: A Commentary on the Greek Text*, NIGTC (Grand Rapids: Eerdmans, 1991) 365.

> [10][I want] to know him [Christ] (τοῦ γνῶναι αὐτόν)—[that is, to know] the power of his resurrection (τὴν δύναμιν τῆς ἀναστάσεως αὐτοῦ) and participation in his sufferings (κοινωνίαν παθημάτων αὐτοῦ), becoming like him (συμμορφιζόμενος) in his death, [11]and so, somehow (εἴ πως), to attain to the resurrection from the dead (εἰς τὴν ἐξανάστασιν τὴν ἐκ νεκρῶν).

Beginning with an articular infinitive that probably functions to highlight design or purpose (τοῦ γνῶναι), the passage picks up on the clause "the surpassing greatness of knowing Christ Jesus my Lord" in v. 8 and explicates more fully what *knowing* Christ means for Paul.

There are a number of exegetical matters in these two verses that demand a more detailed treatment than can be given here. Yet some issues must be dealt with here, even if in a somewhat superficial and tentative fashion, in order to proceed further.

One major issue has to do with the object of Paul's knowing: whether it is threefold ("Christ *and* the power of his resurrection *and* the fellowship of his sufferings"), as commonly expressed in the translations,[20] or unitary, with then a twofold explication of the nature of such knowledge ("Christ—[that is, to know] the power of his resurrection *and* the fellowship of his sufferings"), as often argued by commentators.[21] The first

---

[20]Cf., e.g., KJV, ASV, RSV/NRSV, NIV—though not always in the more paraphrastic translations of individual translators (such as Moffatt: "I would know him in the power of his resurrection and the fellowship of his sufferings"; Williams: "that is, the power of His resurrection and so to share with Him his sufferings").

[21]Cf., e.g., H. A. W. Meyer, *Critical and Exegetical Handbook to the Epistles to the Philippians and Colossians*, trans. J. C. Moore and W. P. Dickson, Critical and Exegetical Commentary on the New Testament (Edinburgh: T. & T. Clark, 1875) 160; J. B. Lightfoot, *Saint Paul's Epistle to the Philippians*, The Epistles of St. Paul 3 (London: Macmillan, 1881) 150; M. R. Vincent, *A Critical and Exegetical Commentary on the Epistles to the Philippians and to Philemon*, ICC (New York: Scribner's, 1897) 104; Bonnard, *L'Épître de Saint Paul aux Philippiens et l'Épître aux Colossiens*, 66; J. Gnilka, *Der Philipperbrief*, Herders Theologischer Kommentar zum neuen Testament 10, faszikel 3 (Freiburg: Herder, 1968) 195; J. F. Collange, *L'Épître de Saint Paul aux Philippiens*, CNT 10a (Neuchâtel: Delachaux & Niestlé, 1973) 131; G. F. Hawthorne, *Philippians*, WBC 43 (Waco: Word Books, 1983) 143; O'Brien, *Epistle to the Philippians*, 402; G. D. Fee, *Paul's Letter to the Philippians*, NICNT (Grand Rapids: Eerdmans, 1995) 327-28.

reading views the two occurrences of καί ("and") as simple conjunctions; the second takes the first to be epexegetical and explicative, with only the second functioning as a simple connective. The question cannot be decided on the basis of grammar alone. Also to be considered are the immediate context of the passage and the other references in Paul's letters to the focus of his life. And when such contextual matters are taken into account, it seems best to view the object of the apostle's knowing in v. 10 as being unitary ("Christ"), with then the nature of his knowledge explicated by means of the two clauses that follow.

Another matter concerns the relations between these two explicatory clauses, "the power of his resurrection" and "participation in his sufferings." The better manuscripts ($\mathfrak{p}^{46}$, ℵ*, B) omit the articles before κοινωνίαν ("participation" or "fellowship") and παθημάτων ("sufferings"), leaving only one definite article τήν ("the") before the two clauses. Therefore, these two clauses, being united by a single article, are to be viewed as (in some sense) a single unit—that is, probably to be understood as follows: "to know him [Christ]" is to experience both "the power of his resurrection and participation in his sufferings."

But what does it mean to know "the power of his resurrection"? Most have assumed that these words have to do with the impact of the risen Jesus on the Christian. Probably, however, they should rather be taken to refer to the power of God himself, which was expressed in the resurrection of Jesus from the dead and is now manifest in the new lives of believers.[22] And what does it mean to know "participation in his sufferings"? Some have restricted these words to the generosity of the Philippians in support of Paul, and so understand the reference being to their financial aid of the gospel. Others have taken them as equivalent to a Christian's

---

[22]Cf. F. W. Beare, *A Commentary on the Epistle to the Philippians*, Harper's New Testament Commentaries (New York: Harper, 1959) 122; J. A. Fitzmyer, " 'To Know Him and the Power of His Resurrection' (Phil 3.10)," in *Mélanges Bibliques en Hommage au R. P. Béda Rigaux*, ed. A. Descamps and A. de Halleux (Gembloux: Duculot, 1970) 411-25 (esp. 420: "It emanates from the Father, raises Jesus from the dead at his resurrection, endows him with a new vitality, and finally proceeds from him as the life-giving, vitalizing force of the 'new creation' and of the new life that Christians in union with Christ experience and live."); F. F. Bruce, *Philippians*, A Good News Commentary (San Francisco: Harper & Row, 1983) 90; O'Brien, *Epistle to the Philippians*, 404-405.

faith in the work of Christ, which is epitomized by suffering and death, and so to be interpreted simply as believers having shared Christ's sufferings at their conversion. There may, of course, be some derivative truth in these suggestions. More likely, however, Paul's intended referent when speaking about "participation in his sufferings," as George Caird has expressed it, was "the discharge of his missionary duties"—that is, "the sufferings which come, unsought though not unexpected, in the course of his Christian service," and which "draw him ever closer to his Lord."[23] Or as Ralph Martin says, what is in view here are Paul's own "apostolic sufferings," which he "regarded as an extension of the 'dying of Jesus' borne in his mortal body (2 Cor. iv.10; cf. Rom. viii.36)."[24]

Accepting, then, that Paul's explication of what it means "to know him [Christ]" has to do with (1) experiencing God's resurrection power in one's life and (2) participating in Christ's sufferings in one's ministry—which may be spoken about as two features in a believer's knowledge of Christ, yet are inseparable factors and so must always be understood and experienced together—there enters here into Paul's autobiographical statements of Philippians 3 the concept of mutuality: that the same divine power that raised Jesus from the dead is also present in Paul's life (and present in every believer's life), which Paul wants to experience more fully, and that the same note of suffering that epitomized Jesus' ministry is also present in Paul's ministry (and present in every believer's ministry), which Paul gladly accepts and is prepared to experience more fully. And this note of mutuality is struck further at the end of v. 10 by the inclusion of the συν-compound participle συμμορφιζόμενος, "becoming like," which is used with respect to "his [Jesus'] death."

In his own life and ministry, therefore, Paul saw the pattern of Jesus' life and ministry being reproduced—a pattern characterized by divine power in one's daily life and by suffering in one's Christian ministry, with

---

[23]G. B. Caird, *Paul's Letters From Prison: Ephesians, Philippians, Colossians, Philemon, in the Revised Standard Version*, New Clarendon Bible (London: Oxford University Press, 1976) 140.

[24]R. P. Martin, *The Epistle of Paul to the Philippians: An Introduction and Commentary*, TNTC (London: Tyndale, 1959) 149; cf. also his introduction, 47-50. Martin adds: "There can hardly be any other meaning of these verses which so dramatically set forth the significance which Paul gives to his sufferings for Christ's sake" (149).

that suffering involving even the real prospect of physical death. It was a pattern of mutuality between himself and his Lord. It was also a pattern that caused him to know Christ better. And he longed, as v. 11 has it,[25] to have eventually the pattern of Jesus' resurrection worked out in his life as well.

4. The Concept of Mutuality in Colossians 1:24

Colossians 1:24 has been a *crux interpretum* from the earliest days of the church to the present:[26]

> Now I rejoice in what was suffered for you (τοῖς παθήμασιν ὑπὲρ ὑμῶν); and I complete (ἀνταναπληρῶ) in my flesh (ἐν τῇ σαρκί μου) what is still lacking (τὰ ὑστερήματα) with respect to Christ's afflictions (τῶν θλίψεων τοῦ Χριστοῦ), for the sake of (ὑπέρ) his body (τοῦ σώματος αὐτοῦ), which is the church (ὅ ἐστιν ἡ ἐκκλησία).

The verse, as Peter O'Brien notes, "appears to express ideas that go beyond Paul's statements elsewhere and which seem to have no parallel in the rest of the NT."[27] And, as O'Brien goes on to point out, it raises several significant questions:

> What are Paul's sufferings and how can they be an occasion for rejoicing? In what sense can these sufferings be for the body of Christ (ὑπὲρ τοῦ σώματος αὐτοῦ), or for the Colossians (ὑπὲρ ὑμῶν), a congregation which he had neither evangelized nor visited? Then, what

[25]On Paul's use of εἴ πως, "so somehow," M. R. Vincent's judgment still holds: "Much unnecessary difficulty has been made over the apparent uncertainty expressed in these words, and the fancied inconsistency with the certainty elsewhere expressed by Paul, as Rom. viii.38, 39, v.17, 18, 21; 2 Cor. v.1ff.; Phil. i.22, 23. . . . His words here are an expression of humility and self-distrust, not of doubt" (Vincent, *Epistles to the Philippians and to Philemon*, 106). G. B. Caird's comment is also apropos: "In view of 1.6, 1.21-3, and 3.20-1, and not withstanding 1 Cor. 9.27, it would be absurd to suppose that Paul harboured any serious doubts about his eternal destiny. He puts his passionate longing in this hypothetical form solely because salvation is from start to finish the gift of God and he dare not presume on the divine mercy" (Caird, *Paul's Letters from Prison*, 140).

[26]On the history of interpretation, see J. Kremer, *Was an den Leiden Christi noch Mangelt: eine interpretationsgeschichtliche und exegetische Untersuchung zu Kol. 1, 24b*, BBB, Bd. 12 (Bonn: Hanstein, 1956).

[27]P. T. O'Brien, *Colossians, Philemon*, WBC 44 (Waco: Word, 1982) 75.

is meant by the phrase "Christ's afflictions"? How can it be meaningfully said that something is "lacking" in these afflictions, and in what way can Paul (or other Christians if it applies to them) fill this deficiency?[28]

Not every matter of importance in this verse can be dealt with here. Three issues, however, are germane to the purposes of this essay. The first concerns the meaning of "what was suffered for you" (τοῖς παθήμασιν ὑπὲρ ὑμῶν), concerning which Paul says he rejoices. The second concerns the meaning of "I complete (ἀνταναπληρῶ) in my flesh (ἐν τῇ σαρκί μου) what is still lacking (τὰ ὑστερήματα) with respect to Christ's afflictions (τῶν θλίψεων τοῦ Χριστοῦ)," asking what the apostle means by such expressions as "complete" (or "fill up"), "in my flesh," "what is still lacking," and "Christ's afflictions"—and, further, how he saw such action to be "for the sake of his body, which is the church." And the third has to do with how these two clauses are to be related.

Almost all commentators have viewed the first statement of the verse, νῦν χαίρω ἐν τοῖς παθήμασιν ὑπὲρ ὑμῶν, as quite clearly speaking of Paul's sufferings in the course of his apostolic ministry.[29] The definite article denotes sufferings that have actually been experienced; the first person singular is used in saying "I rejoice" (following on from v. 23b); and the statement appears at the head of the section of the letter in which the apostle's own pastoral concerns are clearly expressed (1:24–2:5). It seems reasonable, therefore, to conclude that the article τοῖς denotes possession, and so should be read as signalling Paul's own

---

[28]Ibid., 75.

[29]Cf., e.g., J. B. Lightfoot, *Saint Paul's Epistles to the Colossians and to Philemon* (London: Macmillan, 1882) 164; E. F. Scott, *The Epistles of Paul to the Colossians, to Philemon, and to the Ephesians*, Moffatt New Testament Commentary (London: Hodder & Stoughton, 1930); G. H. P. Thompson, *The Letters of Paul to the Ephesians, to the Colossians and to Philemon*, CBC (Cambridge: Cambridge University Press, 1967) 138-39; E. Lohse, *Colossians and Philemon: A Commentary on the Epistles to the Colossians and to Philemon*, trans. W. R. Peohlmann and R. J. Karris, Hermeneia (Philadelphia: Fortress, 1971) 68; R. P. Martin, *Colossians: the Church's Lord and the Christian's Liberty; an Expository Commentary with a Present-Day Application* (Exeter: Paternoster, 1972) 62; O'Brien, *Colossians, Philemon*, 75-77; M. J. Harris, *Colossians & Philemon*, Exegetical Guide to the Greek New Testament (Grand Rapids: Eerdmans, 1991) 65; W. T. Wilson, *The Hope of Glory: Education and Exhortation in the Epistle to the Colossians*, NovTSup 88 (Leiden: Brill, 1997) 238-41.

sufferings. The inclusion of the pronoun "my" (μου) in a corrected version of the fourth-century Codex Sinaiticus (א[3]), in a seventhth-century Syriac translation (sy[h]), and in an eleventh-century minuscule Greek manuscript (81) clearly indicates that at least some scribes read the statement in this way—though most commentators have concluded that "the meaning is plain enough without this explanatory addition."[30]

Furthermore, almost all commentators have treated the two clauses as having the same referent and understood the first clause as being more fully explicated by the second. So having established—or, more frequently, simply accepting as fact—that the writer is speaking about his own sufferings in v. 24a, they have focused their attention on the fuller exegetical data of v. 24b. Eduard Lohse, for example, says of v. 24a: "This phrase [τοῖς παθήμασιν ὑπὲρ ὑμῶν] is more closely explained in the clarifying clause which follows the 'and' (καί): 'and in my flesh I complete what is lacking in Christ's afflictions for the sake of his body, that is, the church.' "[31] And Jacob Kremer's history of the interpretation of Colossians 1:24 does likewise in its almost exclusive focus on the second part of the verse, as its title suggests.[32]

A better understanding of these clauses and their relationship, I suggest, is provided when one takes the definite article τοῖς to be referring *not* to Paul's sufferings, but to the sufferings of Christ spoken about just a few verses earlier—that is, to the sufferings of Christ referred to at the end of the confessional portion of 1:15-20 in v. 20b ("making peace *through his blood, shed on the cross*") and highlighted in the writer's comment on this portion in v. 22 ("But now he has reconciled you *by the body of his flesh through death*, to present you holy in his sight, without blemish and free from accusation"). The article, indeed, points to sufferings that have actually been experienced. But rather than understanding it as denoting possession with Paul as its referent, and so to be more fully explicated by the second clause of v. 24, I suggest it is better understood as denoting possession with Christ as its referent, and so to be picking up from the earlier references to *peace* having been brought about

---

[30]O'Brien, *Colossians, Philemon*, 76.

[31]Lohse, *Colossians and Philemon*, 69.

[32]Cf. Kremer, *Was an den Leiden Christi noch Mangelt.*

"through his [Christ's] blood, shed on the cross" (v. 20b) and *reconciliation* effected "by the body of his [Christ's] flesh through death" (v. 22a).

On such an understanding, the "now" (νῦν) of v. 24 is not to be seen as having in mind the time of Paul's imprisonment (as often assumed by commentators), which is not referred to until 4:3, but should be taken as the first word of a sudden outburst of thanksgiving ("Now I rejoice") for God's great redemption, which has been provided in the work of Jesus Christ. The expression "I rejoice" (χαίρω) has as its object what God has effected by means of the suffering of Christ—that is, "through his blood, shed on the cross" and "by the body of his flesh through death." It probably also signals something of the difference between Paul and the "hollow and deceptive philosophy" (τῆς φιλοσοφίας καὶ κενῆς ἀπάτης) that someone (τις) was promulgating among believers at Colosse (cf. 2:8). For whereas the errorist and others at Colosse may have been embarrassed—even repelled—by references to Christ's "physical body," "blood," "cross," "sufferings," and "death" in effecting human redemption, Paul's attitude was just the reverse: he rejoiced in the sufferings of Christ!

On such a reading, therefore, τοῖς παθήμασιν ὑπὲρ ὑμῶν refers to Christ's sufferings on behalf of believers at Colosse—as well as, of course, all believers "in Christ" more generally—and so should be translated either "that which was suffered for you" or "what was suffered for you." And on such a reading, this first part of the verse (1) picks up on the theme of Christ's physical sufferings highlighted in vv. 20 and 22; (2) restates in dramatic fashion Paul's attitude toward those sufferings ("I rejoice in what was suffered for you," probably in contradistinction to the attitude of the errorist and some Christians at Colosse who started to believe him); (3) ties together what Paul said earlier about Christ's sufferings and what he says in what follows about sufferings in his own ministry; and (4) furnishes a platform for the presentation of his own ministry, which he designates as his service (διάκονος) on behalf of the gospel (τοῦ εὐαγγελίου) in 1:23b and describes more fully in 1:24b–2:5.

The second part of v. 24—"and I complete in my flesh what is still lacking in regard to Christ's afflictions, for the sake of his body, which is the church"—clearly has the apostle's own sufferings in view. And this is in line with the fact that while the expression τὰ παθήματα τοῦ Χριστοῦ / αὐτοῦ ("the sufferings of Christ" or "his sufferings") is used elsewhere in Paul's letters for both Christ's sufferings and Paul's sufferings (cf. 1 Corinthians 1:4-7; Philippians 3:10), neither the noun θλίψις ("oppression," "affliction," "tribulation") or the phrase αἱ θλίψεϛ τοῦ Χριστοῦ ("Christ's afflictions") appear in the apostle's other writings with reference to Christ's sufferings, but are always used in a derivative fashion of the apostle's own sufferings (cf. Romans 5:3; 8:35; 2 Corinthians 1:4, 8; 4:17; 6:4; 7:4; Ephesians 3:13; Philippians 1:17; 4:14; 1 Thessalonians 3:3, 7) or those of other believers (cf. Romans 12:12; 2 Corinthians 1:4; 8:2, 13; 1 Thessalonians 1:6; 2 Thessalonians 1:4, 6) on behalf of Christ.[33]

How, then, should "Christ's afflictions" (τῶν θλίψεων τοῦ Χριστοῦ) in this second part of v. 24 be understood? Further, what are the things that are "still lacking" (τὰ ὑστερήματα)? And what did Paul have in mind when he said "I complete (ἀνταναπληρῶ) in my flesh (ἐν τῇ σαρκί μου) what is still lacking with respect to Christ's afflictions"?

Some have supposed that Paul believed that there was something lacking in the vicarious sufferings of Christ and that he needed to complete Christ's redemptive work in his own ministry.[34] But as Eduard Lohse points out, "Paul and all other witnesses in the NT unanimously agree that the reconciliation was truly and validly accomplished in the death of Christ, and that no need exists for any supplementation."[35] Others have proposed some type of mystical union with Christ's passion that calls for "his body, which is the church," to so enter into the experience of Christ's sufferings that believers individually and the church corporately will be able to complete experientially what Christ began objectively.[36] The majority of interpreters today, however, view the

---

[33]The only place in the Pauline letters where αἱ θλίψεϛ τοῦ Χριστοῦ could be taken to refer to Christ's own sufferings is in Col 1:24b, but that is plainly not the case (contra *BAG*, 363, col. 1).

[34]Cf. H. Windisch, *Paulus und Christus: ein biblisch-religionsgeschichtlicher Vergleich*, Untersuchungen zum neuen Testament 24 (Leipzig: Hindrichs, 1934) 236-50. In Windisch's view, Col 1:24 is to be interpreted as Paul bearing the sufferings "that Christ could not carry away completely" (244).

[35]Lohse, *Colossians and Philemon*, 69; citing his *Märtyrer und Gottesknecht*, 200-203.

[36]Cf. A. Deissmann, *Paul: A Study in Social and Religious History*, 2nd ed., trans. W. E. Wilson (London: Hodder & Stoughton, 1927) 162-63, 181-82, 202; O. Schmitz, *Die Christus-Gemeinschaft des Paulus im Lichte seines Genetivgebrauchs*, Neutestamentliche Forschungen 2 (Gütersloh: Bertelsmann, 1924) 190-96; J. Schneider, *Die Passionsmystik des Paulus ihr Wesen, ihr Hintergrund und ihre*

statement "I complete in my flesh what is still lacking with respect to Christ's afflictions" in an apocalyptic context—a sentiment that parallels the Jewish expectation of an increase of "Messianic travail," or woes of the Messiah, which must come about before the final culmination of human history—and so see Paul speaking about the Messianic afflictions that he must accomplish in his ministry on behalf of the church before the end of time.[37]

My suggestion, however, is that what is presented in Colossians 1:24 is a juxtaposition of (1) what Christ accomplished in his physical sufferings (the τοῖς παθήμασιν ὑπὲρ ὑμῶν of the first clause), which vicariously effected redemption for all believers, and (2) what Paul experienced in his ministry on behalf of the entire church generally and Christians at Colosse in particular (the τῶν θλίψεων τοῦ Χριστοῦ . . . ὑπὲρ τοῦ σώματος αὐτοῦ, ὅ ἐστιν ἡ ἐκκλησία of the second clause), which he saw as completing that redemption by extending it to all people. It was Christ's mission to *effect* redemption; it is the church's mission—and particularly Paul's mission—to be involved in the *extension* of what Christ effected.

On such an interpretation, the feature of mutuality between the mission of Christ and the mission of Paul is highlighted. For what Christ effected once-and-for-all by his vicarious sufferings on behalf of humanity yet needs to be extended through the apostle's sufferings on behalf of the church. Nonetheless, even if both clauses of v. 24 are understood to refer to Paul's own suffering—and so not seen as setting up a parallel between what Christ effected and what Paul was doing by way of extension—such a note of mutuality is still present in the juxtaposition of the person and

---

Nachwirkungen (Leipzig: Hinrichs, 1929).

[37]Cf., e.g., Lohse, *Colossians and Philemon*, 69-72; O'Brien, *Colossians, Philemon*, 79-80: "The apostle, through the suffering which he endures in his own flesh . . . , contributes to the sum total of these eschatological afflictions. By helping to fill up this predetermined measure Paul brings the end, the dawning of the future glory, so much closer"; Caird, *Paul's Letters from Prison*, 184: "*Christ's afflictions* will not be complete until the final victory over evil is won. Someone must carry the burden, and the strong may take over the share of the weak (Gal. 6.2). Paul is glad that he has been able to do enough of the heavy lifting to spare his churches some of their load. It is almost as if he is thinking of a fixed quota of suffering to be endured, so that the more he can attract to himself the less will remain for others."

work of Christ in 1:15-23 and the ministry of Paul in 1:24–2:5. For, as Tom Wright points out with respect to "the whole paragraph" of 1:24–2:5 (with allusions also to 2 Corinthians 1:3-7 and 4:7-12): Paul "applies to himself the same pattern, of suffering on behalf of others, that was worked out on the cross."[38]

5. Conclusion: Mutuality as a Theological Basis for Witness

The concept of "interchange" was significant for Paul's and the early church's understanding of the work of Christ and soteriology generally, as Morna Hooker has frequently pointed out.[39] Concomitant with the idea of interchange was the concept of "mutuality," particularly with respect to understanding relations between Christ's mission and the church's mission. Other factors of a political and sociological nature were undoubtedly at work in the motivation, conditioning, and expression of the church's mission, as Professor Trites has ably demonstrated. At the heart of the early church's understanding of mission, however, was the theological concept of mutuality.

Such a concept seems to have been particularly lively in Paul's own self-understanding and his rationale for a mission to Gentiles, as his highly personal statements of Romans 8:17, Philippians 3:10-11 and Colossians 1:24 suggest. It would also have continued to be an important concept among his immediate followers, which may be argued if Colossians was written by a later follower of the apostle. In all likelihood, therefore, it was from such a concept of mutuality that Luke derived the theological basis for his theme of witness. And it is in the concept of mutuality that the individual believer and the church corporately find theological grounding for their witness today.

---

[38]N. T. Wright, *The Epistles of Paul to the Colossians and to Philemon: An Introduction and Commentary*, TNTC (Grand Rapids: Eerdmans, 1986) 89.

[39]See n. 7 above.

Epaphras and Philip: the Undercover Evangelists of Hierapolis

Larry J. Kreitzer
Regent's Park College, Oxford

In a recent commentary on Ephesians, I put forward a new suggestion concerning the setting and authorship of the epistle.[1] I proposed that the letter was originally intended for the Christian congregation at Hierapolis within the region of Phrygia in Asia Minor, and that it was written by an unnamed disciple of Paul who was a member of the church at Colossae. Furthermore, I also suggested that this disciple might have been given special responsibility for the neighboring congregation in Hierapolis by his home church in Colossae. Such a proposed scenario offers a new way of reading the epistle as a whole, and opens up the possibility of interpreting the letter as one in which the interchurch relationships between the three congregations in the Lycus valley are being addressed. In short, the suggestion is that the church at Hierapolis is a daughter-church of the church at Colossae, and that many of the difficulties of interpreting the letter are eased when it is read against that backdrop. Within this short study, I would like to pursue these proposals a step further by examining the possibility that, within his letter, the writer of Ephesians makes a veiled allusion to both Epaphras, the special envoy of Paul, and Philip, the archetypal evangelist of Acts. Both these men can be connected to Hierapolis. This allusion occurs in 4:11 amidst a listing of the offices and ministries bestowed upon the church by the Spirit of God.

The list in Ephesians 4:11-13 is dependent upon similar passages in 1 Corinthians 12:27-28 and Romans 12:4-8. The essential terms may be compared as follows, in the chart below.

As can be readily seen, there are several common offices or ministries within the three passages, as well as some individualized features. "Apostles" head the lists in both 1 Corinthians and Ephesians, while "prophets" are listed in all three letters; this is not surprising given the importance of both offices within the life of the early church. Most importantly for

---

[1]L. J. Kreitzer, *The Epistle to the Ephesians*, Epworth Commentaries (London: Epworth, 1997).

1 Cor 12:27-28	Rom 12:6-8	Eph 4:11-12
apostles		apostles
prophets	prophets	prophets
		evangelists
		pastors
	service	service
teachers	teachers	teachers
		exhorters
		contributors
		benefactors
		givers of mercy
miracle workers		
healers		
helpers		
administrators		
tongues speakers		

our consideration here, however, is the fact that a mention of "evangelists" (εὐαγγελισταί) occurs *only* in Ephesians.[2] This seemingly insignificant mention of "evangelists" in Ephesians 4:11, one item in the list of six offices and ministries[3] given by God to the church through his grace, is a small piece of evidence that might be relevant in attempts to reconstruct the historical circumstances surrounding the introduction of Christianity to the region. My contention is that this is a deliberate inser-

---

[2]The same is true of "pastors" (ποιμένας), which may reflect a close connection between the two, either within the writer's mind or within the life of the church in Hierapolis.

[3]Several good recent studies of the terms used in the Pauline epistles to denote the titles and offices of Christian ministry are available. Included are R. J. Banks, *Paul's Idea of Community: The Early House Churches in Their Historical Setting* (Exeter: Paternoster, 1980); C. G. Kruse, *New Testament Foundations for Ministry*, Marshall's Theological Library (London: Marshall Morgan & Scott, 1983) 171-76; E. E. Ellis, *Pauline Theology: Ministry and Society* (Grand Rapids: Eerdmans, 1989) 87-121; C. G. Kruse, "Ministry," in *DPHL*, 602-608; E. Schweizer, "Ministry in the Early Church," in *ABD* 4:835-42; E. E. Ellis, "Coworkers, Paul and His," in *DPHL*, 183-89. Unfortunately, the precise meaning of "the evangelists" in Eph 4:11 receives little, if any, discussion in these works.

tion made by the writer of the letter, one that is intended to remind the congregation in Hierapolis not only of its own history in the Christian faith, but also its indebtedness to two persons in particular—Epaphras and Philip the Evangelist.

I offer this study to my friend and colleague Allison, whom I first met almost twenty years ago when he was on sabbatical leave at Southern Baptist Theological Seminary in Louisville, Kentucky while I was a student there. One of my fondest memories of that time is of Allison, wearing his dressing gown and slippers, regally reclining on my living-room sofa, as together we made a weekly ritual out of watching the thirteen episodes of the Public Broadcasting System's television broadcast of Robert Graves's *I, Claudius* (1976).

The figures of Epaphras and Philip the Evangelist are mentioned only in passing in Trites's seminal work, *The New Testament Concept of Witness* (1977), but they do conveniently serve as illustration of one the central points of the book. For example, as part of a survey of how the Apostle Paul uses the ideas of testimony and witness within his letters, Trites remarks:

> In Col. 4:13 Paul pays Epaphras a tribute by saying "I bear witness that he has worked hard for you and for those in Λαοδικεία and in Hierapolis," but here Paul is certainly not using μαρτυρῶ with any reference to a law court; it is simply a matter of vouching for a faithful colleague.[4]

Clearly, Paul held Epaphras in high esteem and offers a word of testimony, or witness, on his behalf. What is equally clear in Paul's tribute to his colleague is Epaphras's involvement with all three of the Christian congregations located in the Lycus Valley. However, the precise relationship between the churches in Colossae, Laodicea, and Hierapolis, and what Epaphras's role was in this regard, are matters about which there remains much mystery. Various suggestions have been put forward by scholars over the years, most of which have concentrated on passing references contained in Paul's letters to the church at Colossae and to Philemon.

---

[4]*NTCW*, 207. The assumption that Paul's witness carries with it the idea of testimony offered in a lawcourt is nevertheless maintained by many interpreters, including J. D. G. Dunn, *The Epistles to the Colossians and to Philemon: A Commentary on the Greek Text*, NIGTC (Grand Rapids: Eerdmans, 1996) 281.

In light of these allusions, and keeping in mind the close connection that we know existed between Paul's letters to the Colossians and to Philemon on the one hand, and Ephesians on the other, I would like to suggest that Epaphras was one of the evangelists mentioned in Ephesians 4:11. In support of this proposal, I shall first examine the person and ministry of Epaphras, reviewing what is known about him from various passages within the Pauline letters themselves. Then, I shall consider briefly the function of evangelists within the early church, particularly as they related to the apostles, as well as the role that evangelists had in the missionary efforts in unchurched regions. Finally, I shall consider some suggestions concerning the identity of "the evangelists" about whom the writer of Ephesians 4:11 speaks.

1. Epaphras of Colossae[5]

Epaphras is mentioned by name only three times in the New Testament (Colossians 1:7; 4:12; and Philemon 23). Yet, the terms that Paul uses to describe him in these verses are very significant.[6] He is described as a "beloved fellow slave" (ἀγάπητος συνδοῦλος) in Colossians 1:7a; as "a faithful minister of Christ on your behalf" (πιστὸς ὑπὲρ ὑμῶν διάκονος τοῦ Χριστοῦ)[7] in Colossians 1:7b; as a "slave of Christ Jesus" (δοῦλος Χριστοῦ Ἰησοῦ) in Colossians 4:12; and as "my fellow prisoner in Christ Jesus" (ὁ συναιχμάλωτός μου ἐν Χριστῷ Ἰησοῦ) in Philemon 23.

---

[5]Epaphras has a short entry in many of the standard reference dictionaries for biblical studies. For example, see: J. M. Norris, "Epaphras," in *Interpreter's Dictionary of the Bible* 2:107; F. F. Bruce, "Epaphras," in *Illustrated Bible Dictionary*, 459; S. F. Hunter, "Epaphras," in *International Standard Bible Encyclopedia*, 2nd ed., 2:108; F. M. Gillman, "Epaphras," in *ABD* 2:533. Also worth consulting is D. E. Hiebert, "Epaphras, Man of Prayer," *BSac* 136 (1979): 54-64.

[6]I assume Paul was the author of Colossians.

[7]Some manuscripts, including 𝔭[46] A B D* F G P, read "our" (ἡμῶν) instead of "your" (ὑμῶν) within the phrase. "Our" is almost certainly the original reading. E. Lohse, *Colossians and Philemon: A Commentary on the Epistles to the Colossians and to Philemon*, Hermeneia (Philadelphia: Fortress, 1971) 23, suggests the alteration from ὑπὲρ ἡμῶν to ὑπὲρ ὑμῶν is due to the influence of 4:12 (where ὑπὲρ ὑμῶν also appears). For more on the fluctuation between first and second person pronouns in the letter, see C. F. D. Moule, *The Epistles to the Colossians and to Philemon*, CGTC (Cambridge: Cambridge University Press, 1957) 27-28.

In addition, in Colossians 4:12 Epaphras is said to be "one of you" (ὁ ἐξ ὑμῶν), which is commonly taken to mean that he was a member of the church at Colossae, and, presumably, a native of the city. Indeed, Paul goes on to declare Epaphras's pastoral concerns for the Colossians in the same verse, by saying that he is "always agonizing on your behalf in his prayers" (πάντοτε ἀγωνιζόμενος ὑπὲρ ὑμῶν ἐν ταῖς προσευχαῖς). As we noted above, Paul further commends him in Colossians 4:13, going on to say that "he has worked hard for you and for those in Laodicea and Hierapolis" (ἔχει πολὺν πόνον ὑπὲρ ὑμῶν καὶ τῶν ἐν Λαοδικείᾳ καὶ τῶν ἐν Ἱεραπόλει). Taken together, these references suggest not only that Epaphras was valued by Paul as a trusted friend and colleague in the faith, but that he was intimately involved in the life of the three Christian churches known to have been located in the Lycus valley, and worked tirelessly on their behalf.[8] Indeed, a small measure of the degree to which Paul viewed Epaphras's labors as equivalent to his own is to be found in the fact that the same evocative participle, "struggled" (ἀγωνιζόμενος), is used of Epaphras in 4:12 as is used in 1:29 to describe Paul's own labors in Christ.[9] In all likelihood, Epaphras was a Gentile believer, given the fact that in Colossians 4:10-11 Paul lists Aristarchus, Mark (the cousin of Barnabas) and Jesus (who is called Justus) as Jewish fellow workers, describing these three as "men of the circumcision" (οἱ ὄντες ἐκ περιτομῆς). Mention of Epaphras then follows immediately in 4:12, and the simplest reading of the passage is that Epaphras is outside of this racial-religious grouping.

---

[8]The reference to Epaphras's "hard labor" (πολὺν πόνον) in 4:13 is somewhat unusual. E. F. Scott, *The Epistles of Paul to the Colossians, to Philemon, and to the Ephesians*, Moffatt New Testament Commentary (London: Hodder & Stoughton, 1930) 90, suggests it might refer to Epaphras's role in helping to set up disaster assistance for those living in the Lycus Valley following the great earthquake of 60 CE (see Tacitus *Annales* 14.27). It may even be that Epaphras came to Rome in order to enlist the financial aid from wealthy Christians there for the relief work back home.

[9]Also, note the use of "struggle" (ἀγῶνα) in Col 2:1, and the use of the compound verb "to struggle together with" (συναγωνίσασθαι) in Rom 15:30. On this matter see P. T. O'Brien, *Colossians, Philemon*, WBC 44 (Waco: Word, 1982) 90, 254-55. V. C. Pfitzner, *Paul and the Agon Motif*, NovTSup 16 (Leiden: Brill, 1967) 125-26, also offers a useful discussion.

It is generally agreed that Epaphras was instrumental in the foundation of the Christian churches in the region, particularly since Paul himself implies that none of them had ever seen him (Paul) in the flesh (Colossians 2:1). Luke certainly mentions the region of Phrygia (in which the Lycus valley was situated) as one through which Paul traveled on his so-called second and third missionary journeys (see Acts 16:6 and 18:23), but the term "Phrygia" is geographically imprecise and cannot be used to confirm Paul's presence in any of the three cities concerned. It seems probable that Christianity spread to the Lycus valley through the agency of Epaphras, who may well have come to know Paul during the apostle's three-year stay in Ephesus (Acts 19; cf. 1 Corinthians 16:8-9, 19; 2 Corinthians 1:8; Romans 16:5). Moreover, it appears that Epaphras paid a visit to Paul and shared his concern about the well-being of the Christians in the Lycus region.[10] Thus, Paul's knowledge of the Colossians is primarily through what he has *heard* about them from others, notably Epaphras (Colossians 1:4, 9).

At the same time, Paul befriends the runaway slave Onesimus (also from the city of Colossae) and brings him to faith in Christ. Indeed, F. F. Bruce proposed that Epaphras may have been responsible for bringing Onesimus to Paul while the apostle was in prison, presumably in the city of Rome.[11] The combination of a visit from Epaphras and the need to regularize the situation with Onesimus and his master Philemon prompts Paul to write the various letters to the Christians concerned. Thus,

---

[10]Thus prompting A. T. Robertson, *Some Minor Characters in the New Testament* (Grand Rapids: Baker Books, 1976) 87, to describe Epaphras as "the News-bearer." G. B. Caird, *Paul's Letters from Prison: Ephesians, Philippians, Colossians, Philemon in the Revised Standard Version*, New Clarendon Bible (London: Oxford University Press, 1976) 160, downplays any suggestion that the visit of Epaphras to Paul was due to an emergency in the life of the church at Colossae. He says: "Epaphras was traveling to Rome on business and took the opportunity of consulting his old friend and father in God about a bothersome problem."

[11]So E. K. Simpson and F. F. Bruce, *Commentary on the Epistles to the Ephesians and the Colossians*, NICNT (Grand Rapids: Eerdmans, 1957) 164-65; F. F. Bruce, *Paul, Apostle of the Heart Set Free* (Grand Rapids: Eerdmans, 1977) 400, 407-408; idem, *The Epistles to the Colossians, to Philemon, and to the Ephesians*, NICNT (Grand Rapids: Eerdmans, 1984) 197, 208, 224; idem, *The Pauline Circle* (Grand Rapids: Eerdmans, 1985) 68.

Colossians is written to the church at large, while Philemon is written to a member of the congregation there, and another letter was written to the church in neighboring Laodicea (Colossians 4:16).[12] Occasionally, it has been argued that Epaphras himself was the author of this (now-lost) letter to the Laodiceans,[13] but it is difficult to imagine why Paul fails to mention it as coming from Epaphras if that was indeed the case.

In any event, it appears that Epaphras himself remained in Rome with Paul, possibly under guard as Paul's fellow prisoner in the faith (Philemon 23). Meanwhile all three of the Pauline letters were probably delivered by Tychicus, accompanied by the runaway slave Onesimus who was being returned to his master Philemon in Epaphras's hometown of Colossae.

To summarize: Epaphras was Paul's envoy to the Lycus Valley, and was responsible for the founding of the churches in the area, including the one in Hierapolis to which a later letter (our Ephesians) was directed.

2. Εὐαγγελιστής in Early Christianity

As noted above, the writer of Ephesians includes a reference to "evangelists" (εὐαγγελισταί) in his discussion of the gifting of God's people in the church. Evangelists are generally regarded as successors to the apostles in the early church, although originally there must have been very little difference between the two offices in terms of function. It seems clear that both apostles and evangelists served as proclaimers of the gospel message about Jesus Christ. However, several questions remain about the role of the "evangelists" (εὐαγγελισταί). Are there any indications of how and where the term came to be used in the Christian church? And to what extent can they be described as "gospel missionaries"?[14]

---

[12]J. B. Lightfoot, *Saint Paul's Epistles to the Colossians and to Philemon* (London: Macmillan, 1882) 37, dates the three letters to 63 CE and assumes the letter to the Laodiceans is a copy of the circular letter of Paul, which we now know as Ephesians. M. Barth, *Ephesians*, 2 vols., AB 34, 34A (Garden City: Doubleday, 1974) 2:15-39, also thinks Ephesians is the lost letter of Paul to the Laodiceans.

[13]C. P. Anderson, "Who Wrote the Epistle from Laodicea," *JBL* (1966): 436-40. Anderson, somewhat bizarrely, equates Epaphras with Epaphroditus of Philippi within his argument, invoking Phil 2:25 and describing Epaphras as Paul's "fellow-soldier" (συστρατιώτης).

[14]Largely on the basis of a comment in Eusebius's *Ecclesiastical History* 3:37:3,

The noun εὐαγγελιστής is rare in the classical literature and appears infrequently outside Christian circles. In the New Testament itself, the term is found only three times (Acts 21:8; Ephesians 4:11; and 2 Timothy 4:5), which makes it very difficult to define precisely what it means. It has been asserted by some commentators in years gone by that the title of εὐαγγελιστής arose among the Hellenistic Jewish-Christians and that it was intimately associated with missionary activity.[15] The figure of Philip the Evangelist is especially important in arguments along these lines, with both Acts (6:5; 8:5-40; 21:8-9) and Eusebius (*Ecclesiastical History* 3:31:3-4; 3:39:9; 5:24:2) commonly cited as supporting evidence (more on Philip below). For many scholars the association of the role of "evangelists" with the proclamation of the gospel message into new, unchurched regions is central.[16]

However, other commentators dissociate the role of the evangelists from explicit missionary activity and instead see their function in more general terms. In the words of Georg Strecker:

> the εὐαγγελισταί are placed after the apostles and are not primarily missionaries, but instead serve the church through the proclamation of the gospel. A clearly demarcated church office is not apparent.[17]

Similarly, U. Becker remarks:

> The term *euangelistes* is thus clearly intended to refer to people who carry on the work of the apostles who have been directly called by the risen Christ. But it is difficult to decide whether the reference is to an

---

D. Y. Hadidian, "Τοὺς δὲ εὐαγγελιστάς in Eph 4:11," *CBQ* 28 (1966): 317-21, argues that the term refers to the office of the gospel writers, rather than to the missionary preachers.

[15]So H. G. Friedrich, "εὐαγγελιστής," *TDNT* 2:736-37; W. Schmithals, *The Office of Apostle in the Early Church*, trans. J. E. Steely (Nashville: Abingdon, 1969) 226, 260.

[16]T. K. Abbott, A *Critical and Exegetical Commentary on the Epistles to the Ephesians and to the Colossians*, ICC (Edinburgh: T. & T. Clark, 1902) 118; J. A. Robinson, *St. Paul's Epistle to the Ephesians* (London: Macmillan, 1928) 181; Barth, *Ephesians* 2:438; C. L. Mitton, *Ephesians*, NCB (London: Marshall, Morgan & Scott, 1976) 150, are cases in point.

[17]"εὐαγγελίζω," *Exegetical Dictionary of the New Testament*, ed. H. Balz and G. Schneider (Grand Rapids: Eerdmans, 1990) 2:70.

office, or simply to an activity. These evangelists may have been engaged in missionary work (Acts 21:8), or church leadership (2 Tim. 4:5).[18]

To adopt a slightly different tack, Andrew T. Lincoln argues that since the mention of "the pastors" (τοὺς δὲ ποιμένας) in Ephesians 4:11 seems to cover church leadership in general, the meaning of "evangelists" must be something other than this. Thus, Lincoln says:

> [I]t is likely that here "evangelists" are to be seen as those engaged in mission and the founding of churches and, therefore, as having responsibilities beyond the local congregation. A further reason for their mention here could be that the churches in Asia Minor, which are being addressed, were not founded directly by Paul but by just such people, coworkers and followers of Paul who continued his type of missionary activity.[19]

In any case, the work of "evangelists" was closely connected to the ministry of "apostles," and is best viewed as an extension and development of it. In this sense, the fact that "evangelists" follows the mention of "apostles" and "prophets" in Ephesians 4:11 is not only historically accurate but also theologically sound. It thus fits well with the only other mention in the letter of "apostles" and "prophets," namely, Ephesians 2:20, where the writer expands upon the image found in 1 Corinthians 3:9-17 and suggests that succeeding generations of the church are built upon its apostolic substructures.[20] Whether evangelists were primarily concerned with bringing the gospel message to an unchurched area, or were more actively involved in ministry within the Christian congregations themselves is quite difficult to determine. What does appear clear, however, is that evangelists were an important part of the overall armory of the church as she engaged in battle against the hostile forces of the world and sought to bring the message of Jesus Christ to bear within human

---

[18]U. Becker, "Gospel, Evangelize, Evangelist," *NIDNTT* 2:114.

[19]A. T. Lincoln, *Ephesians*, WBC 42 (Dallas: Word, 1990) 250.

[20]R. Schnackenburg, *Ephesians: A Commentary* (Edinburgh: T. & T. Clark, 1991) 296-98, offers a fine discussion of this. Also see his R. Schnackenburg, "Die Kirche als Bau: Eph. 2.19-22 unter ökumenischem Aspekt," in *Paul and Paulinism: Essays in Honour of C. K. Barrett*, ed. M. D. Hooker and S. G. Wilson (London: SPCK, 1982) 258-72.

lives. We can safely assume that evangelists served an important function in the life of the congregation being addressed in Ephesians, as Ephesians 4:11 makes quite clear by ranking them in third place superseded only by apostles and prophets. The further question thus presents itself: Whom did the writer of Ephesians have in mind when he mentions these evangelists?

3. Un(der)covering the Evangelists of Hierapolis (Eph 4:11)

On the strength of Ephesians 4:11, it seems beyond doubt that the church of Hierapolis—assuming my proposed scenario about the original recipients of the letter is correct—was familiar with the ministry of evangelists in its midst. Interestingly, the critical phrase in the verse is put in the plural, "the evangelists" (τοὺς δὲ εὐαγγελιστάς), rather than "an evangelist," as if to suggest that there was more than one person involved in God's gifting to the church in this regard. Given what we noted above about the place of Epaphras within the life of the church in the Lycus Valley, it seems highly likely that Epaphras himself was one of the evangelists originally sent to the church in Hierapolis. The question therefore is: Who else might have served as an evangelist to the church located there?

Some scholars have plausibly suggested that Epaphras may have worked with a co-evangelist in bringing Christianity to the area. Barnabas is sometimes mentioned in this regard, on the assumption that the reference in Colossians 4:10 to Mark as "the nephew of Barnabas" (ὁ ἀνεψιὸς Βαρναβᾶ) is so familiar as to suggest that Barnabas was known to the church there.[21] The open-ended description in Acts 13:48-49 of the gospel spreading "in the whole country" possibly supports this. However, this associates the introduction of Christianity to the Lycus region with the so-called first missionary journey of Paul and Barnabas, rather than with Epaphras. Given the arguments above for Epaphras's role in the churches of the Lycus valley, such a scenario seems extremely improbable.

---

[21]See B. Reicke, "The Historical Setting of Colossians," *Review and Expositor: A Baptist Theological Journal* 70 (1973): 432. For a critique of this suggestion see H. Blanke and M. Barth, *Colossians: A New Translation with Introduction and Commentary*, trans. A. B. Beck, AB 34B (New York: Doubleday, 1994) 18-19.

Another possibility is that Aristarchus the Macedonian from Thessalonika was Epaphras's coevangelist. Aristarchus has an impressive list of credentials that well qualify him for the title. He was one of Paul's traveling companions and had been with Paul in Ephesus during the life-threatening encounter with Demetrius and the silversmiths (Acts 19:29). He traveled with Paul on his return from Greece to Macedonia and then went ahead of him to Troas (Acts 20:1-5); he also journeyed with Paul from Caesarea to Rome and probably shared the apostle's imprisonment there (Acts 27:2). In addition, Paul describes him as one of his fellow workers (Colossians 4:11; Philemon 24), and one of his fellow-prisoners (Colossians 4:10). Aristarchus was present with Paul when the letters to Colossae and Philemon were being composed, and sends his greetings within both, thus demonstrating his interest in, and commitment to, the Christians concerned.

A third possibility to consider is Timothy, particularly since he is exhorted to "do the work of an evangelist" (ἔργον ποίησον εὐαγγελιστοῦ) and thereby fulfill his ministry (2 Timothy 4:5). Timothy undoubtedly enjoyed a special relationship with the apostle Paul and is mentioned more frequently in his letters, and with greater variety of expression, than any other person. He is described by Paul as a "brother" (ὁ ἀδελφός) in 1 Thessalonians 3:2; 2 Corinthians 1:1; Philemon 1; as a "fellow-worker" (ὁ συνεργός) in 1 Thessalonians 3:2 and Romans 16:21; and as "my beloved and faithful child in the Lord (ὅς ἐστίν μου τέκνον ἀγαπητὸν καὶ πιστὸν ἐν κυρίῳ) in 1 Corinthians 4:17. In Philippians 2:20-22 Paul speaks of Timothy as a father would speak of a much-beloved son. The fact that Timothy's name appears in the prescript of five of Paul's letters (1 Thessalonians 1:1; 2 Corinthians 1:1; Philippians 1:1; Colossians 1:1; and Philemon 1) is generally taken to indicate his role as Paul's co-writer or amanuensis. On the strength of 1 Thessalonians 2:6, it could be argued that Timothy should be regarded as an apostle. Timothy also figures frequently in Acts, predominantly as one of Paul's traveling companions on the various missionary journeys. In short, Timothy certainly was in the thick of things as far as the spread of Christianity in the initial stages was concerned. However, neither Timothy nor Aristarchus is explicitly described as "an evangelist" (εὐαγγελιστής), as one might reasonably expect to be the case. Indeed, there is only one person in the New Testament who is accorded that title, namely Philip the Evangelist (Acts 21:8). Could Philip, as well as Epaphras, have exercised his evangelist's ministry within the church at Hierapolis?

Much circumstantial evidence is supportive of this suggestion. Philip appears in several passages in Acts, many of them portraying him as a wandering preacher with considerable gifts and abilities. We first encounter Philip in Acts 6:5-6 where he is listed as one of the seven deacons selected from among the Hellenists to assist the apostles. Following the death of Stephen (recorded in Acts 7:54-60), Philip leaves Jerusalem and goes to Samaria where he is instrumental in the conversion of Simon (Acts 8:4-13). He next appears on the road between Jerusalem and Gaza where he encounters the Ethiopian eunuch (Acts 8:26-39), before going on to the city of Azotus and eventually settling in Caesarea (Acts 8:40). It is in Caesarea where we find Philip the Evangelist and his four daughters entertaining Paul and his traveling companions for a few days as they are on the way to Jerusalem (Acts 21:8-10). This ends the biblical testimony about Philip the Evangelist. However, he surfaces elsewhere in early Christian writings, which link him closely with the city of Hierapolis in Phrygia.

An association with Hierapolis is made at several points in the writings of Eusebius (ca. 260–340), the bishop of Caesarea. Four passages in Eusebius's *Ecclesiastical History* (*HE*) are of special note in this regard, although it appears that by this stage the fusion of Philip the Apostle with Philip the Evangelist is complete. The first appears in *HE* 3.31.2-3 where Eusebius discusses a letter from Polycrates, the bishop of Ephesus, which was written to Victor, bishop of Rome. Eusebius says of the letter:

> In this he mentions both John, Philip the apostle, and Philip's daughters as follows: "For great luminaries sleep in Asia, and they will rise again at the last day of the advent of the Lord, when he shall come back with glory from heaven and call back all the saints, such as was Philip, one of the twelve apostles, who sleeps at Hierapolis with his two daughters who grew old as virgins and his third daughter who lived in the Holy Spirit and rests in Ephesus. And there is also John, who leaned on the Lord's breast, who was a priest wearing the mitre, and martyr and teacher, and he sleeps at Ephesus."

Substantially the same section of the letter from Polycrates to Victor and the church is repeated in *HE* 5.24.2, although in this instance it is invoked as one of the reasons for the bishops of Asia to insist on a traditional chronology in what has come to be known as the Quartodeciman controversy.[22] The relevant section from *Ecclesiastical History*, which quotes from the letter of Polycrates, reads:

> Therefore we keep the day undeviatingly, neither adding to nor taking away, for in Asia great luminaries sleep, and they will rise on the day of the coming of the Lord, when he shall come with glory from heaven and seek out all the saints. Such were Philip of the twelve apostles, and two of his daughters who grew old as virgins, who sleep in Hierapolis, and another daughter of his, who lived in the Holy Spirit, rests at Ephesus.

The third passage comes from *HE* 3.31.4 in which Eusebius mentions another source, this time one that is attributed to a man named Gaius. We read:

> And in the dialogue of Gaius, which we mentioned a little earlier, Proclus, with whom he was disputing, speaks thus about the death of Philip and his daughters and agrees with what has been stated. "After him the four daughters of Philip who were prophetesses were at Hierapolis in Asia. Their grave is there and so is their father's."[23]

Fourthly, Eusebius mentions Philip in *HE* 3.39.3 and channels a story about him through the figure of Papias (ca. 60–130) the bishop of Hierapolis.

> It has already been mentioned that Philip the Apostle lived at Hierapolis with his daughters, but it must now be shown how Papias was with them and received a wonderful story from the daughters of Philip; for he relates the resurrection of a corpse in his time and in another place another miracle connected with Justus surnamed Barabas, for he drank poison but by the Lord's grace suffered no harm.

---

[22]This was a debate about whether or not it was proper for Christians to follow the Jewish calendar and always to observe Easter on Nisan 14, regardless of the day of the week on which it fell. The Asiatic churches refused to comply with the dictates of Pope Victor on the subject, and Polycrates of Ephesus was excommunicated for his role in the matter. See F. E. Brightman, "The Quartodeciman Question," *JTS* 25 (1923): 254-70.

[23]Eusebius then goes on to cite Acts 21:8-9 about Philip and his four daughters living with their father in Caesarea in Judea (*HE* 31.3.5).

One other ancient document is worth mentioning here, in that it too associates Philip the Evangelist with the city of Hierapolis in Phrygia in Asia Minor. This is the *Acts of Philip*, a work that probably dates to the late fourth or early fifth century, but that includes many interesting legends and stories about Philip (the Apostle and the Evangelist have become identified in a single person here). The complete text of the work is no longer extant, although sections have survived in Greek, Syriac, Latin, Slavonic, and Coptic. It appears that originally the work contained fifteen sections, or acts, together with an account known as the *Martyrdom of Philip* (apparently an earlier independent work that was incorporated at some stage into the *Acts of Philip* although it still exists as a separate document in some manuscripts). The most important section for our consideration is found at the beginning of *Acts of Philip* 13 where Philip and his companions arrive in Hierapolis:

> In the days of Trajan, after the Martyrdom of Simon, son of Clopas, bishop of Jerusalem, successor to James, Philip the apostle was preaching through all the cities of Lydia and Asia. And he came to the city of Ophioryme, which is called Hierapolis of Asia, and he was received by Stachys, a believer. And with him were Bartholomew, one of the Seventy, and his sister Mariamne, and their disciples. And they assembled at Stachys' house. And Mariamne sat and listened to Philip discoursing. He spoke of the snares of the dragon, who has no shape in creation, and is recognized and shunned by beasts and birds. For the men of the place worshipped the snake and had images of it; and called Hierapolis Ophioryme.[24]

This identification of the city of Ophioryme ("Snakes' Way") with Hierapolis is explicitly made in some, but not all, of the surviving manuscripts of the *Acts of Philip*.[25] It is not clear whether such identification is made in the so-called *Martyrdom of Philip*.[26] In fact, one intriguing

---

[24]J. K. Elliott, *The Apocryphal New Testament: A Collection of Apocryphal Christian Literature in an English Translation* (Oxford: Clarendon, 1993) 516.

[25]For details, see F. Bovon, "Les Actes de Philippe," in *Aufstieg und Niedergang der römischen Welt: Geschichte und Kultur Roms im Spiegel der neueren Forschung*, ed. H. Wolfgang and T. Hildegard (Berlin: De Gruyter, 1988) 4493-94.

[26]Bovon, "Les Actes de Philippe," 4450-52, suggests that the *Mart. Phil.* raises doubts about the identification between Ophioryme and Hierapolis that occurs

manuscript of the *Martyrdom of Philip*, at the Bodleian Library in Oxford, explicitly distinguishes between Ophioryme and Hierapolis in that it describes the removal of the Apostle Philip's remains from Ophioryme to Hierapolis, where a fifth-century church was later built in his honor.[27] This manuscript, designated *Codex Broccianus* 180, was part of the collection of Giacomo Barocci and came into possession of the Bodleian Library in 1629. It dates to the twelfth century and contains 219 leaves, twelve of which are given over to the *Martyrdom of Philip* (folia 70b-82a). The first page of the *Martyrdom of Philip* gives the title of the work along with an opening line:

> The Mart. Phil. the holy Apostle, when Philip, the Apostle of Christ, was locked up in the temple of the snake by the governor.
> (μαρτύριον τοῦ ἁγιοῦ ἀποστόλοῦ Φιλίππου, ὅτε δὲ Φίλιππος, ὁ τοῦ Χριστοῦ ἀπόστολος, κατεκλείσθη ἐν τῷ ἱερῷ τῆς ἐχίδνης ὑπὸ τοῦ ἡγέμενου.)

However, some manuscripts of the *Acts of Philip* do explicitly identify Ophioryme with Hierapolis. In short, it seems that one strand of tradition goes a step further than the legends recorded in the *Martyrdom of Philip* in that it identifies the "Snakes' Way" with a particular place—the Phrygian city of Hierapolis. The key question thus becomes: Why is such an identification made? One important recent proposal is worth considering briefly.

The legendary story of a conflict between Philip and the snake-worshippers of Hierapolis has been the subject of a fascinating study of the *Acts of Philip* by Frédéric Amsler.[28] Amsler builds upon the numismat-

---

in the *Acts Phil.*

[27]The ruins of the Philip Martyrium are located in the upper part of the city, east of its impressive amphitheatre. The building has a square outer foundation, measuring approximately 20x20 meters, and housed an octagonal complex that included a cross-shaped central aisle. For more on the church ruins, including a map and photographs, see G. E. Bean, *Turkey Beyond the Maeander: An Archaeological Guide* (London: Benn, Rowman & Littlefield, 1971) 243-45; K. Tevhit, *Pamukkale* (Istanbul: Hitit Colour, 1996) 68-71.

[28]F. Amsler, "The Apostle Philip, the Viper, the Leopard, and the Kid, the Masked Actors of a Religious Conflict in Hierapolis of Phrygia (*Acts of Philip* VIII-XV and *Martyrdom*)," in *Society of Biblical Literature Seminar Papers*, ed.

ic evidence from Hierapolis, noting coins issued by the city which depict snakes as an animal associated with cultic worship of the Phrygian goddess Cybele. As it presently stands, the *Acts of Philip* contains a number of fantastic stories and is littered with bizarre images, but Amsler nonetheless detects a thread of continuity in the work, a reading of it that is supported by hints of the geographical features of the city of Hierapolis itself. In the end, he suggests that the *Acts of Philip* contains a sustained polemic by the Christians of Hierapolis against the cult of Cybele and suggests that this debate probably dates to the second half of the fourth century. I would concur with Amsler's creative suggestion in every respect except one—the date of the conflict between the Christian believers in Hierapolis and the followers of the cult of Cybele. There is really no reason for such a clash to be dated as late as the second half of the fourth century; the essential components are all in place well before that time. Christians are known to have been in the Lycus Valley since the time of the Pauline mission, and worship of Cybele in the region was considerably earlier than that. In other words, there is every reason to suppose that the conflict may have taken place much earlier, perhaps soon after Philip the Evangelist (Apostle?) arrived in Hierapolis and participated in the establishment of the Christian congregation there.

The passing references to Philip in Eusebius's *Ecclesiastical History*, together with the material in the *Acts of Philip*, certainly make for interesting reading. They suggest there was a long-standing association between Philip the Evangelist and the city of Hierapolis, and this, together with his explicit designation as an evangelist, lends credence to the proposal that the writer of Ephesians may be alluding to him in 4:11 when listing "evangelists" among those given by God through his Spirit to the church.

Summary

I began this study by noting what is a new proposal for reading Ephesians, one that sees it as an epistle written by an unnamed disciple of Paul to the church in Hierapolis in the Lycus valley. The proposal was then made that the reference to "the evangelists" (οἱ εὐαγγελισταί) in Ephesians 4:11 is a deliberate allusion by the writer to the church's own

---

Eugene H. Lovering, Jr. (Atlanta: Scholars, 1996) 432-37.

history and harks back to the founding ministries of Paul's special envoy Epaphras and of Philip the Evangelist. In support of this proposal, the New Testament witness to the life and ministry of Epaphras, meager though it is, was summarized, and his close connection with the Lycus Valley churches was noted. Next, the role of evangelists within the overall ministry of the church was discussed and their connection with apostolic ministry observed. Various characters in the pages of the New Testament who could have been evangelists in these churches, or whose ministry was evangelistic in nature, were then examined, including Barnabas, Aristarchus, Timothy, and Philip the Evangelist. Finally, the testimony of Eusebius's *Ecclesiastical History* and the apocryphal *Acts of Philip* was noted as especially important, given that they link Philip with the city of Hierapolis.

Clearly, the writer of Ephesians includes a reference to "evangelists" in 4:11 for a reason, and the evidence suggests the reason is bound up with the ministries of Epaphras and Philip to the church in Hierapolis. Together these two men are Hierapolis's undercover evangelists.

"In Christ": Key to the Tension in Paul's Eschatological Thought

Manfred T. Brauch
Eastern Baptist Theological Seminary

A continuing, much-debated area in Pauline Studies is the Pauline eschatology with its complexity and variety in eschatological formulations and concepts. At the heart of this debate is the question: How is this diversity in Paul's eschatology to be understood? Or more specifically, how are apparently contradictory elements to be reconciled? It is the purpose of this study to make a constructive contribution to this discussion by a review and an assessment of representative solutions and by exploring how Paul's understanding of the relationship between Christ and the believer may provide a key for the juxtaposition of diverse (and contradictory) eschatological ideas in Paul.

It has long been recognized that the Pauline writings contain essentially two distinct formulations of Paul's conviction about the destiny of believers. On the one hand is the conviction that "the age to come," which has already broken into history in the event of Christ (1 Corinthians 10:11), will come to its climax in the parousia and that this event will be accompanied by the resurrection of the dead and their being gathered into eternal fellowship with Christ (1 Thessalonians 4–5; 1 Corinthians 15). On the other hand, Paul seems convinced that death cannot separate the believer from Christ (Romans 8:23) and that therefore the individual believer's death is that event where transition takes place from this earthbound existence into eternal fellowship with Christ (Philippians 1:23-24; 2 Corinthians 4:16–5:10).[1] Various solutions for this apparently contradictory duality have been proposed.

The Theory of Development in Paul's Thought

A dominant theme in the study of Paul's eschatological thought is that his ideas developed rather dramatically, that environment, historical

[1] G. B. Caird, *New Testament Theology*, ed. L. D. Hurst (Oxford: Clarendon, 1994) 243-46.

realities, and personal experiences forced him to undergo significant changes in his thinking and that these can be traced in his correspondence.[2] If Paul, as an apocalyptic Jew,[3] shared with the earliest Christian community an eschatology with its end-historical expectations, then it is likely that as he carried the gospel into an increasingly Hellenistic environment his eschatology would need to be modified and transformed in keeping with Hellenistic ideas.

The pressures of such a changing environment have not been seen as the only factors in Paul's alleged thought development. Much discussion has centered on the concept of the delay of the Parousia.[4] It is argued that Paul, together with the early church, expected the imminent return of Christ and the establishment of the messianic kingdom in all its apocalyptic glory.[5] When this expectation remained unfulfilled, the belief in the Parousia of Christ was brought into association with the apocalyptic vision of the resurrection of the dead, in order to make it possible for those Christians who had died before the Parousia to participate in this glorious event (thus 1 Thessalonians). However, as the fervent expectation of the Parousia faded even more into the background due to its delay, and as Christians became ever more Hellenized, intimations of immortality came to the fore, replacing a distant Parousia with immediate blessedness at death.[6]

---

[2]See, e.g., the treatment of developmental theories in J. Lowe, "An Examination of Attempts to Detect Development in St. Paul's Thought," *JTS* 42 (1941): 129-42; and in V. P. Furnish, "Development in Paul's Thought," *Journal of the American Academy of Religion* 38 (1970): 287-303. Cf. the more recent proponents of developmental theories in Paul's eschatological thought, such as C. L. Mearns, "Early Eschatology and Development in Paul," *NTS* 27 (1981): 137-57; U. Schnelle, *Wandlungen im paulinischen Denken*, Stuttgarter Bibelstudien 137 (Stuttgart: Verlag Katholisches Bibelwerk, 1989) 37-48.

[3]J. C. Beker, *Paul the Apostle: The Triumph of God in Life and Thought* (Philadelphia: Fortress, 1980), reflects the dominant view that Paul's faith was deeply grounded in and influenced by the apocalyptic strain within Judaism.

[4]E.g., E. Grässer, *Das Problem der Parusieverzögerung in den synoptischen Evangelien und in der Apostelgeschichte*, Beihefte zur Zeitschrift für die neutestamentliche Wissenschaft und die kunde der älteren Kirche 22 (Berlin: Töpelmann, 1960).

[5]Acts 1:6 reflects this expectation; cf. 1 Cor 7:26, 31.

[6]Texts such as 2 Cor 4:16-5:10 and Phil 1:21-24 were understood to support

Beside the movement in the early church from Judaism to Hellenism and the issue of the delay of the parousia as factors in the development of Paul's eschatology, some scholars have accounted for it on the basis of personal crises in the life of Paul. Thus, as Paul became increasingly subject to the threat of persecution and the possibility of his own death, he found the prospect of lying in the grave until the Parousia increasingly unappealing and realized that his older views did not correspond with Christ's own *immediate* resurrection.[7] This experience resulted in the adoption of Hellenistic or Hellenized categories with which to describe the fate of the individual at death and beyond it.

While it is impossible within the compass of this essay to do justice to the complexity and immensity of the discussion which has centered around the issue of development in Paul's thought, some important, representative contributions need briefly to be discussed.

1. The Pressure of Environment

Studies of Pauline eschatology have been dominated by the supposition that the early Pauline conception of a future resurrection was eventually displaced by the hope of immediate entrance into the full blessings of redemption upon death. A classical statement of this idea is that of R. H. Charles, who outlines the movement of the Pauline eschatology in a chapter entitled "The Pauline Eschatology in Its Four Stages."[8] Charles finds in Paul "no single eschatological system," but rather eschatology "in a state of development" from "an expectation of the future that he had inherited largely from Judaism"[9] to a spiritual conception of resurrection at the time of the believer's departure in

---

this view.

[7]See C. H. Buck and G. Taylor, *Saint Paul: A Study of the Development of His Thought* (New York: Scribner's, 1969).

[8]R. H. Charles, *Eschatology: The Doctrine of a Future Life in Israel, Judaism, and Christianity. A Critical History*, with an introduction by G. W. Buchanan, Schocken Paperbacks (repr.: New York: Schocken Books, 1963; orig. 1899) 437. Cf. A. M. Hunter, *Paul and His Predecessors*, Hastie Lectures in the University of Glasgow 1939, new rev. ed. (London: SCM, 1961) 98, who essentially follows Charles's scheme.

[9]Charles, *Eschatology*, 437.

death.[10] For Charles, this development—"in the course of which the heterogeneous elements were for the most part silently dropped"—took place "under the influence of great formative Christian conceptions," particularly the conception of the believer's spiritual fellowship with Christ.[11] It is clear in Charles's treatment that he views the transformation of Pauline eschatology, though motivated internally by the apostle's deepening faith, as dependent upon increasingly Hellenistic conceptions.

A very clear statement of the supposed Hellenization of Paul's eschatological thought is that by W. A. Knox.[12] Knox argues that Paul's experience at Athens (Acts 17:16-34) convinced him that the eschatological presentation of the Gospel would not make sense in a Gentile world, and that "from this point forward his epistles show a progressive adaptation of the Christian message to the general outlook of the Hellenistic world.[13] He sees this process already apparent in 1 Corinthians, with its doctrine of a "spiritualized resurrection," though Paul did not go far enough here. "It appears," says Knox, "that Paul's admission of the immaterial nature of the risen body . . . was not enough to satisfy the Corinthians. The second epistle is largely devoted to a complete revision of Pauline eschatology in a Hellenistic sense."[14] According to Knox, then, the Hellenization of Paul's eschatological thought arose out of a crisis of thought. It was the result of a need felt to restate the Gospel in terms understood by the Hellenistic world.

2. The "Delay of the Parousia"

Other scholars, though remaining within the orbit of a movement from Judaism to Hellenism in Paul's eschatology, view the pressure of the delay of the Parousia as the basic factor in Paul's development. A distinction is made between a sleep-like interim, connected with the assurance of a Parousia experience, and a Hellenistically oriented assurance of immediate union with Christ at death. "The delay of the expected parousia . . . and the increasingly exclusive grounding of

---

[10]Ibid., 456-63.

[11]Ibid., 437, 449.

[12]W. L. Knox, *St. Paul and the Church of the Gentiles* (Cambridge: Cambridge University Press, 1939).

[13]Ibid., 26.

[14]Ibid., 128.

Christianity in Hellenistic soil, led to this historic transformation."[15] Similarly, O. Kuss explains the supposed later conceptions in Paul's eschatology as the result of the further development of previous conceptions, motivated by the delay of the Parousia, and asserts that the later conceptions betray the influence of Hellenistic thought.[16]

3. Personal Crises as Motivating Forces

Some find the central motivating force for what they see as transformation in Paul's eschatology in the personal crises of the threat of death and reject the idea of the Hellenization of his thought as the cause. This line of interpretation was particularly emphasized by C. H. Dodd in his noted lectures on "The Mind of Paul: Change and Development."[17]

Dodd's understanding of Paul's thought is greatly influenced by his conviction that Paul underwent considerable spiritual and psychological development, centering in a kind of "second conversion" around the time of the writing of 2 Corinthians. Dodd argues that initially, Paul's faith was fitted into an apocalyptic framework which persisted, with but slight change in emphasis, through 1 Corinthians. Thereafter, "the thought of the imminence of the Advent retires into the background."[18] With reference to 2 Corinthians 1:8-9, Dodd argues that the extreme danger of death in which Paul had recently stood altered his outlook in this respect. He has faced the possibility that he will "go to stay with the Lord" through death, for he "has become reconciled to experience."[19]

In their full-scale treatment of the idea of development in Paul's thought, Charles Buck and Greer Taylor[20] identify two crises that forced

---

[15]P. Hoffmann, *Die Toten in Christus: Eine religionsgeschichtliche und exegetische Untersuchung zur paulinischen Eschatologie*, NTAbh 2 (Münster: Aschendorff, 1966) 9.

[16]O. Kuss, *Der Römerbrief Übersetzt und Erklärt* (Regensburg: Pustet, 1959) 322-23.

[17]C. H. Dodd, *New Testament Studies* (Manchester: Manchester University Press, 1953) 80-113.

[18]Ibid.

[19]Ibid., 108; cf. W. D. Davies, *Paul and Rabbinic Judaism*, Torchbook Edition (New York: Harper & Row, 1957) 319, who contends that 2 Cor reflects the result of a "crisis of experience, the necessity to reconcile himself to death as a physical event," and that it is not the result of a process of Hellenization.

[20]Buck and Taylor, *Saint Paul*.

Paul to shift his position within a very short period of time: the death of some Christians before the parousia and, even more significant for his new position, the experience of persecution in Asia and the threat of his own imminent death (cf. 2 Corinthians 1:8-10).[21] Paul's eschatology is portrayed as developing in unilinear fashion primarily as modification, extension, elaboration, and revision of his own earlier teaching, in dialogue with those who are responding to that teaching. The authors contend that the teaching of 1 Corinthians 15 about a spiritual resurrection of Christians who have died before the parousia and a similar spiritual transformation of those who are still alive at the parousia carries Paul's teaching "one step further" than it was in 1 Thessalonians. They assume that the "mode" of resurrection in 1 Thessalonians 4 is other than in 1 Corinthians 15. The next step in the development is seen to result largely from the second crisis in Paul's experience and is reflected in 2 Corinthians. Whereas in 1 Corinthians 15 the transformation of the believer is seen as instantaneous, in 2 Corinthians 4–5 it is seen as lifelong and gradual (cf. 2 Corinthians 3:18)

Further, in Philippians 1:23, and possibly already in 2 Corinthians 5:6, Paul seems to conceive of the individual's resurrection immediately upon death, rather than being delayed until the parousia, as in 1 Thessalonians 4 and 1 Corinthians 15.[22] The presence of the Parousia motif in Philippians 3:20-21 is accounted for by placing the writing of Philippians between 1 and 2 Corinthians as a "transitional" letter where "both systems" (that of an awaited parousia and that of an immediate resurrection upon death) operate.[23] Thus, Paul is pictured as a man constantly in the process of "reexamining" and "revising" his thought so that no random elements remain.[24]

Tension and diversity within Paul's mature thought are excluded.

Evaluation of Development Theories

We have briefly presented the main directions that the thesis of development in Paul's eschatology has taken. Whatever factors are

---

[21]Ibid., 58.
[22]Ibid., 42, 54, 56.
[23]Ibid., 71, 234, 239.
[24]Ibid., 16.

isolated as the cause or motivation for the supposed development in Paul's thought, it is understood by all advocates of development to move from an early (Jewish/Early Palestinian Christian) view, as expressed in 1 Thessalonians, toward an increasingly "spiritualized," "Christianized," or "Hellenized" view, as expressed in 2 Corinthians 5 and Philippians 1.

A fundamental assumption behind this understanding of Paul's eschatological development is that a clear distinction could be drawn between Palestinian Judaism and Hellenistic Judaism in the time of Paul, and that therefore the "Hellenistic" and "Jewish" elements could be isolated and traced in the writings of Paul.[25] However, the existence of such a dichotomy has been increasingly questioned.

It is the considered judgment of Davies that "in Paul, Athens and Jerusalem are strangely mixed . . . because the Judaism within which he grew up, even in Jerusalem, was largely hellenized, and the Hellenism which he encountered in his travels, largely Judaized."[26]

Davies and others[27] have clearly demonstrated that many elements in Paul's thought, which are often labeled as Hellenistic, might well be

---

[25]A. Schweitzer, *The Mysticism of Paul the Apostle*, trans. W. Montgomery (London: Black, 1931), who understands Paul as dominated by Palestinian apocalyptic ideas; and C. G. Montefiore, *Judaism and St. Paul: Two Essays* (London: Goschen, 1914), who interprets Paul in terms of Hellenistic categories, both by way of Diaspora Judaism and direct contact with pagan Hellenism. Cf. S. Sandmel, *The Genius of Paul* (New York: Schocken Books, 1969); and E. R. Goodenough, "Paul and the Hellenization of Christianity," in *Religions in Antiquity: Essays in Memory of Erwin Ramsdell Goodenough*, ed. J. Neusner, Studies in the History of Religions 14 (Leiden: Brill, 1968) 23-68.

[26]Davies, *Paul and Rabbinic Judaism*, vii, x-xi.

[27]See, e.g., the studies by S. Lieberman, *Greek in Jewish Palestine: Studies in the Life and Manners of Jewish Palestine in the II-IV Centuries* C.E. (New York: Jewish Theological Seminary of America, 1942); and idem, *Hellenism in Jewish Palestine: Studies in the Literary Transmission, Beliefs and Manners of Palestine in the I Century* B.C.E.*–IV Century* C.E., Texts and Studies of the Jewish Theological Seminary of America 18 (New York: Jewish Theological Seminary of America, 1950); also R. Meyer, *Hellenistisches in der rabbinischen Anthropologie: Rabbinische vorstellungen vom Werden des Menschen*, BWANT 22 (Stuttgart: Kohlhammer, 1937): "[E]ven Rabbinic Judaism did not shut itself off against the religious-philosophical thought of Hellenism. . . . It is evident that the Palestinian Judaism of the Hellenistic period learned in the school of the Greeks."

derived from Palestinian Judaism. So we need not look to Paul's Hellenistic environment (in his later mission activity and correspondence) as the source for certain aspects of his thought.

The discovery of the Qumran literature has further undermined the thesis of the supposed clear dichotomy between Hellenistic and Hellenistic-Jewish thought on the one hand, and Palestinian-Jewish thought, on the other.[28] If Hellenistic influence can be traced in the New Testament, argues Cullmann, it is thereby not automatically late.[29] It is a false idea that Christianity was at first merely Jewish and later became Hellenistic. There was a Jewish Hellenism—by which Cullmann does not mean Diaspora Judaism—before there was a Christian Hellenism. Thus, "the evolution which is generally supposed from early narrow Judaistic Christianity to a later universalistic, Hellenistic Christianity is an artificial scheme that does not correspond to historical reality."[30] Both tendencies existed in the primitive church and "the history of primitive Christianity is the interplay of these two tendencies, both of them present from the beginning in the primitive church . . . because both found their roots in forms of Judaism present in Palestine."[31]

Thus, the assumption of a rather rapid, linear movement in the early church from Judaism to Hellenism and with it a transformation from "apocalyptic eschatology" to "Hellenistic eschatology" in Paul's thought must be called into question. The rejection of these dominant assumptions also has implications for the other aspects of developmental theories in Paul's eschatology.

The early Christian hope certainly included the intense expectation of the return of Christ, of the coming of the Son of Man in triumph. Paul shared that hope, as is evident from 1 Thessalonians 4:13-18. But can it be demonstrated that this intense expectation of the parousia was Paul's only eschatological expectation and that it was replaced, because of its

---

[28]F. M. Cross, "The Contributions of the Qumran Discoveries to the Study of the Biblical Text," *Israel Exploration Journal* 16 (1966).

[29]O. Cullmann, "The Significance of the Qumran Texts for Research into the Beginnings of Christianity," *JBL* 74 (1955); reprinted in *The Scrolls and the New Testament*, ed. K. Stendahl (New York: Harper, 1957); page references below are to the reprint.

[30]Ibid., 19.

[31]Ibid., 30.

delay, by the concept of immediate union with Christ at death? Is it possible that even as early as 1 Thessalonians, the idea of being with Christ at death is present side by side with the expectation of the yet outstanding parousia? Some exegetes place 1 Thessalonians 5:10 ("so that whether we are awake or sleep we may live with him") on the same level as 2 Corinthians 5:6-8 and Philippians 1:21-23, claiming that it affirms continuing fellowship with Christ at death.[32]

In addition, if we date 1 Thessalonians in 50/51 CE and 2 Corinthians in 55/56 (together with the broad scholarly consensus[33]) why would the delay of the parousia have effected such a radical transformation within five years, when during Paul's formative period, from his conversion in the early 30s to the writing of 1 Thessalonians almost twenty years later, the intense expectation of the parousia continued undiminished? Such a radical shift in such a short period of time appears inherently improbable.[34] On the basis of his meticulous study of Pauline chronology, mission strategy and theology, Reiner Riesner concludes that far-reaching divergences in Paul's eschatological views "seem to be the result of overly astute constructions. Although chronology was indeed an important factor in the *development* of Pauline theology, it cannot bear the burden of demonstrating radical, fundamental *transformation*.[35]

Complementing these observations is the recognition that in the late Pauline letters (Romans, 56/57 CE; Philippians, 60-62 CE[36]), the fervent

---

[32]P. Feine, *Theologie des neuen Testaments* (Berlin: Evangelische Verlagsanstalt, 1951) 283; cf. J. Müller, *Der Lebensbegriff des Heiligen Paulus* (Wien: n.p., 1940) 62, who holds that the expression "the dead in Christ" in 1 Thess 4:16 expresses the idea of a continuing fellowship with Christ immediately upon death.

[33]See, e.g., B. Witherington, *The Paul Quest: The Renewed Search for the Jew of Tarsus* (Downers Grove: InterVarsity, 1998) 304-31; *DPHL*, 115-22.

[34]A. L. Moore, *The Parousia in the New Testament*, NovTSup 13 (Leiden: Brill, 1966) 61.

[35]R. Riesner, *Paul's Early Period: Chronology, Mission Strategy, Theology* (Grand Rapids: Eerdmans, 1998) 415. Cf. B. Witherington, *Jesus, Paul, and the End of the World: A Comparative Study in New Testament Eschatology* (Downers Grove: InterVarsity, 1992) 152-231, for an extensive refutation of the idea that Paul's eschatology changed radically during the course of his writings.

[36]If Phil is dated during an earlier Ephesian imprisonment, around 54/55 CE (thus G. F. Hawthorne, *Philippians*, WBC 43 [Waco: Word, 1983] xxvi-xxxix; R. Jewett, *A Chronology of Paul's Life* [Philadelphia: Fortress, 1979] 103;

expectation of the parousia appears undiminished (Romans 13:11-14; Philippians 3:20-21; 4:5). Particularly noteworthy is the juxtaposition in Philippians of the parousia expectation with the affirmation of immediate fellowship with Christ at death.

A third motivation for alleged transformation of Paul's thought, which is closely associated with the delay of the parousia, is the crisis of impending death. Even in a relatively short period such a crisis could, it is held, bring about the radical change postulated. Paul faces the possibility of his own death; yet the Lord's return is outstanding. The conjunction of these realities forces Paul to rethink his position and the result of that process is reflected in 2 Corinthians 5 and Philippians 1.

The weightiest response to such a construction of events is located in the very text used in support of this idea (2 Corinthians 1:8-10), where Paul speaks of persecution in Asia and the threat of death. For it is clear from 1:10 that Paul has received a stay of execution, a reprieve. He has been rescued from imminent danger and is convinced that God will rescue him from future threats to his life.[37] Nothing in this text hints at anxiety about the prospect of not living until the parousia. Coupled with the fact, as argued earlier, that the parousia expectation is still a lively conviction of Paul in his late letters, it is unlikely that the crisis in Asia caused a major shift in Paul's eschatology.

In summary, the Pauline eschatology is not best understood when seen in terms of significant transformation, whatever the reasons proposed for it. How then can the variety in Paul's eschatological formulations and conception be understood?

G. Lüdemann, *Paul, Apostle to the Gentiles: Studies in Chronology* [Philadelphia: Fortress, 1984] 268), then we have within the same period of about two to three years both expectations of the parousia/resurrection (1 Cor 15; Phil 3:20-21) and belief in an immediate presence with Christ at death (2 Cor 5; Phil 1:21-23).

[37]B. Witherington, *Conflict and Community in Corinth: A Socio-Rhetorical Commentary on 1 and 2 Corinthians* (Grand Rapids: Eerdmans, 1995) 362; E. Best, *Second Corinthians*, IBC (Atlanta: John Knox, 1987) 14; R. P. Martin, *2 Corinthians*, WBC 40 (Waco: Word, 1986) 12-17.

Attempts at a Unified View

Some have attempted to secure for Paul a unified view of end-time expectations, either by appeal to particular exceptions, or by subordinating certain ideas to a larger, dominant view (such as parousia/resurrection) and integrating them into that larger view.

There is, for example, the idea that the expectation of Philippians 1:23 is to be understood as the special privilege of the martyrs. Schweitzer, for whom Paul is a thoroughgoing apocalyptic Jew to the end, reasons that, in view of a martyr's death, Paul expects his union with Christ in imminent resurrection.[38] Commenting on the same text, Lohmeyer states, "if death is gain, it is so exclusively for the martyr. Only for him is it the crown of martyrdom, filled with the blessing of being eternally with Christ."[39]

Others interpret the expectation of believers' presence with Christ immediately after death as an intermediate reality between death and the parousia. Thus, Ridderbos maintains that Philippians 1:21-23 clearly refers to the condition of believers after death, and that the expectation of being "clothed with our heavenly dwelling" (2 Corinthians 5:2) is to be understood in no other way as that which takes place at Christ's coming, in keeping with 1 Corinthians 15:53-54.[40]

Witherington holds that Paul's point in 2 Corinthians 5 "is that he longs to bypass the intermediate condition altogether and allow this mortality to be swallowed up by real life—life in the resurrection body. In short, he would rather live on earth until the resurrection."[41]

---

[38]Schweitzer, *Mysticism of Paul the Apostle*, 136.

[39]E. Lohmeyer, *Die Briefe an die Philipper, an die Kolosser, und an Philemon*, KEKNT 9 (Göttingen: Vandenhoeck & Ruprecht, 1953) 64.

[40]H. N. Ridderbos, *Paul: An Outline of His Theology* (Grand Rapids: Eerdmans, 1975) 497-501. He thinks that Paul is able to present this intermediate state as a temporary deliverance, over against the sufferings of life in the present body. Cf. Hawthorne, *Philippians*, 49-51.

[41]Witherington, *Conflict and Community in Corinth*, 391; W. G. Kümmel, *The Theology of the New Testament according to Its Major Witnesses: Jesus-Paul-John*, trans. J. Steely (London: SCM, 1973) 242; Ridderbos, *Paul*, 506, who holds that "the idea of the *intermediate state* is no strange intrusion here. It comes to the fore of itself, as it were, when the great future is still waiting and death is never-

These attempts to discern a unified eschatological view in Paul appear to be either attempts to remove elements which do not seem to fit, from what "should be" a unified perspective, or to establish Paul as a consistent and systematic thinker. On the other hand, is it enough, with John Lowe, to discount the possibility of a unifying factor in Paul's eschatology and to describe it as a "whole wonderful muddle unarranged and alive"?[42] In that vein, some have concluded that both eschatological expectations simply stand side by side in unreconciled and irreconcilable juxtaposition.[43] Windisch gives this "unreconciled juxtaposition" a psychological rationale:

> Paul's eschatology is no unified whole, but the sum total of both independent conceptions and interdependent fragments. Paul is selective, and chooses variously from the Jewish, Hellenistic, and Christian tradition known to him, depending on his mood or need at the time. Thus it is that at one and the same time he is able to reproduce and develop mutually exclusive ideas. . . . In all this he neither recognizes, nor seeks to eliminate, the contradictory elements, because he is not a dogmatician but rather a man of tradition, intuition, impulse.[44]

---

theless an immediate reality."

[42]Lowe, "An Examination of Attempts to Detect Development in St. Paul's Thought," 142, posits four reasons for what he sees as the "baffling inconsistencies" in Paul's thought: (1) changes in mood; (2) changes in external circumstances; (3) perpetual tension between his Jewish heritage and his Christian experience; and (4) "the most satisfying reason . . . the real justification for his apparent inconsistencies, is the inherent paradoxical character of the Gospel he preaches."

[43]W. Lüken, "Der Brief an die Philipper," in *Die Schriften des neuen Testaments: Neu Übersetzt und für die Gegenwart Erklärt*, 3rd ed. (Göttingen: Vandenhoeck & Ruprecht, 1953) 308; P. Althaus, "Retractionen zur Eschatologie," *Theologische Literaturzeitung* 75 (1950): 253-58; Hawthorne, *Philippians*, 49: "No completely satisfactory resolution to the problem posed by the seeming contradictory views has yet been given, and perhaps none can be given."

[44]H. Windisch, *Der zweite Korintherbrief*, KEKNT 6 (Göttingen: Vandenhoeck & Ruprecht, 1924) 174. Contrast the view of E. P. Sanders, *Paul and Palestinian Judaism: A Comparison of Patterns of Religion* (Philadelphia: Fortress, 1977) 432-33, who does not "see any signs of major theological development in Paul's thought," though he acknowledges "alterations in the way in which he expressed himself. . . . he was not a *systematic* theologian . . . but a *coherent* thinker, despite

One may justifiably ask whether such a view of the apostle's mind—given his thorough grounding in both Rabbinic and Greek learning, as well as the evidence of the epistles, which reveal a man capable of the most complex argumentation—is at all credible.

In Christ: Key to the Dynamic Duality in Paul's Eschatology

For me, neither the various attempts to discern a unified Pauline eschatology, nor its interpretation as a "whole wonderful muddle unarranged and alive," seems to represent adequately the Pauline conception. What is correct about the latter position is the recognition of the presence, throughout the Pauline writings, of the expectation of both the parousia (with its related end-time resurrection) and an eschatological fellowship with Christ that commences with death. On the other hand, we do not agree that we are dealing here with an *unconnected* juxtaposition of these two divergent conceptions. Martin Dibelius seems to point in the right direction when he asserts that

> a juxtaposition of the eschatological expectation of the parousia and individualistic hope regarding the time after death [corresponds to the] uniqueness of Pauline faith. . . . While eschatology dovetails the end of history and final personal redemption in resurrection, faith can transfer "then comes the end" (1 Corinthians 13:10) to one's individual death.[45]

The "uniqueness of Pauline faith" consists in the dialectical, paradoxical juxtaposition of the "already" and the "not yet" aspects of the redemptive event.[46] If, as is evident throughout the Pauline epistles, there is a realized element in his eschatology, namely, that reconciliation with God has been effected (Romans 5:1) and that the new creation has begun (2 Corinthians 5:17), then for Paul this realized dimension cannot simply be suspended by death, only to be resumed in a distant eschaton, for "death . . . will not be able to separate us from the love of God in Christ Jesus our Lord" (Romans 8:38-39). The realized element persists beyond death, or better, in the face of death. At the same time, on the historical

---

the unsystematic nature of his thought and the variations in formulation."

[45]M. Dibelius, *An die Thessalonicher I, II; An die Philipper*, HNT 11 (Tübingen: Mohr, 1937) 69.

[46]Cf. Beker, *Paul the Apostle*, 152-53.

plane, the "not yet" element of eschatological fulfillment is rather conspicuous: "the creation waits with eager longing" (Romans 8:19).

For Paul, the idea of continuing redeemed reality on a personal, experiential level, which even death cannot abrogate or suspend, is not incompatible with the idea of an end-historical cosmic redemptive act involving parousia and resurrection. Both realities are for Paul grounded in the redemptive event of cross and resurrection; neither is possible without this event. Consequently, both the so-called Jewish and Hellenistic perspectives are transformed.

What to us may be inconsistencies are, for Paul, simply two sides of the same coin, two ways of looking at the same reality. From the point of view of personal-relational experience, "to be with Christ" (Philippians 1:23) is simply the continuation and culmination of the present existence "in Christ." Here, external, historical events step into the background, except for the historical event of one's death, though this becomes a rather "personal" event. On the other hand, from the point of view of the cosmic-historical process, there are the objective events of God's redemptive story: the event of Christ in history (his coming, life, death resurrection) and at the end of history (parousia, resurrection, judgment). Thus, the two views stand side-by-side, seemingly contradictory and mutually exclusive, but actually, in Paul's view, two aspects of the same reality: "life in Christ."

For Paul, the risen Christ, whom he experienced as a life-giving (Romans 8:9-10) and life-recreating (2 Corinthians 3:17-18; 5:17) spiritual presence, frees believers from bondage to the reign of sin and death (Romans 5:14, 17; 6:6) and ushers them into an existence in which life reigns. In union with Christ, the "reign of grace" begins (Romans 5:21). It is a reign characterized by life and determined by it (Romans 5:17), one that leads to "eternal life" (Romans 5:21). For those whose present existence is already "hidden with Christ in God" (Colossians 3:3), the *telos* of that existence is eternal life (Romans 6:22).

It is the present fellowship with Christ that is the foundation for life on both sides of death. In Romans, a veritable *symbiosis* between Christ and the believer is declared: "crucified with him" (6:6); "died with him" (6:8); "buried with him" (6:4); "shall be united with him" in resurrection (6:5); "shall live with him" (6:8). The use of the future tenses in vs. 5b and 8b is somewhat ambiguous. Is Paul pointing to the future resurrection of believers (at death or the parousia),[47] or to the present new life in Christ (from the point of view of the past event of "dying with Christ")?[48] While Paul may have the future specifically (or primarily) in mind, the present as qualified and empowered by Christ's resurrection and his presence in and with believers is certainly also within his field of vision here. Christians are "dead to sin and alive to God" (6:11) in the here and now. And yet, union with Christ in the present is also and always eschatologically oriented.[49]

While the conception of the believer's union with Christ is predominantly expressed by the unique Pauline formula "in Christ,"[50] only a few passages mention the dwelling of Christ in the believer. Yet the scarcity of references to this conception need not surprise us when we realize how

---

[47]So E. Lohmeyer, "*Syn Christo*," in *Festgabe für Adolf Deissmann zum 60. Geburtstag, 7. November, 1926*, ed. C. L. Schmidt (Tübingen: Mohr, 1927) 221; E. Schweizer, "Die *Mystik* des Sterbens und Auferstehens mit Christus bei Paulus," *Evangelische Theologie* 26 (1966): 239; P. J. Achtemeier, *Romans*, IBC (Atlanta: John Knox, 1985) 104-105; D. J. Moo, *The Epistle to the Romans*, NICNT (Grand Rapids: Eerdmans, 1996) 370-77.

[48]C. E. B. Cranfield, *A Critical and Exegetical Commentary on the Epistle to the Romans*, 2 vols., ICC (Edinburgh: T. & T. Clark, 1975, 1979); S. E. Porter, *Verbal Aspect in the Greek of the New Testament, with Reference to Tense and Mood*, Studies in Biblical Greek 1 (Frankfurt am Main: Peter Lang, 1989) 422-23, who claims that the future tense in these passages, given the contexts, is not to be understood temporally.

[49]On the eschatological orientation of Paul's "in Christ" mysticism, cf. M. Dibelius, "Paulus und die Mystik," in *Das Paulusbild in der neueren deutschen Forschung*, ed. K. H. Rengstorf, Wege der Forschung 24 (Darmstadt: Wissenschaftliche Buchgesellschaft, 1964) 447-74; and J. S. Stewart, *A Man in Christ: The Vital Elements of St. Paul's Religion* (New York: Harper, 1935) 199-202: "The expression of union with Christ, as Paul describes it, *looks beyond the present to the future*. . . . Eschatology does not begin where mysticism ends, nor does its presence argue a defect in the mystic's position. In point of fact, it proves the reality and intensity of his union. It is not because he has had so little of Christ that he yearns for more. It is precisely because he has had so much of Christ that he is sure God intends him for the perfect experience."

[50]The expression occurs almost 100 times in the generally acknowledged Pauline epistles (including the equivalent terms "in him," "in the Lord," and "in the Spirit").

frequently Paul refers to the indwelling of the Spirit of Christ, the Spirit of God, or simply the Spirit.[51] Thus, in speaking of the eschatological orientation of Paul's conception of the indwelling Christ and union with him, passages about the indwelling Spirit must also be considered.

Both formulations of this relational reality come together in Romans 8:9-10:

> But you are not in the flesh; you are in the Spirit,[52] since the Spirit of God dwells in you. Anyone who does not have the Spirit of Christ does not belong to him. But if Christ is in you. . . .

Not only both formulations (Christ/Spirit) of the indwelling divine reality come together here, but also the reality of life now and life in the future, as the following v. 11 shows:

> If the Spirit of him who raised Jesus from the dead dwells in you, he who raised Christ from the dead will give life to your mortal bodies also through his Spirit that dwells in you.

The indwelling Spirit/Christ[53] gives the divine life in the here and now, though this takes place in the context of "dead bodies"—that is, bodies subject to physical disintegration. However, the same indwelling presence is the basis of and cause[54] for the coming of life even to mortal

---

[51]A. Wikenhauser, *Pauline Mysticism: Christ in the Mystical Teaching of St. Paul* (Freiburg: Herder, 1960) 65-66; L. Cerfaux, *The Christian in the Theology of St. Paul*, trans. L. Soiron (New York: Herder, 1967) 312-13.

[52]F. Neugebauer, "Das Paulinische *in Christo*," *NTS* 4 (1958): 124-38, insists that the preposition "in" as used by Paul in such constructions as "in Christ" as well as "in the flesh" (Rom 7:5; 8:8,9), "in the law" (Rom 3:19; Gal 3:11, 12), "in the Spirit" (Rom 8:9; Gal 3:3; 5:8, 16), must be understood in context as "adverbial determinatives," and rendered "determined by." These realities are to be understood as "powers" which determine one's existence. Thus, to be "in Christ" or "in the Spirit" is to be related to Christ in such a way that the entirety of life is determined by the Christ event and drawn into it.

[53]Cf. A. von Schlatter, *Gottes Gerechtigkeit: Ein Kommentar zum Römerbrief* (Stuttgart: Calwer, 1959) 261: "Where his Spirit is, he is. Where the Spirit is present in faith . . . personal life becomes the place of Christ's presence."

[54]See the discussion concerning the textual variants and their meaning in O. Michel, *Der Brief an die Römer*, KEKNT 4 (Göttingen: Vandenhoeck & Ruprecht, 1963) 194.

bodies.[55] How this takes place, whether by resurrection or by transformation, whether in the event of the individual's death or at the parousia, remains unexpressed. What *is* expressed unequivocally is the certainty that the indwelling Christ, who is the Spirit (2 Corinthians 3:17-18), brings about a total redemption from death to life.[56]

Thus, the new Christian existence has its source in the Christ present in the Spirit. The "making alive" of the "mortal bodies" of believers is traced back to the Spirit who dwells in them (Romans 8:11). But this Spirit is at the same time the "Spirit of Christ" (Romans 8:9), that is to say, "Christ in you" (Romans 8:10). Paul makes this even more explicit in 1 Corinthians 15:14. Christ is, indeed, "life-giving Spirit." As the "life of Jesus" comes to expression "in our bodies" (2 Corinthians 4:10)—that is, in the context of our mortality, our earthbound human existence (2 Corinthians 4:11)—so he, as the "life-giving Spirit," is the guarantee that those "in Christ" shall be made alive (1 Corinthians 15:22).

In 2 Corinthians, the transformation of present Christian existence comes from "the Lord, the Spirit" (3:18). This Spirit-Lord is the same reality as the Spirit who has been given "into our hearts" (Romans 5:5) as a "pledge" (2 Corinthians 1:22),[57] as a guarantee "that the one who raised the Lord Jesus will raise us also with Jesus" (2 Corinthians 4:14). This indwelling presence is at the same time the guarantee (5:5) that "what is mortal may be swallowed up by life" (5:4) when movement takes place "away from the body" to being "at home with the Lord." We have here, side by side, Paul's dual eschatological orientation. And both understandings are equally undergirded by his conception of the indwelling Christ and present life in Christ.

In Philippians, we find the same juxtaposition of union with Christ and the dual eschatological perspectives. To be "found in Christ" ("in him") is the goal of Christian existence (3:9). This "being found in Christ" is defined more specifically in 3:10 in terms of "knowing Christ"

---

[55]The majority of commentaries agree that Rom 8:11 is eschatologically oriented.

[56]F. Guntermann, *Die Eschatologie des heiligen Paulus*, NTAbh 13, 4/5 (Münster: Aschendorff, 1932) 192-93: "A living relationship with Christ is the condition for the resurrection."

[57]Cf. Rom 8:23, where "the first fruits of the Spirit" is seen as the basis for the "redemption of our bodies."

and the "power of his resurrection," as well as sharing in Christ's sufferings. Here we have the expression of complete *symbiosis*, of a community of life with Christ. The goal of this complete sharing in the life of Christ is the realization of the resurrection from the dead (3:11). Paul expresses this reality of "life together" somewhat differently in 1:21-23, but the substance is the same. Life for Paul is so determined by Christ, so penetrated by him, that the very act of living is the expression of Christ's own life ("to me, living is Christ"; cf. Galatians 2:20).[58] Now it is this union in life, this being taken up into the very life of Christ, which becomes for Paul the basis for life "with Christ" (1:23) after the departure from "life in the flesh" (1:22, 24), that is, from earthbound existence. We see that here again comes to expression the close connection between union with Christ and the dual eschatological realities: immediate life with Christ on the other side of "flesh-existence" and resurrection at the parousia.[59]

In Romans we find the same pattern observed above. The bond with Christ, having been included in him and sharing in him, cannot therefore cease with death (Romans 8:38; 14:8),[60] for Christ is "Lord of both the dead and the living" (14:9). In both life and death, the believer belongs to the Lord. The relationship with Christ "that the believer enjoys in this life will continue after death with, indeed, an even fuller measure of blessing (cf. 8:18, 31-39)."[61] With this emphasis on the impossibility of separation between Christ and the believer at death is juxtaposed—in the same letter written toward the end of Paul's missionary work, ca. 56/57 CE—the continuing intense expectation of the parousia and the resurrection (13:11-12; 8:19-23). And, like in 2 Corinthians and Philippians, both eschatological realities can be affirmed on the basis of the believer's present relationship with Christ, present in the Spirit (8:9-11, 22-23; 13:14).

---

[58]Cf. J. Gnilka, *Der Philipperbrief*, Herders theologischer Kommentar zum neuen Testament 10, faszikel 3 (Freiburg: Herder, 1968) 71: "Christ is both the empowering for and the foundation of life." See also Hawthorne, *Philippians*, 44-45.

[59]Cf. Kümmel, *Theology of the New Testament*, 242: "Paul obviously is interested only in the fact that the Christian always remains in fellowship with his heavenly Lord."

[60]Ridderbos, *Paul*, 507.

[61]Moo, *Epistle to the Romans*, 845.

The conclusion to be drawn from our study lies on the surface: In terms of the salvation-historical perspective, it is union with the Christ who was raised from the dead that ultimately leads to the believer's own resurrection at the parousia. In terms of the individual-personal perspective, union with Christ removes the present existence from the dominion of death. In that sense, present existence is already the experience of the reign of life. For since death has lost its grip, the physical event of death is but a transition from the present "life in Christ," tempered by the limitations of earthly, creaturely existence, to the "life with Christ" in the presence of God.

When Paul contemplates his own, or others' death, he is certain in the conviction that "life in Christ" in the now is an eternal reality which death cannot abrogate or even diminish, and in light of which physical death is but a footnote in an ongoing story. On the other hand, when he contemplates God's historical, redemptive purposes, he is equally certain that the Lord of history, who has overcome death in the resurrection of his Son, will also raise "the dead in Christ" into the glorious liberty of the children of God (Romans 8:21).

Though it is clear that both eschatological realities—immediate conscious presence with Christ at death and end-time parousia/resurrection—meet at the point of "life in Christ," they appear to remain, from a temporal and linear/logical perspective, mutually exclusive. This tension, argues Fee,[62] may be resolved by appeal to the inherent tension between the "spatial and temporal elements"[63] in Paul's eschatology. His experience "in Christ" excludes the possibility of ever being in a "place" where Christ is not. Therefore, death ushers one into Christ's presence. But, "at the same time, a person's death did not usher her or him into a 'timeless' existence. Hence, the bodily resurrection still awaits one 'at the end.' . . . At issue is the interplay between 'time' and 'eternity' involved in the implied period of 'time' between death and resurrection." While from our human, timebound existence the timeless is difficult, if not impossible, to

---

[62]G. D. Fee, *Paul's Letter to the Philippians*, NICNT (Grand Rapids: Eerdmans, 1995) 149.

[63]This terminology is suggested by A. T. Lincoln, *Paradise Now and Not Yet: Studies in the Role of the Heavenly Dimension in Paul's Thought with Special Reference to His Eschatology*, SNTSMS 43 (Cambridge: Cambridge University Press, 1981) 106.

conceive, from the perspective of the other side, of eternity, the moments of death and resurrection on the timeline continuum may collapse into an eternal Now.

Such a solution to the tension in Paul's eschatology should not be dismissed too lightly as too modern, and something which the mind of Paul would have been incapable of conceiving. For biblical people were very much aware that "time," from the divine and human perspectives looked quite distinct:[64] "[W]ith the Lord one day is like a thousand years, and a thousand years are like one day" (2 Peter 3:8; Psalm 90:4).

[64]Cf. Caird, *New Testament Theology*, 273, who cites a conversation between Ezra and God (Latin 2 Esdr 5:41-42) as evidence of quite sophisticated thinking about time in early Judaism and its implications for the relationship between death and end-time resurrection.

History and Theology

" . . . a thing begunne rather then fynnesshed . . . " William Tyndale as Witness

James R. C. Perkin
Acadia University

Introduction

Reaction to William Tyndale (ca. 1494–1536) and his work was at first violently negative and then, as the decades and centuries passed, increasingly appreciative. Sir Thomas More (1478–1535), Henry VIII's lord chancellor, called Tyndale a "develish drunken soul,"[1] Cuthbert Tunstall, Bishop of London from 1522 to 1530, stated that Tyndale's 1526 translation of the New Testament was a "pestiferous and most pernicious poison."[2] John Foxe (1516–1587) gave early recognition of Tyndale's significance, describing him as "a special organ of the Lord appointed, and as God's mattock to shake the inward roots of the pope's proud prelacy."[3]

The first rule provided for the translators of the King James Version, which appeared in 1611, stated that the Bishops' Bible of 1568 was to be used as a basis and guide ("as little altered as the truth of the original will admit"), but when the translation was complete fully eighty percent of the language of the King James New Testament was Tyndale's.

The eminent Cambridge scholar B. F. Westcott, whose textual and translation work provided great help to the team that prepared the 1881 New Testament section of the English Revised Version, wrote that

---

[1]Quoted in G. MacGregor, *A Literary History of the Bible from the Middle Ages to the Present Day* (Nashville: Abingdon, 1968) 115.

[2]Ibid., 113-14.

[3]*Acts and Monuments . . . of Matters Happening in the Church*, commonly known as *Foxe's Book of Martyrs*. The original Latin text was published in Strasbourg in 1554; an expanded English version appeared in 1563. This huge work (more than 6,000 pages), while demonstrating strong antipapal bias, nevertheless remains a valuable early source on the work and significance of Tyndale. In 1965 G. A. Williamson edited and provided an excellent introductory essay for an abridged version entitled *Foxe's Book of Martyrs* (London: Secker & Warburg, 1965). The quotation is from p. 118 of that edition.

Tyndale's work had "enriched our language and thought for ever."[4] In 1907 Ira Maurice Price, professor of Semitic Languages and Literatures at the University of Chicago, wrote that "Tyndale set a standard for the English language that moulded in part the character and style of that tongue during the great Elizabethan era and all subsequent time."[5] In 1943 Sir Herbert Grierson, who for many years was professor of English Literature at Edinburgh University and was a noted authority on English seventeenth-century literature, published a generously illustrated, forty-eight-page volume entitled *The English Bible*. In it he describes Tyndale as "The hero and martyr of the English Bible as we have it."[6] The introduction to a recent study of Tyndale, an extended work by David Daniell, a leading authority on the translator, opens with the blunt statement that "William Tyndale gave us our English Bible."[7]

In 2000 the British Library published the text of Tyndale's 1526 translation, using the original spelling. The work was edited for the Tyndale Society by W. R. Cooper, who makes an even more far-reaching claim for Tyndale's work. Cooper's introduction begins with the words:

> The printing in 1526 of William Tyndale's translation of the New Testament from Greek into English was arguably the most important single event in the history of the English Reformation. Its impact on arrival in England was immediate, and almost impossible to calculate in terms of spiritual revival and political upheaval.[8]

Dr. Allison Trites, in whose honour this volume has been prepared and published, has thought long and written extensively on the concept

---

[4]B. F. Westcott and W. A. Wright, *A General View of the History of the English Bible* (London: Macmillan, 1905) 132.

[5]I. M. Price, *The Ancestry of Our English Bible* (Philadelphia: The Sunday School Times, 1907) 246.

[6]H. J. C. Grierson, *The English Bible*, Britain in Pictures (London: Collins, 1943) 10.

[7]D. Daniell, *William Tyndale: A Biography* (New Haven: Yale University Press, 1994) 1.

[8]W. R. Cooper, "Introduction," in *The New Testament: The Text of the Worms Edition of 1526 in Original Spelling*, trans. William Tyndale, ed. W. R. Cooper (London: The British Library, 2000) ix.

of witness in, and in relation to, Scripture.[9] William Tyndale provides a classic example of a witness. In him two dimensions of the word μάρτυς are exemplified. His work as a translator of Hebrew and Greek biblical manuscripts into the vernacular illustrates one meaning—"any kind of human witnessing by hand or eye"; his untimely execution illustrates another meaning—"one who witnessed unto death, a martyr."[10]

In appreciation of Dr. Trites's contribution to scholarship and to the church, indeed to his own life of witness, we will now provide a brief outline of the life of William Tyndale, "the hero and martyr of the English Bible," and comment on the significance of his work. His sixteenth-century language will continue to shape worship and devotion in the twenty-first century and, as Dr. Trites well knows, any attempt to translate scripture is, as Tyndale himself wrote in his preface added to his 1526 New Testament, "a thing begunne rather then fynnesshed."[11]

Tyndale: Life and Work

William Tyndale was probably born in the county of Gloucestershire, in the southwest of England, about 1494. There was an extended family of Tyndales in that area, one branch of which also used the name Hutchins, spelt in a variety of ways. He went to Magdalen Hall, Oxford, in 1506 and received a thorough Latin education preparatory to entering Magdalen College. The university was dominated by clerics and monks, and religious ideas and issues were the source of intense controversies. The atmosphere in which Tyndale undertook his degree studies was charged with the energy that is generated when entrenched beliefs and attractive new ideas collide. Among the factors that made Oxford an exciting, possibly dangerous, place to be in the early sixteenth century we

---

[9]A major contribution from Dr. Trites's pen in this field is *The New Testament Concept of Witness*, a thorough study of the concept of witness based on a detailed linguistic analysis of the use of the relevant terms in biblical and classical texts. In 1983 the Judson Press published *New Testament Witness in Today's World*. For these and his other writings on this subject, see the list of publications in the introduction to this book.

[10]See *BDAG*, s.v. μάρτυς.

[11]From Tyndale's "second address" (preface), "To the Reder," added to the octavo edition, and first complete printed edition, of his New Testament published at Worms in 1526.

may mention the legacy of John Wyclif, the lectures of John Colet, and news from the continent of Europe.

Wyclif (ca. 1330–1384), sometime master of Balliol College, challenged the authority of the pope, stressed that knowledge of Scripture was a key to godly living, and encouraged the translation of the Vulgate into English, a task completed in 1382. He was charged with heresy and retired to a rural parish, but his ideas had taken root and his translation was copied widely. Largely because of Wyclif's influence the "Constitutions of Oxford" were enacted in 1408, forbidding any unauthorized rendering of the Bible, in whole or part, into the vernacular.[12]

During 1496–1499, John Colet (1466/1467?–1519) gave a series of lectures at Oxford on St. Paul's epistles. He rejected the accumulated mass of mythological and allegorical interpretations, stressed the importance of a "literalist" approach, and urged simple Christian discipleship. He became dean of St. Paul's in 1504, but his influence was still strong at Oxford when Tyndale began his studies.

Meanwhile, there were rumours that in Germany radical ideas were being voiced, defying the authority of the pope, underlining the centrality of Scripture as the rule of life and faith, and emphasizing the theme of salvation by faith. Perhaps Tyndale was still at Oxford at the time of Luther's dramatic protest in Wittenberg on 31 October 1517, or perhaps he was spending some time in Cambridge, but there can be little doubt that Tyndale's studies were pursued in an environment where reformation tides were flowing strongly.

One other piece of background information is crucial to any understanding of Tyndale's influence. In 1476 William Caxton (ca. 1422–1491), an Englishman who had learned the art of printing on the Continent, set up a printing press in London. Henceforth, essentially identical copies of a document might be produced more quickly—and usually more cheaply—than by employing a copyist.

---

[12]In 1408, a council of English clergy, under the direction of Archbishop Thomas Arundel, met at Oxford and adopted what are known as the "Constitutions of Oxford." Among other things, the "Constitutions" forbade the translation of the Bible into English, except by permission of the bishop. English translation of the Bible was illegal, and those discovered with copies could be charged with heresy, a capital offence. The "Constitutions" remained in effect for more than 125 years.

About 1520 Tyndale returned to Gloucestershire as tutor to the two young sons of Sir John and Lady Anne Walsh of Little Sodbury Manor. He was able to digest and organize the results of his studies in Oxford (and perhaps Cambridge) and to preach in some of the local churches. The Walsh residence offered hospitality to many clerics and church dignitaries and vigorous discussions took place, some of them involving the new tutor. Tyndale appears to have arrived at some important conclusions: that the clergy were, generally speaking, ill-informed about matters related to the Scriptures, not knowing the original languages, nor aware of the interpretations being discussed in the universities; that the churches received indifferent, and often absentee leadership, resulting in a low level of spiritual life; and, above all, that lay people were inhibited in any attempt to discover for themselves the nature of the gospel because of the absence of a readily available text of the Bible in English.

Describing the state of the church in the early years of the sixteenth century, John Lawson paints a vivid picture of the "materialistic accretions"—shrines, relics, and so forth—added to religious observances by uneducated people, "whilst to the learned the primitive faith of the gospels had become obscured by the elaborate superstructure of scholastic theology no less than by these ignorant peasant cults."[13]

Tyndale's resolve to change the situation is clear in the oft-quoted incident reported by John Foxe:

> And soon after, Master Tyndall happened to be in the company of a learned man, and in communing and disputing with him drove him to that issue that the learned man said, we were better be [*sic*] without God's law than the Pope's: Maister Tyndall hearing that, answered him, I defy the Pope and all his laws, and said, if God spare my life ere many years, I will cause a boy that driveth the plough, shall know more of the scripture than thou dost.[14]

---

[13]J. Lawson, *Mediaeval Education and the Reformation*, The Students Library of Education (London: Routledge & Kegan Paul, 1967) 65-66.

[14]*Foxe's Book of Martyrs*, 121. The parallel between Tyndale's assertion and the statement in the *Paraclesis* with which Erasmus prefaced his 1516 Greek New Testament has frequently been noted. Erasmus wrote: "Christ wishes his mysteries to be published as widely as possible. . . . I wish that the husbandman may sing parts of them at his plow, that the weaver may warble them at his shuttle, and that the traveller may with their narratives beguile the weariness of the way." See

Tyndale, as we shall see, went to great lengths to implement his resolve, but the problem of an uneducated clergy was not easily rectified. Lawson refers to Bishop Hooper's visit to the Gloucester diocese in 1551, some thirty years after the incident recounted by Foxe, and found that "out of 311 clergymen questioned, 170 could not repeat the Ten Commandments, 10 could not say the Lord's Prayer, and some did not even know who was its author."[15]

As his frustration with the local clergy and the general state of the church increased, Tyndale resolved to translate the Greek New Testament into English and to do so legally, that is, with episcopal permission. The prospects were not encouraging. Since 1408 (it was now 1523) no such permission had been given and the English ecclesiastical hierarchy was deeply troubled by events in Europe, where Luther's 1522 German New Testament had just appeared. Tyndale therefore decided to visit London and seek the support of the bishop, Cuthbert Tunstall, a scholarly, moderate man. But the bishop's house was full and he was busy. As Tyndale commented later in the prologue to his translation of the Pentateuch, not only was there no room in "my lord of London's palace to translate the New Testament, but also that there was no place to do it in all England."

Having no employment and no welcome in the bishop's house, Tyndale was dependent on the support of friends, one of whom, Humphrey Monmouth, a wealthy cloth merchant, gave him shelter for several months. According to Foxe, Monmouth interceded with the bishop to appoint Tyndale as a chaplain, but Tunstall would not and so Tyndale lodged frugally with Monmouth, working diligently on his translation.

Meanwhile, news of Luther's activities and some of his pamphlets were reaching London and their influence probably helped Tyndale make up his mind to travel to Germany in order to find a printer for his English New Testament. Once he arrived in Cologne, he arranged with a printer, Peter Quentell, to print three thousand copies of the translation on

---

also Daniell, *William Tyndale*, 79; and S. L. Greenslade, "English Versions of the Bible, 1525–1611," in *The Cambridge History of the Bible*, vol. 3: *The West from the Reformation to the Present Day* (Cambridge: Cambridge University Press, 1963) 141-42.

[15]Lawson, *Mediaeval Education* 3:83.

quarto sheets. The printing was never completed: news of the project was given to the city fathers, who issued orders for the cessation of the work and the impounding of what had already been done. Tyndale and his assistant, William Roye, managed to rescue the translation and some of the printed pages and escaped up the Rhine to Worms. The significance of this incomplete publication (Matthew 1–22) is that it represents the first translation of part of the New Testament to be made into English from the Greek text, and printed.[16]

At Worms, Tyndale realized his dream: his whole New Testament was printed, probably early in 1526.[17] It was a thick octavo volume. Either three or six thousand copies were printed by Peter Schoeffer and many began to appear in England, having been concealed in shipments to England of bales of cloth, sacks of flour, or other merchandise. There followed a systematic attempt to obtain and destroy the books, identify and dissuade those who transported them, and locate and punish those who had bought them. So keen was Bishop Tunstall to secure and burn as many copies of Tyndale's New Testament as possible that he became the victim of a rather delightful plot implemented by one of Tyndale's supporters, a London merchant named Augustine Packington. According to Edward Hall (d. 1547),[18] Packington met Tunstall in Antwerp and, sensing the bishop's keen desire to buy copies of Tyndale's work in order to burn them, offered to buy up the unsold stock, provided the bishop

---

[16]This document is frequently referred to as the "Cologne Fragment." There is an excellent discussion of the translation and detailed analysis of its prologue in Daniell, *William Tyndale*, chap. 5.

[17]The printing at Worms may have been completed before the end of 1525, but copies did not reach England until 1526.

[18]In his monumental work, completed by Richard Grafton who published it in 1548 and 1550, *The Union of the Two Noble and Illustrious Families of Lancaster and York: Being Long in Continual Dissension for the Crown of This Noble Realm, with All the Acts Done in Both the Times of the Princes, Both of the One Lineage and of the Other, Beginning at the Time of King Henry the Fourth, the First Author of This Division, and So Successively Proceeding to the Reign of the High and Prudent King Henry the Eighth, the Indubitable Flower and Very Heir of Both the Said Lineages. Whereunto Is Added to Every King a Several Table*. Understandably, this huge volume (used as a source by Shakespeare) is usually referred to by a much shorter title—*Hall's Chronicle*.

would pay for them. "The bishop thinking he had God by the toe, when indeed he had (as after he thought) the Devil by the fist," handed over the money, which Packington passed on to Tyndale so he could pay his debts and continue his revision of the translation! In a curiously modern-sounding conclusion to the story, Hall comments, "And so forward went the bargain, the bishop had the books, Packington had the thanks, and Tyndale had the money." When Tunstall noticed that, despite his investment, there were still many of the translations in London and commented about this phenomenon, the intrepid Packington offered to buy the plates for the bishop, but his Lordship does not appear to have accepted the offer.

So thorough was the attempt to destroy the translation that until recently only two copies were known to have survived—an incomplete copy in Saint Paul's (London) and a copy lacking only the title page and held in the impressive collection of old Bibles in Bristol Baptist College. The latter volume was sold to the British Library in 1994. In 1996 the seemingly impossible happened. While creating an electronic catalogue of the Bible Collection in the Württemberg State Library (Stuttgart) a librarian realized that she was holding a complete copy of Tyndale's 1526 New Testament, a conclusion ratified by the Bible House Library, Cambridge, and by the British Library. That the copy could be found after more than 450 years and have survived the heavy destruction of the Second World War seems almost beyond belief.[19]

John Foxe was obviously puzzled by the opposition to Tyndale's work and reports the translator's reaction in the following words:

> Some said it was not possible to translate the Scripture into English; some that it was not lawful for lay people to have it in their mother tongue; some that it would make them all heretics. To reduce the

---

[19]There is a brief announcement of the discovery by M. Jannetta of the British Library in the Tyndale Society's journal, "Good News from Stuttgart: A Previously Unrecorded Copy of the 1526 Worms Edition of William Tyndale's New Testament Translation," *Reformation* 2 (1997): 1-6. A more detailed discussion is provided by E. Zwink of the Württemberg State Library, Stuttgart, in "Confusion about Tyndale: The Stuttgart Copy of the 1526 New Testament in English," *Reformation* 3 (1998): 28-48. Zwink provides a fascinating account of the various resting places of the translation, suggesting why the copy has survived and why it was not identified earlier.

> temporal rulers unto their purpose they said it would make the people rise against the king.[20]

When Tunstall became bishop of Durham in 1530 he was replaced as bishop of London by John Stokesley; whereas Tunstall was eager to burn translations he regarded as containing heretical views, Stokesley was quite ready to burn translators and possessors of the vernacular Scriptures as being guilty of heresy. From this point on Tyndale was a marked man and it seems likely that he did not stay long in one spot in Europe, but spent time in Wittenberg, Hamburg, and Antwerp. He completed a translation of the Pentateuch in 1530 and of the Book of Jonah in 1531, and probably translated Joshua–Chronicles before his execution. This was a truly significant point in the history of biblical translation into English. The "Constitutions of Oxford" notwithstanding, there was then a complete New Testament translated from the Greek and a major step had been taken towards the translation of the Old Testament from the original Hebrew.

There is much scholarly debate (and speculation) as to where and when Tyndale learned Hebrew. Before the 1530s there was very limited knowledge of the language in England; Tyndale therefore probably developed his thorough acquaintance while in Europe, that is, after 1525. Even if it was the result of a recently learned skill, Tyndale's Pentateuch is a lively translation, his style matching the vigour and drama of the original story.[21] At some point between 1525 and 1530 it is probable that Miles Coverdale (another expatriate Englishman) and Tyndale worked together. Although Tyndale did not finish his translation of the Old Testament, Coverdale did complete the work. Ironically Coverdale's complete Bible appeared in 1535, a year before Tyndale's execution.

Even while working on the Old Testament, Tyndale was carefully revising his 1526 New Testament, supported in part by the money deviously secured by Packington from the bishop of London. The revision was published in Antwerp by Martin de Keyser in 1534; when mention is made of "Tyndale's New Testament" the reference is usually to this edi-

---

[20] *Foxe's Book of Martyrs*, 124.

[21] Daniell, *William Tyndale*, 283ff., provides a detailed analysis of the language used in Gen 3 and endorses the observation that "Tyndale, exactly like the Hebrew, is raw, comic and tragic all at once" (286).

tion which, according to Daniell "has well over five thousand revisions" when compared with the 1526 edition.[22]

Tyndale was staying in the English House in Antwerp early in 1535 when he was arrested and imprisoned at the instigation of Henry Phillips, a dishonest and impoverished son of an English west-country landed family, who was probably in the pay of antireformation elements in England. Tyndale was taken to the castle at Vilvorde, six miles north of Brussels, whose governor was paid for keeping the prisoner. While Tyndale was incarcerated and suffering considerably from inadequate clothing and the damp conditions of the castle, various forces were at work to bring about his release or death. The merchants in the English house in Antwerp, led by Thomas Poyntz who ran the house, urgently sought Tyndale's release to the point where Poyntz's own life was threatened and he had to escape to England. Phillips single-mindedly sought Tyndale's death for heresy, urging his case in such degree that there was no option for the authorities simply to keep their prisoner indefinitely. King Henry VIII was in no position to make threats; the annulment of his marriage to Catherine of Aragon and marriage to Anne Boleyn and above all the 1534 Acts of Supremacy that confirmed the King as "the only supreme head in earth of the Church of England" had given deep offence to powerful forces on the continent.[23] Finally, Tyndale himself, the pawn in the deadly game that was being played, acted throughout with dignity, not to say with naiveté, continuing his work and awaiting his fate with equanimity. On 6 October 1536 the father of the English Bible was strangled and his body burned. His last words—tradition has it—were "Lord, open the King of England's eyes." William Tyndale's work as a witness and martyr had ended, but the influence of that work had only just begun.

---

[22]Ibid., 330.

[23]The king did authorize Thomas Cromwell, his chief adviser on church matters, to write seeking the release and return to England of the translator. Unfortunately, the letters became the subject of confused transmission and their intent was strongly opposed by Phillips.

Tyndale and the History of Translation

Daniell's assertion that "William Tyndale gave us our English Bible" can easily be illustrated from the history of translation. In 1534, while Tyndale languished in the castle at Vilvorde, Miles Coverdale obtained reluctant permission from Henry VIII to publish a translation of the complete Bible. Coverdale was a Yorkshireman whose sympathy with Reformation ideas had prompted him to leave the Augustinian order and, in 1528, led him to seek safety in Europe, where he worked with Tyndale in both Hamburg and Antwerp. After Tyndale's arrest Coverdale set about the task of preparing a complete translation of the Bible, using as much of Tyndale's work as was available and paying close attention to the Vulgate and German versions. The complete work was published in 1535, probably in Antwerp, and has the distinction of being the first *complete* Bible in English to be made from the original languages and printed. It was Coverdale who brought the books of the Apocrypha together and placed them at the end of the Old Testament. Despite the royal tolerance of this translation, perhaps due in part to the influence of Anne Boleyn, and the strong desire in England to have a Bible in the vernacular, Coverdale's version was not widely popular. It was reprinted four times: 1537 (twice), 1550, and 1553. The 1537 reprints were published by John Nicholson of Southwark and the second of these was licensed by the king. However, true popularity and acceptance was given to the next major version, the Great Bible (also popularly known as the "Treacle Bible" after its translation of Jeremiah 8:22), which appeared in April 1539.

Coverdale undertook this publication at the urging of Thomas Cromwell. The aim was to provide a translation which would be available in all the churches and whose use would be formally authorized.[24] It was decided that the printing should be done in France, but the printers were arraigned there on a charge of heresy. Coverdale, who was supervising the

---

[24]Another edition of the Bible was in circulation at this time having appeared in 1537; it purported to be the work of Thomas Matthew, a pseudonym for John Rogers. It used Tyndale's 1534 edition of the New Testament and Coverdale's Old Testament and Apocrypha. In approaching Coverdale to produce what became the Great Bible, Cromwell was probably seeking to have only one translation in the churches.

printing, fled to England. Later he returned with some friends to "obtain" the equipment and type, which was smuggled across the Channel and set up in London. The resultant Bible was indeed a great book, its "royal quarto" pages (four to a sheet) being as large as 9x15 inches, and a copy was placed in each parish church, usually chained into its place. There are delightful stories of literate citizens reading the Bible to groups of worshippers while the sermon went largely unnoticed! When the *Book of Common Prayer* appeared in 1549 the translation of the Psalms was that of the Great Bible; this continued to be the case in the definitive edition of the *Book of Common Prayer* of 1662.

The brief but violent reign of Mary (1553–1558) saw the execution of several leading churchmen, including Thomas Cranmer, the archbishop of Canterbury, who had played a major role in supporting Henry VIII's policy of creating the Church of England. Surprisingly, there was neither parliamentary nor royal attempt to limit the circulation of the Great Bible. Consequently, when Elizabeth came to the throne, the Great Bible, despite being nearly twenty years old, continued to be sold and used. Coverdale had become bishop of Exeter in 1551, but was deposed by Mary and fled to Geneva where he became an associate of John Knox, who ministered to a large group of English exiles. This group is collectively responsible for the translation and publication (in 1560) of the next major translation, appropriately known as the Geneva Bible.

The basis of the Geneva Bible was still the work of Tyndale; his New Testament remains clearly formative, and the sections of the Old Testament that he had not translated are based on the Great Bible. Frequent, and often pungent, marginal comments are a characteristic of the Geneva Bible. While these notes pleased the more radical wing of the reformers, they were later to annoy King James and led him to forbid exegetical marginalia in the translation that bears his name. It is not clear what there was about the Geneva Bible that commended it to the English people. Perhaps there was a growing familiarity with the text of Scripture, thanks to Tyndale and Coverdale; perhaps some people actually enjoyed the sharply worded notes; or perhaps there was a sense of relief that there was apparent stability in the prospect of toleration by the throne and this version was a symbol of what might be expected from the new queen. (The Geneva Bible was dedicated to Queen Elizabeth and later, as the first Bible published in Scotland, 1579, to James VI of Scotland, who of course became James I of England.) In any case, as Bruce wrote, "The

Geneva Bible immediately won, and retained, widespread popularity. It became the household Bible of English-speaking Protestants."[25]

The last major sixteenth-century translation of the Bible was made because, for all its popularity, the Geneva Bible did not have the approval of the hierarchy of the Church of England. One year after the appearance of the Geneva Bible, Matthew Parker, who had become archbishop of Canterbury in 1559, recommended a revision. The task was completed in 1568 by a group consisting largely of bishops and led by Parker himself. The genealogy of this version—the Bishops' Bible—being what it was, Tyndale's work was again enshrined, as was much of Coverdale's, especially the Psalter, which was reproduced virtually unchanged.

In 1603 Elizabeth died and James VI of Scotland became James I of England. James wanted to reconcile the high church and Puritan wings of the church and called a conference in 1604 at Hampton Court. The conference achieved little except what seemed at the time an innocuous agreement—upon the suggestion of John Rainolds/Reynolds (1549–1607), the Puritan president of Corpus Christi College, Oxford—to make yet another "translation" of the Bible. The severely anti-Puritan bishop of London (that same year elevated to archbishop of Canterbury), Richard Bancroft, reluctantly agreed, and King James supported the suggestion. The king insisted there should be no exegetical marginal notes and assisted in the appointment of forty-seven scholars in six translation panels, two at Oxford, two at Cambridge, two at Westminster. Among the guidelines was the requirement that the wording of the Bishops' Bible was to provide the base for the new work; happily this regulation was not slavishly followed! The work, known in much of the world as the King James Version (KJV), was not published until 1611 and steadily won approval to the point where, for the next 350 years, to mention the Bible in England was understood as a reference to this translation, more

---

[25]F. F. Bruce, *The English Bible: A History of Translations from the Earliest English Versions to the New English Bible* (London: Lutterworth, 1970) 91. The Geneva Bible, the first English Bible to have verse numbers, was the Bible of Bunyan, of Shakespeare, of Cromwell and his army, of the pilgrims to the New World, and of the Mayflower Compact. See, e.g., R. G. Bratcher, "English Bible, History of," in the *Mercer Dictionary of the Bible* (Macon: Mercer University Press, 1990) 250a.

commonly known in Britain as the "Authorized Version" (AV).[26] The sonority and structure of this translation made it ideal for public reading. "Eventually . . . its victory was so complete that its text acquired a sanctity properly ascribable only to the unmediated voice of God; to multitudes of English-speaking Christians it has seemed little less than blasphemy to tamper with the words of the King James Version."[27]

Once again, the work of Tyndale is apparent in the KJV. For instance, in Matthew's Beatitudes (5:3-12) comparison reveals only six words difference between the two.[28] The most detailed recent study of the impact of Tyndale's translations of both the Old and the New Testaments is found in *Reformation* (1998), the result of close comparisons of the Tyndale New Testament and the KJV made by Jon Nielson and Royal Skousen of Brigham Young Univeristy.[29] Many memorable phrases and passages believed to be the work of the KJV translators prove on closer study to be Tyndale's words. The final words in the Parable of the Prodigal Son (Luke 15:32) are identical in the two versions.

Although the discovery of previously unknown manuscripts prompted new translations, the Tyndale-Coverdale tradition remains dominant in

---

[26]There is no *known* official "authorization" by either church or crown of the KJV/AV, not that any official decree was needed to establish it. The "authorized" title may simply have been assumed from the printer's addition to the title page of the words "Appointed to be read in Churches." Or it may have followed from the Puritans' demand at the Hampton Court Conference that there be "one only translation of the Bible . . . declared to be authentical, and read in the church." See, e.g., A. McGrath, *In the Beginning: The Story of the King James Bible and How It Changed a Nation, a Language, and a Culture* (New York: Doubleday, 2001) 161, 164, 206-207.

[27]*Cambridge History of the Bible* 3:168.

[28]In 1907 I. M. Price wrote: "There have been some painstaking calculations to determine just how large a part Tyndale may have had in the production of the version of 1611. A comparison of Tyndale's version of 1 John and that of the Authorized Version shows that nine-tenths of the latter is retained. . . . Paul's Epistle to the Ephesians retains five-sixths of Tyndale's translation." Price, *Ancestry of Our English Bible*, 246.

[29]J. Nielson and R. Skousen, "How Much of the King James Bible Is William Tyndale's?" *Reformation* 3 (1998): 49-74: "[W]e conclude that for the New Testament Tyndale's contribution is about 84 per cent of the text, while in the Old Testament about 75 per cent of his words have been retained."

the English Revised Version (ERV, 1881, 1885, 1889), the ERV-counterpart American Standard Version (ASV, 1901), the Revised Standard Version (RSV, 1946, 1952, 1957ff.), and even the New Revised Standard Version (NRSV, c1989, 1990). Presently, the most widely used translation in the churches of the English-speaking world is one of the many editions of the RSV. A comparative study of one of these editions and Tyndale as regards, for example, the Beatitudes (Matthew 5:1-12), the parable of the Prodigal Son (Luke 15:11-32), or the hymn in 1 Corinthians 13 will illustrate how formative and durable Tyndale's work was.

In the immediate post-World War II era a decision was made to move away from the 300-year-old tradition of translation. At the 1946 general assembly of the Church of Scotland delegates welcomed a resolution from one of the presbyteries, strongly supported by former armed forces' chaplains, "that a completely new translation [of the Bible] should be made, rather than a revision, . . . and that the translators should be free to employ a contemporary idiom rather than reproduce the traditional [that is, of the AV/KJV] 'biblical' English."[30] The project was overseen by a joint committee, representative of the participating denominations and agencies, and carried forward by three panels of translators (for the Old Testament, New Testament, and Apocrypha) chosen solely for their expertise in the biblical field. A literary panel advised on matters related to the use of English idiom. Thus appeared the New English Bible (NEB), the New Testament of which was published in 1961. A second edition of the New Testament appeared, with the Old Testament and Apocrypha, as part of the whole Bible in 1970.

In considering this translation it must be remembered that the discovery of the Dead Sea Scrolls began in 1947, providing major new manuscripts and insights into the nature of biblical Hebrew. The collation of manuscript fragments and attempts to establish a definitive text have continued ever since. In 1974 it was decided to undertake what turned out to be a major revision of the NEB, resulting in the publication in 1989 of the Revised English Bible (REB). As we shall see, the scholars who worked on the NEB and REB, having effectively broken the mould of traditional biblical translation, nevertheless reverted in several significant instances to words and phrases first used by Tyndale.

---

[30]Donald Ebor, preface to *The New English Bible* (London: Oxford University Press/Cambridge University Press, 1970) v.

Tyndale and the Language of Translation

Much of the early hostility toward Tyndale and his work derived from the widespread fear among English church leaders of Lutheran ideas. A focal point of this animosity was the language chosen by Tyndale to translate certain words that had key significance in the theological controversies then raging in England. It was Sir Thomas More who led the attack on Tyndale's translation of the New Testament, asserting that it was full of linguistic and theological errors. Tyndale rendered the word ἀγάπη as "love" instead of the Latin-sounding "charity." Coverdale changed the word to "charity," setting a pattern that was followed by translators down to, and including, the KJV. It was not until the ERV New Testament was published in 1881 that Tyndale's word "love" reappeared; it now occurs in virtually every modern translation of 1 Corinthians 13.

A second hotly debated translation was the English equivalent of the verb μετανοεῖν. Church authorities wanted it to be rendered "to do penance," thus implying a major role for the priest; Tyndale translated the verb "to repent" and the noun "repentance." Once again, Tyndale led the way and gradually other translators followed him to the point at which no modern version uses "do penance." Another key word was χάρις, traditionally translated "grace," but sometimes rendered by Tyndale as "favour." In this instance there was no immediate or widespread acceptance of Tyndale's word; for example, in Luke 2:40 Tyndale's version reads "and the favour of God was with him." The KJV has "and the grace of God was upon him," but the RSV and the NEB, for example, return to Tyndale's "favor/favour."

Tyndale's handling of the word πρεσβύτερος is of particular interest. A traditional translation of this word had been "priest," despite the fact that the word really means "senior" or "elder" and that Erasmus had rendered it "senior" or "presbyter" in his Latin version of 1516. In his 1526 translation Tyndale used the word "senior," but he changed this to "elder" in the 1534 edition. This translation dominates both the KJV and the NEB traditions—yet another example of Tyndale's formative influence.

A final example of a word in Tyndale's translation that became the focal point of controversy is his use of the word "congregation" for ἐκκλησία. When translating the greeting at the beginning of both 1 and 2 Thessalonians, Tyndale wrote "unto the congregation of the Thessalonians. . . . " The KJV and its major successors have "church." The 1961 and 1970 editions of the NEB reverted to Tyndale's "congregation," but the REB has "church," providing a rare example of a change against a Tyndale translation which had been used in earlier editions.

The translation of the first beatitude, particularly in the twentieth century, is an interesting and somewhat curious story. Tyndale rendered Matthew 5:3 "Blessed are the *poor in spirit.*" This was Wyclif's phrase (1382) and with the exception of a few individual translators (for example, Goodspeed [1923] and Phillips [1958]) it was commonly used until 1961. At that point the first-edition NEB translated "How blest are those who know that they are poor." Critics complained that the phrase, while emphasizing the economic aspect of the saying, had eliminated the spiritual. In an attempt to rectify this, the scholars who worked on the 1970 edition of NEB substituted "How blest are those who know their need of God," effectively stressing the spiritual dimension of "poor" while eliminating the economic. Given the criticism to which this rendering was subjected, it is not surprising that the revisers metaphorically threw up their hands and went back to Tyndale's "Blessed are the poor in spirit" (REB). Considering that "poor in spirit" is a most unclear phrase, both in Greek and English, its reinstatement may be seen not only as another example of Tyndale's continuing influence, but an illustration of secondary intertextuality, a case in which a text links not so much with another text, but with a traditional interpretation.[31]

The other example of the way in which, either by profound insight or fortunate happenstance, Tyndale has proved to be ahead of his time may be seen in his translation of Matthew 5:9. The Greek text says that "the peacemakers" shall be called "sons of God." Wyclif translated the verse literally, but Tyndale rendered it "children of God." This phraseology was continued to, and in, the KJV (notably including the 1582 Rheims New

---

[31]"Intertextuality" is a somewhat flexible concept. R. E. Scholes, *Semiotics and Interpretation* (New Haven: Yale University Press, 1982) 145, writes that "an intertext is a text linking inside another, shaping meanings, whether the author is conscious of this or not." In *Merriam-Webster's Encyclopedia of Literature* (Springfield: Merriam-Webster, 1995), the article on "Intertextuality" includes the following statement: "In literary theory, a text's quality of interdependence with all previous and future discourse . . . the idea that every new literary text is an intersection of texts—that it has absorbed and transformed previous works and that it will be absorbed and transformed by future texts."

Testament), but ERV–RSV went back to the more literal "sons." Both editions of NEB use "sons," but the 1989 REB and NRSV—probably for the sake of inclusive language—employs Tyndale's "children."

In his preface to the 2000 original-spelling edition of Tyndale's 1526 translation, David Daniell suggests that Tyndale's work was a landmark because

> The English language in the 1520s was uncertain in its direction, being made up of elements from Norman French, from older Anglo-Saxon and from Latin . . . the idea that the English language was capable of carrying any large freight at all was unthinkable. Yet William Tyndale made for the New Testament an English of great clarity, economy and power. It is worth remembering that he had no models for this.[32]

In this fluid linguistic situation, Tyndale's translation created a model or pattern that was formative for the written and spoken English of several generations.

Tyndale, Education, and Literacy

Throughout this study we have demonstrated the significance for biblical translation of William Tyndale's 1526 New Testament and its 1534 revision. It is of interest to note that Tyndale's translation either helped to promote, or at least coincided with, an increase in the number of schools in England, and a sharp rise in the literacy rate. In a chapter that provides a thorough study of "Henry VIII and the Schools," A. F. Leach documents the foundation of scores of schools during that monarch's reign.[33] Leach concludes that the dramatic activity of Elizabethan England in terms of navigation, commerce, colonization, poetry, drama, philosophy and science was possible because of the educational base laid in Henry's

---

[32]D. Daniell, "Preface," in *The New Testament: The Text of the Worms Edition of 1526 in Original Spelling*, v-vi.

[33]This is the last chapter in A. F. Leach, *The Schools of Medieval England* (New York: Barnes & Noble, 1969). See also W. K. Jordan, *Philanthropy in England, 1480–1660: A Study of the Changing Pattern of English Social Aspirations* (London: Allen & Unwin, 1959) 287, and Lawson, *Mediaeval Education and the Reformation*, 81.

reign.[34] If we ask, "What did the children have to read as a first reader?" one response outweighs all others: "The Bible."

According to T. L. Jarman, the reformers played a major role in establishing schools and promoting literacy. The schools were necessary in order to create a generation that was literate, and the prime purpose of literacy was to have the ability to read the Bible. In his book *Landmarks in the History of Education*,[35] especially chapter 9, "The Struggle for Education: Protestants and Catholics," Jarman offers a fascinating study of sixteenth-century Europe and underlines that the truly new feature of this period was the attention given to elementary education. "Provision of higher education, of some kind or other, there had always been, but any attempt to supply the elementary instruction of the common people was something new." This attempt rested on the Protestant conviction that the Bible, not the authority of the church, was the source of divine truth. It was necessary, therefore, to open this source to all.[36]

It is notoriously difficult to assemble reliable statistical information about literacy rates in England during the sixteenth century. Some estimate can be made based on the proportion of individuals who were able to sign a marriage register as distinct from simply making a mark. The same is true of wills and depositions made before courts. The resulting information may be broken down according to county, gender, and social status. David Cressy has undertaken such work.[37] Recognizing that in some categories, such as the clergy, lawyers, and schoolmasters, literacy would be almost one hundred percent, Cressy discusses its incidence among the gentry, yeomen, husbandmen, tradesmen, and labourers. What emerges from the study of illiteracy in the diocese of Norwich is that in all categories literacy increased significantly between 1530 and 1580. Although he suggests reasons for the cyclical pattern of improvement and then stagnation in apparent literacy rates, Cressy does not specifically link them with the sudden availability of scripture as a first reader, in home,

---

[34]Leach, *The Schools of Medieval England*, 332.

[35]T. L. Jarman, *Landmarks in the History of Education: English Education as Part of the European Tradition* (London: John Murray, 1963).

[36]Ibid., 151.

[37]D. Cressy, "Levels of Illiteracy in England 1530–1730," in *Literacy and Social Development in the West: A Reader*, ed. H. J. Graff, Cambridge Studies in Oral and Literate Culture 3 (Cambridge: Cambridge University Press, 1981).

school, and church. However, it is a reasonable assumption that literacy would be improved when two criteria were met: the availability at moderate cost of something to serve as a first reader, and an educational system, however informal and whether based in the home, church, or school, that taught children (and others) to read. Both criteria were met in the mid-sixteenth century and at the same time there was a strong desire among reformers to encourage firsthand acquaintance with the Scriptures among both children and adults. There can be little doubt of the importance of Tyndale's translation of the New Testament in such circumstances.

In his significant work *English Social History*,[38] G. M. Trevelyan discusses the influence of the group of scholars who gathered around Erasmus, bringing about a resurgence of classical scholarship and biblical exegesis. Trevelyan then adds: "None of those friends thought that their new knowledge of the classics and of the Greek Testament would destroy the 'Mediaeval' Church, which they hoped to liberalise and to reform. More radical was the intention of William Tyndale, as in penury and danger he translated the Bible into words of power and beauty that unborn millions were to have daily on their lips, and to interpret in a hundred different ways disruptive of the past."[39]

The ultimate recognition of the importance of William Tyndale in the story of literacy and literature in England comes from a surprising, but impeccable, source.

On 5 and 19 November 1857, the Philological Society (of London) heard two papers from cleric, biblical scholar, poet, and philologist Richard Chevenix Trench (1807–1886), then dean of Westminster, later Protestant archbishop of Dublin. The papers were entitled "On Some Deficiencies in our English Dictionaries," and subsequently were published in 1858. Together with Trench's previous extensive philological works, these two papers provided the initial stimulus and indeed detailed plans for a new lexicographical work. Thus, from this meeting there was begun the long-term project that eventually resulted in the *New English Dictionary*, then also known as the "Philological Society's Dictionary" (ten

[38]G. M. Trevelyan, *English Social History: A Survey of Six Centuries, Chaucer to Queen Victoria* (London: Longmans, Green, 1942).

[39]Ibid., 95.

volumes, 1884–1928). Since 1933, of course, this massive dictionary has been known as the *Oxford English Dictionary* (OED).[40]

In order to manage the enormous task of identifying, defining, and illustrating the usage of every word in the language, an army of volunteer readers was formed. "The helpers were asked to undertake to read books and to extract quotations illustrating the use of the words in them."[41] K. M. Elisabeth Murray, granddaughter of James Augustus Henry Murray (1837–1915)—editor of the first half of the dictionary and the single individual most associated with the dictionary—then goes on to describe the way in which the work was organized: "For convenience, [Herbert] Coleridge [1830–1861, secretary of the original planning committee] divided English literature into three periods: 1250–1526 (Tyndale's *New Testament*), 1526–1674 (death of Milton), and 1674 onwards."[42] This is a most significant statement. The labours that led to the publication of the OED were of the most painstaking kind and the organization was meticulous as well as extensive. The decision to divide the vast tract of English literature into three main periods would help to shape the results of the research that was undertaken by literally hundreds of people. It is important to note that the reference to 1526 is not simply to a date, nor simply to Tyndale as a writer, but specifically to "1526 (Tyndale's *New Testament*)." The clear implication is that in the eyes of Herbert Coleridge, Trench, and their colleagues, Tyndale's New Testament represented a landmark in the history of English literature. Moreover, the suggestion is that the publication of Tyndale's New Testament is of equal significance to the death of Milton.

Tyndale indeed is a witness, both in the sense of one who provides evidence and in the sense of one who is a martyr. The story of translation was forever changed by Tyndale's work. That story will be continued as

---

[40]See, e.g., J. Green, "The New English Dictionary," in *Chasing the Sun: Dictionary Makers and the Dictionaries They Made*, 359-401 (New York: Henry Holt, 1996).

[41]K. M. E. Murray, *Caught in the Web of Words: James A. H. Murray and the Oxford English Dictionary* (New Haven: Yale University Press, 1977) 137.

[42]Ibid., 137. The reference is to the arrangements set down by Herbert Coleridge (1830–1861), grandson of the poet, and secretary of the original planning committee, on whom fell the responsibility of pulling together and organizing the details of a coherent plan.

long as there is a Bible and a church. Any translation is, and will always be, a contribution to something "begun rather than finished."

"The Gospel Its Own Witness": Deism, Thomas Paine, and Andrew Fuller

Alan P. F. Sell
Milton Keynes
United Kingdom

Andrew Fuller (1754–1815) is widely and rightly remembered as a prominent founder and first secretary—the "rope holder"—of the Baptist Missionary Society (1792).[1] Historical theologians and students of eighteenth-century thought may recall him as one who, in *The Gospel Worthy of All Acceptation* (1785)—a work written under the influence of Jonathan Edwards—repudiated the hyper-Calvinism of those who contended that since salvation was for the elect alone there could be no general offers of the Gospel. Fuller's ground for upholding the free offer is summarized in the subtitle of his book: *The Duty of Sinners to Believe in Jesus Christ.*[2] But there is another aspect of Fuller's work that is not so frequently recalled, or, if recalled, is not discussed in any detail.[3] The pastor, whose only

---

[1]See B. Stanley, *The History of the Baptist Missionary Society 1792–1992* (Edinburgh: T. & T. Clark, 1992).

[2]For the context of this complicated and thorny issue see A. P. F. Sell, *The Great Debate: Calvinism, Arminianism, and Salvation* (Eugene: Wipf & Stock, 1998) chaps. 2 and 3.

[3]This is true whether we consider modern students of Fuller or of Paine. As to the former, an exception is E. F. Clipsham, "Andrew Fuller and Fullerism: A Study in Evangelical Calvinism; Fuller as a Theologian," *BaptQ* 20 (1964): 271-74. Phil Roberts declines to consider Fuller's antideistic and anti-Socinian works because "they were not primarily theological treatises but attempts to demonstrate the ethical superiority of Calvinism versus Socinianism and Deism." In T. George and D. S. Dockery, eds., *Baptist Theologians* (Nashville: Broadman, 1990) 138n.36. But in the eighteenth century that was an intensely theological business! In any case, as we shall see, Fuller makes many specifically theological points in his antideist tract. For his anti-Socinian writings, see my "Andrew Fuller and the Socinians," *Enlightenment and Dissent* 19 (2000): 91-115. As to the latter, Fuller's name is not indexed in S. Edwards, *Rebel! A Biography of Thomas Paine* (New York: Praeger, 1974); A. J. Ayer, *Thomas Paine* (London: Secker & Warburg, 1988); M. Philp, *Paine* (Oxford: Oxford University Press, 1989); E. H.

formal education was at the village school in Soham, and whose life was spent in ministry there and, from 1782, at Kettering, was also a dogged controversialist. He published rebuttals of Socinianism, Sandemanianism, universalism, and deism. It is with the last that we are here concerned. In 1799 Fuller published *The Gospel Its Own Witness* in reply to Thomas Paine's two-part work, *The Age of Reason* (1794, 1795). A more pungent opponent Fuller could scarcely have had, as we shall see. But first we must adjust our sights to the complicated phenomenon of deism.

I

It cannot be denied that in some quarters the deists have received bad press. The erstwhile Anglican, Leslie Stephen (1832–1904), declared that "The deist writings are but shabby and shrivelled little octavos, generally anonymous, such as lurk in the corners of dusty shelves, and seem to be the predestined prey of moths."[4] While there are undoubtedly anonymous deist tracts, there are also the substantial contributions of Collins, Tindal, Toland, and, supremely, Paine, all of which are studied to this day. For his part, the Congregational theologian A. M. Fairbairn (1838–1912) was as lofty as ever: the deists, he informs us, were "irrepressible men like Toland, men of mediocre culture and ability like Anthony Collins, vulgar men like Chubb, irritated and disagreeable men like Matthew Tindal, who conformed that he might enjoy his Oxford fellowship and wrote anonymously that he might relieve his conscience."[5] We need not comment on this *ad hominem* outburst. Finally, in our own time, and without reference to the stated desire of many deists to assist the unlettered to discriminate between truth and superstitious error, Gordon Rupp described the deists as "a self-conscious elite, and, with the exception of Thomas Chubb, the tallow chandler of Salisbury, upper class; aristocrats like Shaftesbury and Bolingbroke, and the landed gentleman

---

Davidson and W. J. Scheick, *Paine, Scripture, and Authority* (Bethlehem: Lehigh University Press, 1994); J. Fruchtman, Jr., *Thomas Paine Apostle of Freedom* (New York: Four Walls Eight Windows, 1994).

[4]L. Stephen, *History of English Thought in the Eighteenth Century* (New York: Harcourt, Brace & World, 1962) 1:72.

[5]Quoted by R. Mackintosh, "Apologetics," in *Encyclopedia Brittanica*, 11th ed., 191.

Anthony Collins, dons like Wollaston, Woolston and Tindal, and the medical man, Thomas Morgan."[6] (We might, however, note that Thomas Morgan, "a poor lad in a farmer's house," was given a free education by the Dissenting minister, John Moore[7]). Chubb—and here we encounter the difficulty of pin-pointing deists—was in some ways closer to the nondeist Samuel Clarke, the moderate Anglican Arian, than Shaftesbury and Bolingbroke were to deism. All of which underlines the fact that the deists did not constitute anything so precise as a school of thought, or even a clearly defined movement. Rather, they were writers who in a general way imbibed prevalent skepticism regarding some of the claims of orthodox Christianity, revelation, Christian "evidences" as generally conceived, the authority of the church, and the probity of the priesthood, whilst being unlike one another on many points of detail. We should also be alive to the fact that in that nicknaming age less-than-careful pamphleteers might apply "deist" as a term of abuse to those whose doctrinal views they ardently repudiated. Thus, for example, in his *A View of the Principal Deistical Writers* (1754–1756) John Leland lumps Hobbes and Hume together with others more generally regarded as deists.[8]

One frequently alleged point of agreement must be completely disavowed: the best-known late-seventeenth- and eighteenth-century deists were *not* united in the belief that God, having created the world, then retreated from it and left it to its own devices, remaining transcendent above it. On the contrary, their major point was that God was the God of the natural order, which testified to his power and wisdom. While some of the earlier deists allowed a supernatural revelation provided it were sanctioned by reason, later writers, notably Tindal, declared supernatural revelation redundant. To put the point otherwise, while it may be argued that deism paved the way for modern naturalism and secularism, its representatives of the period that concerns us were deeply attached to the notion that God is to be known in the book of nature: they were not opposed to religion as such, however much some of them deplored some

---

[6]G. Rupp, *Religion in England, 1688–1791* (Oxford: Clarendon, 1986) 277.

[7]See L. Stephen, "Thomas Morgan," in *DNB*.

[8]For the usage of 'deism' see, e.g., F. E. Manuel, *The Eighteenth Century Confronts the Gods* (Cambridge: Harvard University Press, 1959); R. E. Sullivan, *John Toland and the Deist Controversy* (Cambridge: Harvard University Press, 1982) chap. 7.

of its manifestations and intellectual commitments;[9] and they did not wish to be mistaken for atheists.

It is true that, Samuel Clarke (1675–1729) describes one species of deist who

> pretend to believe in the existence of an Eternal, Infinite, Independent, Intelligent Being; and, to avoid the name Epicurean Atheist, teach also that this Supreme Being made the World: Though at the same time they agree with the Epicureans in this, that they fancy God does *not at all concern* himself in the *government* of the World, nor has any regard to, or care of, what is done therein.[10]

This position, Clarke insists, "leads necessarily and by unavoidable consequence, to *plain Atheism*,"[11] because if God has no regard to what is done in the world, "it will follow that he is not an Omnipresent, All-powerful, Intelligent, and Wise Being; and consequently, that he Is not at all."[12] But Clarke's allusions at this point are to classical sources, not to his contemporaries.

It is also true that by the nineteenth century, when a number of related terms were being more precisely defined, the disputed view came to be known as deism. Thus, for example, one standard encyclopaedia of the period defines "deism" as "that view of God, which, as against

---

[9]For a lucid discussion of this point see further P. Byrne, *Natural Religion and the Nature of Religion: The Legacy of Deism*, Routledge Religious Studies (London: Routledge, 1989).

[10]S. Clarke, *A Discourse concerning the Unchangeable Obligations of Natural Religion, and the Truth and Certainty of the Christian Revelation* (London: printed by W. Botham, for James Knapton, at the Crown in St Paul's Church-Yard, 1706) 19. Clarke found three other varieties of deist: 1. Those who believe in the being and providence of God, in God's governing power in the natural order, but who deny that God is concerned with the morally good or evil actions of human beings: "these things depending, as they imagine, merely on the arbitrary constitution of humane Laws" (26-27). 2. Those who believe in God's providence and moral governance, but who are prejudiced against the idea of immortality (32). 3. Those who believe in providence, moral government, and immortality, but who do so only so far as the light of natural reason permits, and without appealing to divine revelation (37).

[11]Ibid., 23.

[12]Ibid., 24.

atheism, recognizes his real existence; as against pantheism, his distinctness from the world; and, as opposed to theism, represents him not merely as transcendent above the world, and distinct from it, but also as separate, in the sense, that, having once created the world, he is not immanent in it as its providential ruler and guide, but allows it to pursue an independent course." But the author immediately and properly adds, "This philosophical definition is, however, of recent date."[13] On this matter the erudite Robert Flint may have the last word, and lead us to our next point. He refers to the "historical application" of "deism" to the English deists, pointing out that it is wrong to "represent them as having denied that God was present and active in the laws of nature. This is erroneous and unfair. One or two of them may have done so, but certainly what as a body they denied was merely [Flint's "merely" makes the denial seem less significant than it is] that God worked otherwise than through natural laws."[14]

II

We are now in a position briefly to characterize, in chronological order of representative works, some of the main lines of deism as it flowed down to Paine and Fuller. In attempting this intricate task we should have in mind the following contextual points. First, behind the appeal of a number of eighteenth-century deists to reason and natural revelation there lay the memory of the previous century's civil strife and religious unrest—some of it occasioned by the appeals of sectaries to special revelations. The deists desired no repetition of this. Equally, many of them were at best cool towards the 'enthusiasm' of the Evangelical Revival, whose beginnings the later deists witnessed. Thirdly, now that the Toleration Act of 1689 had, for all its limitations, legalized Christian traditions other than that of the Church of England, there was no one ecclesiastical authority to which appeal on religious questions could be made. This

---

[13]G. V. Lechler, "Deism," in *A Religious Encyclopaedia, or, Dictionary of Biblical, Historical, Doctrinal, and Practical Theology Based on the Real-Encyklopädie of Herzog, Plitt, and Hauck*, 3rd ed., 621 (b). Peter Byrne reiterates the point in A. E. McGrath, *The Blackwell Encyclopedia of Modern Christian Thought* (Oxford: Blackwell, 1993) 103.

[14]R. Flint, *Anti-Theistic Theories* (Edinburgh: William Blackwood, 1899) 443.

posed the question, again with regard to societal coherence, whether natural religion might provide common ground—even universally agreed common ground—(analogous to the generalizations of science which the "new" scientists were drawing from their observations of the world's phenomena) on which those of many doctrinal persuasions might stand. None of which prevented critics of deism from alleging that deists sought a wider toleration than was currently available (Roman Catholics, Jews, and Unitarians not enjoying the benefits of 1689) only in order to subvert the state by ruining the established church. That this was the desire of atheists, deists, fanatics, and the "spawn of jesuits" (note the imprecision of scurrility) was precisely the view of the anonymous author of a polemical tract of 1705, *An Essay upon Government, Wherein the Republican Schemes Reviv'd by* Mr. *Lock, Dr. Blackal &c. Are Fairly Consider'd and Refuted.* Two years later, the nonjuror, Charles Leslie (1650–1722) accused Tindal and Collins of espousing Locke's moderately progressive views on toleration for the same purpose.[15] With these considerations and cautions in mind we may turn to the deists themselves.[16]

While we cannot here delve into the continental hinterland of English deism, or trace the intellectual indebtedness of particular deists in detail, we may say in general terms that there were many currents in the intellectual air they breathed. From Francis Bacon (1561–1626) there flowed a strong current of scientific empiricism. It was the task of the scientist, he maintained, not to seek final causes, but to proceed inductively from known facts. While he distinguished between knowledge and faith, natural philosophy and theology—especially with respect to their terms of reference—he did not, as some of his opponents contended, repudiate the idea of a final cause. On the contrary, at the beginning of his celebrated essay "Of Atheism" he famously declared:

> I had rather beleeve all the Fables in the *Legend*, and the *Talmud*, and the *Alcoran*, then that this universall Frame, is without a Minde. And

---

[15]See C. Leslie, *The Second Part of the Wolf Stript of His Shepherds Cloathing in Answer to a Late Celebrated Book Intituled "The Rights of the Christian Church Asserted"* (London and Westminster: n.p., 1707) 3.

[16]I have provided a brief general sketch of deism in my *Dissenting Thought and the Life of the Churches: Studies in an English Tradition* (San Francisco: Mellen, 1990) chap. 2.

> therefore, God never wrought Miracle, to convince *Atheisme*, because his Ordinary Works convince it. It is true, that a little Philosophy inclineth Mans Minde to *Atheisme*; But depth in Philosophy, bringeth Mens Mindes about to *Religion*: For while the Minde of Man, looketh upon Second Causes Scattered, it may sometimes rest in them, and goe no further: But when it beholdeth the Chaine of them, Confederate and Linked together, it must needs flie to *Providence*, and *Deitie*.[17]

With this conclusion, as with Bacon's method and his denunciation of "scandalous priests"[18] many deists were in general accord.

From Thomas Hobbes (1588–1679) some deists learned that no revelation could run contrary to reason, and from him, too, some of them imbibed anticlerical iconoclasm. But from the concluding chapters of *Leviathan* (1651), with their anti-Roman Catholic strictures against purgatory, transubstantiation, and the like, those of a skeptical turn of mind could also learn to challenge doctrines traditionally received as scriptural—the incorporeality of spirits, for example—on the ground that they are not taught in the Bible. This is consistent on the one hand with Hobbes's strictures upon "the vain philosophy of Aristotle" with its talk of separated essences; and on the other hand with his staunch materialism, according to which "(. . . the *universe*, that is, the whole mass of things that are), is corporeal, that is to say, body . . . that which is not body, is no part of the universe."[19]

By exalting reason as the "candle of the Lord"—lit by God and receiving God's light—even the very differently tempered Cambridge Platonists, stalwart upholders of the interdependence of reason and faith, whose prominent representative Benjamin Whichcote (1609–1683) lamented the way in which "Bacon, Hobbes, Puritans, and Prelatists, agreed in treating philosophy and theology as things wholly different in kind,"[20] opened the way to deistic constructions of their phrase with

---

[17]F. Bacon, *The Essayes or Counsels, Civill and Morall, of Francis Lo. Verulam, Viscount St. Alban* (London: Iohn Hauiland for Hanna Barret and Richard Whitaker, 1625) 90-91.

[18]Ibid., 94.

[19]T. Hobbes, "Leviathan," in *The English Works of Thomas Hobbes of Malmesbury*, ed. W. Molesworth (London: J. Bohn, 1839) 3:674, 672.

[20]Quoted by W. R. Inge, *The Platonic Tradition in English Religious Thought* (London: Longmans, 1926) 48.

which they themselves would not have been in sympathy.[21] Note, for example, the terms in which Toland described reason: "Reason is not less from God than Revelation; 'tis the Candle, the Guide, the Judge he has lodg'd within every Man that cometh into this World."[22]

Notwithstanding what I have just said concerning empiricism and the inductive method, the "grandfather of English deism,"[23] Herbert of Cherbury (1583–1648), rested on five *innate* principles, namely, that God exists; that he is to be worshipped; that we honour him by the practice of virtue; that repentance is obligatory upon human beings; and that we are liable to postmortem reward and punishment. The validity of these a priori principles is immediately known independently of revelation (which Herbert did not repudiate, but did not need); they are universal and certain. Herbert inveighed against those clerics who, for their own unscrupulous ends, had obscured these fundamental principles. Herbert's views are found in his *De Veritate* (1624) and his posthumous *De Religione* (1663). D. P. Walker has pointed out that the 1645 edition of *De Veritate* tightens the five principles—now described as a perfect circle from which nothing may be subtracted and to which nothing may be added—in such a way as to make it more difficult to regard them as a foundation on which might be erected a Christian superstructure.[24] Later deists for the

---

[21]I have elsewhere suggested that there is a clearer line to the deists via the "ever memorable" Oxford Latitudinarian author John Hales (1584–1656) than via the Cambridge Platonists, for Hales allowed reason to be the arbiter between truth and falsehood. See his *Of Enquiry and Private Juidgment in Religion*, in *The Works of the Ever Memorable Mr. John Hales of Eaton; Now First Collected Together* (Glasgow: printed by Robert and Andrew Foulis, 1765) 3:141-66; A. P. F. Sell, "Platonists (Ancient and Modern) and the Gospel," *The Irish Theological Quarterly* 44 (1977): 161-62.

[22]John Toland, *Christianity Not Mysterious: or, A Treatise Shewing That There Is Nothing in the Gospel Contrary to Reason, nor Above It: and That No Christian Doctrine Can Be Properly Call'd a Mystery* (London: printed for S. Buckley, 1696) 146.

[23]Though Peter Byrne has drawn attention to elements in Herbert's thought which distance him from subsequent Enlightenment thinkers. See P. Byrne, *Natural Religion and the Nature of Religion*, chap. 2. See also R. D. Bedford, *The Defence of Truth* (Manchester: Manchester University Press, 1979); D. A. Pailin, "Herbert of Cherbury and the Deists," *The Expository Times* 94 (1983): 196-200.

[24]D. P. Walker, *The Ancient Theology* (London: Duckworth, 1972) 167.

most part imbibed Herbert's five principles but generally, in empiricist fashion, construed them in an a posteriori manner as deliverances of experience.

To Herbert's list of five principles Charles Blount (1645–1693), in *The Oracles of Reason* (1693), adds two more: God "governs the World by Providence"; and "our Worship consists in Prayer to him and Praise to him."[25] Blount prefixes his points with a clear definition: "Natural Religion is the Belief we have of an Eternal Intellectual Being, and of the Duty which we owe him, manifested to us by our Reason, without Revelation or positive Law."[26] He ridicules clerics for their myopia, and seeks to undermine the credibility of biblical miracles. His reiterated appeal is to the morality or otherwise of believing that such and such is the case. By this criterion deists could include pre- and non-Christians among the faithful—a degree of ecumenism to which more conservative divines were by no means open. In a section entitled "A Summary Account of the Deist's Religion," Blount discusses the manner of worshipping God, and declares that proper worship is "Not by a Mediator; for, first it is unnecessary; *Miserecordia Dei* being *sufficiens justitiae suae*. Second, God must appoint this Mediator, and so was really reconciled to the World before. And third, a Mediator derogates from the infinite mercy of God, equally as an Image doth from his *Spiritualitie* and *Infinitie*."[27] With some justice Blount has come to be regarded as a forerunner of English free thought.[28]

In 1696, *Christianity Not Mysterious* was published by John Toland (1670–1722).[29] His argument is summed up in the continuation of his title: *Or, A Treatise Shewing That There Is Nothing in the Gospel Contrary to Reason, nor Above It: and That No Christian Doctrine Can Properly Be Call'd a Mystery*.[30] Here we have a clear rationalistic line, the phrase "nor above it" ruling out any appeal to supernatural revelation. Toland hopes

---

[25]C. Blount and others, *The Oracles of Reason* (London: 1693) 195-96.

[26]Ibid., 195.

[27]Ibid., 89.

[28]See further, J. A. Redwood, "Charles Blount (1654–1693), Deism, and English Free Thought," *JHI* 35 (1974): 490-95.

[29]For Toland, see Sullivan, *John Toland and the Deist Controversy*; S. H. Daniel, *John Toland: His Methods, Manners, and Mind* (Kingston: McGill-Queen's University Press, 1984).

[30]See n. 22, above.

Christians will not be offended by him when he endeavours "to confirm and elucidate Revelation. . . . I hope [he continues] to make it appear, that the Use of Reason is not so dangerous in Religion as it is commonly represented."[31] He seeks to show that when the Bible is brought to the bar of reason, insofar at it is vindicated, secure faith in its deliverances is justifiable. If the doctrines of the Gospel are the word of God they cannot be contrary to reason,[32] and they certainly cannot be certified by appealing to mystery, since there is nothing above reason in the Gospel.[33] In Toland's view, "Reason is the only Foundation of all Certitude."[34]

With Anthony Collins (1676–1729)[35] the presuppositions of deism, namely, that human beings are free to employ their reason, and that they are competent to discover truth for themselves (an implicit check upon the authoritarian imposition of beliefs), are brought to the fore. His *A Discourse of Free-Thinking, Occasion'd by the Rise and Growth of a Sect Call'd Free-Thinkers* appeared in 1713. He here contends that those who decline to assent to self-evident truth manifest a "distemper'd State of Mind," and are prey to "the Dictates of artificial designing men or crack-brain'd Enthusiasts."[36] He proceeds on the basis of the following definition: "By Free-Thinking then I mean, the Use of the Understanding, in endeavouring to find out the meaning of any Proposition whatsoever, in considering the nature of the Evidence for or against it, and in judging of it according to the seeming Force or Weakness of the Evidence."[37] Among the matters upon which people have the right to think freely—the denials of the enemies of free thought notwithstanding—are, "the Nature and Attributes of the Eternal Being or God, of the Truth and Authority of Books esteem'd Sacred, and of the Sense and meaning of those Books; or, in one word, of Religious Questions."[38] He feels that great benefits will

---

[31]Toland, *Christianity Not Mysterious*, viii.

[32]Ibid., 23.

[33]Ibid., 67.

[34]Ibid., 6.

[35]For Collins see J. O'Higgins, *Anthony Collins: The Man and His Works* (The Hague: Martinus Nijhof, 1970).

[36]Anthony Collins, *A discourse of free-thinking, occasion'd by the rise and growth of a sect call'd free-thinkers* (London: n.p., 1713) 4.

[37]Ibid., 5.

[38]Ibid., 32.

accrue to society if only people will employ their reason in the way he recommends. By way of encouragement he holds before his readers a galaxy of those he claims as freethinkers, from Socrates, "the divinest Man that ever appear'd in the heathen World,"[39] through Erasmus and others, to Locke.[40]

In his *A Discourse of the Grounds and Reasons of the Christian Religion* (1724), Collins asks, "Of what use is it to consult *reason* and *Scripture* at all, as any means of information, if we are not, upon conviction, to follow their dictates? And what *principles* of religion are men to *profess* (which all say must be) *openly*, and act upon, but those, whereof they are convinc'd?"[41] He charges clergymen with the duty of integrity: "they cannot act more effectually against the design of their own profession, than either by being silent as to the discoveries they make, or by preaching and writing contrary to their own light."[42] Collins pioneers a skeptical approach to the alleged facts of the Bible, and implies that if Scripture is unreliable, apologetic arguments based on the appeal to the fulfilment of prophecy are seriously weakened. Indeed, appealing to the scholarship (though not to the ecclesiastical loyalty) of Hugo Grotius, he concludes that Old Testament prophecies were not fulfilled by Christ. Indeed, "these *proofs* taken out of the *Old*, and urg'd in the *New* Testament, being sometimes, either not to be found in the *Old*, or not urg'd in the *New*, according to the literal and obvious sense, which they seem to bear in their suppos'd places in the *Old*, and therefore not proofs according to scholastick rules,"[43] they are patient of allegorical interpretation only. In part two he argues that in his *Essay towards Restoring the True Text of the Old Testament* (1722) the now deposed Anglican Arian divine William Whiston (1667–1752),[44] who wishes to show that the text of the Old Testament is "the very same now that it ever has been from the utmost antiquity," undercuts his own argument by adverting to the

---

[39]Ibid., 123.

[40]Ibid., 177.

[41]Anthony Collins, *A Discourse of the Grounds and Reasons of the Christian Religion, in Two Parts . . . to Which Is Prefix'd an Apology for Free Debate and Liberty of Writing* (London: n.p., 1724) xiv.

[42]Ibid.

[43]Ibid., 39.

[44]Whiston joined the General Baptists in 1747.

corruptions of the text and to the inconsistencies between it and that of the New Testament.[45]

Thomas Woolston (1669–1733), in his *Six Discourses on the Miracles of Our Saviour* (1727–1730),[46] reveals his agreement with Collins as to the alleged evidential value of prophecy. He believes that the controversy over that issue "will end in the absolute Demonstration of Jesus's *Messiahship* from Prophecy, which is the only way to prove him to be the Messiah."[47] But the method of proof requires that the prophecies be construed not literally, but allegorically, after the manner of the early Fathers; and this despite the fact that "this way does not please our ecclesiastical *Writers* in the Controversy."[48] Woolston now follows up, like Blount before him, with an analogous attack upon apologetic arguments which assume the evidential value of biblical miracles. To his own satisfaction he finds that the accounts of fifteen miracles are deficient and incredible, but he does not, on this account, wish to deny the Messiahship of Jesus. But miracles, no less than prophecies must be interpreted allegorically, after the manner of the early fathers. He finds that some of the miracles recorded in the gospels never took place, but are "prophetical and parabolical Narratives of what will be mysteriously and more wonderfully done by him."[49] Indeed, to construe the miracles literally is to "imply Improbabilities and Incredibilities, and the grossest Absurdities, very dishonourable to the name of Christ."[50] His first discourse ends with the following bold statement:

> The History of *Jesus'* Life, is an emblematical Representation of his spiritual Life in the Soul of Man; and his Miracles are Figures of his

---

[45]Collins, *Discourse of the Grounds and Reasons of the Christian Religion*, 270-71.

[46]Reprinted as *Six Discourses on the Miracles of Our Saviour and Defences of His Discourses* (New York: Garland, 1979): "Reprint of works printed 1727–1730 for the author, London."

[47]Thomas Woolston, *A Discourse on the Miracles of Our Saviour, in View of the Present Controversy between Infidels and Apostates*, 5th ed. (London: Printed for the author, 1728) 1.

[48]Ibid., 2.

[49]Ibid., 3.

[50]Ibid., 19-20.

> mysterious Operations. The four Gospels are in no Part a literal Story, but a system of mystical Philosophy or Theology.[51]

He sustains this position throughout his discourses, and in the sixth, devoted to showing that the resurrection of Jesus is a "monstrous and incredible Miracle,"[52] he argues that when Jesus appealed to his own works and miracles as a testimony to his authority, he "did not properly and ultimately refer to those done in the *Flesh*, but to those mystical ones he would do in the *Spirit*, of which those done in the Flesh are but mere Types and Shadows."[53] He concludes by emphasizing that all he has done has been for "the Demonstration of the messiahship of our Spiritual Jesus."[54]

In 1730 Matthew Tindal (1656?–1733), who claimed his place among the "True Christian Deists," published the work which, by common consent, most adequately sets forth the principles of deism. His title, *Christianity as Old as the Creation: or, The Gospel, a Republication of the Religion of Nature . . .*, precisely announces his theme. By "natural religion" Tindal means "the Belief of the Existence of a God, and the Sense and Practice of those Duties which result from the Knowledge we, by our Reason, have of him and his perfections; and of ourselves, and our own Imperfections; and of the relation we stand in to him and our Fellow-Creatures; so that the *Religion of Nature* takes in every thing that is founded on the Reason and Nature of things."[55] 'True Religion' is thus "a constant Disposition of Mind to do all the Good we can; and thereby render ourselves acceptable to God in answering the End of his Creation."[56]

Tindal argues that God treats all alike in the sense of endowing everyone with the capacity to discern and pursue the path of duty. God's will is immanent throughout the created order—so far is Tindal from the

---

[51]Ibid., 65.

[52]Thomas Woolston, *A Sixth Discourse on the Miracles of Our Saviour, in View of the Present Controversy between Infidels and Apostates*, 2nd ed. (London: printed for the author, and sold by him . . . , 1729) 5.

[53]Ibid., 51. So some miracles at least were done in the flesh? Woolston does not seem here to be at his most logical.

[54]Ibid., 71.

[55]Matthew Tindal, *Christianity as Old as the Creation: or, The Gospel, a Republication of the Religion of Nature*, vol. 1, 3rd ed. (London: n.p., 1732) 11.

[56]Ibid., 18.

allegedly "deist" view that God, having set the cosmic process going has retreated from it. It is "the reason of things, or the relation they have to each other" which "teaches us our Duty in all cases whatever."[57] Supernatural revelation and appeals to the miraculous are thus redundant: Tindal argues "That the Religion of Nature is absolutely perfect; and that external Revelation can neither add to, not take from its perfection."[58] We do not need an incarnate Lord, or an atoning work at the Cross. What Jesus does is simply to republish the religion of nature.

Since "God requires nothing for his own sake,"[59] and since the law of nature is clear, "Religion, even in relation to the Worship of God, as it is a reasonable Service, [cannot] be any thing, but what necessarily flows from the consideration of God, and the creatures."[60] As for our moral duty, no supernatural revelation of it could improve upon the revelation of it in nature, because only commands perceived to be reasonable are obligatory, and such perception is within the sphere of natural religion.[61] For "Whatever is confus'd and perplex'd, can never come from the clear Fountain of all Knowledge, nor that which is obscure, from the Father of inexhaustible Light; and as far as you suppose God's Laws are not plain to any part of Mankind, so far you derogate from the Perfection of those Laws, and the Wisdom and Goodness of the divine Legislator."[62] Hence, "were there an instituted Religion which differs from That of Nature, its Precepts must be arbitrary, as not founded on the Nature and Reason of Things, but depending on mere Will and Pleasure; otherwise it would be the same with Natural Religion."[63]

Tindal proceeds to show how his argument for the clarity of the natural revelation of God's law counters superstition, and how it applies to the whole of religion: "natural and reveal'd Religion can't differ: Because whatever Reason shows to be worthy of having God for its Author, must belong to Natural Religion; and whatever Reason tells us

---

[57]Ibid., 16.
[58]Ibid., 49.
[59]Ibid.
[60]Ibid., 53.
[61]Ibid., 59.
[62]Ibid., 91.
[63]Ibid., 99.

is unworthy of having God for its Author, can never belong to the True Reveal'd Religion."[64]

Towards the end of his work there appears Tindal's appeal: if only people believed "that all, who were equally sincere, were equally acceptable to God," and if they were "wholly bent against Immorality, discoverable by the Light of Nature," there would come, "in the Scripture-Phrase, *a new Heaven and a new Earth*."[65] (At which we may imagine that those divines for whom sin was a reality and atoning grace an urgent necessity uttered the eighteenth-century equivalent of "In your dreams!")

Thomas Chubb (1679–1747), who had been a semi-Arian of the Clarkeian kind, gradually veered towards deism and, in 1731, published *A Discourse concerning Reason*.[66] He sets out to show, as his subtitle indicates, that *Reason either Is, or Else That It Ought to Be, a Sufficient Guide in Matters of Religion*. In *The True Gospel of Jesus Christ Asserted* (1738),[67] Chubb follows Tindal in holding that supernatural revelation is unnecessary, and, under attack, published further works in defence of his view that religion is founded on nature. He believes that moral living renders us acceptable to God, that repentance for sin is rewarded by God's mercy, and that all will be judged. He is, however, skeptical of a number of portions of Scripture, and thinks, for example, that Christ's

---

[64]Ibid., 197.

[65]Ibid., 374.

[66]*Discourse concerning Reason, with Regard to Religion and Divine Revelation. Wherein Is Shewn, That Reason either Is, or Else That It Ought to Be, a Sufficient Guide in Matters of Religion. Occasioned by the Lord Bishop of London's [i.e., Edmund Gibson's] Second Pastoral Letter. To Which Are Added, Some Reflections upon the Comparative Excellency and Usefulness of Moral and Pastoral Duties. Occasioned by the Controversy That Has Arisen . . . upon the Publication of Dr. [Samuel] Clark's Exposition of the Church Catechism* (London: T. Cox, 1731).

[67]*The True Gospel of Jesus Christ Asserted Wherein Is Shown What Is and What is Not That Gospel; What Was the Great and Good End It Was Intended to Serve; How It Is Excellently Suited to Answer That Purpose; and How, or by What Means That End Has in a Great Measure Been Frustrated. Humbly Offered to Publick Consideration, and in Particular to All Those Who Esteem Themselves, or Are Esteemed by Others to Be Ministers of Jesus Christ, and Preachers of His Gospel; and More Especially to All Those Who Have Obtained the Reputation of Being the Great Defenders of Christianity*. To which is added "A Short Dissertation on Providence" (London: T. Cox, 1738).

resurrection in no way proves his divinity. In his *Discourse on Miracles* (1741)[68] he argues that the biblical miracles do no more than offer a "probable proof" of a revelation.

Thomas Morgan (d. 1743), though an Independent minister at Burton, Somerset, was ordained at Frome in 1716 by the Presbyterian John Bowder. He became heterodox, and was dismissed from his church in the early 1720s. He turned to medicine, became a freethinker, and eventually described himself as a Christian deist. He wrote tracts against Athanasian Christology, against Chubb's early works, against enthusiasm, and in defence of the Quaker apologist Robert Barclay. Assailed from many sides, he was ever ready to respond. In *The Moral Philosopher* (1737, with replies to Leland and Chapman in 1739, to Leland and Lowman in 1740, and a final volume, *Physico-Theology* in 1741)[69] he sets out from the principle that whether doctrines have been conveyed by reason, immediate personal revelation from God, or authentic testimony from originally enlightened and supernaturally assisted persons, the proof of the religion nonetheless turns upon "the moral Truth, Reasonableness, and Fitness of the Doctrines themselves, as appearing to the Understanding, upon a fair, impartial Consideration and Judgment of Reason."[70] Morgan divorces the

---

[68]*A Discourse on Miracles, Considered as Evidences to Prove the Divine Original of a Revelation: Wherein Is Shewn, What Kind and Degree of Evidence Arises from Them, and in Which the Various Reasonings on Those Questions That Relate to the Subject Are Fairly Represented. To Which Is Added, an Appendix, Containing an Enquiry into This Question, viz., Whether the Doctrines of a Future State of Existence to Men, and a Future Retribution, Where Plainly and Clearly Taught by Moses and the Prophets? Humbly Offered to the Consideration of the Rev. Dr. Warberton [William Warburton], and All Others That Particularly Interest Themselves in This Question* (London: T. Cox, 1741).

[69]*The Moral Philosopher. In a Dialogue between Philalethes a Christian Deist, and Theophanes a Christian Jew. In Which the Grounds and Reasons of Religion in General, and Particularly of Christianity, as Distinguish'd from the Religion of Nature with Many Other Matters of the Utmost Consequence in Religion, Are Fairly Considered, and Debated, and the Arguments on Both Sides Impartially Represented,* "second edition, corrected" (London: printed for the author, 1738). *Physico-Theology, or, A Philosophico-Moral Disquisition concerning Human Nature, Free Agency, Moral Government, and Divine Providence* (London: printed for T. Cox at the Lamb under the Royal Exchange, 1741).

[70]*The Moral Philosopher*, x.

Old from the New Testament, severely criticizes the former, and repudiates the latter's teaching on the atonement—a corruption, he thought, of Jewish sacrificial ideas. The nub of his case is that "None of the Doctrines of Revelation . . . can be fundamental or necessary, because mistakes in such a Case are easily made, and may be unavoidable; nay, no Man can be certain that he understands the true, determinate Sense of the Holy Ghost, or the inspired Writers, concerning . . . fundamental Truths and Doctrines, which are delivered in ambiguous Terms, and cloth'd with Expressions capable of very different Constructions."[71]

Over one further name we need not long delay. In 1742 Henry Dodwell the Younger (d. 1784) anonymously published *Christianity Not Founded on Argument*. He contends that reason is redundant where questions of faith are concerned; that the faithful are best advised not to question what they believe, but simply to welcome the immediate communications of the Holy Spirit. Some Christians welcomed this as leaving the way open for faith; but Philip Doddridge, in his *Answer to a Late Pamphlet* (1743), and John Leland, both in his A *View of the Principal Deistical Writers* and in his 1744 *Remarks*[72] specifically directed against Dodwell's tract, construed it, correctly in the opinion of most scholars, as an ironic exposure to ridicule of the stated views in order that the superiority of reason would clearly be seen.

---

[71]Ibid., 17-18.

[72]Doddridge, *An Answer to a Late Pamphlet, Intitled, Christianity Not Founded on Argument, &c. in Three Letters to the Author* (London: printed for M. Fenner and J. Hodges, 1743). (Each letter has its own title page with imprint dates 1742, 1743?, 1743. With this are bound both of Leland's *Remarks*.) The orginal publication of Doddridge's first two "letters" was as *The Perspicuity and Solidity of Those Evidences of Christianity, to Which the Generality of Its Professors among Us May Attain . . .* (1742). Leland, A *View of the Principal Deistical Writers That Have Appeared in England in the Last and Present Century; with Observations upon Them, and Some Account of the Answers That Have Been Published against Them. In Several Letters to a Friend*, 3 vols. (London: B. Dodd, 1754–1756). Leland, *Remarks on a Late Pamphlet, Entitled, Christianity Not Founded on Argument: in a Letter to a Friend* (London: R. Hett and J. Stagg, 1744). (Bound with Doddridge, *An Answer to a Late Pamphlet*, which see above: 1743 printing.)

III

If anything, the responses to deism are even more diverse in content than deism itself. They are also exceedingly numerous: Tindal's *Christianity as Old as the Creation* alone provoked more than thirty replies. Our selection of responses to deism as a whole is simply designed to show something of the flavour of the authors concerned, and to place Andrew Fuller's reply to Paine in context.

In 1641, during his first Kidderminster ministry, the Reformed pastor par excellence, Richard Baxter (1615–1691), underwent a period of doubt. This prompted him (in Cartesian fashion) "to dig to the very foundations, and seriously to examine the reasons of Christianity, and to give a hearing to all that could be said against it, so that my faith might be indeed my own."[73] As a result of this enquiry "the being and attributes of God were so clear to me that he was to my intellect what the sun is to my eye." Accordingly, atheism was ruled out, and then Baxter saw that "there is no other religion in the world which can stand competition with Christianity. . . . [M]ere Deism, which is the most plausible competitor, is so turned out of almost all the whole world as if Nature made its own confession that without a mediator it cannot come to God."[74] Although in the seventeenth century "deism" was often used synonymously with "theism," the reference to nature suggests that Baxter has natural religion in mind. He does not go into a detailed critique of deism, but in the reference to the deists' bypassing of the need of a mediator Baxter announces what will be a common refrain in many orthodox critiques of deism, namely, that the deists do not take the full measure of humanity's sinful plight and, accordingly, they do not see the need for the saving remedy but are, on the contrary, overly optimistic that people will behave reasonably, seek the good of others, and prize benevolence. This we might label as primarily a religious response to deism, whereas the response of Joseph Butler, for example, is, as we shall see, more philosophical in character.

---

[73]R. Baxter, *The Autobiography of Richard Baxter*, abridged ed. (London: Dent, 1931) 26-27.

[74]Ibid., 27.

The position of Baxter's contemporary John Locke (1632–1704) with respect to deism has been much discussed.[75] The way in which Locke's friend Anthony Collins added Locke to his honour roll of freethinkers tempted some hostile critics into making Locke guilty by association; but not even the most vociferous of his intellectual foes branded Locke a deist—a not insignificant fact in that nicknaming age when numerous epithets lay to hand. Unlike Toland, for example, Locke did not deny that there are truths of revelation which are above reason, and Leland complimented Locke on having shown, "with great clearness and force, the usefulness of divine revelation, for setting the great principles of the law of nature, and the important duties of religion and morality in a strong and convincing light, and enforcing them with the most powerful motives."[76] Locke's apologetic work, *The Reasonableness of Christianity, as Delivered in the Scriptures*,[77] was directed against the deists. In a letter to his supporter Samuel Bold, reproduced in the preface to his *Second Vindication* of *The Reasonableness of Christianity*,[78] Locke expressed the hope that his results will be helpful

> especially to those, who thought either that there was no need of revelation at all, or that the revelation of our Saviour required the belief of such articles for salvation, which the settled notions, and their way of reasoning in some, and want of understanding in others, made possible to them. Upon these two topics the objections seemed to turn, which were with most assurance made by deists against Christianity; but against Christianity misunderstood.[79]

His own position is clear: "A great many things we have been bred up in the belief of from our Cradles . . . we take for obvious Truths, and easily demonstrable; without considering how long we might have been in doubt

---

[75]See, e.g., A. P. F. Sell, *John Locke and the Eighteenth-Century Divines* (Cardiff: University of Wales Press, 1997) 78-82, 205-13, and passim.

[76]Leland, *A View of the Principal Deistical Writers*, 18.

[77]J. Locke, *The Reasonableness of Christianity, as Delivered in the Scriptures* (London: printed for Awnsham and John Churchil, 1695).

[78]J. Locke, *A Second Vindication of the Reasonableness of Christianity, &c.* (London: printed for Awnsham and John Churchil, 1697).

[79]*The Works of John Locke*, 10 vols., 11th ed. (London: printed for W. Otrige, 1812) 7:188.

or ignorance of them, had Revelation been silent."[80] As for natural religion, it provides insufficient incentives for facing the hardships of the virtuous life, its view of immortality is too vague to serve as a moral sanction, and it has no word for sinners who are incapable of fulfilling its perfect moral law. We may therefore endorse J. C. Biddle's apt conclusion that "although Toland and later Deists drew heavily upon his philosophy, Locke seems not to have been an intentional party to their emphasis upon reason and natural religion. Rather, as an opponent of the Deists and a defender of revelation, Locke sought a simple, moral Christianity based on faith."[81]

Samuel Clarke makes a number of antideist points. First, that "almost all the Things that are said wisely and truly by modern Deists, are plainly borrowed from that Revelation, which they refuse to embrace."[82] Indeed, to have had to discover our duty without the aid of revealed light would have been "like groping for an unknown way in the obscure Twilight."[83] Secondly, "the Rewards and Punishments of another World, the great Motives of Religion, cannot be so *powerfully inforced*, to the influencing of the Lives and Practice of all sorts of Men, by one who shall undertake to demonstrate the reality of them by abstract Reason and Arguments."[84] Thirdly, in answer to the objection (raised, for example, by Blount) that

---

[80]*The Reasonableness of Christianity*, 277-78.

[81]J. C. Biddle, "Locke's Critique of Innate Principles and Toland's Deism," *JHI* 37 (1976): 422. It is an exaggeration to imply that all later deists drew heavily on Locke. Toland and Tindal were most heavily indebted to him. At the end of the eighteenth century and beyond we may still find writers on the one hand invoking Locke's aid against the deists, and on the other hand declaring that Locke has subverted divine revelation. The former are exemplified by Uzal Ogden (1744–1822), rector of Trinity Church, Newark, New Jersey, whose (with Charles Leslie) *Antidote to Deism. The Deist Unmasked; or, An Ample Refutation of All the Objections of Thomas Paine, against the Christian Religion; as Contained in a Pamphlet, Intitled, The Age of Reason; Addressed to the Citizens of These States* (Newark NJ: printed by John Woods, 1795) is a two-volume critique of Paine's *The Age of Reason*. For an example of the latter see *Principles of Nature or, A Development of the Moral Causes of Happiness and Misery among the Human Species* (London: R. Carlile, 1819) by the deist Elihu Palmer (1764–1806).

[82]Clarke, *A Discourse concerning the Unchangeable Obligations*, 254.

[83]Ibid.

[84]Ibid., 257.

the revelation of God's Son is not known equally by all nations, Clarke retorts that, similarly, the obligations of natural religion are not universally acknowledged. Nevertheless, as the benefits of the redeeming work of Christ encompass those who lived before his birth, it cannot be proved "but that the same benefit may likewise extend itself forwards to those who never heard of his appearance, tho' they lived after it."[85] But at the heart of Clarke's plea is the religious point we noted earlier in Baxter's brief remarks: "There was plainly wanting a *Divine Revelation*, to recover Mankind out of their universal corruption and degeneracy," to make plain how God should be worshipped, to show what expiation was necessary for sins, and how the "Authority, Honour, and Dignity of [God's] Laws might be effectually vindicated"; and to give people full assurance of the truth of the great motives of religion, namely, the rewards and punishments of a future state.[86]

Richard Bentley (1662–1742), Benjamin Hoadly and William Whiston were among others who rose to the bait of Collins's *A Discourse of Free-Thinking*. Bentley complained that the Freethinkers' definition of "freethinking" meant simply to "*Think and Judge as you find*; which every Inhabitant of *Bedlam* practices every day." In fact "*Free* with them has no relation at all to outward Impediment or Inhibition . . . but means an inward Promptness and Forwardness to decide about Matters beyond the reach of their Studies, in *opposition* to the rest of mankind."[87] In the following year Thomas Halyburton (1674–1712), professor of divinity at St. Andrews, published *Natural Religion Insufficient and Revealed Necessary to Man's Happiness*, in which he brought Calvinistic orthodoxy to bear upon the views of Herbert and Blount.

From the side of English Dissent, Isaac Watts (1674–1748) rose up against deism. In 1722 he wrote *A Caveat against Infidelity*, though the tract was not published until 1729. By that time he could hold it back no longer, for "deism and infidelity [have] made such violent efforts, of late, in this nation." They have managed "to draw some from the faith of the blessed gospel, and to stagger others in their unbelief."[88] His case is that

---

[85]Ibid., 321-22.

[86]Ibid., 241-44.

[87]R. Bentley, *Remarks upon a Late Discourse of Freethinking*, 2nd ed. (London: Morphew, 1713) 10-11.

[88]*The Works of the Rev. Isaac Watts, D.D.*, 7 vols., ed. Edward Parsons (Leeds:

we cannot hope for the favour of God, or for life eternal, unless we seek them by God's appointed means, namely, through the one mediator, Jesus Christ. While ignorance of the Gospel is not as such a crime, and while those who have never heard the Good News are not culpable, the deists are wilful unbelievers: having seen the light, they reject it. It will not do to say that sincerity in holding opinions is more important than the truth of the opinions, for the Gospel does not ask for sincerity, but "*faith in Jesus Christ*, or trust in the mercy of God through Jesus the Mediator."[89] *The Strength and Weakness of Human Reason* (1731) is a refutation of the deists' claim that "human reason, without any revelation from heaven, is sufficient to guide and conduct mankind in a way of religion, to the favour of God, and future blessedness."[90] The truth rather is that apart from God's supernatural revelation in Christ, humanity is lost. In *The Redeemer and the Sanctifier* (1736) Watts argues, against the deists, that Christ came to do more than restore the religion of nature: he inculcated new doctrines concerning himself, and called for obedience to himself. Watts takes his stand against all who would pare down Christianity by excising references to Christ's propitiation and the sanctifying work of the Holy Spirit: "Have we any good and sufficient Reason," he expostulates, "to subdue the Words of *Christ* and his Apostles down to the Meaning and Sense of infidels . . . ?"[91] There followed *Self-love and Virtue Reconciled only by Religion* (1739), in which Watts contends that "the only Effectual Obligation of mankind to practice Virtue, depends on the Existence and Will of God."[92] While reason can discover "the general rules of virtue, and the chief boundaries of good and evil," the sense of obligation is lacking apart from "the supposition of a God."[93] Finally, in *The Ruin and Recovery of Mankind* (1740), Watts insists that because human beings are in the line of sinful Adam, their reason is depraved. Accordingly, they require the supplement and correction provided by God's revelation in Christ, the Saviour. Watts looks for the time when "The deist will have

---

Edward Baines, 1800) 2:552.

[89]Ibid., 2:571.

[90]Ibid., 3:9.

[91]I. Watts, *The Redeemer and the Sanctifier* (London: J. Oswald, 1736) 12.

[92]Watts, *Works of the Rev. Isaac Watts*, 2:355.

[93]Ibid., 2:368.

no longer cause to triumph in the assurance of his attacks against Scripture."[94]

In 1733, the Nonconformist divine, John Leland (1691–1766) published *An Answer to a Late Book Intituled Christianity as Old as the Creation*. Against Tindal he claims to have shown

> that whatever human Reason may be suppos'd absolutely speaking to be capable of, if carried to the utmost possible Improvement, yet taking Mankind as they are, if left to themselves they wou'd be greatly at a Loss in many Things which it is of great Importance to us to know; that even with respect to those Principles and Duties of the Law of Nature, that seem capable of the clearest Proof to right Reason, yet Men have been under great Darkness and Uncertainty, where they have been left meerly to their own unassisted Reason.

Over and above the principles and duties of the law of nature, there are other matters which unaided human reason could not grasp, for example,

> the Methods God will take with his offending Creatures that have transgress'd his Law; whether and how far and upon what Terms he will pardon their Iniquities; whether he will reward even their imperfect Obedience, and what kind of Reward he will confer. . . . It were therefore greatly to be wish'd that God wou'd give us an express Revelation of his Will on these heads; and if he has done so, we ought to accept it with great Thankfulness, and with a deep Sense of our Obligations to the divine Goodness.[95]

Such a revelation, declares Leland, has been provided.

In addition to *A View of the Principal Deistical Writers* (1754–1756), in which Bolingbroke looms large, Leland published a further two-volume antideist work in 1764, the burden of which is expressed in its title, *The Advantage and Necessity of the Christian Revelation, Shewn from the State of Religion in the Antient Heathen World: especially with Respect to the Knowledge and Worship of the One True God: a Rule of Moral Duty: and a*

---

[94]Ibid., 3:370.

[95]John Leland, *An Answer to a Late Book Intituled, Christianity as Old as the Creation, In Two Parts*, 2 vols. (Dublin: printed by S. Powell for Abraham Bradley, 1733) 204-206.

State of Future Rewards and Punishments. To which is prefixed, A Preliminary Discourse on Natural and Revealed Religion.[96] Here, once more, he reiterates his point concerning the necessity of supernatural revelation.

A distinctly different approach (and style) is found in *The Case of Reason, or Natural Religion, Fairly and Fully Stated: In Answer to a Book, Entitul'd, Christianity as Old as the Creation*[97] by the spiritual writer William Law (1686–1761). In his opinion, prevailing infidelity finds its support in natural religion, and he sets out to counter Latitudinarianism in general and Matthew Tindal in particular. Reason, declares Law, is incompetent either for the defence or for the refutation of Christianity. Utterly distinct from revelation, reason is in no position to judge its deliverances. Rather, we have a faculty of spiritual intuition, and it is this which conveys to us the truth of revelation. Here is a religious response to deism which does not rely upon the accusation of missing doctrines (notably sin and the atonement), but elevates what can only be described as a mystical epistemology that bypasses reason and therefore cannot in the end engage directly with the deists' mode of argument.

Engaging with the deists' mode of argument was exactly what Joseph Butler (1692–1752) did in *The Analogy of Religion . . . to the Constitution and Course of Nature* (1736).[98] Judicious, fair, and balanced, Butler allows as much as he can to the deists, and then shows that the parameters of their method have forced them to omit matters of importance. Thus, for example, he grants that Christianity is "a republication, and external institution, of natural or essential religion . . . intended to promote natural piety and virtue," but adds that Christianity also contains "an account of a dispensation of things not discoverable by reason." Hence, "though natural religion is the foundation and principal part of Christiani-

---

[96]Two vols. (London: printed by W. Richardson and S. Clark for R. and J. Dodsley and T. Longman, 1764).

[97]W. Law, *The Case of Reason, or Natural Religion, Fairly and Fully Stated: In Answer to a Book, Entitul'd, Christianity as Old as the Creation* (London: printed for W. Innys, at the West End of St. Paul's, 1731).

[98]He says as much himself. See Joseph Butler, *The Analogy of Religion, Natural and Revealed, to the Constitution and Course of Nature. To Which Are Added Two Brief Dissertations: I. Of Personal Identity. II. Of the Nature of Virtue* (Repr.: London and New York: Ward, Lock, and Co., 1880–1889?) 192; (1st ed.: London: printed for John and Paul Knapton, 1736).

ty, it is not in any sense the whole of it."[99] We see at once that Butler is assuming with the deists (in a way which would be impossible to us today) that all right-minded persons agree that God is the author of the cosmos. He also holds that the doctrines of natural religion are probable. It is crucial to his case against the deists that he can make this out, for his argument is that if the doctrines upon which the deists rely are probable only, then the deists are in no different case from orthodox believers who, relying upon revealed truth, cannot claim absolute epistemological certainty–not least because of the element of mystery in the deepest theological claims, and the fact that in this life we are on probation and have to make moral judgements in circumstances which are not always clear.[100] Hence the objections the deists wish to lodge against claims to revealed truth can be lodged with equivalent force against their claims made on the basis of natural religion.[101]

Between the writings of Law and Butler there appeared *Scripture Vindicated* (1730–1732) by the Anglican theologian Daniel Waterland (1683–1740). Waterland here invokes Locke against Tindal's *Christianity as Old as the Creation*, and seeks to defend the Old Testament–not least the doctrine of the Fall–from the deist's attack. As an example of more popular opposition from one who clearly felt that his congregation needed to be warned against deism (and who resorts to *ad hominem* tactics rather than to reasoned argumentation) we may turn to the Presbyterian minister Josiah Owen (1711?–1755). In a sermon of 1735 he declared that

> Most of the Objections of Deists center in this, that they mistake the Traditions of men for the Doctrines of God; they charge those Chimera's upon the Almighty, that have no Existence, but in the Brains of Persons, who perhaps of all Others, are the most Superficial,—next to themselves. . . . [T]hese Objections don't affect true Christianity.[102]

---

[99]Ibid., 110.

[100]Ibid., 72.

[101]For a lucid and thorough account of Butler's philosophy of religion see T. Penelhum, *Butler*, the Arguments of the Philosophers (London: Routledge, 1985). See also the papers by D. Brown and B. Mitchell in C. Cunliffe, ed., *Joseph Butler's Moral and Religious Thought* (Oxford: Clarendon, 1992).

[102][J. Owen], *The Difficulties and Discouragements That Attend the Dissenting Ministry with the Most Proper Methods to Remove Them; Impartially Consider'd, in a Sermon Preach'd to a Congregation of Protestant Dissenters* (London: printed for

Two years later there appeared the first volume of *The Divine Legation of Moses* (1737–1741) by William Warburton (1698–1779), bishop of Gloucester. It must be said that his approach was novel—even eccentric. Warburton argued that the doctrine of future rewards and punishments is essential to the moral endeavour of human beings. However, no such doctrine is found in the Old Testament—an *absence* which he explained by invoking divine revelation, which the deists denied. Perhaps not surprisingly Leslie Stephen described Warburton as "the rather knock-kneed giant of theology, whose swashing blows, if too apt to fall upon his allies, represented at least a rough intellectual vigour."[103] Warburton also accused Collins of dishonouring the name of Locke by making it appear that Locke was on his side.[104]

From time to time the eighteenth-century evangelicals, whether Calvinist or Arminian, delivered themselves of opinions hostile to deism. Three illustrations must suffice. In the midst of a debate on the question whether the cause of evangelism would be helped or hindered by the preservation of the Welsh language, Griffith Jones, Llanddowror (1683–1761), upheld the cause of Welsh, among his reasons being the fact that there are "some advantages peculiar to the Welsh tongue favourable to religion, as being perhaps the chastest in all Europe. Its books and writings are free from the deadly venom of Atheism, Deism, Infidelity, Arianism, Popery, lewd plays, immodest romances, and love intrigues."[105] At Carmarthen on 5 May 1748, Solomon Harris was put up to dispute with the Calvinistic evangelist Howel Harris (1714–1773). Solomon Harris, an Arian, said that

> reason was enough to lead us on if it be followed, and when it was objected, that then a Mahomedan was in as good a way as a Christian

---

R. Hett, and R. Ford, 1735) 38. For Owen see *DNB*; but cf. Sell, *Dissenting Thought and the Life of the Churches*, 301-302, regarding Owen's elusive movements.

[103]Stephen, *History of English Thought in the Eighteenth Century* 1:72.

[104]*The Works of the Right Reverend William Warburton, D.D., Lord Bishop of Gloucester: To Which Is Prefixed a Discourse by Way of General Preface, Containing Some Account of the Life, Writings, and Character of the Author*, 12 vols., new ed. (London: Luke Hansard & Sons for T. Cadell and W. Davies, 1811) 1:161-62.

[105]D. Jones, *Life and Times of Griffith Jones* (London: SPCK, 1902) 96.

> he said it was not enough without the help of divine revelation. When we objected to this and said as the first was Deism, this was throwing away the Holy Spirit, he then owned we must have the assistance of the Blessed Spirit.[106]

Finally, John Wesley (1703–1791) was not fooled by Dodwell's *Christianity Not Founded on Argument*. Wesley construed the author's objective as being "to render the whole of the Christian Institution both odious and contemptible."[107] Again, in a letter to Mary Bishop of 7 February 1788 he declared "Nothing in the Christian system is of greater consequence than the doctrine of Atonement. It is properly the distinguishing point between Deism and Christianity."[108] With this we return to the heart of the religious case against deism.

By the time Wesley wrote, the deist controversy was largely exhausted, and in 1790 Edmund Burke asked of the deists,

> Who, born within the last forty years, has read one word of Collins, and Toland, and Tindal, and Chubb, and Morgan, and that whole race who called themselves Freethinkers? Who now reads Bolingbroke? Whoever read him through? Ask the booksellers of London what is become of all these lights of the world.[109]

He received his answer four years later when his intellectual opponent Thomas Paine revived the debate by publishing the first part of *The Age of Reason*. Many read Paine—not least Andrew Fuller.

---

[106]*Howell Harris's Visits to Pembrokeshire*, transcribed by Tom Beynon (Aberystwyth: Cambrian News, 1966) 149.

[107]*The Works of the Rev. John Wesley*, ed. T. Jackson (London: John Mason, 1829-1831) 8:14.

[108]*The Letters of the Rev. John Wesley*, M.A., ed. J. Telford (London: Epworth, 1931) 6:297.

[109]E. Burke, *Reflections on the Revolution in France, and on the Proceedings in Certain Societies in London Relative to That Event in a Letter Intended to Have Been Sent to a Gentleman in Paris*, in *The Works f the Right Honourable Edmund Burke* (London: printed for F. and C. Rivington, 1803–1827) 5:170-71.

IV

This is not the place for a detailed account of the colourful career of Thomas Paine (1737–1809). Suffice it to say that after a diversity of positions in England he adopted Benjamin Franklin's suggestion and went to North America in 1774. He became an editor, gaining prominence for his opposition to slavery and his advocacy of American independence. Returning to England in 1787, he published the first part of *The Rights of Man* in 1791. This was a reply to Burke's antirevolutionary *Reflections on the Revolution in France*. The second part was published in 1792, whereupon Paine was forced to flee to France, whose revolutionaries he supported. Then came the first part of *The Age of Reason* (1794), with the second part, written whilst he was in prison, following in 1795. A number of factors motivated him in sending forth this two-part blast. He was dismayed by the way in which so many clerics were opposed to societal change and supported the forces of reaction. But, like other erstwhile supporters of the French Revolution, he did not approve of the way things were working out. As he wrote in the preface to the second part of *The Age of Reason*, "The intolerant spirit of Church persecutions had transferred itself into politics."[110] He was almost as concerned by the drift towards atheism (opposition to which, he thought, had been a factor in his being imprisoned) as by those clerics who, in his view, wilfully held people under a cloud of superstition. In 1802 he returned to America, where he remained until his death.

A few lines into part one of *The Age of Reason*, Paine announces his credo: "I believe in one God, and no more; and I hope for happiness beyond this life. I believe in the equality of man, and I believe that religious duties consist in doing justice, loving mercy, and endeavouring to make our fellow-creatures happy" (1). He appeals for intellectual integrity, believing that "it is impossible to calculate the moral mischief . . . that mental lying has produced in society" (2). In particular, the action of those priests who subscribe to what they do not believe is destructive of morality. Paine echoes Herbert[111] in understanding revelation to be an

---

[110]T. Paine, *The Age of Reason* (London: Watts & Co., 1938) 60. The page references in parentheses refer to this edition.

[111]See Lord Herbert of Cherbury, *De Veritate*, trans. H. Carre (Bristol: Bristol

immediate communication from God to man—hence "It is a contradiction in terms and ideas to call anything a revelation that comes to us at second hand, either verbally or in writing" (3). This is the root of Paine's critique of clerical and scriptural authority. No more than Thomas, the disciple of Jesus, will he take the resurrection on trust from others, though he does think it probable that Jesus existed and was crucified. In good deist fashion he proceeds to adduce difficulties arising in the Old Testament, especially those concerning prophecy and then, turning to the New Testament, he declares, "Had it been the object or intention of Jesus Christ to establish a new religion, he would undoubtedly have written the system himself, or *procured it to be* written in his lifetime. But there is no publication extant authenticated with his name" (17). The four gospels and Acts are anecdotal, Revelation is an enigma, and it is as probable that the epistles are forgeries as that they are genuine.

Not, indeed, that there is no revelation: "The Word of God is the creation we behold; and it is in *this word*, which no human invention can counterfeit or alter, that God speaketh universally to man" (23). Indeed (here is Paine's ecumenical motive), "It is only in the creation that all our ideas and conceptions of a *word of God* can unite," for this word "preaches to all nations and to all worlds" (24). In creation we see God's power and wisdom. Accordingly, if we wish to know what God is we must "search not the book called the Scripture, which any human mind might make, but the Scripture called the Creation" (25).

The only way by which we come to God is that of reason. By contrast, the Christian system of faith "appears to me as a species of Atheism; a sort of religious denial of God. It professes to believe in a man rather than in God" (28). A devotee of Newton, greatly influenced by scientific intelligence concerning the immensity of the cosmos, Paine argues that science is "the study of the works of God, and of the power and wisdom of God in his works, and is the true theology." By contrast, theology as generally conceived is "the study of human opinions and of human fancies *concerning* God" (28). In a particularly striking paragraph he summarizes many of his objections:

> Putting them aside as a matter of distinct consideration, the outrage offered to the moral justice of God by supposing him to make the inno-

University Press, 1936) 308.

cent suffer for the guilty, and the loose morality and low contrivance of supposing him to change himself into the shape of a man in order to make an excuse to himself for not executing his supposed sentence on Adam . . . it is certain that what is called the Christian system of faith, including in it the whimsical account of the creation, the strange story of Eve, the snake, and the apple, the amphibious idea of the man-god, the corporeal idea of the death of a god, the mythological idea of a family of gods, and the Christian system of arithmetic that three are one, and one is three, all are irreconcilable, not only to the divine gift of reason that God hath given to man, but to the knowledge that man gains of the power and wisdom of God, by the aid of the sciences, and by studying the structure of the universe that God has made. (35-36)

Paine then lambastes the church for its persecution of scientists, and for the foolish way in which it builds on untruths. Small wonder that Christian parents are ashamed to teach their children the principles of Christianity:

[T]he Christian story of God the Father putting his son to death, or employing people to do it (for that is the plain language of the story), cannot be told by a parent to a child; and to tell him that it was done to make mankind happier and better is making the story still worse, as if mankind could be improved by the example of murder; and to tell him that all this is a mystery is only making an excuse for the incredibility of it. (41-42)

Then comes his punch line:

How different is this from the pure and simple profession of Deism! The true Deist has but one Deity; and his religion consists in contemplating the power, wisdom, and benignity of the Deity in his works, and in endeavouring to imitate him in everything moral, scientific, and mechanical. (41)

Paine proceeds to lament the unscientific way in which, against modern knowledge concerning the plurality of worlds, Christianity adheres to belief in one world only. There follows a critique of the ideas of mystery, miracle, and prophecy, all of which "are appendages that belong to fabulous and not to true religion" (52). Part one of *The Age of Reason* concludes with a summary of his main points: the idea of a word of God printed, written, or spoken is inconsistent; creation is God's word; our moral duty is to imitate the moral goodness and beneficence of God; and (while he does not elaborate the point) it is more probable that he will continue to exist after death than that he should have existed in the first place. The one point on which all nations are agreed is that there is a God, and "Adam, if ever there was such a man, was created a Deist" (59).

When Paine wrote part one of *The Age of Reason* he did not have a Bible to hand. This inconvenience was repaired by the time he wrote the second part (a mixed blessing indeed, according to many of his critics). We need not follow him in detail. Suffice it to say that he trawls through the Scriptures pointing to inconsistencies, and repudiating the prophetic and the miraculous. At the end of his Old Testament expedition he says, "I have now gone through the Bible, as a man would go through a wood with an axe on his shoulder and fell trees. Here they lie; and the priests, if they can, may replant them. They may, perhaps, stick them in the ground, but they will never make them grow" (127). He proceeds to employ similar tactics to the New Testament. Since the latter is founded upon Old Testament prophecies, and since these are worthless, the New Testament falls too. Paine is not concerned with the existence or nonexistence of its characters, but he is entirely opposed to "the fable of Jesus Christ . . . and the wild and visionary doctrine raised thereon . . . " (128). He makes merry with the genealogies of the infancy narratives, and regards the Virgin Birth as fantastic:

> Were any girl that is now with child to say, and even to swear it, that she was gotten with child by a ghost, and that an angel told her so, would she be believed? Certainly she would not. Why then are we to believe the same thing of another whom we never saw, told by nobody knows whom, nor when, nor where? (133)

Paine finally reiterates his position on revelation, pointing out that while to the Almighty all things are possible, no supernatural revelation has been given, and thus are prevented "the imposition of one man upon another, and . . . the wicked use of pretended revelation" (160). He underlines his main point thus:

> I totally disbelieve that the Almighty ever did communicate anything to man, by any mode of speech, in any language, or by any kind of vision, or appearance, or by any means which our senses are capable of receiving, otherwise than by the universal display of himself in the

> works of the creation, and by that repugnance we feel in ourselves to bad actions, and disposition to good ones. (160)

Deism teaches us "all that is necessary or proper to be known. The creation is the Bible of the deist" (164). As for Christianity, "Of all the systems of religion that ever were invented there is none more derogatory to the Almighty, more unedifying to man, more repugnant to reason, and more contradictory in itself, than this thing called Christianity" (165).

V

The full title of Andrew Fuller's reply to Paine[112] is, *The Gospel Its Own Witness; or, The Holy Nature and Divine Harmony of the Christian Religion Contrasted with the Immorality and Absurdity of Deism* (1799). In his preface he points out that "The peaceful nature of Christianity does not require that we should make peace with its adversaries. . . . On the contrary, we are required to make use of those weapons of the divine warfare with which we are furnished" (1).[113] Following a passing reference to Paine's begging of the question in his title, and to the fact that if Christianity be of God none of its enemies can overthrow it, Fuller gets down to business.

Fuller agrees with all who hold that reason is the common ground upon which believers and unbelievers must stand in order to decide their contests; but he regrets the way in which so few antagonists have used the weapon fairly: "On the contrary, they are driven to substitute dark insinuation, low wit, profane ridicule, and gross abuse" (4). In this regard Paine is linked with such other culprits as Shaftesbury, Tindal, Morgan, Bolingbroke, Voltaire, Hume, and Gibbon. Fuller has no intention of

---

[112]In the course of his tract Fuller lodges objections also to the views of Shaftesbury, Hume, and Bolingbroke. But his remarks are all part of his general case against deism which was provoked by Paine. For this reason, and also because, as pointed out earlier, Shaftesbury and Bolingbroke—and still more Hume—do not represent the main line of deist thought (blurred though that is) I shall not here delve into their works in order to assess Fuller's criticisms of them.

[113]The page references in parentheses are to the first volume of *The Complete Works of the Rev. Andrew Fuller with a Memoir of His Life* (Boston: Lincoln, Edmands & Co, 1833).

engaging the deists at every point. Rather, he will focus upon one relatively neglected issue: "The internal evidence which Christianity possesses, particularly in respect of its holy nature and divine harmony" (4). While agreeing that "the Scriptures having been conveyed to us through the medium of man, the work must necessarily, in some respects, have been humanized; yet there may be sufficient marks of divinity upon it to render it evident, to every candid mind, that it is of God" (5). The witness of Scripture—for example, to the creation, is endorsed by the created order itself. But when Paine elevates nature above Scripture on the ground that the latter is a disputed collection of texts while "No Deist can doubt whether the works of nature be God's works," Fuller retorts that atheists dispute the latter proposition; and Christians might as well say "No Christian doubts the truth of Scripture: the one proves just as much as the other" (6). Fuller's strategy is to show that Christianity is self-authenticating in that it is the only religion which inspires the love of God and man, endues those who embrace it with "a principle of justice, meekness, chastity, and goodness, and even gives a tone to the morals of society at large" (6-7). He hopes to demonstrate that Christianity is "in harmony with itself, correspondent with observation and experience, and consistent with the clearest dictates of sober reason" (7). His final introductory point is that the Christianity he defends is that of the New Testament, not that of popish superstition or of national establishments, both of which corruptions merely furnish weapons to unbelievers.

Fuller's primary claim against the deists is that while professing belief in God they overlook his moral character—presumably because "a *holy* God is not suited to their inclinations" (11). This holy God is to be worshipped. Now Paine believes that our religious duty "consists in 'doing justice, loving mercy'—and what? I thought to be sure he was going to add 'walking humbly with God.' But I was mistaken. Mr. Paine supplies the place of walking humbly with God, by adding '*and endeavouring to make our fellow-creatures happy*' " (14). Paine is offended by the idea of walking humbly with God; he ridicules the practice. He will not consider himself "an outcast, a beggar, or a worm"; he has no need of a Mediator, and he regards "redemption as a fable." Yet "To admit a God, and yet refuse to worship him, is a modern and inconsistent practice" (15). The inevitable conclusion is that "Modern unbelievers are Deists in theory, Pagans in inclination, and Atheists in practice" (17).

Holiness and spirituality inform the Christian standard of morality, and direct us first to love God and then one another. The Bible's precepts "aim directly at the heart" (19). But deism's God takes no cognisance of the heart, and elevates love of self as the highest moral objective. While not disparaging the light of nature on which deists rely, this light in the end only leaves the sinner without excuse: it does not "afford him any well-grounded hope of forgiveness, or answer his difficulties concerning the account which something within him says he must hereafter give of his present conduct" (23). Neither does it recover the sinner, nor "render the *whole will* of our Creator evident, and that in the most *advantageous manner*" (25). The deists have no standard of morality above their own inclinations, but Christians have God's will and heart revealed in Jesus Christ.

Fuller next considers the motives to moral living. While some deists admit the doctrine of a future life, "the greatest truth, if dissevered from other truths of equal importance, will be divested of its energy" (29). Among such truths is that concerning rewards and punishments—a truth repudiated by many deists, who find it easier to contemplate "the hope of happiness beyond this life" than the thought of giving an account of the manner in which they have lived on earth: this latter prospect, says Paine, would "render him 'the slave of terror' " (33).

To the deists' charge that Christianity has been the mother of persecution and war, Fuller replies that such evils predate Christianity; that those who ordinarily perpetrate them are not real Christians; that many courts of Christian princes have been composed more of deists than of serious Christians; and that unbelievers themselves have no remedy for the wickedness of which they complain. Against Paine's claim that "men, by becoming Deists, would 'live more consistently and morally than by any other system,' " Fuller contends that it is better to be inconsistently good than uniformly wicked, while as for morality, "if Mr. Paine could coin a new system of morals, from which the love of God should be excluded, and intemperance, incontinency, pride, profane swearing, cursing, lying, and hypocrisy, exalted to the rank of virtues, he might very probably make good his assertion" (43). Moreover, if the Bible is as immoral a book as Paine says it is, how has it managed to reclaim so many from immorality? "How is it, also, that to say of a man, He rejects the Bible, is nearly the same thing, in the account of people in general, as to say, He is a man of a dissolute life?" (43). Indeed, "The morality, such as it is, which is found among Deists, amounts to nothing more than a little exterior decorum. The criminality of *intention* is expressly disowned" (45).

There follows a catalogue of the hypocrisies of deists. By contrast, Christianity produces good effects in those who believe it, and these permeate society. Fuller gives instances of nonchristian societies, ancient and modern, which indulge in practices of which he disapproves, and he challenges the deists to produce, if they can, a cause other than Christianity for the higher moral calibre of Christian societies. Even the nobler moral characteristics of the deists themselves accrue from the Christian society in which they have been reared: "So long as they reside among people whose ideas of right and wrong are formed by the morality of the gospel, they must, unless they wish to be stigmatized as profligates, behave with some degree of decorum" (65).

Deists, claims Fuller, espouse a shallow view of human happiness. Christians find that "all natural pleasure, when weighed against the hopes and joys of the gospel, will be found wanting" (68). Indeed, "Who but Christians can contemplate the loss of all present enjoyments with satisfaction?" (68). Furthermore, as sinners whose souls are depraved, human beings stand in need of mercy. The gospel alone can meet this need, and those who overcome are those who believe that Jesus is the Son of God. As for society, its evils are causes not so much by ignorance as by depravity, and its hope lies in the espousal of Christian principles. But the charge is that Christianity has been tried and found wanting—to which Fuller replies: "That [Christianity] has not been, as yet, sufficient to banish unjust wars from the earth is true; and it were more than wonderful if it had, seeing it has never yet been cordially embraced by the majority, nor perhaps by the preponderating part of any nation" (76-77). Nevertheless, "the kingdoms of this world shall become the kingdoms of our Lord and of his Christ" (77).

In part two of his work Fuller seeks to show that the harmony of the Christian religion is an evidence of its divinity. He first addresses Paine's charge that the biblical prophecies are poetic statements unfulfilled in history. Where Paine says that the prophecies are "a book of falsehoods," Fuller cites examples—not least Jesus' prediction of the fall of Jerusalem—as counterevidence. Secondly, he argues that Scripture harmonizes with the dictates of an enlightened conscience. Nominal Christians and deists shrink from seeing their own vices portrayed in the Bible, but the Bible does more than this: it makes clear that the root cause of all evil is human depravity, and in terms of this, the persecutions and wars which are laid at the door of Christianity are entirely explicable. As for the style of the Bible, whereas Paine "is pleased to censure the writings of Isaiah as 'bombast, beneath the genius of a schoolboy,' " (94) the Bible's literary merits outclass all other writings. Moreover, the spirit in which the Bible is written is one of reverence—the writers when recording history see in it the hand of God, for example; and so it is with prophecy and miracles. Even the alleged inconsistencies of Scripture witness to its truthfulness: it is not a contradiction-free work of imposture. Whereas those who approach Scripture with a candid mind are conscious of its authority, it is not surprising that the prejudiced Paine finds otherwise, for "If men choose delusion, God also will choose to give them up to it." Hence, "if such a scorner had found wisdom, the Scriptures themselves had not been fulfilled" (101).

Paine agrees that we are created by God, that we sin against God, and that we may be called to account for our conduct, but he objects strongly to the notion of a mediator between humanity and God. Fuller's reply is that "it is less *humbling* for an offender to be pardoned at his own request than through the interposition of a third person"; secondly, that "forgiveness without a mediator . . . provided less for the *honour* of the offended"; thirdly, "to exercise pardon without a mediator would be fixing no such *stigma upon the evil of the offence* as is done by a contrary mode of proceeding"; and finally, "To bestow pardon without a mediator would be treating the offence as *private*, . . . an affair which does not affect the well-being of society" (102-103). The only one qualified to be a mediator is one who is in no way implicated in the offence, namely, Jesus Christ. Paine protests that "The doctrine of Redemption has for its basis an idea of pecuniary justice, and not that of moral justice." But Fuller explains that the pecuniary language concerning our being bought with a price is not to be taken literally, and "As sin is not a pecuniary, but a moral debt, so the atonement for it is not a pecuniary, but a moral ransom" (111).

It should be noted first, that while deists and Socinians think of grace in terms of God's liberality, and set aside the idea of satisfaction, "Free grace, according to Paul, requires a *propitiation*, even the shedding of the Saviour's *blood*, as a medium through which it may be honourably communicated" (112-113). Secondly, forgiveness is thereby bestowed while God's displeasure at sin and regard for righteousness are maintained.

Thirdly, God's righteousness "continues to be manifested in the acceptance of believers through his name" (113). Fourthly, all other spiritual blessings are freely communicated on the same ground. As a final retort to Paine's abhorrence at the innocent suffering for the guilty, Fuller declares, "The truth is, the atonement of Christ affords a display of justice on too large a scale, and on too humbling a principle, to approve itself to a contracted, selfish, and haughty mind" (116). [So there!]

Fuller finally addresses Paine's charge that while science now thinks in terms of a vast cosmos, the Christian religion focuses upon one world only, namely, ours. He seeks to show that "there is nothing in the Scripture doctrine of redemption that is inconsistent with the modern opinion of the magnitude of creation" (119). It is true, he agrees, that the Scriptures do not teach that there are many worlds, but they do not deny it either. The Bible is not a textbook of astronomy or geography: "The great object of revelation is to instruct us in the things which pertain to our everlasting peace; and as to other things . . . they are only touched on in an incidental manner, as the mention of them might be necessary to higher purposes" (121). The Christian doctrine of redemption is strengthened rather than weakened by recognition of the vastness of the universe, for "*The mediation of Christ is represented in Scripture as bringing the whole creation into union with the church or people of God*" (125). It is by revelation alone that we discover things of which human beings would never, by themselves, have conceived.

Fuller's work concludes with brief addresses to deists, Jews, and Christians. He urges deists to consider what they owe to their Christian inheritance, and warns them that although some of them when faced by death may, like Hume and Paine, "brave it out," "For one unbeliever that maintains his courage, many might be produced whose hearts have failed them, and who have trembled for the consequences of their infidelity" (138). Conversely, there is no single instance of a Christian who was troubled at death "*for having been a Christian*" (138). He therefore expresses his earnest desire for their salvation, reminds them that "The door of mercy is not yet shut," and warns them that "to be crushed to atoms by falling rocks, or buried in oblivion at the bottom of mountains, were rather to be chosen than an exposure to the wrath of the Lamb" (140).[114]

---

[114]Fuller likewise urges Jews to receive the Gospel and flee the wrath to come. He urges the Christians to be sincere, to embrace vital, practical

VI

In this essay we have been introduced to some of the varieties of English deism, and to a number of varied responses to it. In particular, we have recounted the arguments of Paine and his opponent Fuller. How successful was Fuller, and, two hundred years on, how far can his performance guide us in our Christian apologetics today?

Fuller and Paine agree that God is known in his works. They are at one with Butler and all the rest in believing that there is well-nigh universal consent that there is a God. This assumption is by no means as open to us as it was to them. Neither, in the wake of Hume's demolition of the cosmological argument for God's existence,[115] and of Mill's devastating articulation of nature's red-in-tooth-and-claw-ness,[116] can we presuppose as they all did that in the book of creation the word of God is plain for all to see.

As for Paine's denial of supernatural revelation, he was, we recall, anxious to preclude the imposition of belief by one person upon another, and to rule out the wicked use of revelation. While not denying that God could reveal himself in speech and writing if he so chose, Paine contended that he never had done so, but had only revealed himself immediately to the individual. For this view Paine presents no argument, and Fuller does not challenge him directly on the point. Instead, Fuller offers an assertion which, interestingly, is the obverse of Butler's. Where Butler cautioned the deists that their case against supernatural revelation could be turned against their own claims made on the basis of natural religion, Fuller declares that the "sacred writings may contain such *internal* evidence of their being what they profess to be as that it might, with

---

Christianity, to cultivate a good understanding among themselves, and not to fear the onslaughts of infidels.

[115]D. Hume, *Dialogues Concerning Natural Religion*, ed. N. K. Smith (Oxford: Clarendon, 1935) part IX, 231-36.

[116]J. S. Mill, *Three Essays on Religion* (London: Longmans, 1885) 28. For contemporary responses to Mill see A. P. F. Sell, *Mill and Religion: Contemporary Responses to Three Essays on Religion*, Key Issues 17 (Bristol: Thoemmes, 1997).

equal reason, be doubted whether the world was created by the power of God, as whether they were written by the inspiration of his Spirit."[117]

Fuller and Paine agree that reason is the common ground upon which intellectual "contests" may be settled. Two points should be made here. First, Butler, as we saw, agreed with this policy, and, of all the opponents of deism, he was the most faithful in adhering to it, and the most gracious in applying it. But by restricting himself to rationalist ground, he was, as he realised, unable to introduce many of the Christian considerations to which he himself was committed. This raises the question of starting points in Christian apologetics: How far ought we to accept the argumentative parameters of our intellectual opponents, whether deists then or latter-day positivists now? Perhaps the most pressing question as we reflect upon the dusty path we have travelled is, "How far can Christian apologetics proceed without invoking the supernatural?" This is a question to which few clear answers have been given of late. On the other hand, the question "Is it possible to make God so 'wholly other' that he might as well not exist at all?" has received one answer in the death-of-God theologians, some of them erstwhile disciples of Karl Barth.

Secondly, Fuller in fact appeals to considerations—notably the saving work of Christ—which fall outside rationalistic confines. In particular, like Baxter, Clarke, and Wesley before him, Fuller is apprised of the realities of a holy God, a sinful humanity, and the need of a Mediator between them. Paine will not have this; and Fuller, in replying that the fact of the innocent suffering for the guilty "is seen every day, in every part of the world,"[118] does not do as much as he might have done to draw the sting of the hoary deist view that the angry God punished the innocent Son. Fuller might have invoked Paul's words at this point—"God was in Christ reconciling the world to himself" (2 Corinthians 5:19)[119]—and allowed trinitarian considerations to remind him that no wedge must be driven between the Father and the Son, and that the work of redemption is the work of all the persons of the Trinity. Be that as it may, the general question arising for apologetic method today is, What are the implications

---

[117]Fuller, *Complete Works* 1:5.

[118]Ibid. 1:114.

[119]It might appear that that minority of radical feminists who accuse the Father of child-battering the Son are doing the deist's work in our own time—and overlooking Paul into the bargain.

of W. P. Paterson's verdict upon deism, namely, that "it makes upon God a claim which is too small in view of human needs, and also too small in view of the magnanimity of God"?[120]

Fuller correctly charges Paine and all deists with overlooking God's moral character as holy, and he has a strong point in emphasising the way in which the quest of holiness and spirituality illuminates the Christian moral standard and motivates moral practice. Paine's omissions, Fuller contends, give him no right to the moral high ground. But Fuller's attempted demonstration of the moral superiority of Christianity, and of its influence for good upon society is one which can easily be turned around by skeptics who, like Collins, can produce their own lists of moral exemplars; and it certainly requires careful handling in the pluralist society of which we are increasingly consciously a part. It may be more obvious to us than it was to Fuller that people can lead morally good lives whilst believing non-Christian—even fantastic—doctrines, or no doctrines at all.[121] We recall his claim that Christianity is "the only religion in the world" which inspires love to God and man.[122] This throws into relief the question of truth, which Fuller's method of adverting to the moral influence of Christianity sidesteps—despite the fact that he constantly presupposes the truth of such propositions as that "Jesus is the only Mediator." The question, What is the epistemological status of such a claim? is not answered by a demonstration (even if it were possible) that Christians lead morally better lives than everybody else.

Fuller's reply to Paine's charge concerning the evils allegedly perpetrated by Christianity is cogent, though we should no doubt wish to revise his adverse interpretation of some pre- and non-Christian societies. But we cannot rest content with his response to Paine's attacks on

---

[120]W. P. Paterson, *The Rule of Faith* (London: Hodder & Stoughton, 1912) 320.

[121]The attitude of Joseph Barber (1727–1810), who became a tutor at Hoxton Independent Academy, is representative of that of many evangelical Christians of the time. Barber refers to those who say that "we are to have charity for all sorts of Heretics; to have charity for Jews, Deists, Atheists, &c., i.e., we are to believe, they may be very good men, and may be saved, notwithstanding any erroneous principles they have imbibed. But the Gospel knows nothing of this sort of charity." See his *Sermons on Regeneration* (1770) 16.

[122]Fuller, *Complete Works* 1:6.

prophecy and miracles. In fact, from our side of modern biblical criticism, we cannot be satisfied with either of their positions, nor with the allegorising proposal of Blount, Collins, and Woolston. They pit text against text in a way which is now precluded by modern biblical scholarship (though it is still practised by some Christians, and by their secular opponents also[123]). But the question how prophecy and miracles are to be construed is still open, as is the question of their place in apologetics: How far can or do they constitute evidence of a kind likely to convince a skeptic? Related to this is Fuller's conviction that the Bible is self-authenticating. But it was not so understood by Paine. How, then, would Fuller demonstrate the fact to Paine? He offers no adequate arguments at this point. Certainly his appeal to the fine style of the Bible is weak (a) because not every portion of the biblical texts is elevated in style—remember the 'begats'; and (b) because to appear to rely upon the kind of assumption in the title of a celebrated collection of purple passages, *The Bible Designed to Be Read as Literature*, can be a wonderful way of missing the main point of the Bible, which is a means of divine revelation and not a resource book for aesthetes or elocutionists. When Fuller further argues that the Bible's reliability is shown by the fact that its historical narratives are written by those who see the hand of God in history, we may feel that he speaks the truth, but this will not commend the Scriptures to any who do not first believe; they are more likely to accuse the biblical writers of special pleading.

As for Fuller's parting shot concerning the deist's need to flee the wrath of the Lamb: in the absence of a considerable amount of interpretation this is more likely to challenge the godly than to move genial secularists at the turn of the second millennium. On the other hand, insofar as the deists stood against untoward authoritarianisms whether

[123]In the very week in which I began to write this paper, Ludovic Kennedy, broadcaster, writer, atheist, and scourge of Christian fuzziness published an article entitled, "How Can the Resurrection Be a Metaphor?" He accuses a number of modern theologians—Tillich, Cupitt, and others—of substituting belief in myth for belief in fact. The starting point of his article? Paine's demolition of the Virgin Birth! See *The Observer*, 17 January 1999, 28. One hundred years ago the pages of *The Freethinker* were rehearsing the same, tired argument. See J. Herrick, *Vision and Realism: A Hundred Years of The Freethinker* (London: G. W. Foote, 1982) 24 et passim.

biblicist or ecclesiastical, and for honest religion, and a moral deity, they, for all their one-sidedness, elevated concerns to which not all Christians have yet paid heed.

Andrew Fuller thought the Gospel witnessed to its own truth, and that those who believed it in turn leavened society for good. What can we say today concerning the apologetic value (if any) of Christian witness? In order to answer this question we shall need first to scrutinize the concept of witness. Where better to start than with the writings of Professor Allison Trites?[124]

---

[124]What we cannot say, I think, is, "A plague on apologetics: let us give ourselves to witness!" For not the least important part of witnessing is honestly (which includes being agnostic where necessary) addressing the pressing questions which are posed to Christian faith. Nor do all of the questions come from outside the fellowship of the church. I suspect that more of these questions remain unarticulated within Christian congregations (perhaps because the puzzled feel guilty about their doubts, or think that they would be slapped down or deemed deficient by the godly) than we realize.

"The Liquid Sepulcher of the Gospel": Baptismal Practice and Popular Belief among Regular Baptists in Maritime Canada

Daniel Goodwin
Atlantic Baptist University
Moncton, New Brunswick

When I was invited to prepare a paper for this *Festschrift* in honour of Allison Trites, I immediately began to consider something related to Christian witness and Maritime Regular Baptists, two themes that have interested Allison Trites throughout much of his distinguished academic career. Allison Trites has always encouraged my research in the field of Canadian Baptist history and culture, and was in fact the second reader of my Master of Divinity thesis in 1989, which focused on the baptismal controversy in Nova Scotia during the first half of the nineteenth century. While this present effort does not deal directly with that theological controversy, it does explore the key role that baptism played in Maritime Regular Baptist witness to Christ and in the creation of denominational identity and community during the first half of the nineteenth century.[1]

Maritime Regular Baptists were a largely indigenous religious movement that emerged in the aftermath of the late eighteenth-century Great Awakening in Nova Scotia (including present-day New Brunswick), which had been led by the enthusiastic revivalist Henry Alline. Believing that ecclesiastical structures "quenched" the work of the Holy Spirit, and that religious rituals such as the sacraments were "nonessential," Alline established a series of loosely connected congregations that persisted well beyond his premature death in 1784. One of the surprising developments among many of these New Light Christians between 1790 and 1810 was their adoption of immersionist baptism as valid and, in some cases, "essential." Far from being a purely theological decision, this acceptance of believer's baptism by immersion was motivated by a host of often-

[1]This lecture was presented in honour of Dr. Allison Trites as the 2001 Acadia Centre for Baptist and Anabaptist Studies Lecture, Acadia University.

conflicting interests such as the desire for additional postconversion religious experiences and a longing for Calvinistic religious respectability as a way to provide distance from some of the antinomian excesses of the New Lights. However, the ambiguous understanding of believer's baptism by immersion that developed among Maritime Regular Baptists proved to be a crucial component of the denomination's identity and unity as it developed in the first half of the nineteenth century.

This move toward immersionist baptism was often deeply personal, as can be seen in the life of individuals such as William Bishop who died in Nictaux, Nova Scotia—in the Baptist heartland of the province—on 6 December 1833, in his seventy-fifth year. The son of New England planters, Peter and Elizabeth Bishop, William grew up in Horton Township where as a young man he was moved by the charismatic preaching of Henry Alline. The words of the Falmouth evangelist—it was noted in the obituary carried in the *Baptist Missionary Magazine*—had "powerfully arrested his conscience, and his mind became solemnly and deeply impressed with a sense of his lost condition as a sinner before God; and he began anxiously to inquire, what he should do to be saved."[2] With an "aching heart and burning conscience" unable to find immediate solace for what William James once described as the "sick soul," Bishop had become increasingly convinced that he would never share the ecstasy of conversion.[3] Eventually, however, the troubled William Bishop experienced the purifying of his soul as he cast himself upon God for all eternity. His was a classic New Light-New Birth in the Allinite tradition.[4] "His tongue broke out in unknown strains," it was recorded, "and sang [with] surprising grace."[5]

After the fire of his New Birth experience cooled, William Bishop found that "he was still in a world of conflict, and exposed to many temptations."[6] Longing to recover the ecstasy and assurance of salvation he had experienced at conversion, he began to pray, study the Bible, and

---

[2]*BMM*, September 1834.

[3]W. James, *The Varieties of Religious Experience* (New York: New American Library, 1958) 112-39.

[4]See G. A. Rawlyk, *The Canada Fire: Radical Evangelicalism in British North America, 1775–1812* (Montreal: McGill-Queen's University Press, 1994) 1-18.

[5]*BMM*, September 1834.

[6]*BMM*, September 1834.

keep company with New Light Baptists. Although Bishop's search for a deeper spirituality cannot be exactly pinpointed, it almost certainly occurred during what Anglican Bishop Charles Inglis has called "the rage for dipping," and what New Lights and Baptists referred to as the "Great Reformation." In 1800, the Anglican leader lamented that

> a rage for dipping or total immersion prevails over all the western counties of the Province, and is frequently performed in a very indelicate manner before vast collections of people. Several hundreds have already been baptized, and this plunging they deem to be absolutely necessary to the conversion of their souls. On the Saturday preceding these solemnities the preacher sits above the congregation with a number of select brethren on lower benches appointed to assist him.[7]

Bishop Inglis did not understand that the "rage for dipping" was more than just a period in which literally hundreds of New Lights rushed to the watersides of Nova Scotia and New Brunswick to receive baptism by "plunging." He could not have known that immersionist baptism was being fused with conversion and revivalism in the minds and experiences of many Maritime evangelicals to produce a resilient and broadly based "trilateral" religious identity for those who would eventually regard themselves as Maritime Regular Baptists.[8] This threefold religious core, later known as the "Faith of the Fathers" among second-generation Regular

---

[7]E. M. Saunders, *History of the Baptists of the Maritime Provinces* (Halifax: John Burgoyne, 1902) 115.

[8]This paper will explore the ritual meaning of believer's baptism by immersion and its importance to the formation of the Regular Baptist community in the Maritimes. It is not intended to chart the changes in practice or understanding of the ritual. In fact, I am suggesting that the ambiguity over meaning and breadth of experiences surrounding the ritual were crucial in creating a sense of Baptist belonging and the glue that held together an often diverse people. One of the most important studies which explores an evangelical ritual is L. E. Schmidt, *Holy Fairs: Scottish Communions and American Revivals in the Early Modern Period* (Princeton: Princeton University Press, 1989). See also D. D. Bruce, Jr., *'And They All Sang Hallelujah': Plainfolk Camp-Meeting Religion, 1800–1845* (Knoxville: University of Tennessee Press, 1974); P. K. Conkin, *Cane Ridge: America's Pentecost* (Madison: University of Wisconsin Press, 1990); R. Isaac, *The Transformation of Virginia, 1740-1790* (Chapel Hill: University of North Carolina Press, 1982).

Baptists, proved to be so endurable and adaptable that it provided a basis for common identity and at the same time a malleability that fostered Regular Baptist growth, geographically and numerically, in the Maritimes.

As William Bishop was baptized by immersion in the "name of the Father and the Son and the Holy Spirit," he entered into a completely new realm of the "spirit."

> In this way, the Lord was pleased to proceed with a work which having already effected the connexion of this redeemed soul with the church militant, was finally to result in his happier union with the church triumphant.[9]

Shortly after his baptism and what must have seemed to him a second work of grace, William Bishop began a lifelong career as lay preacher, exhorter, and deacon. Bishop would have regarded his baptism by immersion, in what A. M. Gidney called "The Liquid Sepulchre of the Gospel," as the day his salvation became fully realized.[10] It was a formative religious experience where Bishop believed he was wed to Christ and the Regular Baptists for all eternity. So profound was the ecstasy of baptism that his religious identity was firmly cast in the Regular Baptist mould for the rest of his life. While much of his New Light spirituality remained intact, Maritime Regular Baptists largely jettisoned the ambiguity of Allinism over the externals of religion in the nineteenth century in favour of immersionist baptism as an identity-giving ritual.

If William Bishop's baptism by immersion became as important to him as his New Birth experience, the same can be said for many other New Lights and evangelical pedobaptists who were looking for more in their spiritual pilgrimage. Charlotte Prescott Boyle of Chester is another example of a New Light-turned-Baptist in this period. She was converted during a revival led by John Payzant and Thomas Handley Chipman, both contemporaries of Henry Alline. Under the powerful preaching of these two Allinites, Boyle experienced the "dark night of the soul" as she concluded that her sins would never be forgiven. "My heart sunk within me under a load of guilt. I knew that God would be just if I were sent to hell; but how he could save me consistently with the claims of justice I

---

[9]BMM, September 1834.

[10]A. M. Gidney to Edward Manning, Pleasant River, Nova Scotia, 19 May 1834. AUA.

knew not." In a way similar to William Bishop, and even Henry Alline, Boyle felt abandoned by God as she cried out for mercy and the solace that she believed would accompany the New Birth. Her period of gloom was soon ended by the experience of great joy and peace as "I beheld by faith the bleeding suffering Saviour, bearing my sins on the cross."[11] So profoundly affected by this experience was Charlotte Prescott Boyle that she began the lifelong practice of public service to God as an exhorter and lay evangelist. Joseph Dimock, the Regular Baptist patriarch from Chester, recalled:

> Religion was the business of her life—her house was a house of prayer, where ministers of the Gospel and the pious of every name, found a welcome and quiet retreat. Her conversation was savory, imparting instruction to the young, comfort to mourners, and edification to all her friends. In religious conversations, her affections would often kindle into a flame of holy extacy [*sic*], that she appeared as one on the borders of Heaven.[12]

Sometime following her conversion, Boyle underwent a second crisis of faith. In her diligent reading of the New Testament, she discovered the words of the Apostle Peter in Acts, "He that believeth and is baptized shall be saved," along with other similar passages. These verses raised the question of whether or not she had appropriated the fullness of God's salvation. If conversion plus baptism was necessary to be saved, she feared that she would not spend eternity with God without believer's baptism by immersion. Joseph Dimock records that Charlotte Prescott Boyle was "baptized about the year 1788, by T. H. Chipman, whom she always respected as her spiritual father."[13] Even if some of the Baptist patriarchs would not have accepted the populist "sacramental" understanding of baptism, Boyle and others in late-eighteenth-century New Brunswick and Nova Scotia seemed to have shared, what George Rawlyk once called, "a growing popular belief . . . that without both conversion and believer's baptism, one could not 'enter the Kingdom of Heaven.' "[14]

---

[11]*BMM*, January 1835.
[12]*BMM*, January 1835.
[13]*BMM*, January 1835.
[14]Rawlyk, *The Canada Fire*, 165.

There are certainly other examples of New Light laypeople who participated in the rage for dipping and became Baptists, for example, Isaac Whitman, Loran DeWolf, Hannah Smith, and Timothy Weatherby.[15] However, the stories of Bishop and Boyle are representative of the widespread phenomenon of the New Light to Baptist transition in which the Regular Baptist trilateral of revival, conversion, and believer's baptism by immersion emerge. But, what these memoirs do not reveal is why baptism by immersion became the identifying evangelical ritual for so many New Lights when "speaking in tongues" or "divine healing" or "intense sanctification" were possible options. George Rawlyk argued that baptism became the defining ritual because it was practiced by the primitive New Testament church and was laden with folk belief and permeated by "a sense of almost medieval magic" as can be seen even in the heavily edited memoirs of Boyle and Bishop.[16] Rawlyk further argued that the increase in the practice of this evangelical ritual was exacerbated in 1800 by millennial expectations popularly held in Nova Scotia and New Brunswick that the physical return of Jesus was imminent.[17]

If there was a willingness at the grassroots to adopt immersionist baptism because of some sense of millennial anticipation, there was also the desire of many New Light preachers to break with the past. This evangelical ritual had the potential to provide a new identity for disillusioned Allinites. During the 1790s, the freedom granted to New Lights because of Allinite ambiguity over the externals of religion, such as church discipline, led to an extreme form of antinomianism that became known as the New Dispensation. Following his exit from the New Dispensation movement, Edward Manning, who would become one of the Regular Baptist patriarchs, recorded:

> Mr. Alline's lax observance of divine institutions fostered in the minds of his followers such ideas, as these: that the ordinances are only circumstantial, outward matters and not mere nonessential; that the scriptures are not the only rule of faith and practice; and that no person is under any obligation to perform any external duty until God immediately impresses the mind to do so. . . . Several began to question the

[15]*BMM*, November 1835; April 1835; April 1832; and *CM*, 1 October 1852.
[16]Rawlyk, *The Canada Fire*, 163.
[17]Rawlyk, *The Canada Fire*, 165-66.

> propriety of having anything to do with external order or ordinances, and soon refused to commune with the church. . . . As they have no rule to go by but their fancies, which they called "the Spirit of God," great irregularities ensued.[18]

The "great irregularities" that ensued culminated in the 1796 public confession of New Light preacher Harris Harding to impregnating Mehetable Harrington, a teenage resident of Liverpool, Nova Scotia. Six weeks later, a child was born to the couple. Not surprisingly, since most of the New Light preachers sought to distance themselves from the antinomianism of the New Dispensation, there emerged an increased desire to create a new identity within religious respectability.[19]

If there were New Light leaders in 1796 who were still undecided about the potential for antinomianism behaviour within Allinite freedom, the "Babcock Tragedy," in the winter of 1805, removed any doubt. Following the 1804 New Light revival in Shediac, New Brunswick, Sarah Babcock began to prophesy the imminent return of the Lord, which would immediately follow the conversion of the nearby Acadian population. So affected was Sarah's father, Amasa, by his daughter's message that it drove him insane. In a rather bizarre religious ritual, he fatally stabbed his daughter, for which he was tried and hanged.[20]

In the minds of many Maritimers, the antinomianism of the New Dispensation Movement and the "Babcock Tragedy" remained forever connected, in their minds, to uncontrolled enthusiastic religion and the Allinite ambiguity over order or the externals of religion. Even John Payzant continued to be characterized as a radical antinomian New Light. Although he never participated in the New Dispensation Movement and, it may be argued, had always sought to establish a certain degree of order in his congregation. However, he and his Congregational church in Liverpool, Nova Scotia, never adopted the key Regular Baptist scheme of immersion only. And, as late as 1834, the respected Baptist layman Angus

---

[18]J. M. Cramp, "A History of the Maritime Baptists." AUA.

[19]See G. A. Rawlyk, *Wrapped Up in God: A Study of Several Canadian Revivals and Revivalists* (Burlington: Welch, 1988) 76-95.

[20]G. A. Rawlyk, *Ravished by the Spirit: Religious Revivals, Baptists, and Henry Alline*, 1983 Hayward Lectures (Kingston: McGill-Queen's University Press, 1984) 100-101.

M. Gidney wrote about the "anti-Christian" nature of the "pedobaptist newlightism" which pervaded Payzant's Congregational church in Liverpool.[21] The evidence suggests that at least some Baptists came to regard the excesses of New Lightism as the result of ambiguity about the ordinances. It was believed that if the New Lights had adopted the Regular Baptist principles of believer's baptism by immersion and church order, the embarrassing events of the 1790s and 1805 certainly could have been avoided. By consciously distancing themselves altogether from Allinism and pedobaptism, the early Baptist leaders, including T. H. Chipman, Edward Manning, T. S. Harding, and Joseph Crandall, forged a new identity with the aid of Calvinistic Baptist leaders from Maine such as Isaac Case and Henry Hale in the post-1800 period. This shift in direction by the leadership consolidated the Regular Baptist position in Nova Scotia and New Brunswick and insured the institutional adoption of immersionist baptism.[22]

What is clear, however, is that although the first third of the nineteenth century witnessed a remarkable shift toward order and religious respectability among Regular Baptist leaders, there was also an equally strong spiritual dimension to the Maritime Regular Baptist ethos. A popular radical evangelical spirituality rooted in New Lightism endured well into the nineteenth century within the parameters of church discipline and order. In fact, had there not been a firm continuity with the religious practices and experiences of the First Great Awakening, including revivalism and conversionism, it is doubtful whether the former Allinite and new Regular Baptist preachers would have been able to lead so many New Lights and Congregationalists into the Baptist fold during the first decade of the nineteenth century. Revivals, rapturous conversions, and intense ecstatic religious experiences were not only transferred to the Maritime Regular Baptist experience, but were recast into a distinct framework centred around the evangelical ritual of believer's baptism by immersion. The marriage of Allinite religious experience and immersionist baptism created an almost irresistible baptismal spirituality. And it was clearly this hybrid of two traditions along with the move to order and religious respectability that glued together many Maritime

---

[21]A. M. Gidney to Edward Manning, Pleasant River, Nova Scotia, 19 May 1834. AUA.

[22]This theme has been explored in Rawlyk, *Ravished by the Spirit*, 118-19.

Regular Baptists throughout the first half of the nineteenth century, despite ethnic, class, and geographical differences.

Part of the success of the Regular Baptists from the 1790s to the 1850s was due to outdoor baptismal services. This religious ritual was a complex, multifaceted, and evangelical practice that was laden with richly textured layers of personal, social, and spiritual meaning. Whether baptismal candidates were recent Irish immigrants from the Mirimachi River, New Brunswick, members of the petite bourgeoisie in Halifax or Saint John, or daughters of New England planter families in the Annapolis Valley, they found their religious identity in immersionist baptism, usually preceded by conversion within the context of revival. Regardless of the differences among them, this ritual set these people apart from society and united them together as "Regular Baptists."

While Maritime Regular Baptists did not produce a manual for baptismal services, the extant evidence points to a dynamic religious ritual which could be easily adapted to a host of variables such as the seasons, time of day, and geographic setting. One of the most poetic, if not complete, accounts of a Regular Baptist baptismal service is found in Angus M. Gidney's 11 June 1834 letter to Edward Manning. Gidney was a well-educated Regular Baptist layman from Cornwallis Township who often wrote theological pieces for the *Baptist Missionary Magazine*. In his letter to Edward Manning, Gidney depicts the familiar sight of a late afternoon baptismal service in Nictaux, the heart of Nova Scotia's Annapolis Valley. Although Gidney did not recount all of the common features of that evangelical ordinance, the letter nevertheless serves as an appropriate basis for a broader ritual analysis.

> The day was one of uncommon loveliness and beauty. The sun shone on green fields and bright flowers—the birds sang—and indeed, all nature seemed dressed in its sabbath-day clothing, that it might in its best attire, behold the holy ceremonies of the christian religion. On both sides of the clear stream were multitudes standing of all ages, whose solemnized appearance plainly indicated that they were not indifferent spectators. Every cloud seemed to be rolled away, that nothing, on this occasion, might intercept the intercourse between earth and heaven.
>
> The eye, as it looked upward into the bright blue vault above, seemed lost in the unclouded purity of boundless ether, stretching far away towards the peaceful mansions of everlasting blessedness. The water was so pure, so calm, and unruffled that it reflected all above it.

> When the first recipient arose from the watery tomb, a swallow, making a perpendicular descent from above, almost touched him, and then glided away through the soft air, rejoicing in the sunshine, and seemed to twitter its praises to Him, who was thus blessing man with unmerited Mercy. This little incident led my mind back to the banks of Jordan, when the whole Trinity eighteen hundred years ago, sanctioned this ordinance; and when the Spirit, like a dove, descended from on High and perched upon the Saviour, bearing from his Father a message of divine Love and approbation. During the performance of the ceremony, ever and anon, a loud sob of either grief or joy would burst upon the ear, and when looking around among the multitude, to ascertain by the countenance from whence it proceeded, a hundred faces deeply imbued with a kindred solemnity met the view.
>
> The scene before me naturally drew my contemplations far back into Ages and Centuries that have passed like morning dreams away; and are only embalmed in the Eternal Divinity of Sacred Writ. Man's primitive state—his transgression and fall—the promise of the woman's seed—the judgments and mercies of Heaven—God's dealings with his ancient people—the birth of the Saviour, his Baptism—his ministry—his sufferings and death—his resurrection—and the prophecies of both the old and new Testaments nay fulfilling mankind brought unnumbered images of the Lord's glorious Sovereignty to my view. . . .
>
> After returning to the Meeting-House, there was "a feast of love"; for the Christians all seemed drinking of that "river the streams whereof make glad the city of God." It was sunset before the people would go away; and many a heart, hitherto careless, was deeply solemnized under the presence of Jehovah![23]

The site for the baptismal service on that warm sunny day in June 1834 had been carefully chosen. A small stream had been selected so that eager spectators could line up on both banks, giving ample space to stand for a sizeable crowd if necessary. Indeed, some consideration had to be given to the size of the community in which the baptismal service was to take place. For example, if outdoor baptisms were to be performed in Saint John or Halifax, it might be necessary to choose a site that would allow room for some three thousand onlookers. Even in remote and sparsely populated areas, crowds of one hundred were not uncommon. One report of a May 1834 baptismal service in Liverpool states that

[23]A. M. Gidney to Edward Manning, Nictaux, N.S., 11 June 1834. AUA.

onlookers watched the "solemn proceedings" closely from a number of boats that created a circle of spectators on land and sea.[24] The ritual site also required at least four to five feet of water in order to baptize adults with ease. The depth of the water was as crucial a factor as any in choosing a place for the sacred event. During winter, ice would often have to be cut out before the ritual could take place. The Fredericton, New Brunswick, preacher Samuel Elder recorded on 3 December 1848, that as "the [Saint John] river is frozen over to the depth of a foot or more, a place for baptism had to be cut through the ice for a considerable distance from the shore. The labour thus imposed on the brethren who volunteered its performance was great."[25]

Although baptismal celebrations could last an entire day, they could also be very brief indeed. In a manuscript fragment dated 4 February 1834, it is recorded that during harsh winter conditions twenty people could be properly baptized in about twenty minutes.

> "[O]n Lord's day morning, the 4th, we repaired to the water (a beautiful lake). The ice was cut and twenty candidates, with brother Porter and myself, surrounded the baptismal waters in the presence of a large concourse of spectators. It was a solemn sight. We sang, prayed, and addressed the people very briefly on account of the coldness of the day, and in little over twenty minutes the whole number was buried with Christ in baptism. . . . The reformation advances gloriously on the mountain and the valley."[26]

A somewhat less tangible, though no less important, factor in choosing a site for outdoor baptismal services was its "otherworldliness." These rites were most effectively orchestrated when water, shorelines, trees, and sky merged to create a sense of sacred space. In reading Gidney's romantic account, it is clear that all of nature "seemed dressed" for the occasion so that nothing might "intercept the intercourse between heaven and earth." For many at the waterside, the beauty found in nature

---

[24]A. M. Gidney to Edward Manning, Pleasant River, N.S., 19 May 1834. AUA.

[25]Samuel Elder Diary, 4 December 1848. Provincial Archives of New Brunswick.

[26]Manuscript fragment, 4 February 1834. AUA. I am grateful to G. A. Rawlyk for this citation.

was more than just ornamental but a means of communing with God directly, a means of grace. In an anonymous letter published in the *Christian Messenger*, 8 January 1841, the author captures the romantic, if not pantheistic, quality found at an unidentified baptismal service held at the height of a Maritime summer.

> It was a Sabbath morning; one of those hushed . . . seasons when the functions of the soul cannot operate save to adore and worship. Summer wore her richest garniture of leaves and flowers, and the glorious sunshine was abroad with its softest and holiest influences.
>
> In a wild and secluded spot, shut in by surrounding hills, and occupying the shore of a small lake, so very small that it scarcely merited the name, was collected a congregation . . . to the number of nearly two hundred. The rich and interwoven foliage of the trees formed their canopy, and the mossy banks afforded easy and convenient seats. The services were performed quietly and devoutly. The knees bowed upon the verdant and, the clasped and elevated hands, the . . . imploring eyes were but the visible expressions of a deep and fervent adoration.[27]

Since many candidates for baptism would remember their baptismal day as long as they lived, the thoughtful choice of a site could enhance the long-term impact of the occasion. Speaking to his fellow Regular Baptist pastor, Ezekiel Masters, William Chipman recalled in 1829 the "blessed" day in Billtown, Nova Scotia, on which they were "buried with Christ."

> "Pointing to the lovely lake, I said, 'Brother, you remember the great baptismal day when you and I were baptized by Father Manning, in that placid sheet of water, into the name of the Father, Son, and Holy Ghost?' "
>
> Masters replied with great emotion, "I do." And with big tears swelling in his eyes he added, "I shall meet you above."
>
> Chipman replied "God grant it my brother."

Many years after this baptismal service, both Chipman and Masters were emotionally moved at the mere recollection of that day. The "beauty of the lake," the "placid sheet of water" in which they were baptized, the Baptist Patriarch, Edward Manning, who performed the ritual, and the

---

[27]CM, 8 January 1841.

words of institution created an event that for a few stirring moments brought heaven on earth.[28]

As time went on, repeated baptismal services in the same place created a sacred sense of permanency about the space itself. (This was similar to clearings that were continually used for camp meeting sites.) The extant evidence suggests that previously immersed onlookers would often experience a reenactment of the day they had been "buried with Christ." Ellen Weiss makes the point that the ongoing use of space for evangelical rituals often transformed an area physically, and in the minds of the people it became a mystical place where God was intensely present.[29] It is only within the context of sacred space that the choreography of the outdoor baptismal service itself can be properly understood.

Since baptism was the "visible gospel" dramatically portrayed, all who participated in the service had clearly defined roles. Orchestrating the ritual was, without exception, a properly ordained Baptist minister. There is no known evidence in Maritime Regular Baptist church records, for the nineteenth century, of a single baptism being performed by anyone except an ordained preacher. In spite of an unyielding commitment to the priesthood of all believers, baptism remained the sole responsibility of the clergy. It would seem that at the popular level there was a commitment to clergy-controlled baptisms for heterodox reasons. Many people believed quite emphatically that baptism by immersion needed to be performed by an ordained Regular Baptist minister because of its sacramental, almost regenerative quality. During the spring revival of 1834 in Liverpool, Nova Scotia, led by I. E. Bill—a young preacher from Nictaux—it is recorded that "the Lord, in vindication of an ordinance in which Christ participated came down and hushed all around into reverential silence; and the Holy Dove rested on Bro Bill, while he stood in the permanent footing of Bible ground and delineated the design and divinity of the Lord's mode of Baptism."[30] Ordained men, it was believed, had been especially endued by God with the Holy Spirit to make effective the spiritual blessings of

---

[28]I. E. Bill, *Fifty Years with the Baptist Ministers and Churches of the Maritime Provinces of Canada* (Saint John: Barnes, 1880) 77.

[29]E. Weiss, *City in the Woods: The Life and Design of an American Camp Meeting on Martha's Vineyard* (New York: Oxford University Press, 1987).

[30]A. M. Gidney to Edward Manning, Pleasant River, N.S., 19 May 1834. AUA.

baptism by immersion. A baptism performed by a layperson was considered to be without power and therefore worthless and to be avoided. The authority of the ordained preacher, it was believed, was the key to the ritual's spiritual power. This was a central tenet of the faith embraced by the Fathers of the denomination. It became a way for patriarchs such as Edward Manning to exercise more control over their people.

These heterodox beliefs, while wide-ranging, may be referred to collectively as grassroots baptismal spirituality. The ambiguity of meaning and varieties of religious experiences surrounding the outdoor baptismal service proved to be key factors in the formation of Regular Baptist religious identity. Men, women, and converted youths often held conflicting notions about immersionist baptism but they were nevertheless bound together by a common ritual that united them and identified them as belonging to the Baptist community. Indeed, baptism, for many Regular Baptist laypeople, was far more than an outward sign of inward spiritual grace. From the very beginning of the transition from New Light to Regular Baptist, a firmly established connection was maintained between baptism by immersion and the coming of the Holy Spirit. While it was readily acknowledged that God gave a certain measure of the Holy Spirit at conversion, a second portion or work of the Spirit was believed by some to infuse the believer during the ritual itself. Writing about the baptism of the New Light preacher, Harris Harding, on 28 August 1799, James Manning—a leading New Light Baptist and brother of Edward Manning—recorded: "It seemed as though he had a double portion of the Spirit."[31] This is not to suggest that Regular Baptist ministers no longer considered conversion to be a prerequisite for baptism. In fact, the evidence strongly supports the long-held practice of the candidate being interviewed by the ordained minister before baptism. Maritime Regular Baptist ministers also tried to squelch "immorality" in their communities by withholding the rite from some who had not been sufficiently "changed in heart." By controlling who was baptized and who was a church member—through church discipline—preachers believed they could

---

[31]Cramp, "History of Maritime Baptists," 73. See also D. G. Bell, ed., *The Newlight Baptist Journals of James Manning and James Innis*, Baptist Heritage in Atlantic Canada 6 (Saint John NB: Acadia Divinity College and the Baptist Historical Committee of the United Baptist Convention of the Atlantic Provinces, 1984).

effectively preserve the pure church ideal.[32] Heterodoxy and immoral behaviour could thus be monitored by ordained leaders. And it was only when the preacher was satisfied that the candidate was indeed converted and committed to basic Christian morality that baptism was permitted. While most Regular Baptist ministers during the first half of the nineteenth century would have rejected outright the notion of a baptismal regeneration, the evidence suggests that a modified form of this understanding of baptism persisted at least at the grassroots with the knowledge, if not consent, of some preachers. This suggests that while baptism became a means to bring some semblance of order to New Light Baptist churches, it provided a way for ordinary evangelicals to pursue the limits of Allinite spirituality within the confines of church structures.

"The Lord gave her much of his presence in the ordinance" of baptism, wrote an itinerant Baptist preacher about a woman he had baptized from "Bucktush" in 1840.[33] Earlier in the century an angry Bishop Inglis had stated, "this plunging they deem to be absolutely necessary to the conversion of a sinner."[34] After a February 1837 baptismal service at the refined Granville Street Baptist Church in Halifax, Nova Scotia, it was recorded that baptisms were "seldom administered without being honoured in a greater or lesser degree, by the effusion of the Holy Spirit."[35] In February 1858, "J.B." of Lower Stewiacke, Nova Scotia, expressed in verse the role of the Holy Spirit in baptism.

> How sweetly solemn is this sacred scene!
> Surely the Holy Spirit hovers near—
> His dove-like form to mortal eyes unseen,
> But humble hearts must feel his presence here—
> Descend then heavenly Messenger of peace—
> Shed o're our souls the beams of sacred love;
> Here let all doubts, and fears, and conflicts cease,
> And holy joy pour on us from above.[36]

---

[32]The pure church ideal consisted of ensuring that only converted, orthodox, and morally upright individuals were included in membership.

[33]CM, 18 September 1840.

[34]Bill, *Fifty Years*, 190.

[35]CM, 17 February 1837.

[36]CM, 14 April 1858.

J.B.'s verse expresses the underlying assumption that immersionist baptism was an occasion in which God, by his Holy Spirit, blessed his people with his felt presence, peace, love, and joy. In Angus Gidney's detailed description of the Nictaux baptismal service recorded more than twenty years before the verses penned by J.B., Gidney notes that when "the first recipient arose from the watery tomb, a swallow, making a perpendicular descent from above, almost touched him, and then glided away through the soft air, rejoicing in the sunshine, and seemed to twitter its praises to Him who was thus blessing man with unmerited Mercy." Indeed, for many Regular Baptists, God was performing an additional work of grace through the waters of baptism.[37] God was sending his Spirit to bless his Baptist children, as he had his own son eighteen hundred years before. While Henry Alline may have been the ideal religious leader in the minds of some Baptists in the early nineteenth century, they rejected the Falmouth preacher's contention that the sacraments were nonessential.

In 1836, a concerned Calvinistic Baptist from a Scottish settlement in Cape Breton wrote an extended letter "To Unbaptized Believers" and took issue with those pedobaptists who regarded the sacrament—as understood by the Regular Baptists—as "nonessential." One major point of the letter was that unbaptised believers—those not immersed—had denied themselves a more complete experience of God.

> Let us again advert to the sacred Scriptures, and endeavour to inform ourselves of the views our Lord had of that ordinance which, at the close of his own earthly ministry, he concluded in the general commission, 'Go ye therefore, teach all nations, baptizing them in the name of the Father and of the Son, and of the Holy Ghost;' and at the same time for their encouragement annexing the gracious promise, 'Lo !, I am with you always even unto the end of the world.' Let us then bear in mind that when the ordinance of baptism is scripturally administered, we may look with confidence for the *especial* presence of the Redeem-

[37]While it must be acknowledged that Gidney may have romanticized or embellished the baptismal account, his stylization still confirms my contention that the "otherworldliness" of the scene was a crucial aspect of this ritual.

> er—and dear Christian Brethren is this a nonessential? Is it of no importance?[38]

Implicit in this baptismal spirituality was an experienced closeness with Jesus through the Holy Spirit that profoundly moved many candidates into a lifelong devotion to Regular Baptist piety and identity. If conversion had transformed sinners into believers, baptism by immersion made believers into Regular Baptists. The enthusiastic response of many Maritimers to the "gospel made visible" in immersion sparked a vigorous debate in pulpits and print, especially in the 1830s, between Regular Baptists and those who accepted pedobaptism.[39]

While the theology of this "second blessing" of the Holy Spirit was never fully developed or articulated, the extant reports clearly indicate that Maritime Baptist beliefs about baptism occasionally approached a sacramental view not unlike those of High Anglicans and Roman Catholics.

> In this ordinance we [Halifax Regular Baptists] believe that God is especially present with his people; and that as in the baptism of our Saviour, the Holy Ghost descended in the form of a dove, so in the baptism of his followers now the Holy Spirit descends, though not in a visible shape, to bless and sanctify and enlighten the minds of men.[40]

According to this anonymous Baptist writer, there was a threefold benefit to be received in the waters of baptism. The simple blessing of a greater degree of the Holy Spirit in one's life meant that Baptists would be closer to God than pedobaptists. Secondly, the sanctifying work of the "dove come down" meant that the likelihood of the baptized person sinning would be significantly reduced. Since sanctification implied holy living, baptism by immersion was believed to actually wash away not only sins, but also the very desires that led to breaking God's command. In the instant that the baptismal waters rippled over the body of the candidate, the Holy Spirit, it was believed, cleansed the soul and purified the will.

---

[38]*BMM*, May 1836.

[39]An outline of this debate is found in D. C. Goodwin, " 'The Very Vitals of Christianity': The Baptismal Controversy and the Intellectual Awakening in Nova Scotia, 1811–1848," *Nova Scotia Historical Review* 15 (1995): 72-87.

[40]CM, 17 February 1837.

The third benefit of "dying with Christ" was an enlightened mind that was enabled to oppose more effectively the untruth of pedobaptism, among other things. "Without the aid of the Spirit of God, we can do nothing; it is through his influence and grace, that we are brought to repentance, and by the same spirit are enabled to persevere unto the end," stated the same 1837 report from Halifax. If the conversion experience changed one's status before God, the baptismal experience granted, to the convert, power to live a holy and productive Christian life and rewarded the individual with an assurance that he "that hath begun a good work in us, must carry it on until the day of Jesus Christ." Although it is nowhere explicitly stated, the implication seems to be that apart from "scriptural" baptism, these "blessings" from the Holy Spirit could not be received in their fullness. This was the power of immersionist baptism. And it was also the central ritual of the trilateral "Faith of the Fathers." That this ritual was understood and experienced differently from person to person allowed more people to become Regular Baptists than would have been the case if the denomination had been strictly creedal or narrowly confessional.

If immersion fostered internal aspects of religious faith, it was also connected, in the minds and experiences of some, to the outward response to "God's call" to effective Christian service. This theme was developed in verse form by J. D. Casewell, a British Baptist who preached in New Brunswick in the 1830s and 1840s.[41] Casewell implies in these lines that the New Testament evangelist was successful in converting people to Christianity because "obedience [to believer's baptism] brought more strength to him."

Paul's Baptism

1

Obedience to his Lord's command
Did Saul of Tarsus rise;
Went to the limpid waters, and
In them was baptized.

2

Obedience brought more strength to him
To cheer disciples eyes

[41]See Saunders, *History of the Baptists of the Maritime Provinces*, 475.

He lov'd his Lord and hated sin,
Arose and was Baptized.
3
The people saw the wondrous change
And asked as much surprised,
"To kill he did not come?" how strange!
He arose and is Baptized.
4
He preached the Saviour crucified,
And sinners that despised,
Call'd from the refuge of their lies,
To arise and be Baptized.
5
The more in strength he did increase,
Proving the Lord is Christ;
Believe! and with him be at peace,
Arise and be Baptized.[42]

The remarkable point about Casewell's argument is that the New Testament text of Acts 9:18, upon which these verses are based, makes only passing reference to Paul's baptism. Nevertheless, this example indicates how important this ritual was in interpreting the Bible and understanding the Christian faith for Maritime Calvinistic Baptists.

Many accounts of nineteenth-century Regular Baptist baptismal services point to the centrality and deeply spiritual meaning surrounding believer's baptism. Why would the very young and the very aged risk their health, which was constantly threatened, to be baptized in the frigid winter waters of the Maritimes? William Chipman—a preacher from Cornwallis Township, Nova Scotia—recorded in 19 March 1829 that

> unwilling to delay their baptism longer . . . we had the ice cut out, and proceeded through snow and storm, to administer the divine rite. After the baptism, we returned to the house to give the hand of fellowship. There the presence of the Redeemer was . . . manifested.[43]

If the power "unto salvation and holiness" was often experienced in the "watery grave," the "power of healing" was at least occasionally

[42]CV, 15 July 1853.
[43]Bill, *Fifty Years*, 77.

encountered. In his 14 December 1849 letter to the *Christian Visitor*, James Trimble described the nine-week-long revival in Waterborugh, New Brunswick.

> Our baptismal seasons are solemn; the spirit of God rests on the congregations at the waterside; one dear sister so infirm that she was very seldom out of her house for nine years, felt it her duty to follow her Lord in the ordinance of Baptism, and although many thought she would die in the water, yet the love of Christ constrained her, and she was carried to the water in a chair, and after she was baptized she felt happy in the Lord, and her health is improving since.[44]

What makes this account so remarkable is not just the improved health of the infirmed woman, but that she risked further physical decline by being immersed in the chilly waters of a late New Brunswick autumn. For some Maritimers it would seem that baptism by immersion could also mean an opportunity to experience the "healing power of God," even if improved heath was sometimes only temporary, as it was for Isaac Titus, a twenty-six-year-old resident of Weymouth, Nova Scotia.

> During the revival here in the spring of 1858, he experienced a change of heart. Although extremely weak at the time, he was very desirous to follow his Saviour in the ordinance of Baptism; that privilege he was permitted to enjoy: he was taken in a carriage, and seated in a chair at the water's edge during the preliminary services, and then he was baptized in the name of the sacred Trinity. From that time and during the summer months he appeared to rally, so that he was able to attend many of the meetings, but with the return of autumn he began to decline, and with increasing rapidity.[45]

Suffering from "consumption" and apparently near death, Isaac Titus surrendered to the call to repent and be baptized in the healing waters of "Jordan's flood." It seems clear that the young Weymouth resident expected that the Spirit of God would meet him in the water to restore his soul and perhaps, for a time, even his body. For some people, such were the expectations of baptism by immersion. Its lack of finely articulated theological dogma permitted individuals to adopt their own under-

---

[44]CV, 14 December 1849.

[45]CM, 6 July 1859. Titus died within a few months.

standing of the ritual's meaning and still sustain their religious identity as Regular Baptists in the tradition of the "Faith of the Fathers."

If Regular Baptist baptismal spirituality often included a populist understanding, it also incorporated an intensely evangelistic bent from its Allinite heritage. Since services of believer's baptism were public meetings, often lasting an entire day and, in some cases, several consecutive days, they frequently attracted large and attentive crowds. In the early part of the nineteenth century, Regular Baptist preachers and missionaries actually relied upon the spectacle caused by outdoor baptisms to obtain a hearing in areas where a small or even no Baptist presence was to be found. Baptisms were often held at night not to avoid detection, but to create a glowing representation of the "gospel made visible." Early Maritime Regular Baptists would select a prominent ritual site and hold the service by torchlight that created a spectacle for all to see.

The crowd itself would often contain those individuals who were decidedly unsympathetic. Congregating at the periphery of the "sacred space," these men and women would mock and scoff and attempt to disrupt and heckle. Although clearly identified as "sinners" who needed to be converted and baptized, they were, in spite of their hostility, almost always welcomed by Baptist preachers and laypeople for it was hoped that the gospel preached and "made visible" would change their perspective and eventually lead to their conversion and baptism. David Jones, a preacher from the Baptist Missionary Society of Massachusetts, recorded during his February 1826 visit to the Irish settled along the Miramichi River, New Brunswick, that

> On the Sabbath a great crowd of people came together, and many were in tears. I believe that the Lord was in the place. On Monday, two persons, a man and a woman, offered themselves for baptism. Some of the people threatened to mob me and the candidates. And the woman's mother said that she wished somebody would drown her daughter. I was somewhat afraid of a riot, but the Lord softened the hearts of these persecutors.—On the Sabbath I preached on the subject of baptism, and I think, the Lord blessed the service to many. At the time the ordinance was administered, the persons, who threatened to mob us, came forward with tears and assisted in singing at the waterside, and some that were under concern of mind found comfort.[46]

---

[46]*BMM*, January 1827.

Dangerous activities, such as baptizing believers by immersion among a strongly Irish Presbyterian and Roman Catholic population, were frequently accompanied by evangelistic success for Regular Baptists. Jones's efforts show how immersionist baptism became a way for Regular Baptists to convey their distinct gospel message to populations outside their New England planter ethnic stronghold. Enthusiastic opposition to the evangelical ritual created an atmosphere ripe to "harvest converts" and to baptize them in the "liquid grave." Although hecklers did not always experience conversion, it was hoped that they might become at least sympathetic and move inward from the perimeter of the ritual and join the seekers.

The seekers were persons who might or might not have been converted, but were curious about baptism by immersion which was an unusual practice since almost all Christians in this period, except Baptists, were infant baptisers. From their vantage point within the ritual, seekers could participate in the service by singing, praying, listening, and witnessing the "visible gospel" without making a commitment. Indeed, it would seem that during many Regular Baptist revivals there were those who found themselves out on the boundary between pedobaptist and Calvinistic Baptist religion. Thomas Todd, a Regular Baptist preacher writing from Woodstock, New Brunswick in 1849, noted that

> sinners have been converted to the knowledge of the Lord. I had the unspeakable happiness of baptizing nine willing disciples on the last two Sabbaths, who came forward and gave a scriptural relation of the dealings with God with their souls. The ordinance was administered in the beautiful river Saint John, in the presence of a thousand spectators. . . . [However, while some] have cried for mercy others are halting between two opinions . . . [as] people have been warned from house to house of the danger and sin of listening to our doctrines.[47]

While facing opposition, however, it is clear that the Regular Baptists' baptismal service—the reenactment of the New Testament salvation message—was often too powerful for many people to resist. Thus, at the time of "invitation" it would seem that countless numbers of seekers made their way to the waterside and surrendered themselves to Jesus and his "sacred rite," which was often performed the following week if sufficient

[47]CV, 25 May 1849.

evidence of conversion and a desire to live a "holy" life were provided to the preacher.

Those closest to the water's edge comprised the Regular Baptist community. They were individuals who had already been "buried with Christ," or were about to receive the ordinance. This section of people was responsible to help with the singing of baptismal hymns that were almost always led by the presiding minister. J. D. Casewell, writing from Fredericton in November 1853, described a moving outdoor service where the baptismal hymn "rose upon the air and floated over the broad expanse of our beautiful [St. John] River."[48] In his hymn, simply entitled "Baptism," "J.D." declared:

How sweet the notes of the Baptismal hymn
Float o'er the stillness of the Sabbath morn!
So to the mercy-seat—between the Cherubim
May grateful incense from our hearts be borne.[49]

Hymns comprised a very important part of the outdoor baptismal ritual. In 1834 the *Baptist Missionary Magazine* published a series of "Original Baptismal Hymns" which were to be used by the Regular Baptist constituency at the waterside. Taken together these hymns reflect the collective consciousness of those who had made the journey from New Light pedobaptism to Regular Baptist. Rudolph Otto argued in the *Idea of the Holy* that it is in singing that the rational and existential dimensions of the faith converge, enabling believers to describe the spiritual events of their lives.[50] In the hymn entitled "The Strait Path" (printed below), the anonymous author spoke for many who had been inspired by the "unbending path" of Christ which led to "Calvary's fiery tempests" because of single-minded obedience to God. This example of Christ had led many New Lights and others from "Sodom's deluge raining round" to conversion. From the New Birth experience the "unbending path" led to "rites sublime" or the ritual of baptism. In the face of "Frowns of his creatures," surely a reference to anti-immersionists, "My Saviour's smiles."

---

[48]CV, 18 November 1853.

[49]CM, 14 April 1858.

[50]R. Otto, *The Idea of the Holy*, 2nd ed. (London: Oxford University Press, 1957) 70-71.

The hymn culminates in a plea to follow the "Father's voice," through conversion and baptism, "to counsels all divine."[51]

The Strait Path

1.

Unbending was the path he trod,
Who, scorned of man and bruised of God,
The garden's baptism—tears and gore,
And Calvary's fiery tempests bore.

2.

Unbending was the path we faced,
From Sodom's deluge raining round;
When Mercy urged our lingering feet,
And Faith first sought her last retreat.

3.

And if unbending still the path
That leads us from God's coming wrath—
Foes press us on—and seas our way—
'Onward' commanded, we obey.

4.

Frowns of His creatures, clouds of time,
May gather round these rites sublime;
My Saviour's smiles, and truth adored
Dispel the gloom—"It is the Lord!"

5.

He leads in love; the Father's voice,
And Spirit's presence, bid rejoice:—
Follow in love—your steps resign,
Ye saints, to counsels all divine.[52]

In the collection of baptismal hymns, "The Strait Path" was designated number one because it clearly conveyed the religious pilgrimage of so many within the Regular Baptist fold. By the 1830s, it must be remembered that the communities of the Maritimes were beginning to be more fully integrated which meant that the Regular Baptists had a much greater opportunity to expand into communities that had been previously closed to them. "Pilgrims" from pedobaptism to the Regular Baptist position had

---

[51]*BMM*, March 1834.
[52]*BMM*, March 1834.

discovered the truth of Matthew 7:13-14, the verses upon which the hymn was based, that "strait is the gate, and narrow is the way, which leadeth unto life, and few there be that find it."

Although, in Calvinistic fashion, a limited number of Regular Baptists would have stressed the necessity of election to salvation from the "foundation of the world," they nevertheless pleaded for the conversion and baptism of all people at the waterside—believing those predestined by God to respond would in fact experience the New Birth and be immersed. While several of the "Original Baptismal Hymns" stressed the central elements of the New Birth such as repentance and regeneration, all of the gospel songs contained a call to go beyond conversion to baptism in the watery grave.[53] As will be seen, for at least the first two generations of Regular Baptists, their spirituality included a rejection of infant baptism and an acceptance of the intense experience of the "peculiar rite." Since their religious identity was not tied exclusively to the New Birth but also to its dramatic re-enactment in baptism, the evangelistic call to faith during this ritual included a passionate call to obey "the Lord's command." Perhaps the best example of this kind of exhortation is encapsulated in the hymn entitled "Unscriptural Delay Examined" in which the singing baptized congregation debates unimmersed individuals. The essential argument is based on Acts 22:16, "And now why tarriest thou? Arise, and be baptized, and wash away thy sins, calling on the name of the Lord."

1.
Why tarry ye, whose price was blood,
Poured from a dying Saviour's veins,
To make your best friend's purchase good,
And yield the fruit of all his pains?

2.
Why tarry ye? perdition yawns,
At every trifler's palsied feet:
Why tarry? opening glory dawns,
The obedient child of grace to greet.

---

[53]The full collection of these original hymns may be found in *BMM*, March 1834; May 1834; July 1834; September 1834.

3.
Confessors only are confessed
Of Christ, in judgment's awful morn.
Yield we to God's own will expressed!
High honour of the doubly born.
4.
Arise to seek for guilt a grave'
And bury sin in all men's sight'
'Tis purity's own parting wave,
That waits to wash it from the light.
5.
Weak in thyself from Him on high
Who braved the roughest deeps for thee,
Seek strength—he heard thy weaker cry,
And turned to love thine enmity.[54]

In these verses of exhortation, the New Birth and baptism are so closely linked that it is not clear if sin is washed away by "your best friend's purchase" or "purity's own parting wave, That waits to wash it from the light." As this hymn was sung at countless baptismal services in the Maritimes, it is likely that many unimmersed people "tarried not" as they came forward to receive the sacred rite in order to avoid eternal damnation. It would seem that the ambiguity over regeneration and immersion was intentional so that the eternal reality of a hell for the "unwashed" might be seen as a possibility. This theme of judgment was often tempered by heart-warming exhortations, based on personal experience, of baptismal candidates and members of Regular Baptist churches. The themes of perdition and ecstasy found in the gospel songs contributed a valuable dynamic to the evangelistic effectiveness of the ritual itself.

Perhaps no less important to the baptismal service was the sermon preached by the ordained minister. Although preachers, such as Edward Manning, chose to conduct the ordinance first at the waterside and then "repair to the meeting house," the majority of surviving baptismal accounts suggest that (for at least the first half of the nineteenth century) the sermon would be offered immediately before the baptisms, or directly after the sacred rite. Depending on the time of year, the minister might preach an entire sermon waist-deep in water and close the service by

[54]BMM, March 1834.

lifting his hand, dripping with water, and asking "What is to prevent you from being baptized?" Writing to Edward Manning from Halifax, Nova Scotia, on 9 June 1828, A. Caswell reported:

> I took my stand on a rock which rose above the water and addressed them at some length from Matthew 28:19. The air was quite calm and suppose mostly the whole assembly (a large concourse of people) could hear distinctly. The attention was fixed and the countenances of many not without indication of deep feeling.[55]

While the ritual was the "gospel made visible," it was still necessary for the preacher to explain in simple terms the biblical support for immersionist baptism.

Often the sermon would contain a rather polemical tone such as J. D. Casewell's sermon from the Saint John River in the fall of 1853 when he gave an "address upon the nature of the ordinance and the exactitude of its accordance with Holy Scripture." Placing "it in contrast with infant sprinkling, which is unmeaning and without any shadow of support and authority from the word of Jehovah," the Fredericton pastor challenged attentive pedobaptists to break with human traditions and embrace the truth.[56] This kind of aggressive preaching often proved to be effective in areas where discussions about baptism among laypeople were heated. The goal of the ritual, however, was always to make more immersed Christians.

The transformations that took place at outdoor baptismal services were not just personal in nature. As the distinctions of "sinner," "seeker," and "saint" began to break down during the religious celebration, a spontaneous sense of community was often created. Even hardened opponents of the Baptist cause were swept up into the fervour of the moment and became convinced of the immersionists' way, leaving pedobaptism behind. At least for the duration of the baptismal service all baptized persons possessed a certain equality, for even women and children were given the opportunity from the water to exhort husbands and fathers to accept this "better way." If all who were baptized into Christ had equal standing before God, then theoretically, that equality should have manifested itself in some aspect of Regular Baptist church life, but there is little evidence

---

[55] A. Caswell to Edward Manning, Halifax, N.S., 9 June 1828. AUA.
[56] CV, 18 November 1853.

to suggest that it did. Nevertheless, receiving the rite of baptism by immersion built a strong sense of identity and community among the Baptists. That William Chipman and Ezekiel Masters would feel spiritually connected to one another after so many years because they were baptized together suggests the social bonding effect the ritual had on many people.

The Maritime Regular Baptists had a very developed sense of a community of committed believers who had been baptized by immersion to form the "visible church." The doorway through which one had to pass was baptism by being totally submerged under water by a properly ordained minister of the gospel. The leadership of the denomination attempted to sustain the integrity of this "holy collective" by insisting upon the practice of close communion with the recognition that baptism by immersion created this ideal Christian community. That existing relationships within communities were strengthened through baptism by immersion was evident during the spring revival of 1832 in Wilmot and Upper Granville, Nova Scotia. With fifty-three reported to have gone down into the "watery grave," it was noted by a church observer that personal relationships were strengthened as

> Husbands and wives, brothers and sisters, were seen together rejoicing in God, and following him in His ordinances [baptism]. Parents who had long borne their children in the arms of faith and prayer, had the unspeakable satisfaction of seeing them bathed in tears of penitence, and then rejoicing in God's pardoning love.[57]

Wellington Jackson, the Regular Baptist minister from St. Martin's reported in May 1849 that he baptized "our sister who . . . is a married woman, and I have no doubt but her union with the church will prove a blessing to herself and her family, as well as a blessing to the church. Her grandfather is the oldest member of this church." Jackson was overwhelmed with emotion when, following the baptism, the elderly man took "his grandchild by the hand, and welcome[d] her" into the fellowship of the church.[58] Indeed, baptism by immersion often became a family affair and a means of identity as one generation followed the next into the "placid sheet." For example, during a revival led by the home missionary James Blakeney in New Jerusalem, New Brunswick, John W. Moore, who

---

[57]*BMM*, October 1832.

[58]*CV*, 25 May 1849.

had settled in the Saint John area in 1826, with his parents, would not submit to baptism by immersion until his parents had first experienced the rite.[59] Very often when a parent received baptism by immersion, the children were powerfully influenced to seek the ordinance as well. One woman in the "Bucktush" area of New Brunswick was baptized near her own place of residence.

> When coming up out of the water she prayed fervently that the Lord would have mercy upon her family. This took a great effect on the mind of her children. Her eldest daughter could not refrain from acknowledging it was her duty to follow the example of her mother.[60]

In a somewhat different context, N. S. DeMill of Saint John, New Brunswick, wrote a lengthy article on his reasons for embracing believer's baptism by immersion. An inquiry from his young son had led him to examine the evidence in favour of the immersionists' claim.

> The investigation of *truth*, through the good Providence of God, is frequently brought about by very slight circumstances—so it was in my case. The asking of a simple question by my little son, Viz.: for one proof from the Scriptures for "INFANT BAPTISM," led me to examine the word of God upon that subject; and for twenty-three months that examination was closely followed up, and at last, closed by my giving up my adherence to "INFANT BAPTISM," and consequently my connexion with the Episcopal Church and necessarily my offering myself as a Disciple of Christ to the baptized Church of Christ in this city.[61]

What is remarkable about this account is that it was the child's challenge of the religious assumptions of his father, with regard to baptism, which led to the immersion of the parent.

On 8 January 1841, the *Christian Messenger* recorded the unusual events of a baptismal service that included the wedding of a young couple immediately before their "burial with Christ."

> [T]he minister walked forth . . . and stood upon the shore of the lake. Immediately from among the crowd followed a young maiden, leaning upon the arm of her lover. They stopped up on a small mound that

---

[59]CV, 18 November 1853.
[60]CM, 18 September 1840.
[61]CV, 28 January 1853.

> sloped down from the trunk of a spreading maple. The maiden was young and fair. A sweet spiritual expression rested upon her countenance, which was pale, and almost infantile in its freshness and delicacy. Her eyes rested sometimes pensively upon the ground, and were sometimes turned tenderly upon the face of her betrothed.
>
> The minister, an aged and venerable man, lifted his hands and invoked a blessing upon their love. Their hands were joined, and, in a low but distinct voice, he pronounced them wedded for joy and for sorrow, for sickness and for health, for life and for death, and spiritually, it might be for eternity.
>
> Once more the minister invoked a blessing, but it was upon a new rite. He prayed that the baptism which was about to be conferred by water might be an outward emblem of the more perfect baptism of their spirits in the fountain of eternal life. . . .
>
> Tears gathered into many eyes, and a gentle awe pervaded the lightest hearts. The [minister] arose from his knees, and, taking the bride and bridegroom by the hand, led them into the water. Immediately after the rite was administered, a multitude of voices broke forth. . . .[62]

The anonymous reporter makes a very strong connection between the relationship-building potential of baptism by immersion and the marriage. In fact, the wedding itself takes on a certain "spiritual quality" because it is performed in the sacred space of the baptismal site. In the first rite, the young man and woman were married to each other and in the second, there is a sense in which they totally identified themselves with Christ. In both rituals they were "wedded for joy and for sorrow, for sickness and for health, for life and for death," and spiritually to Christ for eternity. Baptism could bond relationships between people if both had received the ordinance, especially at the same time.

The ritual of baptismal services fostered community, but not without qualifications. The coming together of great numbers of people for worship seldom ended in total solidarity. This ritual that could collapse divisions between individuals could at the same time establish new boundaries. Immersed individuals discovered a new family of baptized brothers and sisters, but often at the expense of straining relationships with siblings and parents. Nevertheless, the Regular Baptists of the Maritimes were able

---

[62]CM, 8 January 1841.

to create during the nineteenth century a religious community that had the capacity to include people from different regions and walks of life, because of the identity-creating ritual of believer's baptism by immersion. That its participants understood this evangelical rite in often radically different ways cannot be doubted. The attraction of the ordinance itself was to be found in its many layers of personal and social meaning. Whether one was a sacramentalist seeking for "more" of the Holy Spirit, an elderly or ill person longing for spiritual and physical restoration, or the only unimmersed member of a family, the ritual as it was popularly understood could effectively accommodate a variety of religious needs and expectations. Regardless of how heterodox the understanding of the ritual may have been, it gave thousands of people in nineteenth-century Maritime Canada a common sense of belonging. The Regular Baptist trilateral that found its centre in immersionist baptism set them apart from their Allinite and pedobaptist backgrounds, gave them a distinctive religious identity, and created a separate Christian community.

During the first half of the nineteenth century the evangelical ritual of believer's baptism by immersion became the definitive mark of Regular Baptist spirituality and identity. So powerful was this rite that the thousands of people, from rural, urban, New England planter, Loyalist, Scottish, and Irish communities, sought the Saviour in the "watery grave" and united into a fairly inclusive and dynamic Christian denomination.

From Revivals to Evangelism: Changing Patterns of Growth among Maritime Regular Baptists, 1850–1900[1]

Robert S. Wilson
Acadia Divinity College

It is difficult to assess the long-term impact of a person's life in the history of a denomination. In the case of Allison Trites, however, his role in the education of most of two generations of theological students at Acadia Divinity College makes that evaluation somewhat easier. As a scholar, his two loves are Biblical Studies and Atlantic Baptist History. He passed on these two loves to his students. As a product of Atlantic Baptist churches and a student of their history, Dr. Trites has embodied the concept of being a witness to the Gospel. The focus of this present study is the movement of the Baptists of the nineteenth century—especially as reflected in the life of that great Maritime evangelist/pastor Isaiah Wallace—from being dominated by revivals to becoming agents of evangelism; the means of "bearing witness" changed. Their concern, like Allison Trites's in this generation, was to be faithful witnesses to the Gospel. It is therefore a rare privilege to be involved in this tribute to a wonderful and inspiring colleague.

Revivals and revivalism were key ingredients in the growth of Baptists in the Maritime Provinces during the nineteenth century. While a fair amount of work has been done on the era of the Second Great Awakening and the leaders of that generation, little has been done to examine the period following the formation of the Regular Baptist Convention in New Brunswick, Prince Edward Island, and Nova Scotia in 1846. This essay therefore will just touch some of the areas of interest, and is merely the beginning of studies that are needed to give a full understanding of the long-term impact of revivals. The materials used for this study are the

[1]The term "Maritime Provinces," or the abbreviated "Maritime" or "Maritimes," includes New Brunswick (NB), Prince Edward Island (PEI), and Nova Scotia (NS). The terms "Atlantic Provinces," and "Atlantic Canada" include the Maritime Provinces and Newfoundland (NFLD).

rather obvious ones such as periodicals and convention reports, and Isaiah Wallace's *Autobiographical Sketch with Reminiscences of Revival Work*. These illustrate the importance of revivals and the changing pattern during the latter part of the nineteenth century. Isaiah Wallace embodies many of the traditions and changes because his ministry was often touched by revival and his ministry spanned the period under discussion.

During the nineteenth century, the Regular Baptists in the Maritimes grew from a few hundred to more than fifty thousand. Very little of this growth came from immigration although some Baptists did come from Britain and the United States. Many of those who did come to the area from Britain were pastors or teachers.[2] The growth was by conversion of people of other backgrounds to the Baptist position. Edward Manning Saunders commented: "It has been in revivals chiefly that people have been induced to embrace and practise Baptist principles."[3] Writing just into the twentieth century, Saunders considered revivals to be the factor that shaped Baptist culture, institutions, morals, and people.[4] Even those who sometimes looked askance at revivals were assured of their importance. The president of Acadia College from 1851 to 1869, Dr. J. M. Cramp, wrote the following in 1878:

> Educated and trained in England, and in a church which was not remarkable for liveliness, I was a stranger to the scenes which have fallen under my notice in this land, and in some degree prejudiced against them. . . . I am free to declare that as a genuine revival of religion is an undoubted blessing, Christians should regard it as a standing obligation to seek renewed bestowments by earnest prayer and individual efforts for the conversion of souls. Revivals would be more frequent if the members of our churches were truer in their responsibility as witnesses for Christ.[5]

---

[2]R. S. Wilson, "British Influence in the Nineteenth Century," in *Baptists in Canada: Search for Identity Amidst Diversity*, ed. J. K. Zeman (Burlington: G. R. Welch, 1980) 21ff.

[3]E. M. Saunders, *History of the Baptists of the Maritime Provinces* (Halifax: John Burgoyne, 1902) 466.

[4]Ibid., 307-308.

[5]J. M. Cramp, "Sketches of the Religious History of Acadia College and Horton Collegiate Academy," in *Memorials of Acadia College and Horton Academy for the Half-Century 1828–1878*, ed. J. M. Cramp (Montreal: Dawson, 1881) 50.

Revivalism had become a way of life for many Baptists by 1850 and this was passed on from generation to generation. Isaiah Wallace tells of visiting Theodore Seth Harding in the company of other young preachers and sometimes alone "to receive his [Harding's] judicious counsels and to listen to his ministry."[6] Harding had been pastor of the Horton Church in Wolfville, Nova Scotia, for more than fifty years when Wallace met him, and Harding had heard Henry Alline preach while still a boy.[7] Saunders perceived this kind of influence when he preached a Semi-Centennial Sermon in 1888 at the Jubilee of Acadia College. He recounted some of the revivals that had taken place there and made the following assessment: "The uneducated ministers gave in exchange to the educated their 'newlight' zeal for the mental quickening which they received. From this centre, life and power have been diffused."[8]

The pattern for revivals had become well established. Emotionalism, crying out, and even unconsciousness were accepted manifestations into the 1850s. Isaiah Wallace, the son of a pastor in Albert County, New Brunswick, had been born into that tradition. The whole of Albert County had been swept by revivals until the majority of the population was Baptist.[9] Just after he had completed his training at Acadia, he was involved in a revival at Washadomoak Lake in 1857. He said the meetings were "sometimes noisy and full of excitement" and he had to "ask God for a steadying hand."[10] In Guysborough, Nova Scotia, in 1852, there were reports of sinners crying aloud during revival meetings.[11] It was not unusual for the night to be filled with the sounds of people crying aloud to God for mercy. One particularly sad case took place at Harbourville, Nova Scotia, in 1875 where Wallace was holding revival services.

---

[6]I. Wallace, *Autobiographical Sketch with Reminiscences of Revival Work* (Halifax: John Burgoyne, 1903) 18.

[7]G. E. Levy, *Baptists of the Maritime Provinces: 1753–1946* (Saint John: Barnes Hopkins, 1946) 45.

[8]E. M. Saunders, "The Semi-Centennial Sermon, Aug. 29, 1888," in *Jubilee of Acadia College and Memorial Exercises* (Halifax: Holloway Bros., 1889) 37.

[9]Wallace, *Autobiographical Sketch*, 1. Isaiah Wallace was born January 17, 1826.

[10]Ibid., 23.

[11]CM, 19 March 1852, 94.

As the people walked home after a meeting, they heard voices crying for help and assumed they were the voices of sinners under conviction. The next morning they discovered the voices had in fact been two young fishermen crying for aid after their boat capsized. Both drowned in the night, although each had made a profession of faith a few days earlier.[12]

One of the more remarkable revivals of the time took place in Belldune in northern New Brunswick in 1859. On an October Sunday, Wallace had visited the community and preached on Isaiah 33:14: "The sinners in Zion are afraid; fearfulness hath surprised the hypocrites. Who among us shall dwell with the devouring fire? Who among us shall dwell with everlasting burnings?" A woman became convicted of sin and one evening, while sixty young people were dancing in the next room, she was at prayer. A young man picked up a piece of paper and found it to be a page from the Bible. He read: "and these shall go away into everlasting punishment." He fell prostrate and called for mercy. The dance ended when five others joined the young man. The Presbyterian minister and Isaiah Wallace were called to help, and hundreds joined the Presbyterian Church and a Baptist Church was formed. Wallace said it was similar to events he had heard about in Coleraine, Ireland. He added: "Such a revival I had never before witnessed, nor have I ever seen anything like it since." During the preaching, convicted ones would cry aloud for mercy and fall back in a state of physical prostration, and would thus remain for several hours.[13] They were usually converted when they regained consciousness.

The nature of the revivals, however, began to change in the late 1850s. The 1855 revival at Acadia College was a part of that change because of the way it developed there and because of its widespread impact by the number of students who later entered pastorates. It began with a Sunday morning prayer meeting held by the students as "tears of penitence flowed" during prayers for the unsaved.[14] President Cramp did not know how to deal with the situation and so "gave the special services over to the students," with his "sympathies and prayers."[15] He later said

---

[12]Wallace, *Autobiographical Sketch*, 119.

[13]Ibid., 30.

[14]Ibid., 16.

[15]Ibid., 16.

that "it was not got up, it grew."[16] There was a sense of oppression throughout the whole College before a bursting of bounds saw fifty students converted and baptized. Special meetings were held at the college and at the local Baptist church where Cramp was interim pastor. Wallace said that he and other ministerial students received "a fresh impulse heavenward."[17] Fifty years later he commented: "Whatever success may have attended my life's work in the Lord's service, it now seems to me, is traceable in some degree, at least, to that gracious renewing of 1855."[18]

For the students from Acadia and for an increasing number of churches, this quiet type of revival became the norm. In Little River, New Brunswick, Wallace became the catalyst for a revival when he announced to the congregation one day in 1857 that he felt more like praying than preaching, and he asked others to join him. A revival broke out in that prayer meeting.[19] This was not unusual, and by 1859 there were a number of reports in *The Christian Messenger*, the local Baptist periodical, with comments like that which came from Cornwallis, Nova Scotia. In seven Sundays seventy-seven people were baptized. "The work has been characterized with no undue excitement. . . . Circumstances have greatly changed from former years, yet no one can doubt that this revival is the work of the Holy Spirit."[20] A similar report from Cape Breton, Nova Scotia, said that there was no groaning or shouting.[21] In Hopewell, New Brunswick, a revival broke out in 1861, and the report commented: "The work is free from excitement, those who have come forward, acting on the voluntary principle, without being called up to be prayed for—as is sometimes done on such occasions."[22] After mid-century, revival often began in and was sustained by the prayer meeting.[23]

---

[16]Cramp, "Sketches of the Religious History," 49.

[17]Wallace, *Autobiographical Sketch*, 17.

[18]Ibid., 17.

[19]Ibid., 17.

[20]CM, 23 March 1859, 94.

[21]CM, 2 March 1859, 69

[22]CM, 20 February 1861, 62.

[23]Stephen DeBlois, "Historical Sketch of the First Horton Church: 1778–1878," quoted in D. A. Steele, "Pastor DeBlois," in *The Religious Life of Acadia*, ed. A. C. Chute (Wolfville: Kentville Pub., 1933) 27-28; CM, 18 March 1863, 86; CM, 22 April 1863, 126; CM, 6 May 1863, 142.

The changing nature of revivals caused some discussion of what constituted a revival. Saunders argued that revivals were not to be measured by excesses of psychological manifestations, but by whether "there is a reform of character and life."[24] W. B. Boggs, who had observed many of the revivals at Acadia near the end of the nineteenth century, listed three major "Proofs of Genuine Revival," which included transformed characters, new aspirations and life plans, and the quickened and renewed life of the church.[25] Certain times seemed to be more propitious for revivals than were others, and so the study of revivals caused certain expectations. *The Christian Messenger* published an article in early 1875 suggesting that "probably the time never was when our churches so generally as now expected to enjoy a revival of religion in their midst."[26] Because the economy was experiencing a downturn, the week of prayer was expected to have a large impact.[27] Revival was defined as "a reviving of spiritual emotions and enjoyment, a renewed engagedness in the service of Christ."[28] Revivals therefore were expected to renew Christians, to bring new people to meet Christ, and to change society in the area where it was manifested.

In the latter connection, comments abound of the impact of revivals upon Maritime communities. Several illustrations will have to suffice. After 1850, there was often a relationship between revivals and the size of local temperance societies. In 1859, it was reported that a number of people in Upper Wilmot, Nova Scotia, had been baptized into the local church, and liquor sales fell while the numbers of those joining the temperance society grew.[29] At Hantsport, Nova Scotia, in 1861, twenty-nine had been baptized into the local church, and the commentator said: "there appears to be scarcely a house in the village where God is not pouring out his Spirit."[30] Sunday schools like those in Hebron, Nova Scotia, in 1863, were enlarged as well as the prayer meetings, with

---

[24]Saunders, *History of the Baptists of the Maritime Provinces*, 304ff.

[25]A. C. Chute, *The Religious Life of Acadia* (Wolfville: Kentville Pub., 1933) 31.

[26]CM, 3 February 1875, 52.

[27]Ibid.

[28]Ibid.

[29]CM, 30 March 1859, 101-102.

[30]CM, 20 February 1861, 62.

increased attendance.[31] Wallace commented in 1887 that, following the addition of more than one hundred to the church, life at sea became different: "Many of the converts were seafaring young men, and it is said that there was a great change in character of many of the crews that went from Shelbourne County to the Grand Banks that Spring."[32] Illustrations could be multiplied of the changes wrought by revivals, but no community was more regularly visited nor had so much impact upon the broader community than Acadia College.

Acadia had experienced a number of revivals in previous years, but it was the 1855 revival that set the pattern for those that followed.[33] Between 1828 and 1878, more than five hundred students were converted at the institutions at Horton.[34] E. A. Crawley commented in 1878 that "those visitations of Divine grace which we term revivals very early became a marked feature of the Academy and subsequently of the College."[35] While many of these revivals were spontaneous, President Cramp tells of the situation in 1874 when students who had been at the College for three or four years were concerned that they would leave and not have experienced a revival and so they "prayed and wrestled, and worked, and the Lord has at last laid bare his arm to save."[36] These revivals continued into the twentieth century and shaped the lives and expectations of many potential leaders in the Baptist community. A. C. Chute tells of one such movement in 1905: "As a result of special services, begun early in March, the Lord moved quietly but mightily on the hearts of his people, as also upon the unsaved ones, and brought many to Himself."[37]

---

[31]CM, 1 April 1863, 102.

[32]Wallace, *Autobiographical Sketch*, 96.

[33]Ibid., 17.

[34]Cramp, "Sketches of the Religious History," 51.

[35]E. A. Crawley, "Address: 'The Rise and Progress of Higher Education in Connection with the Baptist Denomination in the Maritime Provinces,' " in Cramp, *Memorials of Acadia College and Horton Academy*, 31.

[36]A. Caldwell, "History of Acadia College: The Vaughan Prize Essay," in Cramp, *Memorials of Acadia College and Horton Academy*, 115 and 117; Cramp, "Sketches of the Religious History," 51.

[37]Steele, "Pastor DeBlois," 30.

This tradition meant that Acadia provided revival-orientated leadership to the Baptist churches. In 1878, Albert Caldwell commented that "many who are now successfully preaching the Gospel began their religious life at these revivals, and hundreds of others bless God today for the Christian influences thrown around them at the Horton institutions."[38] By 1888, more than 150 graduates had entered the ministry from Acadia, and Calvin Goodspeed contrasted that figure with the very small number of those entering the Baptist ministry from any other university. The College professors emphasized evangelism.[39] Many supporters of Acadia therefore gave sacrificially, for they believed, with Saunders, that if they kept Acadia strong, the denomination would be strong.[40]

Isaiah Wallace was a lifelong supporter of Acadia, and several times was called upon to raise money for the College. In 1877, he became an agent to raise an endowment for the College. One man on the Board of the College remarked: "Mr. Wallace would make a good agent, but it would be hard to keep him to his work, for he would be likely to bolt and engage in the promotion of revivals."[41]

This is just what he did, for he raised money in the daytime and preached at night.[42] He also encouraged many students to go to Acadia for he considered the "prosperity of our institutions of learning at Wolfville" to be vital for Baptist work in the Maritimes. He was also concerned for the spiritual development of the students, and in 1889 accepted an invitation to hold special meetings there. In spite of his nervousness at the beginning, "a powerful work of grace" led to about fifty being baptized.[43] He believed that special services should be held "as often as possible" for the benefit of students at Acadia.[44]

While Acadia produced many pastors and others came from Britain, the lack of pastoral leadership was still a problem. The number of

---

[38]Caldwell, "History of Acadia College," 115-16.

[39]C. Goodspeed, "The Claims of the College on Its Constituency," in *Jubilee of Acadia College and Memorial Exercises* (Halifax: Holloway Bros., 1889) 59; Steele, "Pastor DeBlois," 30.

[40]Saunders, "Semi-Centennial Sermon," 41.

[41]Wallace, *Autobiographical Sketch*, 48ff.

[42]Ibid., 50ff.

[43]Ibid., 110 and 176; D. A. Steele, "Pastor DeBlois," 59.

[44]Wallace, *Autobiographical Sketch*, 111.

churches always remained far in advance of the number of pastors. Many of the smaller churches, therefore, had to depend upon periodic revivals for their continued existence. In 1871, there were 161 ordained men among Regular Baptists in the Maritimes, and by 1900 there were 250.[45] In 1903, however, there were only 183 pastors to minister in 418 churches. Even with multiple-church fields, 101 churches had no pastoral leadership.[46] As a church planter, Isaiah Wallace was perplexed by the "difficulty of securing missionary pastors."[47] The leadership problem is partially explained by the fact that so many Acadia graduates had to go elsewhere to receive seminary training. By 1900, one-half of the Acadia graduates were going to the United States and very few returned. Theological Schools at Rochester and Chicago had many Acadia graduates, while Newton had more Acadia graduates than from any other single college or university.[48] Those who did return often lacked the revivalist tradition.

Isaiah Wallace had a real concern for the small churches and communities without pastoral leadership, and therefore the larger part of his ministry was among the little villages and towns of the Maritimes. He served several association and provincial home mission boards, all of which shared the stated purpose of the Nova Scotia board, which defined its role in 1857 as "preaching the Gospel throughout Nova Scotia and Prince Edward Island, the assistance of feeble churches, and the planting of new ones."[49] In 1883, Wallace became general missionary for the newly formed Home Mission Board of the Maritime Baptist Convention. He says he accepted the post because of "an inward consciousness that my duty ran in the line of evangelistic work, and that I could in that way accomplish most for the Master."[50] An example of his ministry would be 1888, when he traveled 3,100 miles, preached 220 sermons, baptized 134

---

[45]Levy, *Baptists of the Maritime Provinces*, 227.

[46]*The Baptist Yearbook of the Maritime Provinces of Canada* (Halifax, 1903) 229.

[47]Wallace, *Autobiographical Sketch*, 100ff.

[48]Saunders, *History of the Baptists of the Maritime Provinces*, 454.

[49]Wallace, *Autobiographical Sketch*, 44-45; Levy, *Baptists of the Maritime Provinces*, 160-61; CM, 16 September 1857, 282.

[50]Wallace, *Autobiographical Sketch*, 65.

people, organized two churches, and visited 854 families.[51] He remained as general missionary for twelve years, leading evangelistic services and solving local church problems.[52]

In many of the communities, the revival meetings often overlapped denominational boundaries. Wallace tells of numerous occasions when revivals added numbers to many churches.[53] There were other occasions when the local people would call in other preachers, often a Free Will Baptist, to complete the work begun by Wallace.[54] Some revivals might have a half-dozen preachers in a five- or six-week period.[55] This common concern for preaching the Gospel as well as the similarities in polity led the two Baptist groups to join in 1905/1906. The pooled leadership allowed many more churches to have pastors by combining congregations in places where there were both Free Will Baptist and Regular Baptist churches.

Revivals remained of major importance to men like Wallace until well into the twentieth century. The revivals did not always appear and if the expected growth in the denomination or a local church did not happen, there was often a lot of soul searching to discover the reason. In January 1856 a letter appeared in *The Christian Messenger* entitled "Revivals—Why Do We Not See them?" The letter was written because the pages of the paper had been barren of reports of revivals in the Maritimes for several months, and so the following reasons were suggested as hindrances to revival: "coldness"; "lack of family altar"; "lack of prayer"; and "lack of attention to the sermon."[56] Until 1867, the same paper carried a separate section on revivals that reported any extraordinary manifestation of the Holy Spirit where large numbers were converted.[57] This included news from around the world, and so Maritime Baptists were aware of the wider movements. In 1858, the revivals in the United States were reported and

---

[51]Ibid., 106.

[52]Ibid., 68ff.

[53]Ibid., 91-92 and 114; CM, 23 April 1852, 133.

[54]CM, 21 April 1858, 142; Levy, *Baptists of the Maritime Provinces*, 249; Wallace, *Autobiographical Sketch*, 40ff.

[55]CM, 30 April 1852, 140.

[56]CM, 23 January 1856, 29.

[57]CM, 14 August 1867, 262.

the writer of an article wondered if they would spread to the Maritimes.[58] 1859 was a year of revivals in many areas and 2,576 people were baptized in the Baptist churches of the Maritimes.[59] 1860, however, was a year of dryness and again an article appeared asking why the great outpourings of revival continued in Britain, Europe, and the United States, and yet had ceased in the Maritimes.[60]

Solutions to the problem of how a church generated a revival were often offered. J. M. Cramp, in his "State of the Denomination Report" in 1867, asked why there was only 1.7 percent growth among Baptists, and suggested that people and churches were at fault: "Of this at any rate, we may be assured, that if the churches devoutly seek from God the guidance and grace which in our present circumstances are so much needed, a merciful bestowment will be the result."[61] Pastors like Elder Charles Tupper expected periodic seasons of revival in his churches and when these did not come, he would hold special meetings. In 1854, he had baptized eighty-five in Aylesford, but by 1856 he felt the people had grown cold. He therefore held special meetings twice a day for a month and baptized twenty-nine in twenty-nine days. A number of preachers took part in these services as various pastors from nearby churches would come and preach for a couple of days and then return home.[62] This became a pattern in many churches like the one at Horton where special meetings were used to dispel the "darkness and coldness" that "pervaded the community."[63]

Probably no church experienced a more consistent cycle of revivals than did the Horton, later Wolfville Baptist Church. Whenever revival came to either Horton Academy or Acadia College, the church would hold extra meetings. Many students dedicated themselves to Christ and

---

[58]CM, 20 October 1858, 330.

[59]See appendix, below.

[60]CM, 31 October 1860, 346.

[61]*Minutes of the Twenty-Second Session of the Baptist Convention of Nova Scotia, New Brunswick and Prince Edward Island, 1867* (Halifax: Christian Messenger Office, 1867) 19.

[62]CM, 14 May 1856, 154; I. E. Bill, *Fifty Years with the Baptist Ministers and Churches of the Maritime Provinces of Canada* (Saint John: Barnes & Co., 1880) 723.

[63]CM, 1 April 1857, 93.

were baptized into that church, while others dedicated themselves to Christian ministry as a result of the revival meetings. The pastoral leadership of that church had a profound effect upon the students from the time of Theodore Seth Harding on into the twentieth century. Rev. Stephen DeBlois, who succeeded Harding, "preached conversion in season and out of season."[64] He was unique in that, when he finished his message, he would walk down the aisle and go home, "leaving the message to do its work in the manner of our old ministers."[65] Rev. Thomas Trotter, pastor of the church during the revivals of the mid-1890s and a "clear, strong, eloquent, and persuasive preacher of the Gospel," played a key role during the special meetings at the Wolfville church. He resigned his charge to become president of Acadia in 1897.[66]

Sometimes special services were not enough to stir a congregation. In one of his few negative comments, Isaiah Wallace tells of a revival effort in Salisbury, New Brunswick, in 1889: "Want of earnestness and cooperation on the part of the church, and probably lack of faith on my own part, may have been the cause of our not enjoying the abundant blessing we hoped for."[67]

J. M. Cramp wondered in 1860 why there never seemed to be two years of revival in a row.[68] This concern for revival prompted denominational leaders to make it the occasional theme of circular letters and numerous Convention reports.[69] When the 1861–1862 revivals in Jamaica were reported, there was an editorial in *The Christian Messenger* entitled "Revivals: Will They Become General?" in which it was observed that there were revivals on every hand but few in the Maritimes.[70]

During the 1860s, there was a downturn in the number of recorded baptisms with only 892 reported in 1861 and three more years in the decade in which baptisms fell below the 1,000 mark. The 1862 annual

---

[64]Steele, "Pastor DeBlois," 18, 28-30; DeBlois, "Historical Sketch," 27-28; Cramp, "Sketches of the Religious History," 50.

[65]Cramp, "Sketches of the Religious History," 18.

[66]Chute, *Religious Life of Acadia*, 29.

[67]Wallace, *Autobiographical Sketch*, 111.

[68]*Minutes of the Baptist Convention of Nova Scotia, New Brunswick and Prince Edward Island* (Saint John, 1860), 20.

[69]CM, 6 August 1856, 255.

[70]CM, 17 December 1862, 402.

convention meeting in Moncton heard a call from the leadership for a time of revival to dispel the gloom. It was decided that as a denomination they would set apart the first Thursday of December as a day of humiliation and prayer.[71] The edition of *The Christian Messenger* following the special day of prayer reported that many churches observed the day because "religiously our mountains are yet cold and bleak and our valleys dry."[72] There was a significant increase in the number of baptisms the following year when they rose to 1,659, and credit was given to the day of prayer. It therefore became a standard ingredient in the Baptist calendar for the next few years.[73] In spite of this, the 1860s were lean years and in 1869 J. M. Cramp complained, "believing penitents do not 'fly as a cloud,' they drop in by twos and threes. This is not a satisfactory state of things."[74] He challenged Baptists to search their hearts for surely they were "at fault somewhere."[75]

A look at the statistics of growth for the Baptists in the last half of the nineteenth century reveals a rather steady growth with periods of rapid expansion that are accounted for by revivals. Baptist increases went over the 2,000 mark in 1859, 1874, 1875, 1876, 1885, 1886, 1894, 1895, 1896, and 1897.[76] One reads comments like "seasons of remarkable revival, and numerous conversions have gladdened the hearts of God's people."[77] In 1885 the report on denominational growth commented: "Revivals of great power have swept over several districts of our Convention."[78] These periods of revival, however, only touched a few churches

---

[71]*Minutes of the Baptist Convention of Nova Scotia, New Brunswick and Prince Edward Island* (Halifax, 1862) 25.

[72]CM, 17 December 1862, 406.

[73]*Minutes of the Baptist Convention of Nova Scotia, New Brunswick and Prince Edward Island* (Halifax, 1863) 19; Minutes of the Baptist Convention of Nova Scotia, New Brunswick, and Prince Edward Island (Saint John, 1864) 25.

[74]*Minutes of the Baptist Convention of Nova Scotia, New Brunswick and Prince Edward Island* (Saint John, 1864) 36.

[75]*Minutes of the Baptist Convention of Nova Scotia, New Brunswick and Prince Edward Island* (Halifax, 1869).

[76]See appendix, below.

[77]*Minutes of the Baptist Convention of Nova Scotia, New Brunswick and Prince Edward Island* (Halifax, 1859) 21.

[78]*The Baptist Yearbook of the Maritime Provinces of Canada* (Halifax, 1885) 37-

and each year many churches recorded no baptisms. In 1876, J. M. Cramp, as chairman of the committee in charge of reports, stated that in spite of the 3,463 baptisms there were some churches with no additions. He added: "It is easy to ascribe this difference to the sovereignty of God, who saves by many or by few, at his pleasure, but surely it is not wise or safe to content ourselves with such a solution to the problem."[79] The Home Mission Board made efforts to organize revival or evangelistic efforts. The very fact that organization became a part of the concept of revivals caused a loss of spontaneity and changed the concept of what constituted a revival.

Isaiah Wallace reflects both the revival tradition and the changed image of revivals, and his methods illustrate the shift. E. M. Keirstead suggested that Wallace's autobiography affords a glimpse into the "inner life of the denomination as cannot be obtained elsewhere."[80] An indication of the changing emphases of the late nineteenth century was Wallace's choice of texts for his messages. The sermon that sparked the Belldune revival was 'hellfire and brimstone,' while the ones he mentions from a later period are based on texts like Exodus 32:26: "Who is on the Lord's side?"[81] He also mentions using John 3:7: "Marvel not that I say unto you, ye must be born again." Of the sermon preached on this text, Wallace said:

> Regeneration was our theme, its Nature, Importance, and Evidence. Soon the great power of God was manifest. In his discourse the preacher had emphasized the fact that regeneration is divine in its source, and it seemed as if the divine power was manifest, swaying the minds and hearts of the people and producing conviction for sin and faith in the atoning blood.[82]

He also tells of asking during meetings for a positive response to an invitation and tells of people "rising up to speak" or coming for prayer.[83]

38.

[79]*Minutes of the Baptist Convention of Nova Scotia, New Brunswick, and Prince Edward Island* (Saint John, 1876) 31.

[80]Wallace, *Autobiographical Sketch*, i.

[81]Ibid., 62.

[82]Ibid., 92ff.

[83]Ibid., 102; CM, 23 November 1864.

Wallace baptized more than 3,000 people during his ministry and there were many others who were baptized by the local pastor where he was preaching. He says he had "no stereotyped methods for promotion of revivals," but did consider the preaching of the Word to be "the most prominent factor in his success."[84] Next in importance was a church in condition to "travail."[85] A third characteristic was a preacher willing to visit and become aware of the spiritual condition of the hearers. Last was faith in himself as a servant of God and faith in the power of God. He added: "All this presupposes the habitual exercises of earnest prayer, diligent Bible study, and also correct Christian deportment."[86] He also always sought to be supportive of local pastors. Pastor W. Camp wrote in 1895 of a visit of Wallace to Hillsborough, New Brunswick: "But I would like to say that he is free from all those methods adopted by many evangelists and so objectionable to most of our best-thinking pastors. He allows the pastor to lead and renders him assistance."[87] Wallace therefore reflects the change from revivalism in the mid-nineteenth century to evangelism, which sought by organization and new methods to bring people into the church.

This was reflected in one other way: in the recognition of the growing importance of the Sunday school movement. Wallace early perceived its significance and, as chairman of the Sabbath Schools Committee of the Convention in 1853, urged that every church should have a sabbath school.[88] By 1887, there were 8,639 scholars in Baptist Sunday schools. Of the 1,846 people baptized in Convention churches in 1888, 735 were from the Sunday schools.[89] By 1900, there were 29,182 scholars and 3,327 teachers in Regular Baptist Sunday schools.[90] One wonders if the growth of the denomination after the mid-1890s is not to be understood as a consequence of the number in the Sunday schools rather than revivals or

---

[84]Wallace, *Autobiographical Sketch*, 172-73.

[85]Ibid., 173.

[86]Ibid.

[87]Ibid., 149.

[88]*Minutes of the Baptist Convention of Nova Scotia, New Brunswick, and Prince Edward Island* (Halifax, 1853) 10.

[89]*The Baptist Yearbook of the Maritime Provinces of Canada* (Halifax, 1888) 40-41; Levy, *Baptists of the Maritime Provinces*, 228.

[90]Ibid.

evangelism. Certainly, those responding to the "altar call" were very likely products of the Sunday schools.

There is one final note to be made of the trend that very much disturbed the people of the time: the growth of nonresident members. The idea is inconsistent with Baptist polity, but by 1886 it was calculated that there were as high as 7,000 nonresidents being maintained on Regular Baptist membership lists.[91] Emigration to the United States and the larger Canadian cities made this issue increasingly important. Much of the decline in members in the early twentieth century may reflect the removal of some of the nonresident names from church roles.[92]

In conclusion, several observations can be made. First, Baptist growth during the early part of the nineteenth century was maintained by revivals and that tradition permeates Baptist life for the rest of the century. Second, the nature of revivals changed to reflect a more organized church structure. Third, when times of revival ceased to come, growth was slow or there was none at all. Last, people continued to long for revivals, but the churches had institutionalized the ways the Holy Spirit had moved in earlier days with the result that there was evangelistic activity, but not the traditional revival.

---

[91]Saunders, *History of the Baptists of the Maritime Provinces*, 409; *The Baptist Yearbook of the Maritime Provinces of Canada* (Halifax, 1886) 16-19; *The Baptist Yearbook of the Maritime Provinces of Canada* (Halifax, 1891) 17-20.

[92]See appendix, below.

Appendix

There are some years for which statistics are incomplete.

YEAR	CHURCHES	BAPTISMS	TOTAL	%GROWTH	COMMENTS
1851	193	1280	16,000		
1852		750	16,298	1.9	
1853		585	16,580	1.7	
1854		1180	17,035	2.7	84 baptized by C. Tupper
1855					
1856	216	1309	17,759		
1857	248	1411	18,976	6.9	140 baptized by I. Wallace
1858	251	1396	19,506	2.8	
1859	249	2576	20,760	6.5	138 baptized by C. Tupper
1860	265	1615	21,861	5.3	
1861	266	892	22,908	4.8	
1862	283	1010	23,677	3.4	
1863	271	1659	24,595	3.9	
1864	268	879	24,649	2.2	
1865	274	866	24,740	.4	
1866	276	1317	25,362	2.5	
1867	277	976	25,781	1.7	
1868	287	1481	26,715	3.8	
1869	294	1372	27,461	3.5	
1870			27,905	1.6	
1871	311	1214	28,316	1.5	
1872	311	804	28,977	2.3	
1873	318	766	29,357	1.3	
1874	323	3021	31,693	8	252 baptized by I. Wallace
1875	328	2030	32,942	3.9	
1876	346	3463	35,535	7.9	330 baptized at Berwick, NS by I. Wallace in 3 yrs
1877	344	1580	36,691	3.3	
1878		1735	36,761	.2	
1879	353	1353	37,017	.7	

1880		1883?			200 baptized by I. Wallace
1881	355	1260	37,393		
1882	344	1098	37,480	.2	
1883					
1884		1986	35,060?		
1885	396	2135	41,637		
1886	357	2508	43,463	4.4	
1887	375	1768	43,553	.2	
1888	378	1946	43,746	.4	
1889	384	1817	43,995	.6	
1890	389	1171			
1891	392	1772	42,777		
1892	392?	1772?	42,777?		Yearbook gives 1891 figures
1893	397	1652	44,697	4.5	
1894		2219	44,953	.6	
1895	404	2729	47,108	5	
1896	405	2580	48,830	3.5	
1897	414	2324	50,424	3.3	
1898	409	1741	50,551	.3	
1899	410	1362	50,846	.6	
1900		1384	51,390	1.1	
1901	409	1292	50,821	-1.1	
1902	400	1637	50,185	-1.3	
1903	418	1458	51,946	3.5	
1904	416	1051	51,463	- .9	
1905	418	1790	50,942	-1	

"This Little Light of Mine" in a Postmodern World[1]

Roy Williams
Acadia Divinity College

You are the light of the world. . . . [L]et your light shine before men, that they may see your good deeds and praise your Father in heaven.
(Matthew 5:14, 16 NIV)

I frequently ask new students a few questions to give me an idea of their knowledge of theology. An example is, "What place do good works have in the Christian faith?" Not surprisingly, my students rarely have a good word for good works! At best one might say, "We are not saved by good works but by faith in Christ." Some simply say, "None!" They have gotten the message that good deeds or keeping God's Law does not justify. Most Protestants would find some ground of agreement here. After all, they reflect Luther's doctrine of justification by faith alone, a doctrine that the Swiss Reformer Heinrich Bullinger called "the head and foundation . . . of evangelical and apostolic doctrine." However, there is a disturbing aspect to this. In most Protestant's minds, good works are in the same situation in which comedian Rodney Dangerfield finds himself when he says "I don't get no respect around here." And while that may make for good comedy, it does not make for good theology. Students find puzzling the title of Bullinger's book by which he intended to express the consensus of all Protestants: *The Grace of God that Justifies Us for the Sake of Christ through Faith Alone, without Good Works, while Faith Meanwhile Abounds in Good Works.*[2]

This paper draws attention to the second part of Bullinger's title, *Faith . . . Abounds in Good Works*, that expresses the strong consensus amongst Reformation theologians. While the first part of the title received considerable attention in the twentieth century,[3] the second half of

---

[1]This lecture was presented in honour of Dr. Allison Trites as one of the 2001 Hayward Lectures, Acadia University.

[2]J. J. Pelikan, *Reformation of Church and Dogma (1300–1700)*, Christian Tradition (Chicago: University of Chicago Press, 1984) 4:139.

[3]Writing in 1990, Carl E. Braaten observes, "The history of twentieth-century theology may be read in terms of the rise and fall of the place of justification."

Bullinger's title is the church's orphaned child. This is as true in the Evangelical branch of Christendom as in any other. It is inexplicable that the branch of Protestantism that stresses biblical authority and frequently sees itself as the continuation of classic Reformation theology[4] should lose its grip on this doctrine that receives so much attention in the New Testament. To put it more boldly, there is more positive material in the New Testament dealing with good works than material dealing with justification by faith.

In this neglect, recent Protestant theology is failing to follow the example found in the Reformers' works, catechisms, and confessions. This is weakening the church in a critical way at a critical time. To effectively minister in the twenty-first century with its postmodern interest in pragmatism, we need to restore the theology and practice of good works.

This essay explores the concept of good works in the theology of the Protestant Reformers, Martin Luther and John Calvin, and in the thinking of Karl Barth, one modern theologian who develops the topic. Added to these, a brief look at New Testament material will form the background for an Evangelical theology of good works that is biblical, Reformed, and pertinent to a postmodern world.

Luther

In his "Ninety-five Theses" of 1517, Luther wanted to debate the misuse and abuse of indulgences—not their legitimacy, for he did not yet question that. Justification by faith does not really find a place in the theses,[5] but good works do. Six theses speak of them.

Braaten reminds us of the central place the doctrine played in the work of many prominent theologians (e.g., Karl Barth, Emil Brunner, Rudolph Bultmann, Paul Tillich, and others) in the twentieth century, while theological trends at the end of the century (e.g., feminist, liberation, and process theologies) have lost interest. C. E. Braaten, *Justification: The Article by Which the Church Stands or Falls* (Minneapolis: Fortress, 1990) 10-11.

[4]See A. E. McGrath, *Evangelicalism & the Future of Christianity* (Downers Grove: InterVarsity, 1995); and B. L. Ramm, *The Evangelical Heritage: A Study in Historical Theology*, foreword by K. J. Vanhoozer (Grand Rapids: Baker, 2000).

[5]It is possible that Luther had not yet established his position on justification by faith. Scholars debate the date at which Luther made his breakthrough with arguments giving a range of dates from 1513–1515 to 1518–1519. See A. E.

Luther's understanding of good works is based on the Aristotelian concept of *habitus*, that is, that virtue is acquired by the habitual practice of good acts and states of mind. To put it another way, by doing good we become good.[6] Further study leads Luther to adopt the Augustinian view of human nature reflected in his 1525 work, *The Bondage of the Will.*[7] This allows no room for people to do good works, or to be good, through their own efforts. Preaching on Titus 3:4-8, Luther said: "[N]o one can do good unless he himself is good first. Therefore he does not become good through good works, but the works become good through him. But he . . . becomes good through this washing of regeneration, and in no other way."[8]

Two other ideas in Luther's mature theology require attention. The nature of works is first. As a Roman Catholic, in addition to helping the poor, Luther thought of saying or receiving the mass, not eating meat on certain days, scourging one's self, the singing of matins, and observing the seven daily hours of prayer, fasting, invoking the saints, going on pilgrimages, and other such activities as good works.[9] In time it became apparent to Luther that, with the exception of helping the poor, these ideas were not grounded in Scripture. He therefore replaced them with more biblical and practical notions: "A servant is doing good works when he . . . leads his life in obedience to his master[,] . . . maintains moderation and decency, serves his neighbor, cleans the stable, gives the horses

---

McGrath, *Luther's Theology of the Cross: Martin Luther's Theological Breakthrough* (Oxford: Blackwell, 1985) 141-47.

[6]See G. Ebeling, *Luther: An Introduction to His Thought*, trans. R. A. Wilson (Philadelphia: Fortress, 1970) 141-58; A. E. McGrath, *The Intellectual Origins of the European Reformation* (Oxford: Blackwell, 1987) 75-93; and Aristotle, "Nicomachean Ethics," in *A New Aristotle Reader*, ed. J. L. Ackrill (Princeton: Princeton University Press, 1987) 2:1-6.

[7]For Luther's Augustinianism, see McGrath, *Intellectual Origins*, 86-93; McGrath, *Luther's Theology of the Cross*, 63-71; and Pelikan, *Reformation of Church and Dogma (1300–1700)*, 139-44.

[8]E. M. Plass, *What Luther Says: an Anthology* (Saint Louis: Concordia, 1959) 3:1510.

[9]*Sermons on the Gospel of St. John, Chapters 14–16*, in *Luther's Works*, ed. J. J. Pelikan et al. (Saint Louis: Concordia, 1961) 24:229; *Sermons on the First Epistle of St. Peter*, in *Luther's Works* 30:82-83; and *Sermons on the Gospel of St. John, Chapters 6–8*, in *Luther's Works* 23:15.

fodder, etc. . . . He knows that whatever he does in his calling pleases God."[10] And a servant girl when she washes the pots, lights the fire in the oven, and makes the beds does good works when she does these things unto Christ. "So it is with a son who is obedient to his father. If he is sent to do his lessons, . . . and thinks: 'This is my father's command, and it is pleasing to God.' "[11] Obviously this changes the nature of good works.

More important is the shift in the role of good works in salvation. Late medieval theology was influenced by a number of intellectual streams. One of them, the *via moderna*,[12] argued that God had entered into a covenant with humanity. If a person met the conditions of the covenant by doing his best, *quod in se est*, God would justify him.[13] Luther found this to be lacking and argued it is "impossible to be justified by works."[14] Discussing Romans 3:28, he says, "Certain it is that since Christ or the righteousness of Christ lies outside us and is foreign to us, our works are unable to lay hold of it." However, "faith, which the Holy Spirit infuses into us when we hear about Christ, lays hold of Christ." Therefore "faith alone justifies without any works of ours."[15]

Luther's opponents accuse him of being against good works. The charge is rebutted from Luther's own writings. Commenting on Galatians 3:22, he states, "Apart from the issue of justification, no one can adequately praise true good works."[16] One reason is those New Testament passages that speak of judgment according to works. Here Luther reasoned that "even though God judges us according to our works, it nevertheless remains true that the works are only the fruits of faith. They

---

[10]Plass, *What Luther Says*, 3:1518.

[11]*Lectures on Titus*, in *Luther's Works* 29:66. In part, Luther is trying to encourage political stability: see E. Grislis, "The Meaning of Good Works: Luther and the Anabaptists," *Word & World* 6 (1986): 170-80.

[12]See McGrath, *Intellectual Origins*, 75-85.

[13]Ibid., 81, 116-17.

[14]*Theses Concerning Faith and Law, 1535*, in *Luther's Works* 34:113. For the development of Luther's doctrine of justification by faith, see McGrath, *Luther's Theology of the Cross*, 128-36; and A. E. McGrath, *Iustitia Dei: A History of the Christian Doctrine of Justification* (New York: Cambridge University Press, 1986) 188-206.

[15]Plass, *What Luther Says*, 2:707.

[16]*Lectures on Galatians*, 1535, in *Luther's Works* 26:334.

are the evidence of our belief or unbelief. Therefore God will judge and convict you on the basis of your works."[17] Rejecting *habitus*, he says works acceptable to God are obviously those He produces: "A good work comes completely and entirely from God; for grace alone sweeps away, draws, and moves the will."[18]

Luther wanted balance when dealing with good works and this requires a great deal of pastoral acumen:

> It is difficult . . . to teach that we are justified by faith without works and yet to require works at the same time. . . . Both topics, faith and works, must be carefully taught and emphasized, but in such a way that they both remain within their limits. Otherwise, if works alone are taught, as happened under the papacy, faith is lost. If faith alone is taught, unspiritual men will immediately suppose that works are not necessary.[19]

In summary, Luther gives good works biblical content. He argues they do not justify, but they always accompany saving faith.

When reading Luther's *Freedom of a Christian* or his *Sermon of Good Works*, a question comes to the mind of Karl Barth.

> What was really on Luther's heart? What did he really want to say to us? That we must do good works to please God and help our neighbor, or that good works can issue only from faith, and that without faith they are dead and in themselves at least neither good, demanded, nor necessary? Undoubtedly both. But you will clearly find that Luther's real interest is in the second point and not the first, not the step into life and the doing of works, but in the fact that when they are done they are done in faith.[20]

Barth stresses that in making this observation there is no dishonor to Luther;[21] whose theological method and concern for Christian freedom demanded it. However, "it is a historical fact that Luther's heart concern

---

[17]*Sermons on the First Epistle of St. Peter*, in *Luther's Works* 30:34.

[18]Plass, *What Luther Says*, 3:1514.

[19]*Lectures on Galatians*, 1535, in *Luther's Works* 27:62-63.

[20]K. Barth, *The Theology of John Calvin*, trans. G. W. Bromiley (Grand Rapids: Eerdmans, 1995) 75-76.

[21]Ibid., 76.

was with the basis of works and not the will for them, with fighting *against* papist works and not fighting *for* works of the Spirit and love, remarkable and vital though what he said about these might be."[22]

Calvin

To observe a theology that stresses both parts, good works do not save but come from a living faith and are for love of God and neighbor, Barth directs us to Calvin. Calvin's own edifice is built upon the same sure foundation that Luther used: the Holy Scriptures interpreted through an Augustinian hermeneutic.[23]

Calvin made a fourfold classification of humanity. People are idolaters; baptized but impure in their lives and hence Christian in name only; hypocrites who are wicked in heart; or "regenerate by God's Spirit" and making "true holiness their concern."[24] Not one of these has a hope of being justified by good works. The first three, even when they do good, "deserve no reward . . . because . . . [of] the pollution of their hearts."[25] It is only the fourth group, those regenerated by God's Spirit, whose good

---

[22]Ibid. Of Luther, Barth says, "Without the negative gestures of the Enthusiasts [he sought] only to proclaim directly to housewives, servants, princes, and soldiers the forgiveness of sins, simply trying to tell things as he saw them in Romans and the Psalms, no matter what the outcome might be in the empire of Charles V—that was Luther, the reformer of the first turn, and I would not hesitate to concede that in this regard Zwingli and Calvin, though they, too, knew what he knew, are not to be compared even remotely with him." Ibid., 89.

[23]As with Luther, the origin of Calvin's Augustinianism is debated. See, e.g., A. E. McGrath, *A Life of John Calvin: A Study in the Shaping of Western Culture* (Cambridge: Blackwell, 1990) 40-47; and McGrath, *Intellectual Origins*, 86-107. McGrath observes that with the passing of time, it is Calvin's model of justification by faith rather than Luther's that will gain the ascendancy among Protestants outside the Lutheran camp, McGrath, *Iustitia Dei*, 226.

[24]J. Calvin, *Institutes of the Christian Religion*, ed. J. T. McNeill, LCC 20 (Philadelphia: Westminster, 1960) 3:14, 1.

[25]Calvin does not say that the virtues and good works of the unregenerate are without value, just that they are without saving merit. He acknowledges that "they are God's instruments for the preservation of human society in righteousness, continence, friendship, temperance, fortitude, and prudence." Ibid., 3:14, 1-3.

works are going to be acceptable to God. Calvin grounded this notion in his doctrine of justification by faith.

In his doctrine of justification by faith, Calvin was obviously indebted to Luther, but he gave the concept his own stamp.[26] Luther's model was based upon Augustine's with a significant difference. Luther's view was forensic, that is, the righteousness God gives remains outside believers rather than within as in Augustine.[27] At times, both Luther's supporters and detractors misread this to mean that righteous living and good works are not necessary. Calvin overcame this difficulty by tying justification tightly to union with Christ. For him, as with Luther, the believer is freely justified by faith through the imputed righteousness of the Savior. Calvin says, "We define justification as follows: the sinner, received into communion with Christ, is reconciled to God by his grace, while, cleansed by Christ's blood, he obtains forgiveness of sins and is clothed with Christ's righteousness as if it were his own, he stands confident before the heavenly judgment seat."[28]

Justification and regeneration are tightly linked in Calvin's thought. "Calvin asserted that faith, which consists of knowledge of the Gospel, persuasion of its truth and trust in Christ, is the conscious human response to the divine work of regeneration."[29] Thus the justified are those in union with Christ through regeneration, which begins the restoration of the *imago dei* within believers.

Calvin asserted that Christians "dream neither of a faith devoid of good works nor of a justification that stands without them." The two must be together. It is within the bounds of regeneration, an experience always accompanying justification, however, that good works find their

---

[26]McGrath, *Iustitia Dei*, 223-26; F. Wendel, *Calvin: the Origins and Development of His Religious Thought*, trans. P. Mairet (New York: Harper & Row, 1963) 255-63.

[27]McGrath, *Iustitia Dei*, 23-36, for Augustine's view of justification; 188-207, for Luther's; and also P. Althaus, *The Theology of Martin Luther*, trans. R. C. Schultz (Philadelphia: Fortress, 1966) 224-50.

[28]Calvin, *Institutes of the Christian Religion* 17:3, 8.

[29]Calvin "viewed regeneration broadly as the whole process of spiritual vivification, inclusive of the new birth, conversion, and sanctification." B. A. Demarest, and G. R. Lewis, *Integrative Theology* (Grand Rapids: Zondervan, 1994) 3:77. See also Wendel, *Calvin*, 242-55, for Calvin's concept of regeneration.

origin.[30] For this reason, God approves of the good works of the believer because "the Lord cannot fail to love and embrace the good things that he works in them through his Spirit."[31] Commenting on Ephesians 2:10, Calvin expounded Paul's teachings as follows:

> When he says, that "we are the work of God," this does not refer to ordinary creation. . . . We are declared to be new creatures, because, not by our own power, but by the Spirit of Christ, we have been formed to righteousness. This applies to none but believers. . . . [B]y the grace of Christ . . . they are spiritually renewed, and become new men. Everything in us . . . that is good, is the supernatural gift of God. The context explains his meaning. *We are his work*, because we have been *created* . . . not to every kind of life, but to *good works*.[32]

But these "good works of believers are never so pure as to be able to please [God] without pardon."[33] They are imperfect because "the godly . . . are still sinners, and their good works are as yet incomplete and redolent of the vices of the flesh."[34] At this point Calvin's doctrine of "double justification" comes into play.[35]

> Therefore, as we ourselves, when we have been engrafted in Christ, are righteous in God's sight because our iniquities are covered by Christ's sinlessness, so our works are righteous and are thus regarded because whatever fault is otherwise in them is buried in Christ's purity, and is not charged to our account. Accordingly, we can deservedly say that by faith alone not only we ourselves but our works as well are justified.[36]

---

[30]Calvin, *Institutes of the Christian Religion* 3:16, 1. For a discussion of "the place of good works in the Christian life" in Calvin's theology, see, J. H. Leith, *John Calvin's Doctrine of the Christian Life*, with a foreword by A. C. Outler (Louisville: Westminster/John Knox, 1989) 103-106.

[31]Calvin, *Institutes of the Christian Religion* 3:17, 5.

[32]J. Calvin, *Commentaries on the Epistles of Paul to the Galatians and Ephesians*, trans. W. Pringle, Calvin Translation Society Publications (Edinburgh: Calvin Translation Society, 1854) 229.

[33]J. Calvin, "The Necessity of Reforming the Church," in *Theological Treatises*, trans. J. K. S. Reid, LCC 22 (Philadelphia: Westminster, 1954) 202.

[34]Calvin, *Institutes of the Christian Religion* 3:17, 5.

[35]For "double justification" see Wendel, *Calvin*, 260-62.

[36]Calvin, *Institutes of the Christian Religion* 3:17, 10.

For Calvin, therefore, faith justifies both the person and the works. If this is the case,[37] what role do good works play in the Christian life? They have several important functions.

Objectively, Calvin tied good works to the chief end of life, bringing glory to God.[38] This idea is tightly connected to the doctrine of regeneration in a circular way. God, by the Holy Spirit indwelling the Christian, works in that life so that glory is brought to God's name. Calvin put it this way:

> We confess that while through the intercession of Christ's righteousness God reconciles us to himself, and by free remission of sins accounts us righteous, his beneficence is at the same time joined with such a mercy that through his Holy Spirit he dwells in us and by his power the lusts of our flesh are each day more and more mortified; we are indeed sanctified, that is, consecrated to the Lord in true purity of life, with our hearts formed to obedience to the law. The end is that our especial will may be to serve his will and by every means to advance his glory alone.[39]

From the subjective side, Calvin sees good works as evidence of adoption and regeneration. They are "testimonies of God dwelling and ruling in us." Such activities show "that the Spirit of adoption has been given to us [cf. Romans 8:15]."[40] The Christian does not look to his good works for salvation, but to gain assurance that he is indeed regenerate[41] and hence one of the elect.[42]

In summary, Calvin argued that good works do not justify, but they always accompany saving faith. Never pure, they are themselves justified

---

[37]Francois Wendel draws attention to the important point that for Calvin the value of faith is its content, Jesus Christ, Wendel, *Calvin*, 262. See, e.g., Calvin, *Institutes of the Christian Religion* 3:18, 8, where Calvin says, "We say that faith justifies, not because it merits righteousness for us by its own worth, but because it is an instrument whereby we obtain free the righteousness of Christ."

[38]J. Calvin, "The Catechism of the Church of Geneva," in *Theological Treatises*, 91.

[39]Calvin, *Institutes of the Christian Religion* 3:14, 9.

[40]Ibid. 3:14, 8.

[41]Ibid. 3:14, 19.

[42]Ibid. 3:14, 20.

by faith. They witness to one's regeneration and election. Because they come from the regenerative activity of God, they are acceptable to him and bring glory to his name.

Barth

Like Luther's and Calvin's, Barth's thought is heavy with biblical content. Although his theology owes much to classic Reformation thought, his is a neoreformation theology. For Luther, wrestling with the burden of personal sin, the question "How can I find a gracious God?" is paramount. For Barth the pressing issue is epistemological. Alister McGrath notes, "For Luther, the gospel was primarily concerned with the forgiveness of sins, whereas for Barth it is primarily concerned with the possibility of the right knowledge of God. Barth has placed the *divine revelation to sinful man* at the point where Luther placed the *divine justification of sinful man*."[43] To put it in Barth's own words: "The *articulus stantis et candentis ecclesiae* is not the doctrine of justification as such, but its basis and culmination: the confession of Jesus Christ, in whom are hid all the treasures of wisdom and knowledge."[44]

However, in his *Church Dogmatics* IV/1, Barth devotes considerable attention to "justification by faith alone" and makes it one of the three foci, along with sanctification and calling, of the doctrine of reconciliation. The depth of Barth's thought, the breadth of his learning, and the strength of his argumentation are all so powerful, interest in the doctrine was rejuvenated and culminated in new ecumenical explorations and understandings of it.[45]

Where justification is concerned, Barth "denies the competence, the relevance, the power, and the value of all human action."[46] And he

---

[43]McGrath, *Iustitia Dei*, 361.

[44]K. Barth, *Church Dogmatics*, trans. G. W. Bromiley and T. F. Torrance (Edinburgh: T. & T. Clark, 1936-1977) IV/I, 527.

[45]E.g., H. G. Anderson, T. A. Murphy, and J. A. Burgess, *Justification by Faith*, Lutherans and Catholics in Dialogue 7 (Minneapolis: Augsburg, 1985); Braaten, *Justification*; D. A. Carson, *Right with God: Justification in the Bible and the World* (Grand Rapids: Baker, 1992); H. Küng, *Justification: the Doctrine of Karl Barth and a Catholic Reflection*, trans. E. Quinn (Philadelphia: Westminster, 1964).

[46]Barth, *Church Dogmatics* IV/1, 626-27.

describes "faith as the humility which involves necessarily the exclusion of works."[47]

Barth carefully defines the term "works." He observes that for Paul it means "the works which the OT demanded of . . . Israel to mark their distinction from other peoples . . . [and] to attest the fact that they belonged to the covenant which He had made with them." In a broader context, Barth says that works "are the thoughts and words and achievements of sinful man, including the works which he is able and willing and ready to do and produce as such in relation to the revelation of God and in obedience to His Law."[48] None of these can justify. Even faith itself is not a work that justifies, but is rather a gift from God.

Although denying works any role in justification, Barth is not about to throw them away.[49] His theology is too enriched by the Scriptures, too informed by Reformation doctrine for that to happen. He discusses "The Praise of Works" under the topic of sanctification. Although sanctification and justification are to be distinguished,[50] they are "indissolubly bound," as "two different aspects of the one event of salvation."[51] Good works are grounded in both of these dimensions of salvation. To begin with, good works are an attestation of one's justification by faith.[52] Furthermore (illuminating what Barth means by "the *praise* of works), sanctification "takes place here and now in works which are really good, that is, which are praised by God and praise Him."[53] As Christians cannot "belong to Jesus Christ as their Lord and Head . . . to no purpose," good works are obligatory for them.[54] It is for these that one is elected, called, and empowered by God.[55] Barth draws attention to numerous biblical examples of these things.[56]

---

[47]Ibid., 628.

[48]Ibid., 621.

[49]Ibid., 627-28. For a discussion of Barth's theology of good works, see Küng, *Justification*, 79-81.

[50]Barth, *Church Dogmatics* IV/2, 504.

[51]Ibid., 503.

[52]Ibid. IV/1, 627-28.

[53]Ibid. IV/2, 596.

[54]Ibid., 585.

[55]Ibid., 597.

[56]Ibid.

Barth's Augustinian anthropology leads him to several conclusions. It is only the regenerate who can truly perform good works.[57] Furthermore, rejecting any hint of Pelagianism, "their works are taken into service by God and are good works, quite irrespective . . . of the fact that even as good works they are full of transgression."[58] Consequently (here Barth sounds like an English Puritan), the Christian will work,

> knowing that he must lay himself and what he wills and does and achieves wholly in the hand of the God who has so graciously chosen and called him to participate in his work. He will constantly commend it to Him, that He may forgive that in which it is sinful, that He may receive it like himself, that He may sanctify it, that He may use and order it, that He may give it the character of a service rendered and acceptable to Himself—which is something that can never be given by the man who performs it.[59]

Considering that Barth's theology is a theology of the Word of God, it is not surprising that he argues, "Works can be good only as they declare what God has done and accomplished—the goodness in which He has turned to man and given Himself for him. . . . All the works which are called good and described as good in the Bible take place in this context."[60] To put it another way, the good works of a person declare the good work of God.[61] This seems to make proclamation the ultimate good work.[62] However, as he brings his discussion to a conclusion, Barth gives practical examples of these things, which expand his concept considerably.

> There is the good cooperation between few or many. There are good meetings and partings. There is the good attempting of big things and the good fulfilment of small. There is good conduct in difficult and testing conditions. There are good achievements in family and social life. . . . There is good speaking and silence; good laughter and weeping; good resolves and decisions. There is good Christian profession. There

---

[57]Ibid., 593.
[58]Ibid., 593.
[59]Ibid., 594.
[60]Ibid., 590.
[61]Ibid., 591.
[62]Ibid., 591-93.

is also good prayer, good hearing and reading and study, and sometimes good preaching . . . .[63]

Barth concludes his exploration with two questions and answers from the *Heidelberg Catechism* which reflect the biblical nature of Reformation theology and his own. The ninety-first defines "good works" as those which are grounded in Scripture rather than the opinions of men. The eighty-sixth teaches that good works are necessary "because Christ, having bought us by His blood, has also renewed us by His Holy Spirit, that we should show ourselves grateful to God for His benefits with our whole lives and that He should be magnified through us. Also in order that we may have assurance of our faith from its fruits, and win our neighbours to Christ by our godly conversation."[64]

New Testament Survey

The quarry out of which these three great Protestant theologians extracted the ore from which comes their finished theologies is primarily the New Testament. As we turn our attention to that source, we will have to limit our excavations to a few crucial texts.

Studying the Gospels, especially Matthew and Luke, one finds a wealth of material describing the righteousness the Kingdom of God requires, and much of this affirms the role and importance of good works.[65] For example, Jesus instructs his followers to practice alms giving, perform good works, "lay up treasures in heaven," and be "rich towards God." Several major parables stress that at the final judgment the righteous will be distinguished from the wicked not because they kept the Law of Moses but because they performed good works, fed the hungry, and clothed the naked.

Of course this is not to say that the Jews of Jesus' day did not think good works were important. They too stressed them in their teachings. For some Rabbis "only meditation on Torah could have outranked charity as a righteous deed." For others, "deeds of charity were seen as greater

---

[63]Ibid., 598.

[64]Ibid., 598.

[65]See H.-C. Hahn, "Work, Do, Accomplish," in *NIDNTT* 3:1147-59; and idem, ἔργον, ἐργάζομαι, *TDNT* 2:645-52.

than all the commandments."[66] However, as the rich young ruler (Mark 10:17-26) and other passages remind us, many saw righteousness to be found primarily in observing the law.

For Jesus, the Law and Prophets are fulfilled in his person, ministry, and crucifixion. In the so-called "Q" material Jesus teaches that the Law and the Prophets were proclaimed until John the Baptist, but now the Old Covenant is superseded by the Kingdom of God (Matthew 11:12; Luke 16:16). For this reason it is not detrimental if the Temple is destroyed (Matthew 24:1-2) and the ritual dimensions of the Law cease.[67] However, as the parables of the shrewd manager (Luke 16:1-15) and the sheep and goats (Matthew 25:31-46) remind us, it is important that his followers continue to practice works of charity until the consummation.

Discipleship is a major focus in Matthew's Gospel. The life of the disciple is patterned after that of his rabbi (Matthew 10:24-25; Luke 6:40). The way the rabbi lives, the piety he practices, and the values and ethics he espouses become those of the disciple.[68] This has a communal dimension in the first gospel. The community of Jesus' disciples is to be characterized by love, forgiveness, and good works (5:16).[69]

> *Good deeds* are characteristic of life in the new age of salvation (cf. Jeremiah 31:31), they bear witness to God's eschatological activity on behalf of humanity. Just as Jesus' life and preaching/teaching bore witness to God's redemptive activity to those who had eyes to see and ears to hear, so the disciple's *good deeds* lead others to recognize the presence of God's transforming power in the world. . . . [Those in darkness will

---

[66]P. H. Davids, "Rich and poor," *DJG*, 704.

[67]See N. T. Wright, *Christian Origins and the Question of God* (Minneapolis: Fortress, 1996) 320-68; K. E. Bower, " 'Let the Reader Understand': Temple & Eschatology in Mark," in *Eschatology in Bible & Theology: Evangelical Essays at the Dawn of a New Millennium*, ed. K. E. Brower and M. W. Elliott (Downers Grove: InterVarsity, 1997) 119-43; C. H. T. Fletcher-Louis, "The Destruction of the Temple and the Relativization of the Old Covenant," in *Eschatology in Bible & Theology*, 145-69.

[68]R. N. Longenecker, "Introduction," in *Patterns of Discipleship in the New Testament*, ed. R. N. Longenecker, MNTS (Grand Rapids: Eerdmans, 1996) 3.

[69]T. L. Donaldson, "Guiding Readers—Making Disciples: Discipleship in Matthew's Narrative Strategy," in *Patterns of Discipleship in the New Testament*, 46.

then] acknowledge God as God and yield to him as their "Heavenly Father."[70]

In the Sermon on the Mount one finds an obedience to God's standard that is revealed by Jesus himself. The instructions he gives relating to "the practice of piety" ("acts of righteousness" in the NIV) begin with the giving of alms (Matthew 6:1-4).[71] Immediately after instructions about prayer and fasting, Jesus again takes up the topic of good works by encouraging his followers to lay up treasures in heaven and then warns about the spiritual dangers of wealth. "Worry" about material things is then discussed and his disciples are instructed to seek first God's kingdom and righteousness. Again, this is probably an allusion to the giving of alms.

In Luke's Gospel, good works are a major theme.[72] Richard Longenecker comments: "Luke wants his readers to know that being a follower of Jesus requires . . . new attitudes towards wealth, poverty, and the use of riches for the benefit of others."[73] The "rich fool" (12:13-21) was foolish because he failed to be "rich towards God" by helping the poor (12:21). The parable of the shrewd manager (16:1-14) also emphasizes giving to the poor.[74] In the parable of Lazarus and the rich man (16:19-31), the latter has the opportunity to have treasures in heaven by helping Lazarus but misses out by ignoring him.[75] The rich young ruler (18:18-30), who has observed all the law since his youth, chooses earthly riches over eternal life and the security of treasures in heaven gained by helping the poor. Only Zacchaeus (19:1-10) the chief tax collector, scorned by Jew

---

[70]R. A. Guelich, *The Sermon on the Mount: A Foundation for Understanding* (Waco: Word, 1982) 129.

[71]For Matthew 6:1, some manuscripts (e.g., L W Z Θ f^{13} and Clement) read "almsgiving" (ἐλεημοσύνη) instead of "practice your piety" (δικαιοσύνη). Scot McKnight notes that "the Hebrew and Aramaic words for righteousness and almsgiving are closely related." McKnight, "Justice, Righteousness," in *DJG*, 414.

[72]R. N. Longenecker, "Taking Up the Cross Daily: Discipleship in Luke-Acts," in *Patterns of Discipleship in the New Testament*, 54, 61, 66-67.

[73]Ibid., 64.

[74]I. H. Marshall, *The Gospel of Luke: A Commentary on the Greek Text*, NIGTC 3 (Grand Rapids: Eerdmans, 1978) 621.

[75]Ibid., 636.

and Gentile, gets it right. He embraces the kingdom of God, receives salvation and gives half of his wealth to the poor.

In such pericopes as these, Jesus and the New Testament writers warn about the dangers of wealth[76] and do not intend to give the impression that only the spectacular gifts of the wealthy count with God. Quite the opposite. The widow's two small copper coins (Mark 12:41-44; Luke 21:1-4) are more pleasing to God than the large gifts of the rich. A cup of cold water given to a disciple in Jesus' name will receive a reward (Matthew 10:41-42). Dorcas's help for the poor and gifts of clothing for the widows are noted by Luke (Acts 9:32-42), while Paul affirms the Macedonian Christians who out of "extreme poverty" give to the poor Saints in Jerusalem (2 Corinthians 8:1-5).

In spite of the abundance of material in the Gospels, little attention is given to this motif in contemporary Protestant writings. In part, this may be because it can be interpreted in a way that conflicts with Paul's teachings about justification by faith. However, this need not be the case. First, it has been observed that "in the context of biblical thought righteous behavior is generally the result of salvation and is required of those who participate in the covenantal blessing."[77] This is obvious in the conversion of Zacchaeus (Luke 19:1-10), but other passages such as that regarding the thief on the cross who believes (Luke 23:42-43) and the parable of tax collector and the Pharisee (Luke 18:9-14), imply, if not teach, justification by grace through faith.[78]

Turning to Paul, it is noted that in his undisputed letters he "speaks of two seemingly irreconcilable things, justification without works of law, and judgment according to works. Both are affirmed."[79] This seeming paradox has received a good deal of attention in the last century. E. P. Sanders's *Paul and Palestinian Judaism*[80] focuses largely on Judaism from

---

[76]See P. H. Davids, "Rich and Poor," in *DJG*, 705-708, for the dangers and right uses of wealth.

[77]S. McKnight, "Justice, Righteousness," in *DJG*, 412.

[78]As the three pericopes appear only in Luke's Gospel, one cannot help but wonder if they do not show the influence of his traveling companion, the Apostle Paul, upon his theology.

[79]Marcus Barth, *Ephesians*, 2 vols., AB (Garden City: Doubleday, 1974) 2:248-49.

[80]Sanders, *Paul and Palestinian Judaism: A Comparison of Patterns of Religion*

200 BC to 200 AD. Sanders claims to have found there a "covenantal nomism," that is, God has entered into a covenant with Israel based upon grace. Salvation is by the grace of God and not works of the Law. Good works and keeping the Law are means of remaining in the covenant. In a second book, *Paul, the Law, and the Jewish People*,[81] Sanders develops more fully his understanding of Paul's theology. He argues that as in Paul's thought salvation can be found only in Christ, the law cannot save, and Gentiles enter into covenant with God without having to undergo circumcision, obey food laws, or observe the Sabbath.

According to Sanders, there are both differences and similarities between Paul's Christianity and Judaism. One of the similarities is that "salvation is by grace but judgment is according to works; works are the condition of remaining 'in,' but they do not earn salvation."[82] To state it in more classic theological terms, salvation is by grace but perseverance therein is by works.

Response to Sanders has been extensive and mixed with few being willing to let him have the last word.[83] One of a number of scholars who have challenged Sanders's presentation is C. F. D. Moule, who argues that the covenantal nomism Sanders describes is more legalistic than Sanders is willing to admit. Furthermore, although "good works" are important in both early Jewish and Christian writings, "in the one they are part of the *means* of 'staying in,' in the other they are a *symptom* of 'staying in.' "[84]

(Philadelphia: Fortress, 1977).

[81]Sanders, *Paul, the Law, and the Jewish People* (Philadelphia: Fortress, 1983).

[82]Sanders, *Paul and Palestinian Judaism*, 543.

[83]E.g., J. D. G. Dunn, *Jesus, Paul, and the Law: Studies in Mark and Galatians* (Louisville: Westminster/John Knox, 1990); H. Räisänen, *Paul and the Law* (Philadelphia: Fortress, 1983); F. Thielman, *Paul and the Law: A Contextual Approach* (Downers Grove: InterVarsity, 1994); T. R. Schreiner, *The Law and Its Fulfillment: A Pauline Theology of Law* (Grand Rapids: Baker, 1993); S. Westerholm, *Israel's Law and the Church's Faith: Paul and His Recent Interpreters* (Grand Rapids: Eerdmans, 1988); N. T. Wright, *The Climax of the Covenant: Christ and the Law in Pauline Theology* (Minneapolis: Fortress, 1992).

[84]C. F. D. Moule, "Jesus, Judaism, and Paul," in *Tradition and Interpretation in the New Testament: Essays in Honor of E. Earle Ellis for His 60th Birthday*, ed. G. F. Hawthorne and O. Betz (Grand Rapids: Eerdmans, 1987) 48-49.

Others argue that although the Reformers tended to read medieval Catholicism into the New Testament text, their paradigm is at its core sound; it simply needs refurbishing.[85] Robert H. Gundry appreciates Sanders' scholarship but writes to refute Sanders's thesis that "Paul is in agreement with Palestinian Judaism. . . . [S]alvation is by grace but judgment is according to works; works are the condition of remaining 'in,' but they do not earn salvation."[86]

Gundry's review of Jewish literature and Paul's writings lead him to conclude that Judaism is "centered on works-righteousness" while Paul's theology is "centered on grace." In Galatians, Gundry notes, contrary to Sanders's view, one enters into salvation by faith and remains there the same way. Regarding Paul's letter to the Romans, Gundry says,

> Even in . . . Romans, staying in by faith in Christ seems to be as much on Paul's mind as getting in, for he devotes chaps. 6–8 to the ongoing life of believers as being not under law, but under grace; and whatever else the phrase "from faith to faith" in 1,17a may mean, it surely means that from beginning to end, faith alone (which Paul expressly contrasts with works—see esp. 4,4-5) forms the overarching principle of soteriology, staying in as well as getting in.[87]

Gundry argues, Paul "makes good works evidential of having received grace through faith, not instrumental in keeping grace through works."[88] An example is 1 Thessalonians 1:3 where he speaks of the "work of faith." Undoubtedly this is a genitive of origin, that is, "your work that comes from faith."[89]

In 2 Corinthians, Galatians, and Romans, good works do not save, but they are nonetheless important. For example, defending his gospel and ministry to the Gentiles, Paul tells the Galatians that James, Peter, and John gave him and Barnabas "the right hand of fellowship." He then adds,

---

[85]In addition to Westerholm, and Schreiner, see R. H. Gundry, "Grace, Works, and Staying Saved in Paul," *Bib* 66 (1985): 7-11.

[86]Ibid., 7.

[87]Ibid., 9.

[88]Ibid., 11.

[89]Ibid., 11 (cf. Rom 1:5; 16:26; Gal 5:6; 2 Thess 1:11; 2:17; Jas 2:14-26; Col 1:6, 10).

"All they asked was that we should continue to remember the poor, the very thing I was eager to do" (Galatians 2:10).[90]

In Romans, when Paul begins to make application of the theology he has presented in the previous eleven chapters, he focuses upon those in the church whose gift is "serving" (12:7), probably a "reference to practical service rendered to those who in some way are specially needy."[91] There is mention of those with the gift of "contributing to the needs of others" (12:8), that is, those who "tend the sick, relieve the poor, or care for the aged and disabled."[92] In the thirteenth verse we find: "Share with God's people who are in need. Practice hospitality." These verses are only samples of the Pauline concern for the poor, especially within the fellowship, and the need to perform good works.

In the contested Pauline literature, good works are brought into sharper focus.[93] For example, Ephesians 2:8-10 establishes that salvation is purely of God's grace, received by faith alone and not by good works. Having said that, many interpreters stop. Paul does not.[94] The argument is not just that one is saved by grace through faith. One is saved by grace through faith *for the purpose of performing good works*. "Salvation is not 'by works' but 'for works.' "[95] The purpose element is strengthened with the word προετοιμάζω, "to prepare or determine beforehand, to predestine." In the words of Marcus Barth:

---

[90]This is probably a reference to Paul's collection for the poor saints in Jerusalem, an activity that was a major concern of the great apostle. See C. K. Barrett, *A Commentary on the Second Epistle to the Corinthians*, BNTC (London: Black, 1973) 216-42.

[91]C. E. B. Cranfield, *A Critical and Exegetical Commentary on the Epistle to the Romans*, 2 vols., ICC (Edinburgh: T. & T. Clark, 1975, 1979) 2:622.

[92]Ibid. 2:627. Markus Barth observes that in Paul's writings good works include "works of trust, obedience, repentance, and praise." *Ephesians* 1:250.

[93]See I. H. Marshall, "Salvation, Grace, and Works in the Later Writings in the Pauline Corpus," *NTS* 42 (1996): 339-58.

[94]"Whether written by Paul or by a follower, Ephesians is now canonical; it has the same authoritative and foundational status for the church's teaching and life as, for example, one of the gospels or Paul's letter to the Romans." A. T. Lincoln, *Ephesians*, WBC 42 (Dallas: Word, 1990) lxxiii. Barth, *Ephesians* 1:36-50, defends the Pauline authorship.

[95]Lincoln, *Ephesians*, 114, who argues that ἐπί with the dative signifies "purpose, goal, or result."

> Eph. 2:10 gives basic information on the necessity of "good works." In eternity, i.e., before the foundation of the world, when God loved his Son and elected the saints in him, he also prepared "good works" for them. If there is meaning in the term "preexistence" at all, then the "good works" of the saints share in it. Still among the preexistent things enumerated in the Talmud "good works" are not mentioned. Thus Paul attributes to them an even higher value than do later Jewish teachers![96]

Having examined selective passages in the Gospels and Paul's writings, still left are those verses in James (2:14-26) which seem to blatantly contradict, if not refute, Paul's doctrine of justification by faith. In the light of James, what can an Evangelical Protestant say? To begin with, James seems to be distinguishing between a head-knowledge faith—"You believe that God is one, you do well. The demons also believe and tremble." (2:19)—and a heart-and-head faith which is life transforming.[97] It is also important to distinguish between "works of the law" and "good works," or just "works," the first not being confused with the last two. Paul, and for that matter the Lord Jesus, do not find a place for the "works of the law"—for example, circumcision, Sabbath rules, dietary regulations—but both do stress the importance of good works. What James is primarily concerned with is charity towards the poor rather than works of the law. "James will not accept any confession of faith without hard evidence of Christian love in action."[98]

Substantially this is not different from Paul who believes that the Holy Spirit accompanies justification with a transformation of life. He "asserts that no one can attain salvation by good works," but he

> also insists that no one can be saved without them, and that they are necessary to obtain an eschatological inheritance. . . . The works that are necessary for salvation, therefore, *do not constitute an earning of salvation but are evidence of a salvation already given*. The transforming work of the Spirit accompanies and cannot be separated from, the justifying work of God. Such good works manifest the work of the Holy Spirit in

---

[96]Barth, *Ephesians* 1:249-50.

[97]Schreiner, *Law and Its Fulfillment*, 206-207.

[98]P. H. Davids, "Controlling the Tongue and the Wallet: James," in *Patterns of Discipleship in the New Testament*, 242. In a similar vein, the author of 1 John stresses a love that acts to relieve the poor (1 John 3:16-24).

> the believer's life. We should also stress that Paul is not demanding perfect obedience, but obedience that is significant, substantial, and observable. Even though the Spirit has been given, Paul's theology still contains a "not yet." The day of full redemption is still in the future (Romans 8:10, 23).[99]

This brief survey of three leading Protestant theologians and of the theme of "good works" in the New Testament provides the foundation for the development of an affirmative theology of good works and its implications for a postmodern world.

Doctrinal Formulation

The stress on works of benevolence reverberates throughout the New Testament. It is one thing, however, to study the Bible as a historical text and another thing to live as a Christian in a postmodern world. This is why systematic theology, or dogmatics, is essential. Systematic theology is not just theological abstractions or even confession; it has a function,[100] a large part of which is practice. "A dogmatic which does not speak of God's commandments is just as inconceivable as a dogmatic which does not deal with man, with sin, with forgiveness, with justification and sanctification."[101]

Several precommitments need mentioning here. One not shared by all since the Enlightenment is the conviction that the Holy Trinity performs illocutionary actions. Kevin Vanhoozer observes that "the Father's activity is locution. God the Father is the utterer, . . . who now speaks through the Son (Hebrews 1:1-2)." Furthermore, "God the Father's locution is the result of his providential involvement in the lives of the human authors of Scripture. God works in and through human intelligence and human imagination to produce a literary account that renders him a mighty speech agent." The Second Person of the Trinity "corresponds to the speaker's act or illocution, to what one *does* in saying." The illocution has both content and intent; it is revelatory. Finally, there is a perlocu-

---

[99]Schreiner, *Law and Its Fulfillment*, 203-204.

[100]O. Weber, *Foundations of Dogmatics*, trans. D. L. Guder (Grand Rapids: Eerdmans, 1981) 1:68.

[101]Ibid.

tionary dimension of the speech-act, that is, the effect it has upon the hearer.[102] This is dependent upon the agency of the Holy Spirit.[103]

Responding to postmodernism, the second precommitment is to hermeneutical realism, that is, the recovery of authorial intent. Vanhoozer argues that "there is something prior to interpretation, something "there" in the text, which can be known and to which the interpreter is accountable."[104] This "does not mean that everything will necessarily be simple and clear. For reality, and this includes the reality of the communicative act, may be extremely complex."[105] As this is the case, our interpretations will never be absolute but they may still be adequate.[106]

The church strives to interpret the Scriptures with a desire to "hear the Word of the Lord." The objective is practical, spiritual, and ethical. Hermeneutics has a strong ministerial objective. The important thing is not the construction of the text but its original meaning and application of such for the church today.[107]

Applying this to good works, Karl Barth is right to discuss good works under the topic of sanctification[108] rather than justification or assurance. It may be true, using the "practical syllogism" popular with the Reformers,[109] that one can argue back from the fruits of faith to assurance of a genuine faith. As observed previously, however, in the Scriptures, good works are not just the evidence of faith; they are the purpose of salvation.

---

[102]K. J. Vanhoozer, "God's Mighty Speech Acts: the Doctrine of Scripture Today," in *A Pathway into the Holy Scripture*, ed. P. E. Satterthwaite and D. F. Wright (Grand Rapids: Eerdmans, 1994) 177. Vanhoozer is applying to theology the speech-act theory of J. R. Searle, *Speech Acts: an Essay in the Philosophy of Language* (London: Cambridge University Press, 1969).

[103]Vanhoozer, "God's Mighty Speech Acts," 178.

[104]K. J. Vanhoozer, *Is There a Meaning in This Text? The Bible, the Reader, and the Morality of Literary Knowledge* (Grand Rapids: Zondervan, 1998) 26; For other presentations of "hermeneutical realism," see D. A. Carson, *The Gagging of God: Christianity Confronts Pluralism* (Grand Rapids: Zondervan, 1996) 57-137; and V. S. Poythress, *God Centered Biblical Interpretation* (Phillipsburg: P & R, 1999).

[105]Vanhoozer, *Is There a Meaning in This Text*, 302.

[106]Ibid., 458.

[107]Ibid., 323.

[108]Barth, *Church Dogmatics* IV/1, 584-98.

[109]Weber, *Foundations of Dogmatics* 2:316-22, 358-62.

It is also true that there will be eschatological judgment of the Christian's works as well as motives and other deeds, good or bad. Part of the Christian hope[110] is not only seeing Christ and being freed from this world but also receiving Christ's commendation for things done in his name. The scriptural teaching of justification by faith must be complemented with the scriptural teaching on good works. The experience of salvation by faith must be accompanied with a transformed life that is oriented towards spiritual practice and deeds of benevolence. Judgment will reveal how fully salvation has been realized.

The church belongs to two ages: it is the people of the kingdom[111] who, having received the eschatological power of the future age, continue to live in the present evil age. As this is the case "it follows that one of the main tasks of the church is to display in this present evil age the life and fellowship of the Age to Come."[112]

The ministry and works of the church bear witness to the kingdom's arrival.[113] Both individual Christians and the collective Body of Christ are "God's workmanship, created in Christ Jesus to do good works, which God prepared in advance for us to do" (Ephesians 2:10 NIV). The church is the messianic community in a fallen world and therefore the love, mercy, and justice that will be fully realized in the age to come are reflected at this present time in the ministry of the church. In the New Testament this includes "the contribution of material possessions for the needs of others,"[114] and "caring for the sick (Matthew 25:36) and providing the medical and spiritual help that they can (James 5:14-15)."[115]

---

[110]J. M. Everts, "Hope," in *DPHL*, 415-17; C. F. D. Moule, *The Meaning of Hope: A Biblical Exposition with Concordance*, Facet Books: Biblical Series (Philadelphia: Fortress, 1963); and E. Hoffmann, "Hope, Expectation," in *NIDNTT* 2:238-46.

[111]G. E. Ladd, *The Presence of the Future: the Eschatology of Biblical Realism* (Grand Rapids: Eerdmans, 1974) 262-77.

[112]G. E. Ladd, *A Theology of the New Testament*, ed. D. A. Hagner (Grand Rapids: Eerdmans, 1993) 113.

[113]Ibid., 114.

[114]E. Ferguson, *The Church of Christ: A Biblical Ecclesiology for Today* (Grand Rapids: Eerdmans, 1996) 369.

[115]Ibid., 289.

Filled with the Holy Spirit, the church continues the ministry of Christ in the world,[116] which is proclamation and deeds and works of mercy. Jesus' ministry was a threefold one including "edification, evangelism, and benevolence."[117] His people are therefore "zealous for good works" (Titus 2:14), "ready for every good wo k" (3:1), and "devoted" to them (3:8, 14). This may be in small things—a cup of cold water (Matthew 10:42), or in great things—selling possessions to give to the poor (Acts 4:32-37). Such activities are expressions of the love of God which inaugurates the kingdom and which unites believers in the fellowship of the church.

Paul argues that gifts of the Spirit will cease in the age to come, but faith, hope, and love will remain (1 Corinthians 13:8-13). The greatest of these three is love. "Love is the eternal activity of the Christian," Karl Barth concludes. "It is the future eternal light shining in the present."[118]

Love is eternal because it is the eternal expression and experience of the Triune God. Although never perfectly realized in this age,[119] the love, which the Father, Son, and Holy Spirit eternally share, is to be reflected in the life of the church and individual Christian. Miroslav Volf rightly argues that "the relations between the many in the church must reflect the mutual love of the divine persons."[120]

Under the broader topic of "The Messianic Community and Individuals," Wolfhart Pannenberg makes similar observations about Christian love and avers that the doctrine and practice must be theologically and experientially grounded in the doctrine of the Trinity. On the one hand, in loving God, Christians "have a part in the intratrinitarian life of God, in the mutuality of fellowship between Father, Son, and Spirit." While on the other hand, by love of neighbor, Christians

> take part in the movement of the trinitarian God toward the creation, reconciliation, and consummation of the world. As the works of the economic Trinity proceed from the life of the immanent Trinity, so love

---

[116]Ladd, *Theology of the New Testament*, 591-92.

[117]Ferguson, *Church of Christ*, 283.

[118]Barth, *Church Dogmatics* IV/2, 840.

[119]M. Volf, *After Our Likeness: The Church as the Image of the Trinity*, Sacra Doctrina (Grand Rapids: Eerdmans, 1998) 207.

[120]Ibid., 195.

> of neighbor issues from love of God, . . .Yet in love of God and love of neighbor we do not have two wholly different realities but two aspects of human participation in one and the same love of God that according to Rom. 5:5 the Holy Spirit has poured into believers' hearts.[121]

Postmodern Considerations

Western intellectual life and culture is passing from the modern era into the postmodern.[122] All this means is not yet obvious; a few things, however, are coming to the foreground. The end of strong foundationalism is rapidly being realized. Reason will play a less significant role in the postmodern world than it did in the modern. Subjectivism, relativism, and pragmatism are characteristics of the new ethos. Metanarratives are suspect along with claims to absolute truth and meaning. Authorial meaning in the text is out and deconstructing it is in. Paradoxically, pluralism opens the door to an even more radical secularism than the modern era knew while at the same time allowing spirituality to be important again. As Graham Ward observes, "the emergence of the postmodern has fostered postsecular thinking—thinking about other, alternative worlds. In the postmodern cultural climate, the theological voice can once more be heard."[123]

---

[121]W. Pannenberg, *Systematic Theology* (Grand Rapids: Eerdmans, 1993) 3:193.

[122]The scope of this paper limits the discussion of postmodernism to the literature of theology. To move beyond this see, e.g., F. Lyotard, *The Postmodern Condition: A Report on Knowledge*, trans. G. Bennington and B. Massumi, Theory and History of Literature 10 (Minneapolis: University of Minnesota Press, 1984); and the many works by such writers as Jean Baudrillard, Zygmunt Bauman, Jacques Derrida, Michel Foucault, and Richard Rorty.

[123]G. Ward, introduction to *The Postmodern God: A Theological Reader*, ed. G. Ward, BRMT (Oxford: Blackwell, 1997) xxii. See also D. Allen, *Christian Belief in a Postmodern World: The Full Wealth of Conviction* (Louisville: Westminster/John Knox, 1989) 1-19, who also argues that theology's voice may again be heard. Supporting this notion would be works like J. Derrida, *The Gift of Death*, trans. D. Wills, RelPos (Chicago: University of Chicago Press, 1995); and J. D. Caputo, *The Prayers and Tears of Jacques Derrida: Religion without Religion*, the Indiana Series in the Philosophy of Religion (Bloomington: Indiana University Press, 1997). However, not all agree that postmodern thought and culture are

How theologians are to respond to this opportunity is being debated. Some liberals and conservatives alike see postmodernism as theology's new handmaid. The first are adapting the theologies of Paul Tillich, Rudolph Bultmann, Alfred North Whitehead, and other liberals to their postmodern methods and agendas.[124] The conservatives draw from sources like the church fathers, medieval theologians, and Karl Barth.[125] Evangelicals, who still tend to work from a classic Reformation paradigm and feel that modern theologians gave the theological farm away, are more cautious about postmodernism. All think it presents opportunities but differ on how much of it can be accommodated. Some like Nancy Murphy have embraced it in method. Murphy says:

> My projection (and hope) is that theologians from both left and right will find resources in the new worldview for many fresh starts in theology—not fresh starts in content so much as fresh approaches to issues of method, to conceptions of the nature of the theological task.[126]

Stanley Grenz is more cautious, stating:

---

necessarily more hospitable to Christianity. See, e.g., B. D. Ingraffia, *Postmodern Theory and Biblical Theology: Vanquishing God's Shadow* (Cambridge: Cambridge University Press, 1995).

[124]E.g., D. R. Griffin, *God and Religion in the Postmodern World: Essays in Postmodern Theology*, SUNY Series in Constructive Postmodern Thought (Albany: State University of New York Press, 1989); D. Cupitt, *The Last Philosophy* (London: SCM, 1995); M. C. Taylor, *Erring: A Postmodern a/Theology* (Chicago: University of Chicago Press, 1984).

[125]E.g., G. Ward, *Barth, Derrida, and the Language of Theology* (Cambridge: Cambridge University Press, 1995); J. Milbank, *The Word Made Strange: Theology, Language, Culture* (Oxford: Blackwell, 1997); E. Wyschogrod, *Saints and Postmodernism: Revisioning Moral Philosophy*, RelPos (Chicago: University of Chicago Press, 1990). For a brief but excellent guide to postmodern theologians, see G. Ward, "Postmodern Theology," in *The Modern Theologians: An Introduction to Christian Theology in the Twentieth Century*, 2nd ed., ed. D. Ford (Oxford: Blackwell, 1997) 585-601.

[126]N. C. Murphy, *Beyond Liberalism and Fundamentalism: How Modern and Postmodern Philosophy Set the Theological Agenda*, Rockwell Lecture Series (Valley Forge: Trinity, 1996) 154.

> The shift from the familiar territory of modernity to the uncharted terrain of postmodernity has grave implications for those who seek to live as Christ's disciples in the new context. We must think through the ramifications of the phenomenal changes occurring in Western society for our understanding of the Christian faith and our presentation of the gospel to the next generation.[127]

Some, like David F. Wells, just resist postmodernism and hold to a historic evangelicalism.[128]

George Lindbeck observes that with the Enlightenment there was a "binary opposition" in "epistemology between reason and faith, theology and spirituality, academy and church."[129] Consequently, spirituality and practice (*praxis* if one prefers) are marginalized[130] and yet it is at this juncture that religion becomes relevant to the postmodern person.[131] Christian response to postmodernism tends to be cerebral and academic. What is being underappreciated is the importance of the practical and spiritual aspects of the faith. Jean-Francois Lyotard reminds us that the postmodern person is not so interested in the question, "Is it true?" as in "What use is it?"[132] or, as Dennis Hollinger observes, "How does that play out in life?"[133] The postmodern person is not looking so much for right

---

[127]S. Grenz, *A Primer on Postmodernism* (Grand Rapids: Eerdmans, 1996) 162. For Grenz's own method for doing theology in a postmodern age, see S. Grenz and J. R. Franke, *Beyond Foundationalism: Shaping Theology in a Postmodern Context* (Louisville: Westminster/John Knox, 2001).

[128]E.g., D. F. Wells, *No Place for Truth, or, Whatever Happened to Evangelical Theology?* (Grand Rapids: Eerdmans, 1993).

[129]G. Lindbeck, foreword to *By the Renewing of Your Minds: The Pastoral Function of Christian Doctrine*, ed. E. T. Charry (New York: Oxford University Press, 1997) xiii.

[130]Ibid.

[131]Wyschogrod, *Saints and Postmodernism*, 243-45.

[132]Lyotard, *Postmodern Condition*, 51. See also R. Rorty, *Consequences of Pragmatism: Essays, 1972–1980* (Minneapolis: University of Minnesota Press, 1982). It has been observed that "Rorty . . . is less interested in whether theories are true or false than whether they are useful and interesting." S. Sim, *The Routledge Critical Dictionary of Postmodern Thought* (New York: Routledge, 1999) 13.

[133]D. Hollinger, "The Church as Apologetic: A Sociology of Knowledge Perspective," in *Christian Apologetics in the Postmodern World*, ed. T. R. Phillips

answers, James White suggests, as for "a caring community of people who can be trusted."[134]

In such a climate, why would one look to Christianity? Secularism's hegemony of the academy and media has successfully disseminated the scandals of Christianity's dirty laundry, while sweeping away the knowledge of its enormous positive contributions to Western life, politics, and culture. Consequently, many rule Christianity out before examining it or its claims.

It is at this juncture that a biblical theology and practice of good works come into play. Sociologist Peter Berger observes that people have plausibility structures from which they construct their world- and life-views.[135] Building on this, Dennis Hollinger contends that "as Christians we can understand that the transcendent reality of the gospel is mediated or at least heard and seen in a social context. What is that social context or plausibility structure? It is the church." It is through the church that people hear the gospel proclaimed and through which they also see it lived. The content of the church's faith is given to it through Holy Scripture; the church then embodies that content.[136] This combination, Scripture and embodiment, becomes the plausibility structure for the Christian and also a basis for engaging the non-Christian. In both proclamation and in life the Christian worldview is expressed and provides

---

and D. L. Okholm (Downers Grove: InterVarsity, 1995) 184.

[134]J. E. White, "Evangelism in a Postmodern World," in *The Challenge of Postmodernism an Evangelical Engagement*, ed. D. S. Dockery (Wheaton: Victor, 1995), 369.

[135]P. L. Berger, *The Sacred Canopy: Elements of a Sociological Theory of Religion* (Garden City: Doubleday, 1969) 45-51; and P. L. Berger and T. Luckmann, *The Social Construction of Reality: A Treatise in the Sociology of Knowledge* (Garden City: Anchor, 1966) 154-63. For a more theological approach, see R. Gill, *Theology and Social Structure* (London: Mowbrays, 1977); and J. Milbank, *Theology and Social Theory: Beyond Secular Reason, Signposts in Theology* (Oxford: Blackwell, 1990).

[136]P. L. Berger, "Different Gospels: The Social Sources of Apostasy," in *American Apostasy: The Triumph of "Other" Gospels*, P. L. Berger, R. J. Neuhaus, and P. T. Stallsworth, Encounter Series 10 (Grand Rapids: Eerdmans, 1989) 8.

a "holistic appeal" to "hearers who will not rely on one mode of reality affirmation."[137]

Raymond E. Brown notes that early "Christian apologists would call upon the impact made by Christian love as a standard argument for the superiority of Christianity."[138] In the postmodern world, where for many "the chief obstacle to being fully convinced of the truth of Christianity is not a scientific view of the world that has no room at all for religion but the existence of rival religions,"[139] we must strive to hold the same ground, to be the "salt of the earth" (Matthew 5:13) and the "light of the world" (Matthew 5:14). If this is to be, beneficence must take precedence over prohibitions. The church must let its light shine through good deeds that people might give glory to our Father in heaven (Matthew 5:16). In the midst of the postmodern era, men and women will estimate the worth and truth of Christianity not just by its arguments and academic methods but also by the lives of Christians whom they see and know. The importance of those lives reflecting the transforming power of God's new creation cannot be overstated. Expounding Ephesians 2:10, Markus Barth captures it well:

> Christians . . . are . . . made a shining light to signal the dawn of a new heaven and a new earth. Thus . . . they are a "new creation" not just for their own sake and benefit but as a "first fruit of all creatures." . . . Christians are not the end of God's ways, but only their beginning. They are an exemplary "work" of God from which all his works will profit. God's work, in turn, calls for works which they do to God's honor.[140]

In light of our study, we are compelled to conclude that good works are essential to any truly biblical Christian theology. They are one of the most fundamental expressions of faith that an individual Christian or church can make. In a postmodern culture, a theology and practice of good works are necessary if our confession is to be authentic and our witness is to be effective.

---

[137]Hollinger, "Church as Apologetic," 187.

[138]R. E. Brown, *The Gospel according to John*, 2 vols., AB (Garden City: Doubleday, 1970) 2:607.

[139]Allen, *Christian Belief in a Postmodern World*, 17.

[140]Barth, *Ephesians* 1:243.

Index

Old Testament

New Testament

Apocrypha

Old Testament Pseudepigrapha

Dead Sea Scrolls and related texts

Josephus

Mishna, Talmud, related literature

New Testament Apocyprypha and Pseudepigrapha

Classical and Ancient Christian Writings